REASON
in
RELIGION

REASON IN RELIGION

THE FOUNDATIONS OF HEGEL'S PHILOSOPHY OF RELIGION

WALTER JAESCHKE

Translated by
J. MICHAEL STEWART
and
PETER C. HODGSON

UNIVERSITY OF CALIFORNIA PRESS
Berkeley, Los Angeles, Oxford

University of California Press
Berkeley and Los Angeles, California

University of California Press
Oxford, England

Copyright © 1990 by
The Regents of the University of California

Translation of *Die Vernunft in der Religion: Studien zur Grundlegung
der Religionsphilosophie Hegels,* copyright © by Friedrich Frommann
Verlag · Günther Holzboog GmbH & Co., Stuttgart–Bad Cannstatt,
1986.

Library of Congress Cataloging-in-Publication Data

Jaeschke, Walter.
    [Vernunft in der Religion. English]
    Reason in religion: the foundations of Hegel's philosophy of
religion / Walter Jaeschke; translated by J. Michael Stewart and
Peter C. Hodgson.
        p.   cm.
    Translation of: Die Vernunft in der Religion.
    Includes bibliographical references.
    ISBN 0–520–06518–2 (alk. paper)
    1. Hegel, Georg Wilhelm Friedrich, 1770–1831—Contributions in
philosophy of religion. 2. Religion—Philosophy—History—19th
century. I. Title.
    B2949.R3V4713   1990   90–33264
                                                                  CIP

Printed in the United States of America
1 2 3 4 5 6 7 8 9

CONTENTS

CONTENTS

FOREWORD

We are pleased to offer in English translation a work that we believe will establish itself as a major critical study of Hegel's philosophy of religion. The author, Walter Jaeschke, is an internationally recognized authority on the texts discussed in this volume, which include not only the *Lectures on the Philosophy of Religion,* newly edited by Jaeschke (1983–1985), of which an extensive analysis is provided, but also other major works such as the *Phenomenology of Spirit,* the *Logic,* and the *Encyclopedia,* as well as Hegel's early theological writings, and a variety of texts from the Jena period the religious and theological aspects of which have not previously been discussed in the detail provided here. The book begins with an analysis of Hegel's break with Kant's moral conception of religion and his relationship to contemporaries such as Fichte, Schelling, Jacobi, and Schleiermacher; and it concludes with the controversy over Hegel's philosophy of religion during the decade following his death, providing informative treatments of the left- and right-wing Hegelians as well as of the speculative theists and the late Schelling. Jaeschke also makes a valuable contribution to present-day discussions of the task of philosophical theology in relation to philosophy of religion and the question of whether and how it is possible to have knowledge of God.

For this translation we have generally followed principles established for our English edition (with Robert F. Brown) of the *Lectures on the Philosophy of Religion* (University of California Press, 1984–1987). Interested readers may wish to refer to the editorial introduction to volume 1 and to the glossary at the end of volume 3 (reproduced in the one-volume abridged edition, 1988). The primary exception is that we have translated *Wesen* as "being" rather than as "essence" when the German term is equivalent to Latin *ens* rather than *essentia*.

With one exception, citations of works by Hegel are referenced both to available English translations and to the German texts used by Jaeschke, employing a system of abbreviations listed at the beginning of the volume. These are cited in-text, with the English translation given first and the German text second. The one exception is the *Lectures on the Philosophy of Religion,* which is referenced only to the English version (*LPR* 1–3). Not only is the pagination of the German edition (*V* 3–5) given in the margins of *LPR,* but also we adhere for the great majority of citations to the English text as it appears in this work (and all modifications are noted, with references in such cases to the German text). By contrast, while being guided by existing translations of other works by Hegel, we have not hesitated to modify these as necessary to maintain consistency with our own translation criteria or in the interests of greater accuracy. Thus we have deemed it advisable to reference both English and German texts in these cases. For works by authors other than Hegel, we cite English translations when they exist or German editions, but not both, also using abbreviations and in-text references for some frequently cited works. Bibliographical information for other titles is often abbreviated in the footnotes; complete information is provided in the bibliography at the back of the volume. From the German edition we have adopted an index of citations, also found at the back of the volume, which lists all the cited texts by Hegel in chronological sequence. Footnotes preceded by [*Tr.*] are the responsibility of the translators; all others are by the author.

We wish to express our appreciation to Walter Jaeschke for reading a draft version of the translation and offering many suggestions for its improvement. He has been unfailingly helpful in other ways as well, and we are pleased to have been able to extend our collaboration with him from the translation of Hegel to the translation of his own work.

J. Michael Stewart
Peter C. Hodgson

PREFACE

The analysis presented below is subdivided into four studies which deal with clearly distinct themes and can also be read independently of one another. Their aim is to cover the entire field required of an interpretation of Hegel's speculative philosophy of religion: its systematic antecedents, the stages in its genesis and development within the system, and finally its subsequent history. This program is based on the conviction that in order to clarify the sorts of problems raised by the speculative philosophy of religion it is wise, if not indispensable, to go both behind and beyond the form in which it found its most mature exposition.

These four studies were preceded by a brief analysis of the "results of research" on Hegel's philosophy of religion.[1] For this reason the author does not here go into further detail regarding the various avenues of research that have been explored. The results achieved are taken for granted and only sporadically identified as such. Another publication preceding the present work, and one of paramount importance for it, is the new edition of Hegel's Berlin lectures on the philosophy of religion (V 3–5, LPR 1–3). It forms the textual basis for the study presented in chapter 3, whose form it also determines inasmuch as for the first time it makes it possible to adopt, as is done in chapter 3, a developmental interpretation.

1. See Walter Jaeschke, *Die Religionsphilosophie Hegels*, Erträge der Forschung, vol. 201 (Darmstadt, 1983). This study of the state of research on Hegel's philosophy of religion forms, from the thematic point of view, a complement to the present work, and those readers who know German may wish to refer to it, especially in connection with chapters 2 and 3.

In this way the new edition of the text, the analysis of the state of research, and the present work form three complementary facets of the study of Hegel's philosophy of religion. In terms of subject matter the studies presented here are more far-reaching than is commonly apt to be the case with works on Hegel's philosophy of religion. The first and the fourth chapters seek to throw light on the speculative philosophy of religion in the context of the approaches adopted in the preceding and immediately ensuing years. They do not, however, aim to write a history of the philosophy of religion in the period in question, one marked by great richness of thought. Their sole purpose is to highlight the distinctive profile of Hegel's philosophy of religion by considering, on the one hand, the historical and systematic preconditions of a philosophy of religion at the close of the Enlightenment and, on the other, the controversies that subsequently surrounded Hegel's work. The second and third chapters, by contrast, enter into more detail, especially in regard to the developmentally differentiated treatment of Hegel's argumentation, both for the Jena period, which saw the genesis of the system, and for the subsequent Berlin lectures. It would seem essential to take into account both the general context and the detail in order to understand the form of argumentation employed in the speculative philosophy of religion, and what it aims to prove. To be sure, the two aspects could be combined only at the cost of leaving aside other themes that are customarily dealt with in works on Hegel's philosophy of religion; but these are in part only loosely related to the problem of the philosophical grounding of Hegel's conception. To this extent these studies form, in regard to content, an explicit contrast, if not a counterpoint, to the themes that have been focused on to date in the discussion of Hegel's philosophy of religion. In regard to method too they seek to follow new paths.

Walter Jaeschke

ABBREVIATIONS

WORKS BY HEGEL

Br   = *Briefe von und an Hegel.* Edited by Johannes Hoffmeister and Friedrich Nicolin. 4 vols. 3d ed. Hamburg, 1969–1981.

BSchr = *Berliner Schriften 1818–1831.* Edited by Johannes Hoffmeister. Hamburg, 1956.

D   = *The Difference between Fichte's and Schelling's System of Philosophy.* Translation of *GW* 4:1–92 by H. S. Harris and Walter Cerf. Albany, 1977.

Enc   = *Encyclopedia of the Philosophical Sciences.* Translation by William Wallace and A. V. Miller of *Enzyklopädie der philosophischen Wissenschaften im Grundrisse,* 3d ed. (Berlin, 1830), with additions by Ludwig Boumann (1845) based on student notebooks and lecture manuscripts. 3 vols. Oxford, 1892 (reissued 1975), 1970, 1971. References by section numbers (§) are identical in the 3d German edition and the English translation, and are given without notation as to edition. References, noted as such, are also made to the 1st ed. (Heidelberg, 1817) and 2d ed. (Berlin, 1827).

ETW   = *Early Theological Writings.* Translation of *J*, pp. 139–231, 243–342, 345–351, 378–382, by T. M. Knox and Richard Kroner. Chicago, 1948.

FK = *Faith and Knowledge.* Translation of GW 4:313–414 by Walter Cerf and H. S. Harris. Albany, 1977.

GW = *Gesammelte Werke.* Edited by the Academy of Sciences of Rhineland-Westphalia in Association with the Deutsche Forschungsgemeinschaft. 40 vols. projected. Hamburg, 1968 ff.

J = *Theologische Jugendschriften.* Edited by Herman Nohl. Tübingen, 1907. Reprint Frankfurt, 1966.

JS¹ = *System of Ethical Life* (1802–3) and *First Philosophy of Spirit* (1803–4). Edited and translated by H. S. Harris and T. M. Knox. Albany, 1979. The first work is translated from *System der Sittlichkeit,* ed. Georg Lasson, 2d ed. (Leipzig, 1923), the second from GW 6:265–331. This volume also contains the fragments of lecture notes on natural law transmitted by Karl Rosenkranz in *Hegel's Leben* (Berlin, 1844), pp. 132–141, as well as pp. 179–193 of this work.

JS² = *The Jena System, 1804–5: Logic and Metaphysics.* Translation of GW 7:3–178 by John W. Burbridge and George di Giovanni. Introduction by H. S. Harris. Kingston, Ontario, 1986.

L = *The Letters.* Edited translation of *Br* by Clark Butler and Christiane Seiler. Bloomington, 1984.

LHP = *Lectures on the History of Philosophy.* Translation of W 13–15, 2d ed., by E. S. Haldane and F. H. Simson. 3 vols. London, 1892.

LPH = *Lectures on the Philosophy of History.* Translation of W 9, 2d ed., by John Sibree. Revised edition. New York, 1900.

LPR = *Lectures on the Philosophy of Religion.* Edited by Peter C. Hodgson. Translation of V 3–5 by R. F. Brown, P. C. Hodgson, and J. M. Stewart. Berkeley, Los Angeles, London, 1984, 1985, 1987.

NL = *Natural Law: The Scientific Ways of Treating Natural Law, Its Place in Moral Philosophy, and Its Relation to the Positive Sciences of Law.* Translation of *GW* 4:417–464, 467–485 by T. M. Knox, with an introduction by H. B. Acton. Philadelphia, 1975.

Phen = *Phenomenology of Spirit.* Translation of *Phänomenologie des Geistes,* ed. Johannes Hoffmeister (Hamburg, 1952), by A. V. Miller. Oxford, 1977. Corresponds to *GW* 9.

PR = *Philosophy of Right.* Translation of *W* 8 by T. M. Knox. Oxford, 1952. References by section number (§) are identical in the German edition and English translation.

PW = *Hegel's Political Writings.* Translation of *Schriften zur Politik und Rechtsphilosophie,* ed. Georg Lasson, 2d ed. (Leipzig, 1923), by T. M. Knox, with an introductory essay by Z. A. Pelczynski (Oxford, 1964).

SL = *Science of Logic.* Translation of *Wissenschaft der Logik,* ed. Georg Lasson (Leipzig, 1923), by A. V. Miller. London, 1969. Corresponds to *GW* 21 (2d ed. of Vol. 1, Book 1), 11:233–409 (Vol. 1, Book 2), 12 (Vol. 2).

TE = *Three Essays, 1793–1795.* Translation of *J,* pp. 3–136, by Peter Fuss and John Dobbins. Notre Dame, Ind., 1984.

V = *Vorlesungen: Ausgewählte Nachschriften und Manuskripte.* Edited by the Staff of the Hegel-Archiv, Bochum. 10 vols. projected. Hamburg, 1983 ff. Vols. 3–5 contain *Vorlesungen über die Philosophie der Religion,* ed. Walter Jaeschke (1983–1985).

W = *Werke.* Complete edition edited by an Association of Friends. 18 vols. Berlin, 1832 ff. Some volumes issued in second editions.

WORKS BY OTHER AUTHORS

B = Kant, Immanuel. *Critique of Pure Reason.* 2d ed., 1787. Translation of Raymund Schmidt's collation of the 1st (A) and 2d (B) German editions by Norman Kemp Smith. London, 1930. The pagination of both editions is given in the margins of the translation.

CJ = Kant, Immanuel. *The Critique of Judgement.* 2 vols. Translated by James Creed Meredith. Oxford, 1928. Vol. 1 contains the Critique of Aesthetic Judgement, and vol. 2 the Critique of Teleological Judgement.

CPrR = Kant, Immanuel. *Critique of Practical Reason.* Translated by Lewis White Beck. New York, 1956.

FGW = Feuerbach, Ludwig. *Gesammelte Werke.* Edited by Werner Schuffenhauer. Vol. 8. *Kleinere Schriften I.* Vol. 9. *Kleinere Schriften II.* 2d ed. Berlin, 1982.

GS = Kant, Immanuel. *Gesammelte Schriften.* Edited by the Royal Prussian Academy of Sciences, the German Academy of Sciences in Berlin, and the Academy of Sciences in Göttingen. Berlin, 1900 ff. The "Akademie-Ausgabe."

HL = Rosenkranz, Karl. *G. W. F. Hegel's Leben.* Berlin, 1844. Reprint, Darmstadt, 1963.

JW = Jacobi, Friedrich Heinrich. *Werke.* 6 vols. Leipzig, 1812–1825. Reprint, Darmstadt, 1976.

KGA = Schleiermacher, Friedrich Daniel Ernst. *Kritische Gesamtausgabe.* Div. 1. Berlin and New York, 1980 ff.

KSA = Schlegel, Friedrich. *Kritische Friedrich-Schlegel-Ausgabe.* Div. 1, vol. 2. *Charakteristiken und Kritiken (1796–1801).* Edited by Hans Eichner. Munich, Paderborn, Vienna, Zürich, 1967.

RWLR = Kant, Immanuel. *Religion within the Limits of Reason Alone*. Translated by Theodore M. Greene and Hoyt H. Hudson. La Salle, Ill., 1934.

SW = Schelling, Friedrich Wilhelm Joseph. *Sämmtliche Werke*. Edited by K. F. A. Schelling. 14 vols. Stuttgart and Augsburg, 1856–1861.

INTRODUCTION
PHILOSOPHICAL THEOLOGY AND PHILOSOPHY OF RELIGION

"Religion gives up its own existence when it gives up the nature of God; it is no longer a truth when it renounces the possession of the true God." These sentences do not come from one of the apologists of traditional religion but from one of its critics, indeed, the one who initiated the radical critique of religion as we still encounter it today, namely Ludwig Feuerbach.[1] One might therefore suspect an element of malice in their formulation. For were it to prove impossible to express the essence of God in a manner compatible with conventional religion, the connection posited by Feuerbach would also compel us to jettison the preexisting forms of religion, which would then be no more than mere idolatry.

Contemporary approaches to the philosophy of religion seem to shy away from the consequences of this logic. Disregarding Feuerbach's warning, they seek to keep the philosophical study of religion separate from the problem of a philosophical theology. This could be taken to imply that the philosophy of religion presupposes the existence of what is commonly named as the object of religion, namely the gods, God, or the divine. But however necessary it may be in the philosophy of religion to regard as disposed of in advance the question left open by Protagoras as to the existence of the gods, whether there are such gods or not,[2] it is nonetheless not self-evident that God can be straightaway subsumed in this fashion among the possible objects of philosophy. Doubts as to the exis-

---

1. Ludwig Feuerbach, *The Essence of Christianity,* trans. George Eliot (New York, 1957), p. 17.
2. Diogenes Laertius 9.51.

1

tence of God have been advanced too early to allow them to be simply disregarded. Of course the philosophy of religion can methodically abstract from them. Yet it will consistently find itself time and again confronted by Protagoras's question—already, for instance, when it takes up the traditional theme of the relationship of the many religions to one another.

Other disciplines that include the word "religion" in their title have an easier task. No one will demand an answer to Protagoras's question from, for example, the sociology of religion. It cannot be inferred from this, however, that a similar abstraction is equally feasible for the philosophy of religion. The very fact that, as philosophy, it has to inquire into the principles of the objects it deals with obliges it to base itself not only upon the undoubted fact that there is a phenomenon called religion but also upon the facts that religion—at least as it traditionally understands itself in our cultural sphere—encompasses the form of the relationship of human beings to God and that the existence of this object of human religious utterances is, in philosophy, no less traditionally (and increasingly) a matter of controversy. To this extent the philosophy of religion is subject to conditions other than those faced by the philosophy of art and perhaps also by the philosophy of history. Without wishing to dispute the foundational problems of the philosophy of art or of history, we can affirm that neither is burdened with the difficulty that weighs on the philosophy of religion, namely that religion intends an actuality that lies beyond it and is thoroughly questionable, but through which alone it receives its sense and right to exist.[3]

The traditional solution to this problem, one that continues to strike an echo today, leads to a further difficulty, which is, however, more methodological in character, and also easier to deal with. It can be argued that it is not the task of philosophy of religion to give the answer to Protagoras's question, and that this falls to another discipline—not, we may surmise, to theology in the nar-

3. In this way of looking at the problem—and not in it alone—the studies presented in this volume converge with a far-ranging but penetrating analysis published at the same time by Falk Wagner, *Was ist Religion? Studien zu ihrem Begriff und Thema in Geschichte und Gegenwart* (Gütersloh, 1986).

rower sense as the systematic exposition of a particular religion's idea of God and thus, more generally, of this religion itself. For this would only remove the problem from philosophy and shift the task of solving it to a sphere to which philosophy had no access. Within philosophy too it was primarily another discipline, metaphysics, to which people looked for an answer to the question of God. And within metaphysics, over against general metaphysics or ontology, the school philosophy of the modern period saw the emergence of a subdiscipline, *theologia naturalis,* whose specific task lay in consideration of this question. Philosophical theology, whether in the form of metaphysics in general or of natural theology, also enjoyed a considerably more dignified status than the philosophy of religion, the existence of which was, by tradition, ultimately dependent on philosophical theology, which was presupposed. To engage in philosophy of religion appeared meaningful only because philosophical theology had removed all doubt concerning the question of God. And it was not only the different tasks assigned to philosophy of religion and philosophical theology but also their differing status that helped to determine the way in which they were regarded by such eighteenth-century school philosophers as Christian Wolff. The philosophical knowledge of God was seen as forming the culminating discipline of theoretical philosophy, whereas what could at all events be called philosophy of religion belonged to *philosophia practica.* At that time it embraced little more than was involved in defining one's *officia erga Deum.* Inasmuch as it was essentially confined to this, it also did not count as an independent philosophical discipline but as part of ethics. The idea that, over and above this practical aspect, religion is capable of philosophical treatment in the framework of an independent subdiscipline was, toward the end of the eighteenth century, still open to contention—the more plausibly so because up to then the very term "philosophy of religion" had been quite unknown.

It was only in the last years of the eighteenth century that a new conception of philosophy of religion emerged, as it rose out of the peripheral position it had previously occupied in the corpus of philosophical studies. Now too for the first time it acquired its name. Yet the very development that facilitated its brief blossoming endangered at the same time the newborn discipline. The newly aroused interest in the *philosophia* or *theoria religionis,* as it was termed in contemporary lecture catalogs, was all too likely to be affected by the fate that had recently overtaken natural theology when the impossibility of all speculative theology had been demonstrated. From this stemmed the complex, indeed paradoxical situation of the philosophy of religion. As long as it seemed as though the idea of God was not only conceivable but indispensable to theoretical philosophy, indeed, properly speaking, its central point, the philosophy of religion had only marginal importance. What first released it from this shadow existence was Kant's demonstration of the failure of traditional philosophical theology. Yet it was this very conjunction that undermined the validity of the philosophy of religion. For this also spelled the end of the phase marked by a certain naiveté in which it seemed as though it could unconcernedly presuppose the idea of God from another discipline. Yet the philosophy of religion was itself no more capable of assuming the task previously assigned to *theologia naturalis.* The verdict as to the impossibility of speculative theology would then have applied to it too. Thus its rise was due to the decline of the very discipline it needed in order to carry out its prescribed role, that of pronouncing on the whole of religion, without leaving aside the most important question of religion, that of the nature and actuality of the divine.

In a book published two decades ago to which too little attention has been paid, Konrad Feiereis described in detail the decline of natural theology and the first stages in the rise of the philosophy of religion. But he gave his interpretation the inappropriate title "The Transformation of Natural Theology into Philosophy of Religion."[4] "Transformation" implies an identical substance that is cast now in one form, now in another. Here, however, this is not the case. The relation between philosophical theology and philosophy of religion at the beginning of the nineteenth century is rather to be understood as conditioned by the demonstration of the im-

4. Konrad Feiereis, *Die Umprägung der natürlichen Theologie in Religionsphilosophie: Ein Beitrag zur deutschen Geistesgeschichte des 18. Jahrhunderts* (Leipzig, 1965).

possibility of the one discipline and its replacement by another, whose contents and methods differ widely from those espoused previously. At all events the new discipline did not succeed in actually taking over from the old, because in order to step into its shoes it could not wholly dispense with the demonstrative procedures with respect to which the earlier discipline had been adjudged to have failed. The transition from philosophical theology to philosophy of religion was facilitated by the fact that initially it seemed as though the idea of God could be safeguarded by an argument pertaining to practical philosophy; this argument was not open to the critique directed at the proofs of God, the foundation of traditional natural theology, but it was wholly suited to provide the fledgling philosophy of religion with the foundations it needed if it was not to forgo the idea of God, and with it the very crux of the concept of religion. Already by the middle of the 1790s, however, the failure of this attempt could no longer be disguised; the moral arguments revealed themselves as inconclusive, and the consequences derived from them led inescapably to the misinterpretation of religion.

In these circumstances there might have seemed no choice but to renounce not only philosophical theology but also the newly founded philosophy of religion. Yet its task was never more urgent. For it was not only the possibility of a natural theology that was contested; the concept of natural religion also had become questionable as the result of Hume. Beyond the frontiers of philosophy, there was a widespread crisis in Protestant theology concerning the scripture principle, and Lessing's polemical writings had undermined the hope of providing a historical basis for Christianity—before historical theology had even established itself.

One lasting benefit derived from the discussions of those years is that for the first time they clearly highlighted a choice with which philosophy of religion is faced. It can lean upon a philosophical theology developed within itself or inherited from outside itself; it can then base itself on its cognitive knowledge of the divine in order to treat of religion and provide an adequate account of how religion conceives of itself. Or else it takes as its starting point the reasoned belief that no such foundation is available to it; then it must in all fairness confine itself to regarding religion as a specifically human expression of life. It has then no right to take what appears as divine to be anything other than human—even if it is experienced as the opposing pole to the human. The divine commandments of which the religions speak, for example, can then only be regarded as human commandments. Moreover, a peculiarity that persists down to the present day here forces itself on our attention. The choice to which we have referred becomes much less weighty and consequential if the lack of a philosophical theology is offset by a certainty of belief derived from nonphilosophical sources. It is then possible for another aspect of the anthropological interpretation of religion to come to the forefront, namely the undoubtedly stimulating impact on the treatment of religion that comes from viewing it as an expression of the *anima naturaliter religiosa* and taking into consideration the historical and geographical plurality of religions. This broadening of viewpoint to include the ethnic religions may be linked to contemporary trends in the philosophy of history (also a newcomer to the scene) as well as other academic disciplines, and a little later to the nascent science of linguistics. The less marked the philosophical intent of such research, the more easily it can forgo the link that binds it to a philosophical theology. The non-philosophical science of religion can view the problematic character of current talk about God as a matter of indifference. Research into the sacred texts and actual practices of such religions is not impaired as a result of being carried out by someone convinced of the illusory character of their particular pantheon—a conviction that is usually determined in consequence of being rooted in one's own faith, the truth of which, however, is not a matter for discussion in the context of the research on which one is engaged.

From the philosophical point of view, however, this way of proceeding did not at the time appear satisfactory, providing after all no way around the choice between acceptance of the existence of God—albeit an acceptance salvaged only by the Kantian doctrine of postulates—and a purely anthropological conception of religion. The critical implications of the anthropological interpretation would also have acquired much more weight in the framework of a philosophy of religion than in the course of investigating the actual practices and texts of the various religions; it would have affected the way in which Christianity too was regarded. A philosophy of religion *etsi Deus non daretur* would have been viewed at that time as a subtle, disguised form of religious critique. What had to be done therefore was to resolve the dilemma we have mentioned by renewed efforts to provide a basis for philosophy of religion in a philosophical theology—provided one could offer reasons to show that the comprehensive critique of prior speculative theology did not necessarily embrace the critique of *all* speculative theology.

The studies presented here concern what was probably the most significant of the attempts made at that time to provide philosophy of religion with a new basis and introduce it into the texture of the individual philosophical disciplines—to recover its conceptual foundations, which alone enable it to take its place in this framework as the successor to philosophical theology. They are also concerned with the philosophical discussions leading up to this attempt, and they follow the concurrent debate up to the point where the failure of speculative theology was again proclaimed, the point where the endeavor to counter the trend toward an anthropological view of religion by again demonstrating the possibility of philosophical theology and claiming that it provided a basis for philosophy of religion was for a second time pronounced abortive. It was then too that the dilemma which had in itself been clearly enough visible earlier was for the first time expressed in radical terms within philosophy: a philosophy of religion that cannot fall back on a philosophical theology has no choice but to regard religion generally as a manifestation of the human, from the point of view of social behavior or certain psychic affects. Any intention to confer on the divine a status other than human requires a philosophical theology, however rudimentary, not even necessarily elaborated as a separate discipline. Failing this, God necessarily becomes a human product or even the essence of human being; and this is no less the case if a philosophy of religion methodically seeks to bracket the problem of God. Unless it can adduce reasons for including God in the totality of possible objects of philosophy, there is no justification for attributing to the idea of God in one domain of philosophy, the philosophy of religion, any meaning other than that what is involved here is a particular kind of expression of human life. And a philosophy of religion that aims to adopt the standpoint of Protagoras and methodically bracket the question of God is wide open to criticism from the side of a determinedly anthropological concept of religion. For even the hypothesis of an *anima naturaliter religiosa* (albeit no longer *christiana*) is quite compatible with the anthropological reduction of religion and even with the interpretation of religion as a collective neurosis; principally it makes it clear that for this very reason religion is best suited, perhaps even indispensable, for overcoming the contingencies of life.

One possible answer to the threat posed by arguments critical of religion to a philosophy of religion not founded on philosophical theology is that the more recent philosophy of religion not infrequently adopts positions formerly associated with critics of religion in order itself to defend the interests of religion. To be sure, this takes the wind out of the critics' sails, but it is still not open to this line of approach to see in religion anything other than a manifestation of the human. To the extent that it spoke of a nonhuman actuality, it would constantly be convicted of its error. Nor does one escape from this dilemma by having recourse to a solely methodological bracketing of the question of God. Other results could be yielded only by a philosophy of religion that views itself as an auxiliary to theology and is prepared to borrow from theology the idea of God. Whoever, on the contrary, regards the link between philosophical theology and philosophy of religion as something not to be given up, in the interests of philosophy of religion itself, will find it worthwhile to subject to detailed analysis that period in the history of philosophy which closed with the second critique of philosophical theology, a critique and rejection that since then has never really been revoked.

The beginning, middle, and end of this half-century are marked by the appearance of Kant's *Critique of Pure Reason*, then by Hegel's speculative philosophy of religion, and finally by Feuerbach's *Theses on the Reformation of Philosophy*. Despite being limited to the time span indicated, the present studies do not aspire in any sense to be a history of the philosophy of religion during this period. They investigate the nexus of problems presented by the relationship between philosophical theology and philosophy of religion from the time of the first sweeping critique of speculative theology, through Hegel's attempt to restore the problem of God to a place in theoretical philosophy, down to the second effective critique of speculative theology and, at the same time, philosophy of religion. For the original exposition of the nexus of problems in regard to philosophical theology and philosophy of religion itself falls into a historical process. This does not mean that we must hark back to the Hegelian idea of a trajectory that has necessarily to be followed "from Kant to Hegel"—even assuming that Fichte and Schelling would find their fitting place as stages on this trajectory. The way from Kant to Feuerbach does not, however, pass through the philosophical positions that Fichte and Schelling propounded in the last years of their lives. The question whether their early positions led consistently to their later works can here be left open. The rational consistency of the history of philosophy, which is here assumed, is not to be understood as knowing only one single, harmonious, forward movement of thought. Nor ought the history of philosophy to be blindly credited with consistency. Some of its prominent and epoch-making decisions could rest on shaky arguments—without this meaning that their reconsideration may be looked or hoped for.

CHAPTER I

TOWARD A SPECULATIVE PHILOSOPHY OF RELIGION: THE HISTORICAL AND PHILOSOPHICAL BACKGROUND

1. The Choice of Interpretative Options

A great philosopher does not merely condemn posterity to the necessity of explicating him.[1] Very often he also obliges it not only to present differing insights but to justify them over against his position. If the greatness of a philosopher were to be judged in the light of the extent to which he calls for the justification of divergent views, Hegel would have to be accorded very lowly status, at any rate today, whereas Kant would occupy one of the foremost places. Such a criterion of greatness does not, however, appear appropriate for the assessment of philosophy in general and Hegelian philosophy in particular. Hegel himself does not seem to have recognized it. Otherwise, so it may seem, he could not, a mere twenty or thirty years after Kant, have arrived at such different views. His approach is widely deemed to be rooted in a supposedly living tradition of the self-certainty of metaphysical thought. This is eloquently reflected in his lament at the disappearance of metaphysics, at the removal of the Most Holy from the temple of philosophy (GW 11: 5–6). The prime evidence for his unbroken attachment to the tradition is provided by his insistence on the ontological proof of God and his categorical rejection of the demand for prior verification of philosophical cognition, its genesis and function.

According to this interpretation Hegel remained largely unaffected by the painful upheaval which took place in Enlightenment thought. If it were correct, his philosophy would be little more than a peculiar throwback to precritical metaphysics. For in Hegel's day

1. Cf. *BSchr* 715.

it was no longer open to thought to adopt the positions of precritical metaphysics—at least not to utilize its arguments; rather, it was incumbent on thought to have recourse to new, improved procedures of proof. Such recourse might seem inconsistent with the general trend of Hegel's polemic against the preceding critique of knowledge. But it is in no way the aim of this polemic to maintain that philosophy can dispense with also proving what it affirms. Hegel emphasizes that philosophy's concern is not merely to set up concepts but to prove them.[2] But for him a prescientific process of proof or one that is extra-conceptual, borrowed from mathematics, must give way to a proof immanent within scientific philosophical exposition itself. He accordingly rejects the demand that speculative philosophy in general or one of its subdisciplines should validate its possibility by a prior process of reasoning. Nor, in his view, can anything be settled as to the possibility of a philosophical theology or the speculative philosophy of religion before embarking on the study in question. It is only in executing it that its possibility thereby becomes apparent. So if we are to take Hegel's program seriously, the foundational problems presented by these disciplines cannot be the subject of prior treatment. In accord with his conception they can only be spelled out in and through the process of inquiry itself. It is, therefore, not possible simply to criticize Hegel for having failed to furnish proof; rather he may be criticized solely on the grounds either that his conception of philosophical proof is not acceptable, involving as it does basic difficulties that warrant reservation in principle, or that he has occasionally, or repeatedly, departed from his (in itself reasonable) program of immanent philosophical proof. A critique not directed along these lines fails to do justice to the strategy employed by Hegel's philosophy in regard to proof and does not rise to its level of reflection. Thus the question to be posed to Hegel's philosophy is whether it conforms to its own criterion. Only to the extent that it does so are its pronouncements philosophically acceptable.

This conception of the demonstration of the possibility and validity of a philosophical science as immanent within it is not an

---

2. *BSchr* 352 (review of Hülsemann's anonymous indictment of pantheism).

arbitrary consequence of the self-sufficiency of speculative thought. Not is it a harking back to one or another arguments lying ready to hand in the *philosophia perennis*; it is, on the contrary, a reply to Kant's demonstration of the impossibility of speculative theology. While the reply may ultimately be rejected as inadequate, it does provide the formal framework within which speculative philosophy can be developed, and it proves that Hegel has not lost sight of the demands formulated in the name of Enlightenment critique. An interpretation that disregards the link between these demands and Hegel's methodological ideal of immanent proof within the framework of the concrete expositions applies a faulty measuring rod with which to assess his philosophy—whether it itself fails to discern this link or criticizes Hegel for not taking it into account. It treats these texts as if it were open to Hegel to incorporate intact into his system the traditional content both of religion and of precritical philosophy, or as if he actually sought to do so. But then it would be incomprehensible how he could make such major modifications in these traditional contents and at the same time claim that his philosophy was well suited to provide a refuge for religion.

What has been said so far defines, in a preliminary and approximate fashion, in what way Hegel's approach was historically conditioned. But it was not so conditioned on the objective plane alone. However much Hegel attacks Kant's philosophy on account of the results it arrives at, he acknowledges no less clearly elsewhere the relationship his philosophy bears to Kant's. He is very well aware, as he indicated in the first edition of the *Science of Logic,* that Kant's philosophy "constitutes the base and starting-point of recent philosophy" (*GW* 11:31, cf. *SL* 61n). But this does not mean that thought can rest content with Kant's results. The second edition adds to the phrase we have just quoted some sentences that epitomize Hegel's view of his relationship to Kant: what in the case of Kant is the result of argumentation becomes, with those who simply echo his conclusions, "a cushion for intellectual indolence," so that a philosophy aiming at cognition and determinate content has to hold to Kant's expositions (*SL* 62n, *GW* 21:46–47)—but assuredly not in order to rest content with his results. The relationship to which this points is not that of mere succession, which, on the contrary, is expressly pilloried. But it is also not to be understood in accordance with the program of the early idealism of the 1790s, as meaning that Kant supplied only the premises. If he had meant this, Hegel would not have laid such weight on the negative side of Kant's work, affirming that it is necessary to counter his arguments by seeking other, better results.

Against this interpretation one could cite doubts as to whether it is appropriate to formulate Hegel's self-understanding in this way. The question is not whether the authenticity of the quoted passages is secure, but rather whether they do not in fact represent later turns of thought in the sense of a teleological systematization of the problems—turns of thought that admittedly have the force of evidence to the extent that they reflect Hegel's later, thoroughly contentious interpretation of the recent history of philosophy, but that do not do justice to the actual development either of post-Kantian or specifically of Hegelian thought. To be sure, it seems as though Hegel's early references to Kant, during his Jena days, are less inclined to recognize the latter's contributions to recent philosophy. The fact that the passage quoted from the second edition of the *Science of Logic* comes from the very last work published by Hegel (1832) could also be adduced in support of this view. But the quotation from the first edition too is sufficiently eloquent concerning the relationship to Kant, and this quotation comes from the first work to be accounted part of the later system (1812)—in other words at a time when the fundamental discipline of the system finds its first comprehensive formulation, and when the solution the system propounds for the relationship of speculative theology and philosophy of religion is first spelled out, at least in part. Hegel's interpretation of his relationship to Kant is not therefore subsequent to the formulation of his position; in point of time it coincides with the mature form of the system.

Moreover, the assessment of Kant as the starting point for modern philosophy—in fact the unavoidable point of transition to modern philosophy—is not confined to the *Logic,* though it is here that it can be most clearly apprehended. Hegel also voices it explicitly in regard to the philosophy of religion. Kant, he tells us, made an important beginning in this area; to him falls the honor of not having merely adhered to the negative viewpoint of the Enlightenment but of having shown that the Christian dogmas too contain "at least some degree of reason."[3] Consequently Hegel's relationship to Kant is not simply that he rejects him but that he carries on from him. Here too, at the same time, one can hear the call to advance beyond Kant's standpoint. And with these words it is Hegel's intention not only to express the contingent relationship of his philosophy to Kant's (a relationship very likely shaped by biographical circumstances) but to arrive at a valid conclusion concerning the relationship to Kant of modern philosophy as a whole—a conclusion that can lay claim to lasting validity at least insofar as Kant's position can be taken as a yardstick for assessing also more recent approaches not derived from his philosophy. In this regard Kant's philosophy forms, in particular, an indispensable corrective to demands that are made on the philosophy of religion from a supposedly uninterrupted tradition—a corrective to illusions over the extent to which it is today possible to ground a philosophy of religion or even a philosophical theology.

Hegel's assessment of Kantian philosophy as the starting point for modern philosophy in general and the philosophy of religion in particular has implications when it comes to portraying the speculative philosophy of religion. It means that in considering the problems that arose at this time in regard to the philosophy of religion, the historical and conceptual starting point must not be looked for in the Hegel of the completed system, nor even the Hegel of the youthful writings, but in Kant. Two methodological consequences ensue, which in effect point in opposite directions. On the one hand we are not here concerned with Kant's position on its own account, but solely in regard to Hegel, so that it might seem unnecessary to enter into Kant's arguments in detail. On the other hand we are not concerned merely with Kant's results, which in their abstract and subsequently popularized form served as a "cushion for indolence," but with the path that led to the unsatisfactory

3. From a transcript by August Diecks of Hegel's 1827–28 lectures on the history of philosophy.

results. Critical analysis of this path alone makes possible what mere reception of the *fabula docet* prevents, namely the discovery of points from which to develop alternative arguments capable of yielding better results.

For this purpose it is indispensable to examine the reasons Kant gives for the failure of the speculative knowledge of God and the arguments he advances to justify the novel fashion in which he then returns to the task of answering the question of God and the basis this affords for the philosophy of religion. Such an examination will, however, be exclusively with the object of identifying possible systematic consequences for the grounding of a philosophy of religion and possible implications for the post-Kantian history of this discipline, and especially that bearing Hegel's imprint—even if this objective is not constantly emphasized in so many words. Nor are we in any way seeking to imply that the arguments to be deployed here were individually present to Hegel's mind in this form. It is not a question of reconstructing Hegel's actual criticisms in their totality, but of gaining insights into the main features of the foundational connection between philosophical theology and philosophy of religion as it was presented in the discussion at that time. Awareness of these features can also be attested in the various stages of Hegel's intellectual development. The extent to which he ever consigned these insights to written form, over and above the passages that have come down to us, may be left an open question. The source materials we have are sufficient to show the general trend of Hegel's critique. They also confirm the fundamental unity that was realized at that time between systematic argumentation and the historiography of the problems.

It is also relevant to the post-Kantian history of philosophical theology and philosophy of religion, starting in the 1790s, that the first systematic exposition of the problems does not take place in the framework of any one of the current philosophical positions but belongs to the history of philosophy of the period in question. This history exposed the problems inherent in the conception much more thoroughly than could have been done by a critical monograph (had one been written at the time). The followers and critics of Kant in this decade also include the young Hegel. This in itself is sufficient reason for examining here this important phase in the changing character of philosophy of religion. Moreover, to do so is not at odds with Hegel's categorical rejection of those who espouse Kant's results. For his critique applies to those who merely receive Kant's affirmation of the unknowability of the divine without entering into the matter by dint of their own intellectual effort. What is involved here, on the contrary, is a discussion of basic questions that is, to be sure, not remotely comparable in importance to Kant's work but even in its faulty developments exerts a major impact on the further history of philosophy of religion. What we have to do here is to pursue this discussion to the point where important decisions are taken for Hegel's subsequent systematization of the relationship between philosophical theology and philosophy of religion.

2. The Unsatisfactory Nature of the Kantian Critique and Restitution of the Idea of God

The starting point of modern philosophy of religion—in the full sense, including the idea of God—is Kant, on the basis of three demonstrations: (1) his "critique of all theology based upon speculative principles of reason" (B 659 ff.); (2) his reestablishment of the idea of God by means of arguments derived from practical philosophy; (3) his elaboration of philosophy of religion in the context of this new grounding of the idea of God. These demonstrations acquired seminal importance for the history of philosophy of religion in the generations following Kant. They form a whole, in which the preceding argument is in each case presupposed if the ensuing stage is to be intelligible. Major modifications in the second stage of the argument, but also in the first, make it probable that similar modifications will be necessary in the third, or second and third, as the case may be. But also the necessity of a change in the final stage would inevitably have consequences at least for the second. So there can be no question of an isolated revision, unless it were to be confined to internal improvement of the demonstrative procedure without affecting the result.

A few years later Hegel took issue with Kant in regard to all three stages and sought to replace his solution by a new, no less closed one. Taking into account the lofty status of Kantian argumentation as well as its claim to exclusivity, which precludes divergent results from the first two stages, such an alternative entails not only the establishment of a new concept but a demonstration of the failure of Kant's argumentation. Here we must spell out the factors by virtue of which Kant's solution could be declared not merely outmoded historically or superseded by a better one but abortive. It is indicative of the status of Kant's solution that in order to proclaim it vanquished it was necessary to modify the systematic philosophical foundations, even though the justification for subjecting it to criticism could not be questioned, and there was also no difficulty in finding possible angles from which to undertake a partial revision. Indeed, the affirmations as to the indemonstrability of God for theoretical philosophy and a new access to the idea of God through practical philosophy are not formulated as self-evident, apodictic truths. What both propositions do rather is to draw out the heart of a lengthy prior presentation. But if these propositions are not regarded as unconditional, then their conditions must be identified and subjected to critical scrutiny in order to assess the systematic credibility of Kant's results and the chances of revising them—not in such a way as to contest the validity of the second, positive result but to find a better expedient in regard to the first. This is what Hegel means when he bids us not merely to hold to Kant's results but to make his reasoning the object of philosophical work. A further question in regard to the history of the philosophy of religion is whether there are grounds for assuming that this kind of systematic consideration as to the justification or even the necessity of a revision was relevant to the actual reformulation of post-Kantian philosophy of religion, or whether the subsequent history was possibly determined by other motives, less conclusive from a systematic point of view. The concern of this first study is to reconstruct the systematic factors that made possible a revision of Kant's critique, taking their historical relevance into account.

2.1. The Indemonstrability of God for Theoretical Philosophy

To reconstruct along these lines the critique to which Kant himself was subjected after his death presupposes agreement at least on the main features of the argumentation by virtue of which Kant proclaimed the failure of speculative theology and worked out a new way of grounding the idea of God and philosophy of religion. For this reason, Kant's conception of philosophy of religion should not be judged in the light of considerations relating specifically to philosophy of religion but in the context of the critique of the metaphysical doctrine of God. The nucleus of this precritical ("dogmatic" in the Kantian sense) theology is the proofs of the existence of God. So it is of prime importance to see the nerve of Kant's refutation of the possibility of a speculative theology in his critique of the ontological proof in particular. Hegel too viewed the matter in this way. This is shown by his repeated assaults on those passages in the *Critique of Pure Reason* that describe very precisely the reasons for the necessary failure of the traditional proofs. Whoever after Kant maintains the possibility of a speculative theology is consequently obliged to refute his arguments.

Hegel's counterargument extends from short, stereotyped passages of invective to comparatively lengthy discussions. It is common knowledge that they do not do justice to Kant's refutation of the ontological proof.[4] It is not solely its differentiated structure that Hegel ultimately fails to perceive; he also does not take due account of the individual steps in the argument. For instance, he erroneously takes the traditional logical objection based on the difference between being (*Sein*) and concept (*Begriff*) to be Kant's central objection, and thus gives free rein to his indignation, pointing out that little is proved by affirming this difference, which is characteristic of finite things, since concept and being are inherently united in the idea of God. And although there is evidence to show that Hegel was familiar with Descartes's *Meditations*, as well as the objections to them and Descartes's responses, he also takes a second traditional objection to be specifically Kantian, namely, that being or existence is not one of the attributes included in the concept of the *ens realissimum*. But the mistaken assumption of Kantian authorship is irrelevant to the systematic function this objection has for Kant's critique. Hegel even goes a long way toward accept-

---

4. Cf. Dieter Henrich, *Der ontologische Gottesbeweis*, 2d ed. (Tübingen, 1967), pp. 137 ff.

ing this criticism: he shares the view that being cannot simply be regarded as one attribute alongside others.[5] In the context of his direct assault on Kant, however, this insight does not play the role that properly belongs to it. Otherwise the inevitable consequence would have been abandonment of the proof of God based on the concept of the *ens realissimum* (Hegel hardly ever speaks of the *ens perfectissimum*).

And there is yet a further respect in which his direct counterargument falls short of Kant's critique. In this connection he does not enter, properly speaking, into the concept of God as *ens necessarium*, nor therefore into Kant's criticism that this concept comprises a mere nominal definition and gives no indication whatsoever as to how such a being is to be thought. It follows from this in turn that in all his numerous attacks Hegel did not actually take cognizance of the very nerve of Kant's refutation, namely the "criticist objection"—in other words, use of the "empiricist objection" to refute the idea of an *ens realissimum*, and the consequent demonstration that this idea could not be used to furnish content for the idea of a necessary being.

Nor is the somewhat unfavorable picture that has come down to us of Hegel's explicit response to Kant's critique affected by the transcripts of the numerous lecture series he gave on the philosophy of religion and more especially on the history of philosophy. The fact that in his lectures Hegel repeatedly presented the same inept arguments in much the same form throws an even more unfavorable light on his dispute with Kant. It might therefore be supposed that his attempt to revise Kant's results is blighted from the start. But it is only Hegel as historian of philosophy who gives rise to this dubious impression. As systematician he cannot be convicted of disregard for the demonstrative steps entailed in revising the Kantian critique.

A reformulation of a post-Kantian program for the theoretical knowledge of God that will not consistently be obsolete from the

---

5. *LPR* 3:353. Already in *Faith and Knowledge*, Hegel identified this argument as the weakest form of the ontological proof (*FK* 85, *GW* 4:338).

outset must above all refute those arguments that exhibit the failure of precritical transcendental theology. For this purpose one can conceive the following steps, each of which could lead independently to the desired result. One step would consist in showing that in addition to the nominal definition it is quite possible to couple with the concept of *ens necessarium* a definite sense by virtue of which this concept can appear suited to serve as the basic concept of a philosophical theology and not merely a demonology. The same is true of the concept of *ens realissimum*. A philosophical theology founded on this concept must be regarded as a failure as long as it does not succeed in conceiving the relationship of being and concept in some other way than that being is a mere positing and not a real predicate. It is indeed difficult to see how such a new conception of this relationship could be arrived at on the basis of metaphysics as previously envisaged. But it cannot be regarded as utterly impossible. It would also be conceivable that the concepts of necessary or most real being, though not themselves being established from the outset as adequate concepts of God, could, in their modified form, again (as previously in dogmatic metaphysics) be placed in a context which, when fully elaborated, would be viewed as the foundation of a renascent speculative theology. Such an attempt would not lie open to the charge of being inevitably refuted in advance by the *Critique of Pure Reason*.

Each of these three solutions independently would present a way whereby the relevant results attained in the *Critique of Pure Reason* could be revised. A common feature of them would be that they remain directly at the mercy of Kant's critique. In order to escape its hold one would have to have recourse to a line of reasoning that did not set itself solely the aim of improving the traditional concepts and connecting them once again as closely as before, but that exposed the unsatisfactory nature of the designation of God as a supremely real or necessary "being," "thing," or actual "entity" (*ens*), and that would also offer a convincing alternative way of speaking of God. This kind of approach would, to an even greater extent than the first one, go beyond the confines of the traditional *metaphysica specialis*. It could even assume a form so different from previous metaphysics that it would not, at first glance, betray that what is involved here is the reestablishment of speculative theology.

This is the kind of advance on which Hegel embarked in his *Science of Logic,* which is not solely a logic in the sense of an ontology but just as much a metaphysical theology. Its reply to Kant's critique of traditional speculative theology contains elements of all three levels of revision outlined here. It redefines the concepts of *ens realissimum* and *ens necessarium,* and does so by means of a changed insight into the character of the concept and its relationship to being. In this way it leaves behind the framework of traditional dogmatic metaphysics, so that one can no longer speak of a mere improvement in the conception of God as an *ens (realissimum, perfectissimum, necessarium, originarium,* or *entium).* It is rather its taking leave of such concepts that marks the new—albeit still metaphysical—theology.

A more detailed interpretation of the *Science of Logic* as speculative theology must endeavor to grasp it as a whole—not simply trace the explicit references to the traditional philosophical idea of God but show the necessity of its comprehensive reinterpretation in a discussion of the key concepts. This could only be done in the framework of a separate study. Individual aspects of the book's philosophico-theological character will, however, be touched on below. At the present juncture, reference may be made to two other problems.

The first of these concerns the historical justification for interpreting the *Logic* in the manner here indicated as appropriate and requisite. No conclusive developmental evidence in support of such an interpretation is available, either in the texts or in reflections in the Kantian style, the total absence of which in Hegel is in itself a source of difficulty when it comes to demonstrating such references. At the same time there is no need to assume a preestablished harmony between the demands for review of the Kantian critique and Hegel's developmental trajectory. Even the evidence that is available gives a clear picture. Right at the start of his first published critique of Kant, in *Faith and Knowledge,* Hegel reproaches Kant for having treated the highest idea he had encountered in his critical operations "as if it were empty musing, nothing but an unnatural scholastic trick for conjuring reality out of concepts" (*FK* 67, *GW* 4:325). Kant, he said, had posited the opposition of freedom and necessity in categorical terms and celebrated "in complete self-confidence and complacency" his triumph over reason, which is "the absolute identity of the highest idea and absolute reality" (*FK* 85, *GW* 4:338). While this criticism could be classed as mere affirmation of the essential nature of reason, the next sentence points to a more restricted meaning. Kant, according to Hegel, took up the ontological proof "in the worst form it is capable of, which is the form given to it by Mendelssohn and others. They turned existence into a property so that the identity of idea and reality was made to look like the adding of one concept to another." This is to endorse, to that extent, Kant's critique of this special form of the proof. It is also to indicate that another solution to the question of the relationship of idea and reality is appropriate—a solution that Hegel had not at that time formulated in a remotely satisfactory way. His awareness of the need for such a formulation, however, is expressed clearly enough in his criticism. He also indicates its scale, pointing out that the task is to show "that infinite thought is at the same time absolute reality, or the absolute identity of thought and being" (*FK* 94, *GW* 4:344–345).

This comparatively early formulation defines the task of all true philosophy in opposition to Kant's critique of the ontological proof. Nor is it superseded later in principle, although it runs far ahead of the form of systematic development that Hegel later regards as necessary in order to discharge adequately the task proclaimed in earlier years. The way to that development could be traced in the drafts on logic and metaphysics from the decade between 1802, which saw the appearance of *Faith and Knowledge,* and 1812, the date of Book I of the *Science of Logic.* It could also be detected where Hegel does not make explicit reference to the traditional form of proof and to Kant's critique—for instance in his reworking of the concept of supreme being in the *Metaphysics* of 1804–1805 (*JS*[2] 177 ff., *GW* 7:170 ff.). These texts attest to the systematic challenge Kant's affirmation of the failure of the speculative knowledge of God presented to Hegel as he gradually elaborated his system. Of greater and more conclusive weight than all explicit evidence in support of this interpretation, however, is the surely indubitable fact that the *Logic* presents seriatim and in programmatic fashion all the arguments to which recourse can and must be made in order to revise Kant's views as to the irreversible failure of philosophical theology.

The second of the two problems referred to concerns once more the conditions of an adequate critique. A restitution of the ontological proof that takes into account the "criticist objection" could not at the same time thereby claim for itself to have escaped censure from the standpoint of the *Critique of Pure Reason*. "Criticist objection" implies a substantive connection with the work in whose context it is first formulated. But although the "criticist objection" owes its name to the *Critique of Pure Reason*, it is not actually based on the *Critique*'s viewpoint. That "being" is not a real predicate is in fact a traditional objection, going back to Gassendi. And that the concept of necessary being is a mere nominal definition and does not suffice for the concept of God because of its emptiness (as well as its uncertainty as to the number of such necessary beings)—this also found expression in the previous critique of metaphysics and can in principle be formulated at its level of reflection. Lastly, the connection posited in the *Critique of Pure Reason* between the concepts of necessary being and *ens realissimum* does not in any way rest on a specifically criticist basis—even if the *Critique* can claim priority in that regard.

This independence of the "criticist objection" from the basic premises of transcendental idealism follows from the structure of Chapter III of Book II of the Transcendental Dialectic (B 595 ff.). Kant starts by spelling out, in Section 2, the concept of the transcendental ideal, i.e., the concept that can seemingly be made the basis for a transcendental theology. But the scope of the ensuing critique in Sections 3–6 does not rest on the point of view of transcendental idealism. It addresses dogmatic metaphysics, and does so at the level of dogmatic metaphysics itself. This is what makes it so convincing and also accounts for its historical impact. But this means that a riposte has the additional task not solely of countering Kant's express objections to dogmatic metaphysics but also of an-

24

ticipating the kind of objections transcendental idealism could level against the ontological proof. Any attempt to revalidate the proofs of God has no chance of success unless it counters, in addition to the explicitly formulated "criticist objection," at least the basic assumptions of critical philosophy, from which the specifically criticist critique of the proofs could stem.

Renascent speculative theology would have to justify its claim in relation especially to the section in the *Critique of Pure Reason* that comes nearest to a philosophical doctrine of God, namely the doctrine of the transcendental ideal (B 599 ff.). Hegel, to be sure, paid little heed to it. For him the refutation of the proofs of God overshadows the doctrine of the *prototypon transcendentale,* though this would have offered an entirely suitable point at which to attack Kant's critique. It is, after all, this passage that goes furthest to meet the demand for a philosophical theology because it preserves the function that the idea of God had to discharge, in dogmatic metaphysics, for knowledge in general. It assigns to the concept of *omnitudo realitatis* even a central significance for knowledge, inasmuch as the principle of the complete determination of each thing invites transcendental comparison with the whole of reality and there can be no talk of complete determination unless such a totality of the material for possible predicates is assumed. Moreover, before ever going on to examine the proofs of God this passage disclosed the transcendental illusion by recourse to which the improper inference is made from such an original or primordial concept to the givenness of an *ens originarium.*

In the interest of grounding a speculative theology one might be tempted to regard this inference as valid. However, it is not solely Kant's verdict that points in the opposite direction, but also the shaky basis from which such a transition starts. Rather than attempt to underpin it, one can therefore turn to the opposing strategy and show that Kant's critique of the inference to the givenness of the *ens entium* does not affect the possibility of a transcendental theology because here there can be no question of such a theology. The flaw in the argument, on this view, does not lie in subreption from the idea of God to the assumed givenness of such an original or primordial being. It lies already in the transition from the idea of *omnitudo realitatis,* which is a necessary condition for the complete determination of each and every thing, to that of a primordial being containing all reality united in itself. Kant spends comparatively little time passing from the thought of the totality of the material of possible predication to the idea of the *ens originarium.* What happens according to him is that the "idea of *the sum-total of all possibility,*" which "serves as the condition for the complete determination of each and every thing," is purified into the "concept of an individual object which is completely determined through the mere idea, and must therefore be entitled an ideal of pure reason" (B 601–602). On the one hand Kant leaves it unclear whether this purification into the idea of something subsisting *in individuo* follows necessarily and how it comes about.[6] Unless the transition is rigorous, the argument has no theological relevance. Admittedly the concept of an *ens realissimum* is the concept of an individual being (B 604). It is just this that suits it for the further specification of the *ens necessarium* in terms of the idea of God. What is problematic, however, is the transition from the idea of the totality of possible predicates to the thought of a single being as a bearer of these predicates. The "material *for all possibility*" (B 601) as the prime presupposition for the transcendental comparison could only with difficulty be directly suited to serve as the concept of God. It only becomes so once it is purified into the sole ideal, properly speaking. And it is only when the conceptual necessity of such purification is demonstrated that the ensuing transition from the primordial concept to the existence of the *ens originarium* becomes possible.

But it is not only the necessity and more precise form of this process that Kant leaves unclear. Such "purification" of the totality of realities into the transcendental ideal, which is presupposed in order to make the transcendental comparison, renders this comparison, which is aimed at the complete determination of each and every thing, impossible. The clearest statement regarding the required purification says "that this idea [i.e., the idea of the sum

6. Heinz Heimsoeth, in his *Transzendentale Dialektik* (Berlin, 1969), pp. 433–443, gives no explanation of this "necessity" either.

total of all possibility], as a primordial concept, excludes a number of predicates which as derivative are already given through other predicates or which are incompatible with others" (B 601–602). Among the derivative predicates Kant includes all realities that are to be thought of as "transcendental negation," i.e., as negation of a material presupposed as reality, which he explicitly distinguishes from merely logical negation. Only because Hegel disregards or does not admit the validity of this distinction can he maintain that "the sum total of all realities becomes just as much the sum total of all negations" (SL 113, GW 21:100), since each reality is negatively determined vis-à-vis all others.

More problematic than this first step in the purification is the second, which excludes from the concept of original being predicates that are mutually incompatible. To be sure, Kant is endeavoring, in line with precritical metaphysics, to exclude contradiction from the concept of the *ens originarium* and to maintain the compossibility of predicates. However, the irreconcilability of predicates is, in itself, no ground for excluding them from the material for all possibility. That predicates "are incompatible" is relevant solely in regard to their attribution to a single subject, but not for their belonging to the "whole store of material" of possible predicates (B 603).

The third stage of purification leads to a further and decisive difficulty. In addition to the two groups of predicates that have been mentioned, Kant would also exclude those of which he says merely that they cannot belong as an ingredient to the idea of the supreme being, such as "reality in the [field of] appearance" (B 607). Thus spatiality and temporality seem to remain excluded from the concept of God, if only because of the doctrine of the transcendental ideality of space and time. But the question arises by virtue of what right this kind of reality—and Kant does continue to speak of "reality"—is excluded from the totality of reality. The purification Kant affirms here broadens its scope until it becomes, as it were, an enhanced transcendental comparison of the *ens realissimum* with the *omnitudo realitatis,* which is distinct from it. Extension, which one would normally term a reality, is, together with a wealth of other predicates, viewed as not belonging to the *ens realissimum,* although this does not mean that nonextension can be affirmed to be the actual reality from which extension derived by way of negation.

If, however, such predicates are excluded from the concept of God—not because they do not denote any realities but because they appear unsuited for the predication of God—then God can no longer be defined as the All of reality. Either such predicates are excluded from the All of reality with good reason, in which case recourse cannot be had to them either for the complete determination of things in the framework of a transcendental comparison, or else the demonstration continues to be concerned rather with the epistemological function of the *omnitudo realitatis* and with the principle of complete determination. But then the purified idea of God proves to be an unsuitable instrument for such a comparison. For the realities that still remain over from the totality of possible predicates after its purification into the transcendental ideal do not suffice for the determination of finite things. It is only on the basis of the unpurified idea of the totality of reality as the material of all possible predicates that finite things can be completely determined by one or another of two contradictory predicates. What makes the concept of the *ens originarium* appear suited as the basic concept of a transcendental theology makes it unsuited for the transcendental comparison and for the complete determination of all things, quite apart from the still open question of the form and necessity of the supposed purification.

Such considerations might give rise to the impression that the problems involved in a theoretical knowledge of God are even greater than was assumed by Kant and that it is simply beyond the capacity of reason to establish an ideal that is without defects. But a different conclusion can be drawn, namely that a philosophical theology which by assigning or excluding predicates seeks to make an initially indeterminate *ens* into the idea of God, and indeed an existent idea, is simply misdirected. It is still too much guided by the procedure of the dogmatic *theologia naturalis* that it has itself rejected. From the failure of such a transcendental theology only one conclusion can be drawn, namely that what is needed is to base the philosophical doctrine of God on a different systematic foundation. Admittedly this does not prove the possibility of doing so. One of the conditions of doing it is to take into account not only Kant's arguments directed against the traditional proofs of God and his warning against hypostatizing and personifying the transcendental ideal, but also a third series of arguments. To be sure, these do not stand directly in the context of the discussion on philosophical theology, but they determine its possibility no less than the parts explicitly devoted to critique of theology, namely the basic postulates regarding the theory of knowledge. Kant's transcendental analytic (B 89 ff.) contains a multitude of arguments disputing the possibility of a speculative theology, arguments that in fact consist of formulae derived directly from transcendental idealism. In the final analysis they amount to no more than the somewhat trivial idea that the concept of God remains empty because God is never given to us in perception—and who would dispute this?

A response to these passages with their at least implied critique of theology has to form an integral moment in any regrounding of philosophical theology. Hegel sought to meet this need—again less so in his explicit and often prominent polemic than in his quest for a new theory of knowledge that takes the *Critique of Pure Reason* seriously as what it itself in no wise claims to be, namely an "exhaustive analysis of the whole of *a priori* human knowledge" (B 27). The temporal and thematic scope of Hegel's discussion— from the early Jena critique of the concept of reflection to the *Logic,* and from the *Logic* to the later lectures—precludes its exhaustive consideration at this juncture, however. Let us therefore only mention some of the themes to which Hegel, partly in agreement with other critics, assigned particular weight.[7]

One first and immediate form of criticism opposes to Kant's assumptions others that in general are more precisely grounded in the context of the shape of Hegel's later system. It embraces virtually all contentious questions, from the themes of the transcendental aesthetic and the doctrine of the transcendental ideality of time and space to the novel definition of what a concept, what *the* concept,

---

7. On Hegel's critique of Kant as a whole, see Klaus Düsing, *Hegel und die Geschichte der Philosophie* (Darmstadt, 1983), pp. 196 ff.

is. But the same problems can also be treated in a second and critically more efficacious way, namely by showing that on the basis of Kantian philosophy it is not possible to ground the type of knowledge that Kant was primarily interested in underpinning, a task he regarded as achieved through his expositions. Certainly Hegel is not concerned to improve Kant's argumentation internally but to demonstrate that it is in principle impossible for transcendental philosophy to make the necessary improvements subsequently. This form of criticism is therefore directly two-edged. In disputing the validity of Kant's arguments, it touches on other objections, of weightier consequence, directed for instance against the possibility of synthetic judgments a priori. Hegel is not interested in demonstrating the impossibility of such knowledge, however, but in compelling an abandonment of the criticist approach as inwardly inconsistent. He is convinced that while Kant failed to ground knowledge satisfactorily, it can be grounded on the basis of speculation, and so he recommends that the criticist approach be sublated into the speculative as the better way to realize Kant's true intentions.

The first, destructive step is undoubtedly easier to accomplish, that of assailing the unsubstantiated differentiation based on the theory of faculties and Kant's assumption as to the concerted action of concept and intuition and in particular his procedure for establishing the categories. As we know, Hegel rejects this as an empirical hodgepodge and thus not appropriate to Kant's intention, but from the criticist standpoint necessarily inappropriate. His attack also bears especially on an appropriate understanding of the original synthetic unity of apperception. Hegel's very first critique of Kant's theoretical philosophy focuses attention on this, at the same time making it a point in the transition from critical to speculative philosophy. Other topics dealt with in the debate over the possibility of a philosophical theology are Kant's doctrines of the paralogisms and of the antinomy of pure reason. Reason can be assigned a new task in regard to the knowledge of God only if Kant's assertion that knowledge based on sheer reason yields solely false conclusions and figments of the brain is invalidated.

It is more especially in the *Science of Logic* that Hegel discusses

these topics. Comprehensive interpretation of the *Logic* as speculative theology is not the task of this or the following chapter. And
this is true a fortiori for the considerably more far-reaching interpretation of the *Logic* as a dispute with the *Critique of Pure
Reason* regarding the foundations of all knowing. It is typical of
the present state of research on the history of philosophy that it is
not possible to refer to an alternative comprehensive treatment of
these problems in the literature. Hegel's polemic against Kant and
his attempt to rehabilitate the ontological proof often, in fact, excite derision. We are still awaiting the promised analysis of the
Logic's ontotheological claims. The fact that no such analysis has
appeared reflects the commonly held view that Hegel's efforts to
win back the problem of God for theoretical philosophy are a failure. His criticism of Kant's attempt to provide the idea of God with
a new foundation derived from arguments of practical philosophy
is judged more favorably. For philosophical theology as well as for
philosophy of religion this leads to the very consequences that Kant
thought himself able to avert with his practical argumentation.

2.2. The Failure of the Attempt to Base the Idea of God on a Practical Foundation

(1) Essentially two motives may be decisive in determining why
theoretical philosophy steers clear of theology: the actual or supposed insight into the impossibility of a philosophical theology, and
the belief—which may be based on different grounds—that such
discussions are irrelevant. Kant's critique marked an epoch because
it secured extensive recognition for the former motive. But his success, which Hegel stigmatizes as the triumph of understanding over
reason, the "victory of nonphilosophy" (*FK* 85, *GW* 4:338), might
well have been less clear-cut had he not also secured acceptance of
the second motive. It is indicative of the twilight of modern ontotheology that Kant not only disputes the power of conviction of the
theoretical knowledge of God but expressly declares that the objects of God, freedom, and immortality are of very small speculative
interest (B 826). Here he does not even mention the regulative function for the use of reason that he himself had assigned to the idea
of God in the shape of the transcendental ideal. Above all, the as-

sessment at which he arrives on this basis must surely have sounded "barbaric"—to use a Hegelian expression familiar in a similar context—in Hegel's ears, and not in his alone, the view, namely, that the theoretical knowledge of God is "a labor so fatiguing in its endless wrestling with insuperable difficulties," and one that can be turned to relatively little useful purpose. This assertion might indeed appear plausible as long as the regulative function of the idea of God for theoretical knowledge seemed secured and one believed oneself in possession of a better solution of the problem of God, namely the practical. But once this lost its force of conviction, renewed efforts in regard to the theoretical knowledge of God seemed very well worth some trouble. And a little later the debate in that regard once again became extremely animated, in the dispute concerning Hegel's philosophy of religion.

Kant's evident lack of concern at taking leave of the transcendental theology that previously had enjoyed unquestioned validity is due to his belief that the idea of God plays a regulative role in theoretical knowledge and is grounded anew in practical philosophy. The former consideration, however, lay more in the background. What actually exerted most effect was the practical regrounding of the idea of God. It even seemed better suited for the assumption of a theological role than when the knowledge of God was anchored in theory, as it had been previously. The combination of a comprehensive theoretical critique with the practical rehabilitation of the idea of God ensured for Kant's viewpoint a relatively rapid acceptance in the 1790s such as no other subsequent philosophy could lay claim to. To ground the idea of God on that of freedom seemed less open to the danger posed by a theoretical critique; at the same time it held out the prospect that all the theologoumena of the former *metaphysica specialis,* down to the deduction of the properties of God, could be repeated virtually *in toto*—even if always with the proviso that it is not here, properly speaking, a matter of theoretical knowledge but of assumptions in the interest of freedom. This blanket limitation is of no significance for the results themselves or for the importance they assumed in the discussion at that time. Nor should the practical argumentation be understood as claiming to be less rigorous. Admittedly it rests on other assumptions, but it must present its results with a logical consistency similar to the theoretical. The proviso that what is involved is practical knowledge is of significance only inasmuch as it invalidates objections founded on theory. It does not therefore operate as a disclaimer, acknowledging a lesser degree of evidential force, but as a weapon conferring immunity against criticism. For who, at that time, was prepared to dispute ethical freedom? Thus a practical grounding seemed to meet a dual need, that of recuperating the whole field covered by philosophical theology and at the same time rescuing it from the theoretical criticism that was already being expressed on certain points. But it soon proved liable to counterattack in the interests of speculative theology, to the extent that the conduct of the practical argument was not subjected to objections of theoretical philosophy but was examined as such in regard to its logical consistency. As was only fitting, this critique preceded the examination of Kant's critique of the theoretical knowledge of God and the ensuing attempts to reestablish a philosophical doctrine of God.

In the first place, however, the practical restitution of the idea of God afforded yet another advantage. In the traditional philosophical corpus the disciplines of metaphysical theology and "philosophy of religion" stood in no very clear relation to each other. They had even belonged to different parts of philosophy, theoretical and practical respectively. But how the God who was conceived as *ens realissimum* was to function as moral lawgiver and as the referent of the *officia erga Deum* was, to say the least, not immediately evident. By contrast, the practical restitution of the idea of God clarified the inner connection between ethicotheology[8] and philosophy of religion. Nor was the connection impaired by the fact that Kant treated the actual philosophical theory of religion separately from his practical explication of the idea of God, elaborating

---

8. [*Tr.*] *Ethikotheologie*. This term is used by Kant in parallel with "physicotheology" in *CJ* §§ 85–86. Physicotheology is a philosophical doctrine of God based on an empirical study of nature and natural teleology, while ethicotheology is a doctrine of God based on a theory of ethics and moral teleology. It is not "moral theology" as that term is commonly used to connote a theological treatment of ethical questions.

it in a text especially devoted to the purpose. The idea of God conceived on a practical basis provided a foundation for the theory of religion—a fact that was not without repercussions for the conception of religion. However, this inner unity made it subsequently appear legitimate to reappraise on the basis of religious actuality the way in which the foundation was conceived in terms of thought.

There is another factor more lastingly prejudicial to the unity of ethicotheology and philosophy of religion than the separate presentation of Kant's theory of religion. Whereas the critique of the theoretical knowledge of God found its comprehensive and valid formulation in the *Critique of Pure Reason,* the practical grounding of theology does not rest on a uniform and comparably self-contained argumentation. It is made up of a series of demonstrations, each reflecting the degree of maturity momentarily attained by Kant's practical philosophy. Each should therefore be examined separately, in the context of the development of the practical philosophy as a whole. Some of the differences that become apparent in this regard can be attributed to individual developmental stages and are consequently defused. But they cannot all be seen in terms of a unidirectional development. Kant's treatment of the relationship between religion and morality is suffused with a conflict between concern for the autonomy of ethics and the concern to make ethics the foundation for the study of religion and theology. Yet this conflict is no indication merely of inadvertence or even private religious problems on the author's part. It testifies rather to a number of problems inherent in the conception. The project of severing the ties linking the idea of God to theoretical philosophy places on practical philosophy a task that ultimately proves beyond its capability. This does not, however, find expression in a progressive insight into the failure of ethicotheology. On the contrary, Kant seeks to bind ethics and "practical theology" more and more closely together. But conceptually as well as historically, his holding fast to ethicotheology as the sole way of ensuring philosophical certainty for the idea of God leads to consequences that run counter to his intention. For they throw doubt on the unconditioned validity and argumentative independence of ethics, without really serving to lay the foundations for an at least rudimentary philosophical theology and a philosophy of religion capable of gaining acceptance.

(2) In the *Critique of Pure Reason* the place where the concept of God is won back for philosophy is, of course, in the doctrine of method and, more precisely, the answer to the question "What may I hope?" (B 833). The ethicotheology there outlined is first introduced on the heels of the answer given to the second question, "What ought I to do?" What is to be done is determined by the moral law that commands categorically, without regard for empirical motives such as happiness. For this purpose there is no need whatsoever to presuppose God as author of such laws. The law of acting is prescribed a priori by the principles of pure reason themselves. Certainly the moral law is holy and divine, but not by virtue of being God-given but because it is categorically binding (B 847).

Kant takes the final step to ethicotheology with the assumption that in the idea of pure reason the system of morality[9] is indissolubly bound up with happiness (B 837). On this condition a further assumption does indeed appear virtually indisputable, namely that the ground of the harmony between merit and happiness[10] as the highest derived good—a harmony that is, to be sure, necessary in an intelligible world but is not to be found in the empirical world—lies in God alone as the highest original good (B 837–838). In conjunction with the first assumption it then necessarily follows that God's existence can lay claim to the same certainty as the principles of morality. And since this harmony is not to be found in the empirical world, Kant concludes, it belongs to a future world, which can therefore be postulated no less certainly. The assumptions of God and immortality are then inseparable from the binding character of pure reason in general (B 839).

Given the validity of the first assumption, this argument is

9. [*Tr.*] *System der Sittlichkeit.* Kant does not distinguish terminologically between *Sittlichkeit* and *Moralität,* and we translate both terms as "morality" so as to set them off from Hegel's special use of *Sittlichkeit* as "ethical life" or "ethical realm."

10. [*Tr.*] *Glückswürdigkeit und Glückseligkeit.* Literally, "the worthiness of happiness" and "the bliss of happiness." The translation loses the word play.

wholly convincing. But it is as a whole hardly suited to make probable the existence of God. Two lines of reasoning can be distinguished in Kant's demonstration. With respect to the first it can be said that, while it is not really conclusive, at least it does not impair the validity of principles. It maintains that the coupling of morally conditioned merit and happiness is necessary to reason, is indeed inherent in reason itself. In a moral world, Kant argues, this harmony is immediately actual since freedom—in part promoted, in part restricted, by moral laws—is itself the cause of universal, self-rewarding happiness. The assumption of the highest original good is therefore necessary for the sake of the highest derived good in the actual, empirical world. In a moral world happiness would automatically follow upon moral action, and it would be unnecessary to presuppose the highest original good. To put it paradoxically, a moral world would not require God as moral *ens originarium*. The only reason for assuming God's existence is in order to be able to maintain the thought of this harmony even under the conditions of a nonmoral world.

It is not difficult to see that the indisputable disproportionality of happiness and merit, in conjunction with the other, likewise indisputable fact that we conceive ourselves as moral beings belonging to a moral world, taken on its own account in no way justifies the conclusion that the guarantor of such proportionality as to ensure the harmony of happiness and morality even in a world that is not merely moral necessarily exists. If there is no reason to postulate the idea of God for a moral world, it is difficult to see why the world's amoral character should give rise to it. The only appropriate way out of the difficulty would be for the two components of the highest derived good to fall apart, for the very reason that our world is not a moral world. The experience of disproportionality could be better taken as an objection to the assumption of God, arguing that if God existed, merit and happiness would not diverge so widely.

The entire force of conviction of the argument rests therefore on the assumption that in the idea of pure reason the system of morality is indissolubly bound up with happiness. For if "happiness" is so closely coupled to the moral law, while on the other hand its realization is dependent on the existence of God, then indeed the existence of God is inseparable from the binding force of pure reason. Kant is well aware of the significance of his assertion. He presents it with a positively biblical pathos: "I say therefore" (B 837). This pathos also serves to blind us, however, to the fact that he adduces no reasons for the assertion. It is injudicious to present a richly empirical content—happiness as the satisfaction for all our inclinations—as indissolubly linked with the idea of pure reason. Doubts would remain, however, even if the empirical content of happiness were exchanged for a moral content. The affirmation that morality and happiness are inseparably joined in the idea of pure reason would remain then too the *prōton pseudos,* the original falsehood, of ethicotheology. Kant never abandoned this affirmation, but he never subsequently presented it in a fashion so vulnerable and so open to misunderstanding as in the *Critique of Pure Reason.* For apart from affirming that it is so, the *Critique* gives no indication why it is so.

If this thesis is accepted as valid, it is assuredly correct that the sole ground for the practically necessary coupling of merit and happiness lies in the ideal of the highest original good (B 839–840). The existence of God cannot then be dissociated from the binding character inherent in the moral law itself. To be sure, this does not yet tell us anything about just how far this binding character goes. To assert that it is binding in the same degree is therefore a two-edged proposition. Properly speaking, it requires that Kant should now emphasize the utterly binding character of the moral law to which he has already given pregnant expression in his answer to the second question. But he now reverses the direction in which the binding character is grounded. Instead of invoking the binding character of the idea of reason as ground for the idea of God, he links the certainty of the moral law to the idea of the highest original and also derived good. Without presupposing God and proportional happiness, it is inevitable, he says, for reason also "to regard the moral laws as empty figments of the brain, since without this presupposition[11] the necessary consequence which it itself connects

---

11. [*Tr.*] Translating *Voraussetzung* as "presupposition" rather than "postulate," which is the term used by Norman Kemp Smith. Reference to "postulates" (*Postulaten*) is found for the first time only in Kant's second *Critique.*

with those laws could not follow" (B 839). This second line of reasoning is surprising in view of what was said a short time before concerning the validity of the moral law, namely that reason gives the laws of freedom, and commands categorically—obviously without regard to whether other conditions, such as the existence of God, are fulfilled, and without regard to the "consequence." Now on the contrary not only proportional happiness but also what was previously the categorically binding character of the moral law are explicitly made dependent on the "presupposition" of God. The idea of God is made the condition for the validity of the moral law, whose binding character is subsequently called upon to ground the idea of the highest derived good and that of the highest original good. The circular structure of the demonstration could hardly be clearer.

This reversal in the process of grounding jeopardizes not only the argument for an ethicotheology at the very moment when success seems within sight—again assuming one accepts the validity of the idea of the highest derived good; it also makes ethics in general dependent on the correctness of the assumption that was to be confirmed by means of a self-sustaining ethics. This would remain incomprehensible if Kant had here conceived ethics as inwardly grounded. But this is not the case. Admittedly the dictates of practical reason are categorical. The actuality of moral action requires, however, not only the moral law to assess such action, but also incentives or springs of action [*Triebfedern*]. Without such incentives, that is, without God and the hope of a future world, "the glorious ideas of morality are, indeed, objects of approval and admiration, but not springs of purpose and action" (B 841). It is only the supreme being that gives effect and confirmation to the practical laws (B 617), and in this way such a being becomes a foundational moment in ethics.

The result Kant here arrives at is indeed precarious. The theoretical demolition of the idea of God has been followed by an attempt to ground it anew on practical foundations. But while this is still under way, the validity of the moral laws is, for their part, tied to the idea of God. Moreover, the last passage we have quoted does not fully reveal the extent of this dependence. It seems after all that the binding character of the "glorious ideas of morality" is not affected by the absence of incentives or springs of action. The passage quoted before the last one puts the emphasis more sharply: without springs for moral action—without God's threats and promises—the moral laws themselves become empty figments of the brain. It is only the threat of divine sanctions that makes them commands. If there were no original being (*Urwesen*) distinct from the world, and if our will were not free and the soul not immortal, moral ideas and principles would lose all validity (B 496). Without this confession the argument for an ethicotheology could at least be freed of its circularity. From the acknowledgment of moral demands in general it would be possible to lead on to the demand for realization of the highest derived good and to ascribe to the idea of God, which has inevitably to be assumed for this purpose, the same binding character as that ascribed to the moral law. It is in this sense that one should understand the assertion that inner practical necessity leads to the presupposition of a wise ruler of the world in order to give effect to the moral laws (B 846). If this argument were consistent, there would be no need for the detour through the highest derived good in order to assume the existence of God. But in confessing the possible illusory character of moral demands, Kant is casting doubt on the argument based on the concept of the highest derived good. The assumption of God has, to be sure, in his view, the same binding character as that of the moral ideas; but since the latter are mere figments of the brain without the idea of God, this idea is needed to lend the argument stringency. But if the certainty of moral demands and their binding character already imply the assumption of God, and if the binding force of the *principium dijudicationis* is tied to the assumption of God as the *principium executionis* (without which it is declared a figment of the brain), then, contrary to what Kant says, the missing condition of binding force cannot be postulated as absolutely necessary (B 661). But then the idea of God is not just the consequence of an inwardly grounded ethics. Rather it forms the condition of its possibility. This would not be a weighty objection if this presupposition were confirmed, as it traditionally was, by recourse to rational theology. But since this is not the case and no other philosophically certified ground for assuming the existence of God presents itself, the conception of ethics outlined in the *Critique of Pure Reason* must be regarded as a failure. In proclaiming the failure of a theoretically grounded doctrine of God, Kant also makes it impossible to ground it on practical considerations.

The first and principal objection was directed against Kant's declaration that merit and happiness are indissolubly united in the idea of reason. This claim formulated in the concept of the highest good is without foundation. It merely betrays a pretension, nurtured by two millennia of Christian promise, that one can claim as a compelling assumption of reason that happiness has to be the consequence of morality. In this fashion the question "What may I hope?" is perverted into the question "What can I demand?" The second objection concerned the circular structure of the attempt to ground the idea of God on the basis of ethics; it is, to be sure, not circular if the binding character of the *principium dijudicationis* is maintained regardless of whether a *principium executionis* is present or not, but it is circular if a moral demand is denounced as a figment of the brain unless a God of promise or punishment is assumed simultaneously. And there are still other aspects of this first attempt at an ethicotheology that issue in contradictory results, namely Kant's deduction of a future life and his judgment as to the primacy of ethicotheology and practical reason over physicotheology and theoretical reason. These two aspects also recur in his later formulations, but the arguments presented in support of them are no longer the same.

From the requisite harmony between merit and happiness Kant infers not merely the existence of God but also the actuality of other conditions for the conjunction he postulates. Since we know ourselves to belong to the moral world and do not find in the world of sense the proportionality between the two elements of the highest derived good that is necessarily present in the moral world, we are entitled to assume that the requisite harmony is actualized in a future world corresponding to the moral (B 839). The basic problem with this transition is the interpretation of the relationship of moral world and world of sense as a relationship of future and present. At roughly the same time, in a lecture on metaphysics,[12] Kant understands the relationship of the two worlds (assuming this distinction to be allowable) in a manner that is not primarily temporal. "Our senses' inability to escape from duration"[13] is no justification for interpreting the moral world as a future one. The mismatch between what we may expect as the consequence of our behavior in a moral world and our fate in the sensible world tells us only that we are members of a moral world but does not provide insight into how moral action is possible in the sensible world. To be sure, an even more obvious inference would be that the lamented disproportion between merit and happiness in the world reveals the demand for harmony to be a product of our poetic imagination; the inference undermines the validity of moral demands rather than entitling us to postulate a future life. It is also possible to criticize the fact that the disproportion is affirmed only in empirical fashion, echoing the fable which alleges that in this world it fares ill with the good and well with the wicked (*LHP* 3:462, *W* 15:594). Finally one has good grounds for regarding as suspect the idea of a God who is only interested in proportionality.

Kant, however, esteems his argument so highly that by virtue of it he regards the primacy of practical reason over theoretical to be securely grounded. He also sees here the way in which to assign to the physicotheological and even to the ontological proof roles for explicating the idea of God grounded in an ethicotheology. But his critical eye is hardly as sharp here as it is in regard to speculative theology. For the idea of God of ethicotheology is no whit better defined than that of theoretical philosophy—even if one acknowledges the ideas of God and of a future world to be results of the ethicotheological argument.

The first obvious course would be to find the reason for the divergence of merit and happiness in the sensible world in the fact

12. Kant, *GS* 28:297–298. On this exposition see Heimsoeth, *Transzendentale Dialektik*, p. 767. In this lecture too Kant does indeed speak of the state of separation of the soul from the body.

13. With this reference Heimsoeth, p. 764, attempts to solve the problem of the temporal succession of the phenomenal and moral worlds.

that the moral original being (*Urwesen*), while the author of moral demands, is powerless to bring about the requisite proportionality in the world of sense, and one has therefore to wait for the future. But there is no plausible ground why the attainment of such a balance should not already be possible in the world of appearance. It is easier to doubt this original being's goodness or omnipotence. The history of Christian heresy offers very colorful material to illustrate that such an objection is in no way a far-fetched thought experiment.

Matters stand no better with the unity of this assumed original being. From moral unity as a necessary law of the world Kant believes himself entitled to infer the existence of that for which he regards the concordance of purposes in nature to be insufficient—namely, one sole, supreme will (B 843). Indeed it remains problematical why a will must necessarily be taken not only as the author of threats and promises but as the source of the moral law—why a lawgiver must necessarily be conceived in addition to the law. The inference to this being a single will also seems open to doubt. The most that can be inferred from the systematic unity of purposes is that there are no such original beings opposed to one another. All the argument succeeds in doing is to exclude a moral dualism.[14] When passing from ethicotheology to physicotheology, in the interests of demonstrating the primacy of practical reason Kant consigns his earlier critique of physicotheology to complete oblivion. If it was not legitimate there to proceed from the idea of the sculptor of a preexistent matter to that of God as the creator and lord of nature, it is not legitimate here either. The supreme lawgiver in the moral world too could make use of available material, and thus remain a demiurge. It would in any event be more plausible to infer from the divergence of the moral and sensible worlds the cosmological incapacity of the supreme moral will, or at least to cast doubts on its alleged omnipotence and regard the moral will

14. On the contrary, Heimsoeth, p. 770, subscribes to Kant's argument, observing that perfect unity could "only be conceived as stemming from a single rational original being functioning as a directing will."

as limited by a resistant matter. It is precisely the stress laid on the disharmony of merit and happiness, in order to safeguard the thought of immortality, that makes the assumption of a unity of freedom and nature seem unconvincing. Since the highest derived good is, according to Kant, to be actualized not in this world but only in a future, and indeed quite different, that is, purely moral world, he abandons the very thought of the unity of the moral and natural orders for the sake of which he depicts ethicotheology as superior to the physicotheological proof. His concept of God is not that of a God who also has power over nature and the sensible order, but of a God who actualizes happiness—corresponding to merit, of course—only in a future antiworld. In theological terms the defect of his solution could be said to lie in the fact that he conceives future life as existence no longer in the world of sense—that he does not conceive it as resurrection of the flesh. That Kant's presentation gives rise to such questions makes it hard to concur with his affirmation as to the primacy of ethicotheology, at least as long as this does not gain conviction in a form less open to criticism.

(3) Kant himself was the first to note the shortcomings of the outline of an ethicotheology contained in the *Critique of Pure Reason*. There is no justification for saying of the highest good in the first *Critique* what he, albeit also wrongly, maintains of the *prototypon transcendentale*, that it is an ideal without flaws. Even the traditional conception of the ontological proof, which he rightly rejects, shows itself greatly superior in its speculative power to the practical arguments. It is only peculiar that Kant incorporates this outline unchanged in the second edition, despite the fact that two years previously *The Fundamental Principles of the Metaphysic of Ethics* presents an ethical schema that marks an improvement in essential respects. And the very next year the *Critique of Practical Reason* portrays the connection between ethics, doctrine of God, and philosophy of religion in a new guise. Indeed, even this does not represent Kant's last word in defining this relationship. All his subsequent approaches to the question after the first *Critique*, however, can be interpreted as a series of attempts to master the problems that arose in that work. By the end of the 1790s at the latest,

it was recognized that they had become more and more deeply entangled in aporias.

The improvements made in the *Critique of Practical Reason* serve on the one hand to provide a new foundation for ethics; this is doubtless the point of view that comes to the fore, and this aspect is well known and has been sufficiently discussed. The second aspect, with which we are primarily concerned, relates to the consequences of this regrounding for an ethicotheology. The changes made in the fundamental principles of ethics necessitate a reformulation of the connection between ethics, doctrine of God, and philosophy of religion. For the really significant argument in the first *Critique* was in fact that only the assumption of God brings into play the incentives or springs of action that must combine with the moral ideas as the *principium dijudicationis* in order that the actuality of moral actions may be perceived. The second *Critique* on the other hand declares the sole incentive to be respect for the moral law. From the standpoint of this profound change in the fundamental principles of the theory of morality, the moral conception of the *Critique of Pure Reason* even appears deeply amoral. To make divine threats and promises incentives for acting morally renders, if anything, such action, as defined in the second *Critique,* impossible. This is not the place to judge whether the new doctrine of regard for the moral law as the sole incentive for acting morally not only helps to make ethics formally self-contained but is also justified. Its immediate consequence for ethicotheology, however, is that the assumption of God—at least to the extent that God was claimed, in the context of the *Critique of Pure Reason,* as the incentive for acting morally—becomes, to say the least, redundant. And if, as a means of defense against such redundancy, one were to accept that the assumption of divine existence can still serve as an additional incentive, then one would certainly ensure a continued place for the idea of God, but it would be a place that jeopardized the possibility of moral action. For such an additional incentive, alongside pure regard for the moral law, would indeed bring about lawful, but not moral, action. The essay entitled "Orientation in Thinking" also stresses that morals would be devoid of value if it were grounded on religion or on the assumption of God. Similar arguments are to be found in the *Fundamental Principles.*[15]

Under the circumstances relating to this new conception of morality, the link to a doctrine of God had at all events to be conceived in a radically different manner. Nor did this escape the notice of contemporary critics, even before the appearance of the *Critique of Practical Reason.*[16] Obviously the labored reasoning of the second, and still more of the third, *Critique* is due to the necessity of deflecting such entirely plausible objections and showing that an ethicotheology can be coupled just as well with the new position too, and how. The realm of morality now comprises the principles of judgment as well as of execution. Now it no longer needs religion. So at least it seems on the basis of the essay on "Orientation in Thinking," *The Fundamental Principles of the Metaphysic of Ethics,* and also the elementary doctrine of the second *Critique.* It is therefore surprising that in order to resolve the dialectic of practical reason Kant reverts to the themes "God" and "immortality" and conceives of both as postulates of practical reason. "God" and "immortality" not only accrue externally to ethics; they serve one of its prime tasks, that of resolving the dialectic of practical reason, i.e., the contradictions that are otherwise present in it. So already the systematic context of the doctrine of postulates makes it impossible to sustain the view that the doctrine of God is to be seen as something that merely accrues to an inwardly grounded ethics as an optional appendix. Only for this reason can Kant attribute to the assumption of God the same necessity as he accords to the demands of the moral law—by virtue of a different line of reasoning, to be sure, but with an outcome similar to that at which he had arrived in the first *Critique.*

The new ethicotheology is also based on the concept of the high-

---

15. See "Orientation in Thinking" in Kant, *CPrR* 298; and Immanuel Kant, *The Fundamental Principles of the Metaphysic of Ethics,* trans. Otto Manthey-Zorn (New York, 1938), esp. pp. 54–55, 82–83.

16. We may think in particular of Theodor Wizenmann, to whom Kant also refers in *CPrR* 149. On Wizenmann see Hermann Timm, *Gott und die Freiheit,* vol. 1 (Frankfurt am Main, 1974), pp. 242 ff.

est good. This concept acquires still greater importance since it has to compensate the loss of the grounding provided by the idea of God as a moral incentive. Its content, however, is new as compared with the first *Critique,* in relation both to the highest original and the highest derivative good. The new definition obviously corrects a defect in the preceding one. If the highest derivative good is made to reside in the connection of merit and happiness, such harmony is also attainable at a far from exalted level: it can consist in eternal damnation. Now on the contrary the highest good is defined as the unity of perfect morality (i.e., holiness) and perfect happiness. A further difference from the *Critique of Pure Reason* follows from the revised form of the fundamental principles of ethics. The highest good is no longer characterized as the determining ground of the moral will but explicitly as its object. To be sure, the moral law, which forms the actual determining ground or motive [*Bestimmungsgrund*] of moral actions, is also implied in this object.

In somewhat simplified form Kant's demonstration can be summarized as follows: (1) The highest good is ordained for us as the ultimate object of the moral will. (2) We must therefore be able to realize it. (3) But morality and happiness, the two elements making up the highest good, are totally different in character. (4) Their conjunction can be thought of as actually achieved only if one presupposes God as lawgiver of the moral as well as of the natural world, and also only if one presupposes immortality. (5) The existence of God and immortality must therefore be accepted as postulates of practical reason.

What has been said involves directly the practical interpretation of religion, namely that religion is the understanding of the moral laws as divine commandments. The problems to which this gives rise for the moral autonomy of practical reason have still to be considered below.

The standpoint of the second *Critique* involves considerable difficulties for the ethical grounding of the idea of God—in regard not only to its exclusion from the incentives for acting morally but also, and no less, in regard to the highest good. We are told that the latter is not a motive for acting morally but its object. One of its two components, morality, does function not only as *principium dijudicationis* but also as *principium executionis*. It is the motive for acting morally, whereas happiness is regarded as forming merely the object of such acting. The evident aim of this construction is to avoid a conflict between striving for happiness and morality. Objections to amalgamating them as motives for acting morally do not consequently apply to Kant's conception inasmuch as it is initially presented as a broad outline. It is, however, easy to object that in excluding happiness from the motives for acting, Kant is merely making an empty assertion, dictated solely by the concern to harmonize the doctrine of the highest good with the new doctrine of incentives, and that in fact the expectation of happiness surpasses morality as a motivating factor and makes a mode of acting based on moral incentives an exception if not an illusion.

There are also a series of other considerations that make Kant's second attempt to ground the idea of God on practical arguments seem equally unsuccessful. One point that invites criticism is the assumption by which Kant seeks to exclude the possibility of the highest good acting as the determining ground of the moral will and so making morality impossible, in other words the designation of the highest good as an object of moral action. This assumption adheres to the idea of the *Critique of Pure Reason,* namely that the expectation of happiness is inseparably linked with the system of morality, and simply gives it an improved form. But even in this form the assumed indissolubility of happiness and morality remains the *prōton pseudos* of ethicotheology. It is now, however, of great importance not only for ethicotheology but for ethics in general.

If the highest good were ordained by pure reason as the object of moral action, the only consequence would be what it is in comparable cases, namely that if we ought to realize it, then we must also be able to realize it—thanks to the causality through freedom that distinguishes us as members of the moral world. How this is possible might remain quite beyond our powers to discover. The moral claim has its counterpart in the certainty of being able to act accordingly. This certainty may involve religious connotations. But it does not necessarily imply that such connotations, once passed through the philosophico-theological mill, could contribute to the grounding of a theory of moral action and throw light on the possibility of freedom.

Quite apart from such an—in other contexts, thoroughly Kantian—argument, we may here stress that the highest good is in no sense an object of the moral will. The fact that pure practical reason ordains a mode of acting that springs from the moral law does not in any way imply that realization of the second, subordinate element of the highest good, namely happiness, is ordained as well. What is ordained is to bring forth merit. This consists, however, in nothing other than precisely morality. It is indeed not a matter of dispute that morality is not solely the determining ground of the will but also the object of action. It is therefore an empty assertion that the highest good is the object of the moral will. This would be the case only if its two components were the object of [moral] action. But there is absolutely no justification for assuming this. If happiness were the object of the moral will, I would have to be able to realize it. But in a world that is not merely moral, I cannot realize it, and I cannot do so in principle.

What first strikes us as the plausibility of the doctrine of postulates rests on the fact that something is incumbent on us that by its very essence goes beyond the bounds of action and can at most be granted by God. All I can achieve is merit and the happiness that springs from consciousness of the morality of my actions—but this is not what we are here concerned with. For such happiness the idea of God would not in any event be a necessary presupposition. If, however, I could achieve happiness in the full sense as first defined, the postulate of God's existence would even be superfluous. I alone would be the author of my morality and also of my happiness. Since this is not the case, however, I cannot achieve happiness, but only hope for it—for the very reason that I am duty bound to let myself be determined solely by the moral law. The second element of the highest good is, at best, a consequence of my actions. But it is in no way necessarily bound up with them. Such a link might possibly be intuited if God were presupposed. But even so, the highest good would never be an object of my action. It would remain that with which my hope is concerned. Nothing gainsays this hope, but nothing follows from it either. All that is incumbent on me is to follow the moral imperative—to use it to assess my possible actions and allow myself to be moved to act by respect for the moral law. This corresponds to the strict concept of morality that is so distinctive of Kant's mature ethics and makes the attempt to ground the doctrine of God on practical arguments so attractive. There are other reasons too why I could not promote happiness. For one thing it would be questionable how it should be defined. For another thing the highest good would require the match of perfect morality and happiness. How the latter is to be measured, however, would be wholly uncertain—in particular, I would have to be my own judge. Happiness matched to morality can therefore never form an object of action. The object always remains morality as the supreme good.

To designate the highest good as an object of my action—and not of divine action—means formulating the task of morality in such a way that it appears as insoluble unless the idea of God is presupposed. But with such a presupposition it remains empty. Nor must we say that the highest good can only be realized by me in an infinite progress. By its very nature it does not form an object of moral action—especially if we apply the strict concept of morality that forms the hallmark of Kant's mature position from the *Fundamental Principles* on. For acting immediately with a view to happiness is here denied any moral character. The sole thing relevant for ethical action is what is moral, and not how happiness is to be realized—even if happiness is not thought of as my own happiness but as a state of the world. Contrary to Kant's explicit assertion (*CPrR* 149–150), there is no duty incumbent on us to realize the highest good to the utmost limit of our capability but only to realize the first component. There is no justification, consequently, for presupposing what is necessary for the realizability of the highest good. The categorical imperative is valid without regard for the conditions that make realization of the highest good possible. Where Kant does not unfold the schema of his new conception of ethics with a view to grounding ethicotheology but remains within the framework of ethics in the narrower sense, he expresses this very clearly. Even if rational beings cannot count on the realm of nature and its appropriate ordering to be in harmony with themselves, that is, to be conducive to their expectation of happiness, the categorical imperative remains in force, for the very reason that it is categorical and not hypothetical.[17] The moral law does not become illusory, as it does in the *Critique of Pure Reason,* if one does not couple it with the idea of God's existence.

This critique of the concept of the highest good differs from that generally proffered, which acknowledges the highest good to be the object of moral action.[18] It has points of contact, however, with criticisms voiced during the immediately post-Kantian history of the philosophy of religion.[19] It is Kant's argument that the highest good is ordained and that it is therefore possible to infer the existence of God and the immortality of the soul with the same certainty as is claimed by this presumed ordinance. If, however, the highest good is not an object, the basis of the argument falls away. At least it would be necessary to formulate it very differently—for example, by asserting that moral action in general is conceivable only if God is presupposed. It would at any rate be necessary first to show the justification for such an assertion, which would again bring ethics into as close a connection with theology as the first *Critique.* But Kant had good reason for revising this conception, in order to promote the independence of ethics.

The difficulties facing the new ethicotheology stem from the fact that it continues to remain Kant's intention to secure for the assumption of God the same binding force as distinguishes the moral law. The demonstrative procedure also remains comparable with respect to form. As in the first *Critique,* what is inferred is the condition whereby a state of affairs demanded by practical reason becomes possible. If the inference were justified, practical philosophy

17. *Fundamental Principles of the Metaphysic of Ethics,* pp. 56–58.

18. Thus for example Klaus Düsing, "Das Problem des höchsten Gutes in Kants praktischer Philosophie," *Kant-Studien* 62 (1971): 29–33. Lewis White Beck, in his *Commentary on Kant's Critique of Practical Reason* (Chicago, 1960), p. 275, speaks on the contrary of an "alleged command to seek to establish the *summum bonum*"; cf. also pp. 245 ff., 253.

19. See for example Friedrich Köppen, *Ueber Offenbarung, in Beziehung auf Kantische und Fichtische Philosophie,* 2d ed. (Lübeck and Leipzig, 1802), p. 31, where it is stated that the moral law commands categorically and has nothing to do with happiness.

would in fact have succeeded in grounding the idea of God. It is not a sufficient objection to this argument to say that it is convincing only for those into whose thinking the idea of morality has already entered.[20] At a later stage Kant explicitly excludes so simple a way out of the difficulty (*CJ* 2:120). What we have here are universally discernible demands of practical reason, to which one may, to be sure, pay no heed, but without being able to derive from this a right to moral or theological ignorance.

It would offer no way out of the dilemma to hold fast to the doctrine of the highest good and at the same time abandon the Kantian affirmation that the highest good is the object of moral action. Reversion, for instance, to the solution proposed in the *Critique of Pure Reason*, to the effect that the two components of the highest good are indissolubly joined together in pure reason, would again have the status of a mere assurance, one which, moreover, the new conception of ethics made even more dubious than before. And to direct attention solely to the realization of the highest good would make the argument circular: God, as postulate, would be the condition making possible something that it would be meaningful to assume only if the existence of God is presupposed. There is indeed a necessity attaching to this chain of reasoning, but it is the conditional necessity of the hypothetical judgment. If God exists, the argument runs, the highest good is not merely an empty ideal, and we may rather hope for a happiness in proportion to virtue. This would leave the question of his existence entirely open. Later, too, particularly in Fichte's *Critique of All Revelation*,[21] we find similar arguments formulated in such a way as to show a recurrent tendency to circularity. But circularity is present only when the highest good is not positively required by practical reason. If it were ordained, its possibility would be comprehensible to us only if God is presupposed. At any rate it would also then remain questionable whether the same binding force attaches to the assumption of God as to the principles of morality or whether we do not have to con-

20. Thus Wilhelm Weischedel, *Der Gott der Philosophen*, vol. 1 (Darmstadt, 1975), p. 212.

21. Johann Gottlieb Fichte, *Attempt at a Critique of All Revelation*, trans. Garrett Green (Cambridge, 1978), p. 64.

tent ourselves with the information that we can say nothing as to the realization of the highest good and simply have a duty to place our freedom at its service.

In addition to the foregoing criticisms there are a number of other objections to Kant's form of argument and to its purported results. The postulates of God and of immortality seem to be arrived at in similar fashion. But the grounds on which they are based differ. Thus, the postulate of immortality does not require the detour via the highest good, as it does in the *Critique of Pure Reason*. Even without the element of happiness the infinite nature of the progression is already postulated—if postulates as such are accepted—by the maximal demand represented by moral perfection. At any rate the nerve of the argument can be presented in such a way that the concept of the highest good does not enter into it: (1) The moral law requires perfect morality or holiness. (2) The possibility of such perfection can be assumed, therefore, with the same binding force as distinguishes the moral law in general. (3) But no sensuous being is capable of holiness. (4) Therefore, this requisite state can be realized only in a progression *ad infinitum*.

But even if this form of the proof, which has recourse to the arguments Kant habitually also uses elsewhere, dispenses with the concept of the highest good, the postulate of immortality is not yet invalidated by the objection that the highest good is not an object. It is easy, however, to show that this variant of the proof is likewise unsatisfactory. The fact that I ought to allow my actions to be determined by the moral law alone involves solely the certainty that moral actions must be possible. Otherwise the moral law would indeed be vain. Beyond this no assumptions are justified—neither that of God as the author of a happiness in proportion to morality nor even the assumption that a morality conforming to the moral law will ever become actual. Besides, the assumption of a progression *ad infinitum* does not offer a way of meeting the requirement of holiness. Its infinite character—the fact that the requisite state is nonetheless never attained—robs progress of all achievement, since in an infinite approximation to the unattainable ideal, every single step is equally distant from it. In the same way that the ascent in the chain of conditions only seemingly comes nearer to the unconditioned, so too in the practical realm the infinite gulf remains unbridged.

It is, furthermore, a peculiar consequence of the model that, in the event of the unexpected complete realization of holiness, immortality would become superfluous and death could finally enter in—a limiting assumption that reveals the unsatisfactory nature of the model. This curious consequence follows necessarily from the improvements that distinguish the reasoning of the second *Critique* from that of the first. In the *Critique of Pure Reason* the idea of immortality—the promise of reward or the threat of punishment—serves for moral encouragement or deterrence. It is not, however, determined by the principle of a perfecting of morality. It would consequently be no argument against it that the match of happiness and morality is not already attainable at the close of an average life. Such a match does not at any rate require an infinite progression. Where the two elements of the highest derivative good are in evident mismatch at the end of a life, it would indeed be possible to infer, not immortality, but a finite sequence of further existences until such time as the harmony of happiness and merit was achieved.

A further implication of the postulate of immortality is, moreover, as is well known, that it already presupposes the existence of God. For the assumption of an infinite process of approximation to the ideal of holiness is meaningful only with the additional proviso that this process is a progression. But this can be conceived only if one assumes divine guidance. Otherwise there is no reason why such a process should ever lead closer to the goal and should not rather remain stuck where it is or even veer to the opposite extreme.

Finally, let us refer to a further characteristic feature of the idea of immortality put forward in the *Critique of Practical Reason*. Immortality as a precondition for an infinite process of moral perfecting implies that such perfecting does not in fact occur, as is occasionally assumed, under changed conditions.[22] Rather it must take place under like or at least similar conditions. To assume

22. See Friedrich Delekat, *Immanuel Kant: Historisch-kritische Interpretation der Hauptschriften*, 3d ed. (Heidelberg, 1969), p. 308, who speaks of a "continuation of earthly existence under other conditions."

changed conditions would mean that it would be quite impossible to postulate immortality, since holiness could then result from just one single further existence. The requirement that the conditions should be comparable also stems from the different ways in which the first and second *Critiques* define the highest good. While according to the first *Critique* continued existence serves for the realization of proportional happiness—and this can also be conceived under changed conditions, as occurring in a moral world—a process of moral perfecting presupposes identical conditions. At least the conditions must be similar in the sense that they permit a purification reflecting the difference between nature and morality as a precondition for the possibility of moral actions. The postulate of immortality accordingly appears as a deduction of palingenesis derived from practical reason. The main difference between familiar religious ideas and such a doctrine of palingenesis would lie in its view that the process will never come to a state of rest, to an end. While this is here seen as a positive feature, the difference hardly helps to make the criticist version of karma-doctrine attractive over against the Buddhist. The character of the immortality that does, to be sure, follow from the postulate is consequently profoundly different from other views of the immortality of the soul, for instance the Greek, or even from the Christian belief in resurrection.

A few additional remarks are still called for in regard also to the postulate of the existence of God, in order to fathom the various aspects of the practical grounding of the idea of God that are here implied and to throw light on the characteristic features of the idea of God that is postulated. In the same way as the postulate of immortality, that of God's existence can also, without recourse to the highest good, acquire the degree of conclusiveness that only this concept seemingly confers on it. For the idea of God has to be presupposed not only for the realization of harmony between perfect morality and happiness but also for the infinite approach to holiness. So a critique of ethicotheology would be incomplete if it concentrated on the derivation of the postulate from the concept of the highest good. Nor does recasting the argument help it to attain its goal. The command to act morally, indeed to lead a holy life, does, to be sure, involve the direct certainty that I can comply with it, but it does not involve the assumption of immortality or of God, although such an assumption would be the sole precondition known to me for the infinite approximation to the ideal. This is not the place to discuss the problems to which a divine guidance gives rise for moral freedom.

Above all, however, recourse to the highest good merely complicates the argument, by posing a threat to morality. For it is quite evident that with the hope of happiness seen as a consequence of my action, a consequence possibly delayed but guaranteed by virtue of the idea of God, morality does not remain the sole determining ground or motive; instead the second element of the highest good, namely happiness, unavoidably becomes the second motive for acting, though more probably the actual motive, properly speaking. This objection, a recurrent theme elsewhere, is here relegated to the background compared with those already mentioned. For the most part Kant goes to every conceivable trouble to exclude happiness as a motive for acting. At the same time there remain doubts as to whether, once one introduces the second element of the highest good into the demonstration, this is really possible and whether this does not give rise to a threat to the possibility of purely moral action, a threat that is unintended but no less effective for that. The more successful one is in excluding the striving for happiness as a motive for acting, the less important it becomes to introduce the highest good. At all events the tendency of Kant's demonstration is directly opposed to doing so. Rather he takes the view that it is self-evident that the highest good previously designated as object "is likewise the determining ground of the pure will. This is because the moral law already included and comprehended in this concept, and no other object, in fact determines the will according to the principle of autonomy" (CPrR 114). In this regard it is nevertheless open to doubt whether "everything really stands in the most perfect harmony," as Kant sees himself obliged expressly to assure us in the immediately ensuing sentence. The strange assertion that not only the moral law but also the highest good is the determining ground of our action (although only the moral law included within the highest good determines the will) is probably to be explained only by the difficulty that something is to become the object of our action which is nevertheless in no way involved in the determining ground of our action, since the concept of morality precludes making the striving for happiness a motive in this direct fashion.[23]

A distinction was drawn above (pp. 36 ff.) between arguments that are unable to carry the burden of proof they are supposed to carry but do not impugn the whole conception, and arguments that, in the interests of attaching ethicotheology to practical philosophy, run the risk of making its elaboration less than rigorous. One example of the latter type of argument would be the assertion that without the assumption of God the splendid ideas of morality become figments of the brain. Similarly the new attempt to ground ethicotheology introduces into the demonstration an argument that is ruinous for the very autonomy of ethics Kant has just adduced reasons for affirming. Admittedly this argument keeps within the framework of the argument developed in the first *Critique* against the possibility of an ethics *etsi Deus non daretur*. At the same time extra weight is laid upon it in the second *Critique*, since here—at least as it appears from the Analytic of Practical Reason—the idea of God is no longer involved in the grounding of moral philosophy. In this altered context, therefore, Kant's renewed rejection of the possibility of an ethics without the idea of God can only be termed a self-contradiction.

The reinstatement of the idea of God in the grounding of ethics is accomplished in two stages. The first modifies the doctrine of respect for the moral law as the sole purely moral incentive. Kant himself does not seem to have thought much of its impelling force; otherwise he would not have introduced God into ethics again as a "cause supplementing our incapacity with respect to the final moral end" (*RWLR* 171). This could be a disguised admission of the inadequacy of the new conception (and as such thoroughly justified), and form the first step in a more far-reaching revision of the doctrine of incentives. It was in this sense that Kant's admission was taken up and elaborated in the 1790s. We know how in their early polemics Schelling and Hegel seized on such arguments.

23. [*Tr.*] At the suggestion of the author, our translation of this sentence differs slightly from his German text. We have also followed his suggestion in modifying slightly the translation of the preceding quotation from *CPrR* 114.

Even more important than this revision of the doctrine of incentives, which had after all only just been formulated, was the assertion which, still prior to any of the labored and at the same time unsatisfactory demonstrative steps of the doctrine of postulates, links not only the realization of proportional happiness but also the validity of the moral law itself to the existence of God: "If, therefore, the highest good is impossible according to practical rules, then the moral law which commands that it be furthered must be fantastic, directed to empty imaginary ends, and consequently inherently false" (CPrR 118). Since the highest good is conceivable only if the idea of God is presupposed, the validity of the moral law is likewise tied to the idea of God. To leave it out of account in ethics degrades the moral law to the level of empty caprice. The choice is between acceptance of the idea of God and the collapse of ethics. Moral faith is not, therefore, only the consequence of an inwardly grounded, self-sufficient ethics. Contrary to appearance it is, as in the first Critique, the precondition for its binding character. For the sake of the practical regrounding of the idea of God, Kant abandons both the fact of moral insight and the effectiveness of purely moral incentives as mere illusions. By the measure of his presupposition this is correct: if the moral law commanded promotion of the highest good, it would indeed be unmasked as mere fantasy if the highest good were impossible according to practical rules. Practical reason would then be inwardly self-contradictory. Nothing, however, compels us to assume that practical reason commands anything of the kind—and not rather purely and simply to act morally. But the idea of God can no longer be securely attached to an ethics conceived in this fashion. Through a detour via the highest good, Kant therefore again makes the idea of God the condition of possibility for an ethics. The link to theology is plausible only to the extent that it is constitutive for the binding character of moral demands.

But just to the extent that it appears plausible to link the idea of God to ethics, the foundation of ethics is destroyed. Kant has two irreconcilable aims: he wants to make ethics independent from the idea of God and from religion, and at the same time to make the assumption of God no less binding in character than the moral law. But theology becomes a merely optional appendage of morals as long as morals is not tied to the validity of the idea of God. Either one disregards Kant's assertion and maintains the possibility of pure reason legislating *etsi Deus non daretur,* in which case the basis for an ethicotheology falls away, or else one understands Kant's dictum as expressing a better insight into the actual connection between ethics and idea of God; this insight, which finds little expression elsewhere in the new conception, is then ruinous for the concept of ethics developed by the *Fundamental Principles* and the second *Critique.* The moral law would then no longer command categorically, but only subject to the assumption of God and immortality. Otherwise it would be contradictory. But by this means the categorical imperative would become hypothetical. It would be conditional on the explicit presupposition that God exists. Otherwise it would be vain. The argument designed to safeguard the idea of God thus destroys the second *Critique's* conception of ethics. The sole conclusion appropriate to this conception is that the moral law commands unconditionally, and it is for us to comply with it. That we can do so inheres in the fact of freedom. But how such compliance can come about, how freedom is possible, may lie beyond our powers of judgment. This does not detract from the unconditionedness of the moral commands. To be sure, the unconditionedness of the categorical imperative may be combined with the assumption of a divine lawgiver. This is not the place to discuss the problems to which this gives rise for the autonomy of pure practical reason. This assumption, however, cannot itself provide the basis for the binding force of the moral law without undermining its categorical claim. If one holds fast to the binding character of the moral law, one is well advised to remove the idea of God from ethics—not only because, as we have shown, it is redundant but also because of the threat it poses to pure morality. At least the function performed by the idea of God must be formulated in a way that does not make the unconditionedness of the moral claim subject to the condition that God exists.

One might, to be sure, be tempted to argue in the opposite sense, that the attempt to ground ethics excluding the idea of God shows itself to be a false path. The dialectic of practical reason makes plain that the theoretical decisions taken previously stand in need of correction and that the idea of God has necessarily to be brought into the task of grounding an ethics. But if the idea of God is not secured by theoretical philosophy, it cannot be made one of the foundations of practical philosophy without canceling its binding character. If, however, it is placed in a looser connection with an inwardly self-sufficient ethics, it loses its own evidential character. For this reason alone Kant finally has recourse to an uncompromising argument that shows the path apparently taken by the second *Critique*, that of grounding theology on the basis of the previously demonstrated categorical validity of the moral law, to be impracticable not solely factually but as a matter of principle. Every form of practical grounding of the idea of God leads to the dilemma that in doing so it destroys the binding character of the very thing on which the attempt to achieve such grounding is founded.

(4) These objections to the *Critique of Practical Reason* are not altogether identical with those that caused Kant to revise his moral proof yet again in the *Critique of Judgement*. The scale of this renewed reworking of the argumentation is also much less far-reaching than that found in the second *Critique*. The differences between the comparable passages in the second and third *Critiques* are markedly less than between the first and second, since they do not correspond to a fundamentally new conception of ethics. Present-day as well as contemporary interpreters consequently in large measure overlook them. It is indeed commonly accepted that the *Critique of Judgement* exercised greater influence on German idealism than the first two *Critiques,* but where Hegel comes to speak of the moral proof, he is referring, not to the third, but to the second *Critique*.

This appraisal does not, however, do justice to the actual relationship between the relevant sections of the two works. Some passages reveal all too clearly the traces of a deliberate revision. And the altered form of Kant's replies is occasionally all too clear even where he is not perhaps drawing special attention to the differences or intending his readers to take particular note of them—where what he says is meant as a precaution against possible misunderstandings of what he had said before. In several passages his new arguments are directly convincing, for instance in regard to the subordination of physicotheology to ethicotheology and the resulting doctrine of the primacy of practical reason. And, however much it remains tied to the course pointed by the *Critique of Practical Reason* and beset by the ensuing problems, Kant's new reply to the question of an ethicotheology is also distinguished by new insights and admissions, which, to be sure, make it appear less open to attack but restrict the argumentative value of his expositions.

The second *Critique* designates the highest good as the highest "object" [*Objekt*] of action, whereas the Critique of Teleological Judgment views this object that is to be actualized by our actions in more precise terms as the "final end" [*Endzweck*] (*CJ* 2:121). Apart from this modification the structure of proof remains unaltered. From the affirmation that the highest good is presented to us as final end Kant now infers the existence of God as the condition of possibility of the final end.[24] Our critique can therefore essentially keep to the lines already established. The first point calling for comment is the assertion that the moral law ordains in general a determinate purpose—even if it is the highest good. Using Kantian arguments one can simply take the view that the moral law ordains neither an object nor an end, at all events nothing with material content, but solely an obligation to act under the law itself. If, however, the teleological judgment views the world as a totality cohering according to purposive principles, and comprehends our acting too as directed toward such a final end, then it remains open to question, as was the case in the second *Critique*, whether this final end purportedly demanded by the moral law contains anything other than just morality itself. There is no need to conceive the element of happiness as contained in this final end. The final end of rational beings under moral laws is solely to effect what corresponds to the moral law. The categorical imperative knows nothing of happiness, not even as a consequence of morality. This can be

24. *CJ* 2:144. The existence of rational beings is designated as the final end, indeed of creation (2:116), but so also that quality of the world which coincides with such beings (2:124), as well as the highest good. The complexity thus introduced into the approach and the question as to the reconcilability of these different final ends can here be left open.

criticized as a defect, but it cannot be disregarded. The assumption that the final end ordained by the moral law includes the happiness appropriate to morality involves the *prōton pseudos* of ethicotheology in its third form.

According to the third *Critique,* practical reason ordains as final end the actualization of "universal happiness" in conjunction with the "strictest morality" (*CJ* 2:122). In line with Kant's previous argumentation it would be legitimate to infer from the understanding of this goal as a command of practical reason to the conditions making its realization possible and thus to the existence of God. But Kant interposes yet another mediating thought, namely that the conditions that make realization possible would consist in the fact that the nature of things conforms to this final end, and it is only this conformity between the character of the world and our final end that entitles us to assume a final end of creation. It is the thought of such a creation, a "real existence of things conformable to a *final end"* (*CJ* 2:125), that first provides Kant with a basis from which to infer not only an intelligent but also a moral author of the world. Here again the proof could be conducted without the element of happiness, solely from the requirement that the world should be compatible with the goal of morality. It would, however, then also make use of the concept of end. The same objections as before could be advanced to show why it was not conclusive: "The fulfillment of duty consists in the form of the earnest will, not in the intervening causes that contribute to success" (*CJ* 2:120). Only in the latter case would the moral law entail the assumption of God as guarantor of the execution of moral principles. And in any case this would disregard the role that falls to the concept of happiness in the third *Critique* itself.

The *Critique of Judgement* betrays more clearly than the preceding *Critiques* the source of the element of happiness in the concept of the final end. In so doing it exposes not only Kant's motives but also the points on which criticism could seize. Talk of a final end admittedly presupposes an end-setting agent, and this can be most readily interpreted as a rational being. Then recourse to the moral proof soon enables one to conjure up the personal being seated in heaven (*L* 29, *Br* 1:14). The argument that entitles us to assume such a final end and an end-setting intelligence is then conducted along familiar lines.[25]

Kant's exposition initially seems governed by the thought of the moral. It is not, he argues, human beings as such who are the final end of creation (creation understood generally, not necessarily assuming a creator), nor is it those who make their own happiness their aim, but only human beings under moral laws. This is stressed most insistently (CJ 2:110, 115). Happiness is only incidental to this "as a consequence proportionate to the measure of [human] harmony with that end, as the end of [human] existence," namely morality. Happiness is thus of no account for the status of human being as the final end of creation. It seems unsuited to be the final end, even if humans may invariably make it their ultimate subjective end (CJ 2:100). All that counts is the good will.

In the execution of the moral proof, however, the element of happiness thrusts itself to the fore. The purpose of action is now primarily determined by the striving for happiness. Happiness is an end that finite beings have by virtue of their very nature, an "irresistible end" that reason subjects only to the moral law "as inviolable condition," and thus "makes the furtherance of happiness in agreement with morality the final end" (CJ 2:119). The final end of all rational beings is "happiness so far as consistent with duty" (CJ 2:145). The weight attaching to happiness and morality is thus transposed: happiness does not follow on morality but is the end placed in us by nature and is simply held in check by morality. This leads to the anomaly that the promotion of happiness—one's own happiness, for this is what human beings usually make their goal— is declared by the moral law to be a duty, even with the proviso that the striving for happiness has to be tamed by morality.

25. For this reason Jakob Friedrich Fries criticized both the physicotheological and the ethicotheological proof as circular: "Instead of finding the notion of purposiveness in nature, we find it in the idea and then adjoin it to nature"; we are entitled to infer the existence of God "only on the presupposition of an absolute purposiveness in the world order, which we do in fact believe precisely on the basis of the idea of divinity." See *Neue oder anthropologische Kritik der Vernunft*, 2d ed. (Heidelberg, 1831), 2:293. Our criticism by contrast refers to the way in which the demand for morality is affected by the dominance of the quest for happiness in the concept of the end to be realized.

The transvaluation of the two elements of the highest good affords a deeper insight into the changed conception than the replacement of the concept of object by that of final end. The striving for happiness now stands revealed as the fundamental element in the idea of end: "The subjective condition under which man . . . is able under the above law [i.e., the moral law] to set before himself a final end, is happiness." Happiness is also the highest physical good there can be in the world. Certainly it is subject to "the objective condition that the individual harmonizes with the law of *morality*" (*CJ* 2:118), but this is more by way of being a secondary refinement. It is now less a question how it can be thought possible that happiness actually follows moral action; rather it is a question whether there is a prospect of my realizing my happiness even under the conditions of the moral law.

It is not only by this factual primacy given to the striving for happiness that the emphasis laid on the moral proof in the third *Critique* differs from the second, nor solely in the fact that the necessity of harmony between the character of the world and moral demands thrusts itself to the fore as the ground for the assumption of God. God's existence is no longer demanded as the precondition for the process of moral perfecting, and this also lessens the relative importance of the immortality postulate. What has become important for the further discussion is, in particular, the bringing to light of the assumptions that lead to this mode of proof, and the greater space Kant now devotes, as compared with the second *Critique,* to considering the demonstrative value of his exposition. He stresses more than once the note already sounded in the second *Critique,* to the effect that the moral necessity for presupposing God is subjective, a need, linked, to be sure, to the consciousness of duty, but not itself duty (*CPrR* 129–130); human beings need a moral intelligence in order to have a cause of their ends—their own and the world's (*CJ* 2:113); there is a purely moral need for the existence of an intelligent, moral author of the world. This limits, however, the force of conviction of the moral argument to the level of such a need, that is, to specifically human presuppositions; it becomes a proof not *kat' alētheian* but *kat' anthrōpon* (*CJ* 2:134). Here we have the slogan that was to play a decisive role during the next decade and, more especially, at the end of the period we are here considering.

But the question then is whether the proof can still lay claim to what the previous *Critiques* point to as the achievement of ethico-theology, namely, that it requires the existence of God to be assumed with the same binding force as pertains to the moral law in general (B 839), and that the assumption of the existence of God as the condition of possibility for the highest good "rests solely on *a priori* grounds of knowledge" and is unavoidable, not merely under the conditions of human nature, but "for every rational being in the world" (*CPrR* 117, 150). Even disregarding the connotation of specifically human need, the second *Critique* already presents the evidential claim of the moral argument in the surprising new term "rational faith" [*Vernunftglaube*], and the third *Critique* spells it out—presumably in the light of criticism voiced in the meantime[26]—as "moral faith." God and immortality are "mere matters of faith" (*CJ* 2:142). They are, to be sure, assumed for the sake of the practical use of reason, but are not themselves practically necessary, as is duty (*CJ* 2:145). We might wonder, therefore, whether it is not advisable, now that the validity of the argument has been restricted to human need (instead of to all rational beings), to abandon it and content ourselves with the insight that the idea of freedom is at the same time a fact that attests its own reality, whereas we can only presuppose God and immortality as the sole conditions we can conceive for the possibility of a final end which likewise belongs among mere matters of faith, and the accomplishment of which it is at any rate beyond our powers to grasp (*CJ* 2:146).

Yet here Kant proceeds to what is at first sight his most convincing proof, though ultimately it too fails owing to the very arguments that are supposed to be its principal stay. It is precisely where the link between the moral law and the idea of God is most intimate that the difficulties inherent in all ethicotheology come to the fore. In its new, most pregnant form, however, the argument is not to

26. Cf. Wizenmann's critique, cited by Timm, *Gott und die Freiheit*, pp. 444–445 (see above, n. 16).

be found under the title of the moral proof but in the doctrine of methods of the *Critique of Judgement*. It exhibits clear signs of the conscious revision of earlier formulations. Both the first and the second *Critiques* link the validity of the moral law to the existence of God in general. This has the undesired effect that, since there is no other sure foundation for the assumption of God, the moral law too can be surrendered, as an empty figment of the brain (B 839) or as fantastic and untrue (*CPrR* 118). The *Critique of Judgement* is clearly more cautious in the way it proceeds. Those, it argues, who cannot convince themselves of the existence of God have in no way the right to proclaim themselves free from the binding force of the moral law. It is only the prospect of the final end that has then to be surrendered. In saying this, Kant preserves the autonomy of the moral sphere better than he had done previously. If, however, his statement were not modified by additional clarifications, it would mean that the reasons given for presupposing God became much less convincing. For it would then be a matter of moral indifference whether one merely conformed to the moral law and excelled by acting blamelessly or shared the hope for the consummation of happiness. The progress from ethical teleology to ethicotheology, however, would then be rather a question of changing mental disposition than a problem in regard to the logical consistency of pure practical reason.

Kant therefore seeks to guard against being understood in this way by recourse to two arguments, one logical, the other empirical. The former could be called an application of the principle of noncontradiction. It recalls the fact that it ought not to be in any way optional whether one wishes to promote only morality or at the same time also the final end as a whole. Kant maintains rather that the moral law ordains pursuit of the final end. If, however, this appears an empty demand unless the existence of God is presupposed, then it is not merely the moral demands relating to the realization of happiness that in consequence become untenable. If the moral law here becomes self-contradictory, this also affects its other ordinances. Again it is the element that is primarily supposed to secure the idea of God which simultaneously threatens the moral law's claim to its binding character—in just the same way as in the previous versions of the argument. Kant, however, attaches the right to ultimate consistency to a condition. Because the moral claim is categorical it is not legitimate to gainsay it by holding against it the merely problematic character of God's existence and so making the moral demands self-contradictory. As a matter of logical consistency, practical reason constrains one to subscribe to this problematic assumption on practical grounds. The only thing, according to Kant, that can dispense one from it is the "complete certainty" of reason that the ideas of God and immortality are wholly null and void. According to the *Critique of Pure Reason,* however, such dogmatic certainty of God's nonexistence is out of the question. Since the existence of God and immortality remain, to be sure, problematical but can be thought without contradiction, whereas the assumption of God's nonexistence drives practical reason into contradiction within itself, these ideas must be accepted in order to keep practical reason free of contradiction (*CJ* 2:145).

This formulation of the connection between ethics and theology undoubtedly forms the most complete demonstration Kant achieved. It holds fast to the conviction that the idea of God is indispensable for morality and advances good reasons for not abandoning this idea on the basis of doubts as to God's nonexistence. On the premise that the moral law in fact ordains the realization of the final end, embracing both happiness and morality, the rigor of Kant's argument cannot be denied. The premise itself, however, might be formulated for the sake of the conclusion and be unsupported by other evidence.

Kant's maturest formulation of the connection between ethics and theology thus again makes the existence of God a constitutive element in ethics. If God did not exist, the moral law would contradict itself by demanding something by its very nature unfulfillable. The concluding passage of the third *Critique* is therefore contrary to the facts. It claims that "while morality without theology may certainly carry on with its own rule, it cannot do so with the final purpose which this very rule enjoins" (*CJ* 2:163). This unexpected statement opens up a conflict in regard to the goal Kant is aiming at. On the one hand the assumption of God becomes really binding only if on the basis of the principle of noncontradiction the contrary is excluded as a self-annulling of practical reason. On the other hand the dogmatic atheist must be prevented from declaring himself free of the moral law also. Kant had already envisaged this solution earlier (*CJ* 2:119–120), but he would hardly have repeated it in this form at the close of the work unless he had regarded it as justified and closer to the facts. Yet it reverts to the view that the validity of moral demands can be regionalized. It is in no way, however, only a matter of whether I forfeit a hope in regard to the final end, but rather whether my confidence in the moral law as a whole is shattered. For a system of morals without theology ordains a final end that must by its very nature remain unfulfillable. In this way it is not only one of its demands that becomes illusory; it becomes fantastic as a whole. To be sure, the dogmatic atheist does indeed deceive himself in regard to the right of theoretical reason to dispute dogmatically the existence of God. But when he usurps this right, even if from a lack of insight, then it is not only to be feared that his "heroism"—if such it be, to use the term employed in the second *Critique*—will not suffice as a foundation for morals. Rather does a convinced atheist render himself guilty of inconsistency if he holds fast to the binding character of the moral law; for him moral demands must appear contradictory. This precarious result is the unavoidable outcome of the assumption that the idea of God is constitutive for the inner consistency of practical reason. Thus the binding character of the moral claim is ultimately made dependent on a theoretical insight. Provided he is consistent, a convinced atheist cannot act morally.

This problem of moral atheism recurs at an empirical level. It is not only inconsistency of which Kant accuses the dogmatic atheist, assuming he still feels himself bound to the moral law and does not rather make his own happiness the goal unreservedly. He also contests his possibility of acting morally in real life—though no longer on the grounds he advanced in the first *Critique* or in his lectures on the doctrine of religion as transcribed by Pölitz,[27] namely that

27. [*Tr.*] Karl Heinrich Ludwig Pölitz transcribed and later published (in 1817) Kant's *Vorlesungen über die philosophische Religionslehre*. This work has been translated into English by Allen W. Wood and Gertrude M. Clark as *Lectures on Philosophical Theology* (Ithaca, N.Y., 1978).

dogmatic atheists have no incentives for acting morally. God is no longer invoked as *principium executionis*. But this makes little difference in the outcome. Without the assumption of God and without confidence in the realization of the final end (*CJ* 2:120), the moral disposition is necessarily undermined. Kant's penetrating portrayal of the dangers of attempting a morality without God leaves one with a choice between presupposing God and, at the least, weakening morals. The only logically consistent reaction, albeit built on false premises, would be to abandon the moral law altogether: "But a dogmatic *unbelief* cannot stand side by side with a moral maxim governing the attitude of the mind—for reason cannot command one to pursue an end that is recognized to be nothing but a fiction of the brain" (*CJ* 2:147). But this dilemma itself furnishes an incentive for revising Kant's concept. For the figure he chooses to illustrate a dogmatic unbeliever—Spinoza—teaches rather that the dilemma is false. Even Kant does not seek to assign Spinoza to one or the other side. He does not reproach him with moral laxity, nor does he take the view that his conviction of the nonexistence of God—in the Kantian sense—ultimately gave way to the assumption of a moral author of the world. So his own example confirms the doubt as to the correctness of his thesis that the idea of God has a constitutive function for ethics.

2.3. The Philosophy of Religion between Ethicotheology and Anthropology

(1) The efforts directed to the practical recuperation of the idea of God which we have considered thus far culminate in the designation of God as an object of moral faith. He is understood as the condition of possibility for the final end, but a final end whose form—a goal of all our action ordained by the moral law—and whose content—the harmony of happiness and morality—can be termed highly disputable. So the idea of God is the sole condition we are capable of conceiving for the realization of a problematic final end whose more precise form remains at all events unknowable.

This result invites a comparison with philosophical theology in its theoretical [i.e., Kantian] form. The latter ends, to be sure, with the demonstration of the impossibility of all speculative theology. But measured by the result of the attempt to find a new practical foundation for theology, the concepts of God formulated by theoretical reason do not show up at all so poorly. Kant himself terms the *prototypon transcendentale* "the only true ideal of which human reason is capable" (B 604), an ideal that is quite unique (B 639–640), in fact "an ideal without a flaw" (B 669). If this ideal is not taken as constitutive and hypostatized by means of a transcendental subreption, but rather grasped as a regulative principle of reason, then it can stand up well to comparison with the idea of God based on practical foundations. The third *Critique* also calls the idea of the absolutely necessary being a concept that is, to be sure, unavoidably problematic for human understanding but at the same time an indispensable idea of reason (*CJ* 2:57). A hidden admission of this superiority could be seen in the fact that Kant after all ends up by contesting not only speculative reason's qualification for establishing such an ideal but even its ability to hypothesize God: having regard to the lack of all other conditions of knowledge, such a hypothesis is not justified merely by the fact that the idea of God is free from contradiction (*CJ* 2:139). In that case the practical grounding would indeed enjoy undeniable precedence. But this is not the result of the *Critique of Pure Reason,* and it cannot be presented as the outcome of the theoretical knowledge of God, without retracting the results arrived at in the first *Critique.*

One may therefore be tempted with more justification to relate Kant's renunciation of the theoretical knowledge of God to his attempt to find a new, practical foundation for it; knowledge of God, we might say, is "a labor so fatiguing in its endless wrestling with insuperable difficulties," from which at the same time little useful benefit can be derived (B 826). It was, to be sure, in such usefulness that Kant saw the superiority of the practical method. Its usefulness, however, is evident exclusively in the brief outline of an ethicotheology contained in the *Critique of Pure Reason,* where God is accepted as the sole incentive for morality. For Kant's subsequent conception, by contrast, little store is set by usefulness; and it is even to be feared that it will be more than counterbalanced by the danger conjured up by a practical grounding of the idea of God, namely, that the latter is more threatening than conducive to the binding character of moral demands.

The fact that the practical grounding of the idea of God has not succeeded either is not yet a convincing argument for its theoretical formulation. Furthermore we have not yet paid attention to Kant's allusion to the fact that it is only the practical form of argument that unifies the idea of God and religion. To the question concerning the value of theology, he answers that we "need theology solely on behalf of religion, that is to say, the practical, or in other words moral, employment of our reason, and need it as a subjective requirement" (*CJ* 2:159). To the extent that religion is thus directly identified with the moral use of reason, we do not yet have any kind of relationship between theology and religion. In Kant's view, what he here affirms by way of defining religion, namely that it is morals in relation to God as lawgiver (*CJ* 2:131), applies to the whole sphere of morals. Even the more familiar formula found in the second *Critique,* which he repeats in the third, does not yet allow any differentiation between an ethics that rests ultimately on theological grounds and religion: religion, so the formula runs, consists in the knowledge of our duties as divine commands (*CPrR* 134, *CJ* 2:158). In the strict sense, therefore, one cannot yet speak here of theology's being useful to religion. Paradoxically it could be said that such usefulness consisted in the fact that religion was indistinguishable from ethicotheology. Even a theoretically grounded theology does not sever this link to ethics. But it is just this that causes Kant to reject such a theology, not solely because it was insufficiently grounded but because it modified both morals and religion. For morals would, in this case, have to take theology as its guiding light. "Thus not alone will an extrinsic and arbitrary legislation on the part of a Supreme Being have to be introduced in place of an immanent and necessary legislation of reason but, even in such legislation, all the defects of our insight into the divine nature must spread to the moral code, and religion in this way be divorced from morality and perverted" (*CJ* 2:131). This consideration is highly relevant to Kant's definition of the relation between the two ways to the knowledge of God; the real defect in the theoretical way consists in the fact that it throws into question the exclusively moral interpretation of religion and the purity of the moral law known in religion as divine command. Thus there are for Kant not only no good arguments for the theoretical knowledge of God, but also a weighty objection to it. To the very extent that it would be possible to know something more and something else about God than that he is moral author of the world, religion too would encompass other, nonmoral contents. Then it would be necessary to find a place also in religion for, let us say, dogmatic speculation on God's trinitarian nature.

It was not just for the future that Kant feared such consequences. He could find sufficiently frequent occasion for them in the history of Christianity, and surely also in its present condition. (He does not in any event devote more than a glance to other religions.) To this extent his fear is, to be sure, well founded. It undeniably assumes, however, that religion is really nothing other than knowledge of the moral laws as divine commands. Otherwise the fact that the concept of God and religion form a unity would oblige one, for the same reasons of consistency, to demand that the idea of God should not be based merely on moral grounds. Now it would be easy, in the event of its being impossible to base the knowledge of God on either theoretical or moral grounds, to loosen or even abandon the close conceptual link between the idea of God and religion. The consequence would be that philosophy of religion, in the sense to which Kant adheres, would be quite impossible; but so too would religion. For without having a philosophical theology (even if only rudimentary and however fashioned) which presents the idea of God as an ideal along with its justification for doing so, and without testing the "purity" of this idea by means of this "touchstone," all worship of God would be "idolatry" (*RWLR* 157).

If, however, religion were to be nothing more than morals, Kant's talk of an "unavoidable" and "indispensable" passing over from morals to religion would remain empty talk (*RWLR* 5–7). Indeed the first preface to *Religion within the Limits of Reason Alone* gives the impression that pure practical reason has no need of the idea of God. There is no denying that Kant frequently formulates his ethics without regard to the idea of God. But it cannot be said of this form that it leads unavoidably to religion. The alternative version, by contrast, makes the idea of God the condition for the noncontradictoriness of ethics and regards the moral laws themselves as divine commands. With it there can as a consequence be no question of first "passing over" to religion.

(2) The idea of God as promulgator of the moral law remains in the background in the three *Critiques,* where God is defined rather as the source of promises and threats or as the guarantor of the realization of the highest good. In the definition of religion, and in *Religion within the Limits of Reason Alone* as a whole, this concept comes back into view, however. A first objection to it concerns Kant's argument for assuming such a lawgiver, namely that the unity of the moral law must be grounded on the unity of the moral will of a single supreme lawgiver in the moral kingdom of ends (*CJ* 2:110). That ethicotheology, unlike physicotheology, leads to the concept of one supreme lawgiver has been called in question above (pp. 42f.). This unity of pure practical reason is indeed also not threatened by the way it is manifested in single individuals. From the standpoint of ethicotheology there is no compelling argument why one should not assume, let us say, three or more divine beings, provided they do not enter into conflict. Still less convincing is what we are told in the second *Critique,* that the laws proclaimed by each and every free will must at the same time be regarded as commands of a divine will, since otherwise there is no certainty of the highest good being realized (*CPrR* 134). This simply presupposes the moral author of the world as the condition of possibility for something whose existence can justifiably be assumed only if this condition is fulfilled, without its being credible by virtue of other assumptions. In any event the moral lawgiver remains an empty concept. The binding character of the moral law is not based on it: it is divine because it is binding, not binding because it is divine. Nor is it possible to take as one's starting point the concept of God as moral *ens originarium* and deduce the moral laws from that (B 847). And as far as content is concerned, the introduction of a divine lawgiver does not make it any wider; no new actions are ordained, nor any particular duties vis-à-vis God, which are attributable solely to God's lawgiving—not because we are as yet unaware of any such duties, but because we cannot act upon God (*RWLR* 142). Nor is

it necessary to designate God as a moral lawgiver in order to entrust him with the realization of the highest good, if indeed that seems appropriate, nor in order to assign him the function of the source of moral incentives. In any case the latter matter is regarded as settled since the time of the *Fundamental Principles*. Yet here we have stress laid on the assumption of God as moral lawgiver. The result in any event generates a conflict with the conception of ethics developed elsewhere.

Certainly the resolution of this conflict should not be for Kant to revert without further ado to the standpoint of the first *Critique* and make God undisguisedly the source of the incentives for acting morally. His solution indeed respects the distinction between legality and morality. The line it follows is that designated above (p. 56) as a first step toward modification of the doctrine of purely moral incentives: God becomes the "cause supplementing our incapacity"—but not only, as indicated there, "with respect to the final moral end" (*RWLR* 171) but also in regard to moral action in general. The assumption of God is not viewed as replacing moral incentives but as complementing, enhancing, and animating them. So the question arises whether respect for the moral law and the assumption of God can be combined in such a way that the latter enhances the moral incentives—"purified of the stupidity of superstition and the madness of fanaticism" (*RWLR* 93)—without jeopardizing them in their "purity" or even taking their place. Kant is visibly concerned to make a precise conceptual distinction, especially in the passages dealing with the relationship between godliness and morality (*RWLR* 171 ff.). That the doctrine of God eliminates the otherwise unavoidable inner contradictoriness of the moral law and so removes the objections to its acceptance cannot be regarded as detracting from pure regard for the moral law. The same would have to be said if it could be maintained in isolation that pure regard is "crowned with the hope of the ultimate achievement of all our good ends" (*RWLR* 173). But this hope is linked with the expectation of one's own happiness, and it is difficult to affirm that it has no effect on pure regard, especially since happiness is our immediate and natural aim. Regardless of the conceptual distinction, therefore, enhancement of the purely moral incentives by the idea of God must be accounted an ill-disguised variant of the direct striving for happiness. The only possible exception would be when—as in *The Conflict of the Faculties*—animation of the moral incentives through the Bible occurs as the result of just what we put into it "by a moral cast of mind."[28] Apart from such a self-enhancement of morality it is, to be sure, conceptually possible but illusory in reality to exclude the striving for happiness as a motive for action. Kant even makes other concessions to it, by counting not only the idea of the divine lawgiver but also that of the divine judge as purely religious beliefs. If it is only through God that the moral law becomes command, becomes *lex perfecta,* then the idea of God as judge finds entry into the conception too—and in even more crass fashion than in the idea of the highest good. It is consistent, then, that Kant speaks of eternal bliss and eternal woe as of "representations powerful enough . . . to serve as incentives" (*RWLR* 63).

The doctrine of purely moral incentives that has been obligatory since the *Fundamental Principles* is here expressly surrendered; yet this assertion follows consistently on the main thread of *Religion within the Limits of Reason Alone.* In a later passage Kant explicitly denies that the prospect of reward in a future world has the character of an incentive. He interprets it as "a soul-elevating representation of the consummation of the divine benevolence and wisdom in the guidance of the human race," and as an "object of the purest respect and of the greatest moral approval" (*RWLR* 150). The fact that he does this is certainly understandable in terms of his concern to present the teacher of the gospel as a pure moralist. But it reveals no less clearly the extent to which the talk of a purely moral incentive can be manipulated—and it reveals something else besides. In the *Fundamental Principles* Kant sees the scant influence of morals as due to the fact that "the teachers did not clarify their own ideas. In their desire to be thorough they spoiled them by digging up motives of moral goodness from every quarter in order to make their medicine good and strong" (*RWLR* 27). This warning

28. Immanuel Kant, *The Conflict of the Faculties,* trans. Mary J. Gregor (New York, 1979), p. 125.

against an ethics compounded of moral incentives and impulses can also be turned against one compounded of religious and moral incentives: the effectiveness of the moral incentives is here jeopardized by notions that must inevitably acquire a greater influence over action than do moral incentives. If the moral law is not the sole determining condition, and there is also the threat of eternal damnation and the promise of eternal bliss, then it is illusory to suppose that the moral incentives would actually come into consideration as opposed to the religious ones—even if the two can be conceptually differentiated.

This outcome is not affected even if one disregards the wholesale promise of reward and threat of punishment and speaks solely in terms of the more subtle distinction as to whether an action is done or not done because it is prescribed or prohibited by autonomous practical reason or by a divine lawgiver. In her conversation with Saladin, Sittah bemoans the fact that should Christians ever do good it was only because Christ had commanded it and not because it was good. Actions undertaken from religious motives coincided, it was true, with moral actions, but only because Christ fortunately had been a good man. This does not make such actions moral. The authority conferred by Christ replaces moral incentives by religious ones and autonomous moral decision by heteronomous commandments. From this point of view the problem of heteronomy becomes a matter of no less importance than it has in regard to sensible desire, with which Kant is principally concerned. If one declares God simply to be the author of the moral law, one makes the fact of moral insight (a fact directly bound up with the concept of freedom, but not itself permitting further insight as to its possibility) part of God's doing. What the second *Critique* tells us of the irreducible fact of moral insight then becomes a mere propaedeutic culminating in the avowal *Deus fecit*. It would accordingly stand in need of modification and correction in the light of the religious interpretation.

The conflict between the autonomy of moral reason and the heteronomy of divine legislation is in no way inevitable for Kant's ethics. It manages without assuming a divine legislator, without even assuming God, if it does not (for the sake of grounding an ethicotheology) unnecessarily represent as an ordinance of the moral law what involves a contradiction of moral reason with itself, even without the assumption of God. It is only if it takes the highest good as a morally ordained final end that it has to attach constitutive meaning to the thought of a moral world author and lawgiver. But then it can no longer resolve the conflict between the autonomy and the heteronomy of pure practical reason. It is only in subsequent approaches that a resolution of the conflict becomes possible, in particular in Fichte's *Appelation an das Publikum* (1799)—though in a way that, as we know, drew upon itself the criticism that it surrendered one pole of the tension, namely the personal divine lawgiver.

(3) These objections to naming God as moral lawgiver admittedly impugn Kant's frequently repeated definition of religion. But they adhere to the framework laid down for ethicotheology by the three *Critiques*. Up to this point there is no need for a social phenomenon called religion over and above pure religious faith. The assumption of God as lawgiver does not require one to go beyond the individual's ethicoreligious disposition to religion as a social phenomenon. For this purpose Kant again has recourse to the idea of the highest good, although here too, properly speaking, the "morality" element is sufficient: to promote the rule of the good principle is, he argues, beyond the powers of a single individual and requires an ethical commonwealth, the "establishment and spread of a society in accordance with, and for the sake of, the laws of virtue" (*RWLR* 86). The consideration that in the second *Critique* led to the postulate of immortality is used here to provide a rational basis for ethical communities, which have to perform the same function, *mutatis mutandis,* as immortality did previously. And this time Kant explicitly maintains what is true also of the immortality postulate, that such grounding requires the presupposition of a higher moral being (*RWLR* 90). In the perspective that is valid also for the immortality postulate, this is entirely plausible. Otherwise human nature is portrayed in such somber terms as to threaten the ethical commonwealth no less than the individual: "it suffices that . . . they are men, for them mutually to corrupt each other's predispositions and make one another evil" (*RWLR* 85). Kant,

however, introduces the idea of God in yet another fashion, arguing that the people cannot be regarded as legislating in an ethical
commonwealth, and that the legislator must be someone else—not
the worldly ruler, but God, whose laws are identical with moral
laws (RWLR 90 ff.). Certainly this mode of justification is unconvincing in the extreme. There is no denying that "the people" cannot be regarded as the lawgiver in an ethical commonwealth. It
would, moreover, be unnecessary; the fact of the moral law is sufficient to constitute an ethical commonwealth. In any case it would
be possible for there to be external prescriptions, which it might
very well be the task of the members of this commonwealth to lay
down. Indeed, Kant himself deems it presumptuous to view regula-
tions that are necessary for ecclesiastical organization as statutory
ordinances of God (RWLR 96). It is only the analogy of an evolution from the political natural state to civil society that requires a
formal giving of laws for the sake of an evolution from the ethical
natural state to an ethical commonwealth, even though these laws
are grounded in the autonomy of pure practical reason and possess
unassailable binding force even without the assumption of God as
moral lawgiver. This renewed attempt to save the idea of the divine
lawgiver from the suspicion of redundancy by arguments relating
specifically to the philosophy of religion is unpersuasive also. The
same is true of the credibility of the further expositions, in regard
(for example) to the contrast drawn between pure religious faith
and historical faith based on revelation.

The coupling of ethics with theology presents no less a threat to
religion than to the inclusiveness of ethics and its claim to a binding
character. It reduces religion to moral belief. What people take to
be pleasing to God but cannot be legitimated as moral is denounced
as pseudoworship and fetishism, with a sharpness that falls little short of the radical French Enlightenment (RWLR 181). The
ethicotheological foundation of the philosophy of religion turns out
to be the Procrustean bed of historical religion—in quite a different
fashion than Hegel's subsequent attempt to discern reason in religion. For Hegel in no way reduces religion to ontology. He simply
lets it be understood that religion has this dimension of reason in
the metaphysical sense and has to be regarded first and foremost

from this point of view within philosophy, but he does not reject the aspects of religion that lie beyond reason as idolatry and demonology (to use only Kant's more reticent terminology).

The failure of ecclesiastical faith to meet the moral claim, a failure that prompted Kant's violent polemic, is, however, in no way a matter of chance, the perhaps reversible consequence of past misunderstandings. It stems from human nature, which does all it can to escape the demands of the moral law. All characteristics of cultic faith and, in general, of historical faith based on revelation are attributed by Kant to the weakness and corruption of human nature. The phenomenal form of religion is viewed as a refraction of pure religious faith in the imperfect medium of human nature—a nature that only rarely allows one to rise to pure faith based on reason. Kant can maintain the reasonableness of religion, therefore, only because he rejects its phenomenal form outright as depraved by the conditions of its reception inherent in human nature.

Also doomed to failure is his attempt to discover reason in the strained relationship between pure religious faith and historical religion by conceiving this relationship as something historical. It is historical no longer in a mythical sense, as a subsequent residue of the pure rational faith of an ideal former age, but in the sense of a conception of educational process. Kant's sole attempt to give cultic religion something more than a merely negative function makes it a vehicle for the introduction of pure rational faith (*RWLR* 97–98). Definitions of the relationship of rational and historical religion current at the time may have served as a model in this regard. But Kant's definition of the relation of purely moral religion to cultic religion undermines a consistent conception of educational process similar to Lessing's view or to Johann Salomo Semler's idea of perfectibility.

Two recurrent affirmations by Kant cannot be reconciled: on the one hand, that ecclesiastical faith makes moral religion "comprehensible" (*RWLR* 153) and provides the vehicle for it (*RWLR* 109); and on the other hand, that historical religion never becomes universal, always remains tied to limited conditions, and can thus never be promoted generally. It is not very promising to use as means of conveyance for the religion that is said to be universally intelligible and evident to all a form of faith, namely ecclesiastical faith, which is deficient in these qualities, which runs strictly counter to the moral claim of pure religious faith, and which declares it to be unnecessary, even pernicious. In Kant's day the understanding of "vehicle" was molded by its use in pharmacy: "vehicle" denotes the neutral substance that functions as a carrier of the properly active material. Ecclesiastical faith, however, is no such neutral substance: it tends rather to lead away from pure religious faith and to enhance positivity. It is useless to have recourse to it as a vehicle of educational process, especially since Kant does not really testify to such a pedagogical function of the ecclesiastical faith he elsewhere speaks of so slightingly. He makes use of an apologetic saying currently in vogue, of which an echo is found in Goethe's *Faust*, in the Walpurgis Night's Dream scene:

Ja, für die Frommen, glaubet mir,	The pious need no fancy prop,
Ist alles ein Vehikel;	All vehicles seem sound:
Sie bilden auf dem Blocksberg hier	Even up here on Blocksberg's top
Gar manches Konventikel.	Conventicles abound.[29]

Within the framework of Kant's conception it is only pure religious faith—grounded directly in reason, independent of tradition and historical erudition—that could form the vehicle for refining the historical religion based on revelation. For it to be otherwise, Kant would have to regard pure rational faith as the result of an educational process, and he would have to conceive reason itself as historical. But the primacy of rational revelation robs this schema of its basis: ecclesiastical faith and pure religious faith do not stand in a historical relationship but are viewed according to the paradigm of pure reason and its perversion by human needs.

Kant's emphatic reference to the anthropological conditionedness of ecclesiastical faith prompts us to consider again the question whether what he terms pure religious faith is not itself molded by the weakness of human nature. Attention has already been drawn above (p. 63) to the clearer emergence of anthropological consider-

---

29. [*Tr.*] Johann Wolfgang von Goethe, *Faust*, trans. Walter Kaufmann (New York, 1961), lines 4326–4330 (pp. 394–395).

ations in the *Critique of Judgement*. This viewpoint is even more evident in *Religion within the Limits of Reason Alone*, in regard not only to ecclesiastical faith, whose anthropological roots are beyond dispute, but also to pure religious faith. A footnote to the preface (*RWLR* 5–6) declares openly that the concept of a final end cannot be deduced from the duties prescribed by the moral law. This belated clarification confirms the criticism advanced here: the moral law commands categorically regardless of success. The idea of a final end—and an end is an object of inclination, something one can love—first comes into the argument through the "inescapable limitation" of humanity. It is true that here too Kant defines the final end as presented by pure reason—but explicitly as a subsequent extension of the moral law, brought about by "the natural characteristic of man that, for all his actions, he must conceive of an end over and above the law." But it is just this concept of the object or final end that provides a starting point for the ethicotheology of the second and third *Critiques*. Even if the postulate of God as the condition of possibility for this end were stringent, its foundation could only be the "inescapable limitation" of humanity— not morals but the human incapacity to rise to the level of morals.

This confession concludes more than a decade of constantly improving efforts to provide a new, practical grounding for the idea of God. At an early stage in this process Kant believes it is possible to exclude all anthropological considerations. *The Fundamental Principles of the Metaphysic of Ethics* outlines a system "that is not mixed with any anthropology, theology, physics or hyperphysics, even less with any hidden qualities." It denotes this metaphysics as "an indispensable substratum of every theoretical knowledge of duties which has been determined with certainty," and stresses for its part "that moral principles are not founded upon the properties of human nature, but must subsist *a priori* of themselves."[30] By the close of the decade, however, we have not only the disillusioned description of ecclesiastical faith but also the scarcely disguised admission of the anthropological presuppositions for the postulates

30. Kant, *Fundamental Principles of the Metaphysic of Ethics*, pp. 26–27. [*Tr.* Manthey-Zorn's translation, which is based on the Cassirer edition rather than the Akademie-Ausgabe, lacks the word "theology" in the first quoted passage.]

of divine existence and immortality, postulates that nevertheless at the same time play a constitutive role within ethics. This development can be seen as anticipating the criticism later directed against the one-sided fixation on the concept of duty. It may also form a more suitable answer to the problem of ethics because it explicitly brings human nature into its approach. But this tendency not only detracts from ethicotheology; it is utterly ruinous to it. That the idea of God is a complement of human weakness was an idea not unknown even previously. Nor was it necessary, in order to arrive at it, to imperil the autonomy of ethics and cut religion down to the scale of morality.

3. The Elaboration and Critique of the Moral Concept of Religion

3.1. On Method

Kant's contemporaries were initially faced with a different picture of the moral concept of God and religion from that portrayed here. Certainly there was no lack of critical voices even early on. But individual objections of this kind did not prevent Kant's solution of the problem of the connection between ethicotheology and philosophy of religion from occupying a dominant position at the beginning of the 1790s. This did not rest so much on the fact that the first *Critique* had disposed of the old metaphysical concept of God once and for all. Merely negative consequences of a demonstrative procedure can rarely have such a positive effect, even if they are as rigorous as desired. Kant's solution owed its wide acceptance partly to the fact that the critique of the demonstrability of the existence of God was at the same time a critique of the demonstrability of his nonexistence. In this way the Kantian solution came to the aid of theology by supplying the proof of which it stood in need during the late Enlightenment. At the same time it seemed to make it possible to present all previous theoretical conclusions regarding the existence of God, as well as a direct revelation of God or the attributes of God, as not open to a theoretical critique but as practically necessary. This also offered the advantage of putting one's opponent morally in the wrong. Schelling expressed this in pithy terms: while an opponent of a follower of Wolff had been regarded as someone deficient in philosophy, a critic of the moral concept of God was saddled with the "anathema of moral depravity."[31] The blanket proviso that it was not a matter of theoretical knowledge but of assumptions justified on practical grounds did not limit the scope of these assertions and further strengthened their claim to acceptance.

Only a decade later this reasoning no longer held. The doctrine of postulates of the second *Critique* and the moral proof of the third were not of the same epoch-making importance as the demonstration of the failure of all speculative theology. The moral concept of God and of religion was indeed able to hold sway during the decade following the *Critique of Practical Reason,* which could be called the decade of the moral God. But even in the second half of the decade other conceptions came to the fore. Thus by the end of the decade there remained essentially the alternative of either forsaking the moral grounding of the idea of God and of religion, or else, with Fichte, of holding to its context (albeit in modified fashion) and conceiving the moral world order itself as God.

To show the failure of the moral solution was less of a problem than to replace it by a new one. Kant indeed had recommended ethicotheology as the sole remaining way to a philosophical idea of God. Merely to refute his solution would have resulted in confessing the impossibility of a philosophical theory of God and of religion. Refutation of the moral interpretation did not therefore take the form of merely supplanting it by a new position, in such a way that its demonstrative force would have remained, as it were, uncontradicted, but also without attending to how the gap that would otherwise arise was to be filled. There was not available, however, an inexhaustible arsenal of new interpretations such that when one was shown to be inadequate, it would have been a simple matter to have recourse to the next.

Even so, the criticism to which the moral God and religion

31. Friedrich Wilhelm Joseph Schelling, *Philosophische Briefe über Dogmatismus und Kriticismus,* in *Historisch-kritische Ausgabe,* eds. H. M. Baumgartner, W. G. Jacobs, H. Krings, and H. Zeltner (Stuttgart, 1976 ff.), 3:58.

within the limits of merely practical reason were subjected did not in itself prove the possibility of a new conception. The direction in which such a conception was to be sought was also not yet fixed. The first reactions bear witness to a certain perplexity of mind, which are coped with only by not posing the problems in their full dimension, even though they can be said to reproduce, elaborate, and criticize Kant's viewpoints in a not inconsistent manner. In part they focus on the critique of speculative reason. While they do not seek to bring about any fundamental revision of its theological results, they do voice a hesitant uneasiness in regard to some of them. The fact that their opposition is thus rather half-hearted means, however, that on the whole they remain under the spell of the *Critique of Pure Reason* and accept its verdict (sec. 3.2 below). Of greater importance, therefore, are the attempts made to dispute the power of conviction of ethicotheology. On the one hand they enhance the independence of ethics as opposed to the belated attempt to assign a constitutive function to the idea of God (sec. 3.3). If ethicotheology forms the sole remaining way for the philosophical knowledge of God, this argument, to be sure, leads to negative consequences in regard to the very possibility of such knowledge—even if these consequences are not drawn explicitly. For this reason it also remains more on the margin of the discussion, which centers on the restatement and elaboration of the Kantian assumption that the idea of God is also a necessity for moral philosophy. Nothing contributed more strongly, however, to the decline of ethicotheology than the extension effected on its behalf. What to some appeared elaboration was viewed by others as a compromising of practical reason (sec. 3.4). An alternative conception, instead of entering into the controversy in regard to ethicotheology, sought to interpret religion and the history of religion with the help of Kant's results. The failure of this attempt too led to forsaking the moral concept of God; this development could be seen most clearly in implicit fashion in a change in the concept of religion—a transition to a new concept complete with metaphysical characteristics (sec. 3.5). After the failure of the practical grounding, however, the problem of God did not simply revert to theoretical philosophy. It had first to be shown that this offered a better place for it. A much more obvious course was to remove it wholly from the sphere of philosophy or at least deliberately to pose the question of God and religion no longer *kat' alētheian* but *kat' anthrōpon* (sec. 3.6).

The choice of the viewpoints to be discussed here is guided by the fact that the prime concern of these studies is the foundations of the speculative philosophy of religion. We must leave aside the theoretical philosophy of this decade, as it is determined by Fichte's *Science of Knowledge* and the texts by Fichte and Schelling that followed on it. There is no intention of disputing their importance, but what we are concerned with here is to reconstruct the arguments that led to the replacement of moral theology by speculative philosophy of religion. As a consequence we have to pay attention essentially to the viewpoints that we can show or assume Hegel must have taken into account in affirmative or critical fashion on the way to formulating his philosophy of religion.

3.2. The Hesitant Rehabilitation of the Theoretical Knowledge of God

Despite the dominance of the moral concept of God, there were constant doubts regarding not only the the way the moral line of argument was conducted but also the *"utility* of the whole process." We could, it was argued, be well content with the postulates of practical reason "if we could only see that in this way our concepts of God and immortality rested on a somewhat firmer foundation than the natural illusion of speculative reason. But that is what we must still doubt."[32] Schleiermacher penned these thoughts in the year following the appearance of Kant's second *Critique,* without making them public. Ernst Platner's twenty-four questions on Kant's moral theology[33] had by contrast a major influence on the discussion that took place at that time. What is unsatisfactory about them is not so much the fact that Platner equates the demonstrative claim of the so-called moral proof with that of a theoretical proof and criticizes it accordingly, as that he fails to separate the stages we have here distinguished in Kant's argumentation. The

---

32. Friedrich Schleiermacher, *Über das höchste Gut,* in KGA 1:99.
33. Ernst Platner, *Philosophische Aphorismen,* 3d ed. (Leipzig, 1793), § 941.

sharpest criticism of ethicotheology came from Schelling in his *Philosophische Briefe über Dogmatismus und Kriticismus.* It presupposes other developments we have still to consider (sec. 3.4). But even where the intention was to remain at Kant's standpoint, an interest in linking ethicotheology to themes of theoretical reason manifested itself early on. A typical example is afforded by Karl Heinrich Heydenreich's *Betrachtungen über die Philosophie der natürlichen Religion.* A contemplative ground of faith is here assumed in addition to ethicotheology. Theoretical reason is led to the idea of a necessary, supremely real being, and it identifies this idea with the primordial basis of moral reason and the creator of the future world system.[34]

Interest in a moderate revision of the rigorous exclusion of all theoretical elements was not directed to cosmotheology or even to ontotheology; it concerned solely physicotheology. There was an unquestionable justification for revising the verdict on physicotheology because, contra Kant, the demonstrative force of the physicotheological proof is in no way inferior to that of the moral proof. Moreover, the interest in physicotheology was at that time still so strong that a number of works aimed less at a reanimation of physicotheology than at its naively unbroken continuation—without taking cognizance of Kant's critique. For this reason we need not here take them into account.[35] They ran the scale from an unreflective juxtaposition to deliberate association. Ludwig Heinrich Jakob, for instance, though he took over the results of ethicotheology, tended to do so in a way different from that of Kant, as is already clear from the amount of space his work devotes to physicotheology.[36] Even among committed Kantians the binding

34. Karl Heinrich Heydenreich, *Betrachtungen über die Philosophie der natürlichen Religion,* 2 vols. (Leipzig, 1790–91), 1:173. See Hans Jürgen Gawoll, "Karl Heinrich Heydenreich: Zwischen Spinozismus und Kantianismus" (Manuscript, Ruhr University, Bochum), p. 66.

35. As representative of the attitude that still prevailed at that time, we need only mention the long-winded expositions given in Johann Friedrich Dahlenburg, *Philosophie und Religion der Natur, für gebildete Menschen,* 3 vols. (Berlin, 1797).

36. Ludwig Heinrich Jakob, *Die allgemeine Religion* (Halle, 1797). Jakob's work shows a weakening of the moral understanding of religion in another direction as well, since he lays stress on psychological and anthropological factors; see his preface, pp. xii-xvii.

force of ethicotheology was dwindling at the time Jakob was engaged in this work. But the attempt to reground physicotheology on an ethicotheological basis was in no way new. It could invoke the *Critique of Judgement* itself. In his anonymous *Offenbarungskritik,* Johann Gebhard Ehrenreich Maass had already provided an ethicotheological foundation for a concept of indirect revelation and for this purpose had recourse to physicotheology.[37] And in his letter to Schelling at the end of January 1795, Hegel spoke of a plan to show to what extent, "after having fixed moral belief, we might now utilize the thus legitimated idea of God backwards, for example in the elucidation of goal-directedness, and so on; that is, to what extent we might take the idea of God derived from our present vantage point in ethicotheology with us back into physicotheology, in order to legislate in this second field by means of that idea" (*L* 31, *Br* 1:17).

These approaches to the problem betray a renewed interest in theoretical knowledge. No fundamentally new insight could be expected from them, however, since they purely and simply presuppose the foundational function of ethicotheology. Compared to this, the question of a greater or lesser extension of physicotheology was secondary. Merely to restore physicotheology in its pristine form as a foundational discipline was at all events condemned to failure by the *Critique of Pure Reason.* So no transformations and also no critique of ethicotheology were to be looked for from the renewed interest in physicotheology. To the extent that this interest had any claim to philosophical seriousness, it had necessarily to develop, and could only develop, under the aegis of ethicotheology.

3.3. The Atheism of Moral Reason

Of more importance was the question of the necessity of the connection between ethics and theology, whether theology in fact followed so unbrokenly from ethics as Kant, his theologizing followers, and Kantianizing theologians alleged. We have already in-

37. Johann Gebhard Ehrenreich Maass, *Kritische Theorie der Offenbarung* (Halle, 1792). Maass also departs from the practical standpoint inasmuch as he sees the concept of God given a priori as a first cause and the most perfect being (p. 9). But he too deems the only possible rational theology to be a moral theology (pp. 14–15).

dicated the different points on which a critique of this kind could fasten. We now have to see to what extent they were important for the historical unfolding of the link between philosophical theology and philosophy of religion.

The critique of ethicotheology comprises a series of objections: (1) Even if practical reason were to fall into self-contradiction unless God is presupposed, this would not prove the existence of what could avoid the contradiction. This argument forms as it were a first line of defense. The crucial point is the second: (2) Moral reason does not in any event fall into self-contradiction since the conjunction of virtue and happiness is not an end presented to us. For virtue and happiness to fall apart would thus have no effect on acting morally. But then the justification for postulating the existence of God disappears. There remains indeed the mere wish that virtue and happiness may harmonize with each other. To act morally is required categorically. Its sole presupposition lies in the fact of freedom. The lack of any prospect of happiness does not exempt one from conforming to the claim of the moral law. This line of argument could, however, be taken a step further: (3) Not only is the existence of God not presupposed for the sake of acting morally. Rather it hinders genuine morality, if it does not make it utterly impossible. This argument corresponds to the objections raised by the proponents of ethicotheology to the theoretical knowledge of God. It can with more justification be turned against the attempt to ground knowledge of God on practical reason. For the assumption of God as moral lawgiver or as judge over proportionate happiness includes his activity as executor of the moral law, and with it the notions of reward and punishment. But the incentives that derive from these notions do not enhance the purely moral impulses, that is to say, sheer respect for the moral law; rather they undermine them. The assumption of God is therefore detrimental to acting morally.

In portraying these three stages, we have had in mind the position adopted by "M." in Heydenreich's *Briefe über den Atheismus.*[38]

---

38. Karl Heinrich Heydenreich, *Briefe über den Atheismus* (Leipzig, 1796). The first two stages of the objection are also found, among other places, in Schleiermacher, *Über das höchste Gut* (*KGA* 1:81 ff.).

The stages are to be found similarly in numerous lesser works and essays. These works were on fragile ground, theologically speaking, because they not only stressed the autonomy of ethics but also subscribed to the result arrived at in the first *Critique,* namely the atheism of theoretical reason. The assertion, which was not yet so objectionable on its own account, that practical reason does not advance of itself and necessarily to the idea of God, in other words the atheism of moral reason, led by this path to the atheism of reason as such. That ethicotheology was accounted the sole remaining way to a philosophical idea of God was for a long time the mainstay of its power of conviction. The undesired consequence of its demolition was to play into the hands of philosophical atheism.

An additional factor that went to justify doubts in regard to the coupling of ethics to the idea of God was the style employed to counter objections. It was enough to accuse one's opponent not only of moral atheism but of complete atheism. One could then save oneself the trouble of detailed argument: the only response to whoever gave tongue to such abominations was not argument but pity. There was indeed an alternative, namely indignation at the enormity of the offense committed. Pity inspired by religious motives and moral indignation also remained the two strongest counters to moral atheism. By contrast, the other arguments, such as those advanced by "M.'s" correspondent "R.," remained so feeble as to give rise to the suspicion that it had been the author's intention to leave them so unconvincing. This was already the impression formed by Georg Christoph Lichtenberg.[39] Their clumsiness contrasted too strongly with the warmth with which the position of the moral atheist was presented.

Attempts to refute moral atheism were essentially limited to three arguments. One stock rejoinder was, and is, that the moral atheist disregards the essence of the moral proof, which is not to be understood as a syllogism. But this reply does not really refute the atheism of moral reason. Rather it acknowledges the weakness of the moral proof. Indeed its power of conviction cannot be saved by referring all claims back to its supposed conclusiveness. More-

39. Cited by Gawoll, *Karl Heinrich Heydenreich,* p. 72.

over, the moral atheist's objection does not imply that the moral proof is formulated as a syllogism. Either the idea of God forms the condition for moral demands to be free from contradiction; or the clarity and binding character of the moral law are given even without the idea of God, and the categorical imperative is really valid categorically, not merely under the condition of God's existence and the hope of a well-proportioned happiness. But then moral reason does not need theology in order to achieve harmony with itself. It is after all always open to it to extend its sphere by means of hopes, if it chooses to do so.

A second rejoinder has recourse to the idea of a harmony between nature and morality. It reproaches moral atheism with being unable to conceive such a harmony. This is assuredly true, but it is no conclusive objection. It could pertain to the essence of morality that it should dispense with any such buttressing. If one elevates the harmony of nature and the moral law to the level of a criterion, one jeopardizes the binding character of the law and also only presupposes the idea of God, instead of grounding it on morality.

The least satisfactory reply is the one to the moral atheist's third objection, however. The idea of God, so the reply goes, in no way impairs the purity of moral incentives; it raises still higher the value of acting morally. For it is harder to act dutifully if there is an evident hope of reward and fear of punishment. In these more difficult circumstances morality is for this very reason much more exalted than otherwise. Admittedly this rejoinder constitutes a formal rebuttal of the objection. But it misuses the idea of God by changing its function to that of a solely artificial hurdle for the further exaltation of moral conduct. The meaning of introducing it into ethics would then consist in again banishing it from ethics in a methodological abstraction—a kind of religious asceticism *sub specie Dei.* So unworthy a view of the relationship between the idea of God and morality reveals that no real answer is known to the problem of the purity of moral incentives. This way of resolving the dreaded conflict between morality and the idea of God is better suited to justify the atheist.

Friedrich Karl Forberg drew the consequences of this sorry plight of ethicotheology frankly, not simply placing them in the mouth of imaginary correspondents, and in so doing ushered in the "atheism controversy." He regards the ideal harmony between morality and happiness as no more than a wish of the well-disposed heart that good may prevail in the world; this is not, however, just an idle wish but one that is bound up with earnest moral aspiration toward realization of this ideal.[40] For this conception the existence of God is not necessary. It therefore does not entitle us to postulate such an existence. What is necessary is to act as if one were entitled to presuppose God, as if one believed in God. It is in this acting "as if" that religion consists. It involves accepting the maxims that conduce to the greatest possible furtherance of the good—the maxims of immortality and of the possibility of a kingdom of God on earth—even if one remains doubtful of the possible realization of such a kingdom as well as of the existence of God himself. The question of God's existence stands revealed as the misbegotten fruit of a curiosity to which the answer must remain and can remain uncertain. Since, however, it is only religion—which involves acting on the assumption of the "as if"—that makes possible the prescribed mode of acting, we are bidden to have religion atheistically. But faith that goes beyond the moral maxims is, on this view, superstition. By comparison with Heydenreich's *Briefe über den Atheismus,* this establishes a new variant of the atheism of moral reason. Heydenreich's atheist "M." abandons the concept of religion. Now moral atheism appropriates the concept of religion, while disputing the justification for ethicotheology.

The next step along these lines of returning to the idea of God consists in identifying the moral world order, presupposed on practical grounds, with God, and in identifying religion with belief in this world order, beyond which all further belief becomes superstition. This step is taken by Fichte in his *Ueber den Grund unsers Glaubens an eine göttliche Weltregierung* (1798).[41] This necessarily

40. Friedrich Karl Forberg, "Entwicklung des Begriffs der Religion," *Philosophisches Journal* 8, no.1 (1798): 27 ff.
41. Johann Gottlieb Fichte, *Gesamtausgabe der Bayerischen Akademie der Wissenschaften,* eds. Reinhard Lauth, Hans Jacob, Hans Gliwitsky, Div. 1 (Stuttgart–Bad Canstatt, 1964 ff.), 5:354. This essay has been translated as "On the Foundation of Our Belief in a Divine Government of the Universe," in *Nineteenth-Century Philosophy,* ed. P. L. Gardiner (New York, 1969), pp. 19–26.

brings the concern with ethicotheology to a close, since it does not surrender the independence of ethics and yet avoids the atheism of moral reason. But it does this only at the cost of a far-reaching modification of the concept of God, one that now for the first time really brought down upon itself the charge of atheism—more strongly than the previous varieties of the atheism of moral reason. The further development of this idea in the revisions of the *Science of Knowledge*, from 1801 on, as well as in Fichte's writings on philosophy of religion, occurs under different circumstances. These, however, formed no part of the historical and conceptual background to the speculative philosophy of religion. For its elaboration another strand in the debates concerning ethicotheology assumed importance, even if only as a counterpoint, namely the widening of the moral grounding of the idea of God so as to bring back the religious view in its traditional dimension.

3.4. The Overextension of the Practical Foundation

At the beginning of the 1790s the atheism of moral reason was regarded as an aberration of a diseased mind. It was the linkage that Kant forged between ethics and the idea of God which initially had a powerful impact. From the theological point of view this linkage proved so fruitful that it caused the consequences of the negative critique to be forgotten and Kant promoted to be the prime witness of a professedly enlightened theology. Kant's position received a euphoric welcome because it seemed distinguished by two advantages. The assertion that God was indemonstrable for theoretical reason could be used to support the contention that for theoretical reason the idea of God was irrefutable.[42] And the immediate benefit for contemporary dogmatics lay in the fact that a position now

---

42. Gottlob Christian Storr, *Bemerkungen über Kant's philosophische Religionslehre* (Tübingen, 1794), pp. 21, 4 ff. Hegel owned the Latin version of Storr's work, which was translated into German by Friedrich Gottlieb Süsskind, who, in response to Fichte's *Critique of All Revelation,* appended to the work his own observations concerning the justification afforded by principles of practical reason for believing in the possibility and actuality of a revelation. For this reason the following discussion is based on the German edition. Storr was the leading theologian of the so-called old Tübingen school of precritical supernaturalism. [Note emended by the translators.]

seemed to have been found which, on the heels of the crisis of philosophical theology, made philosophical discourse about God possible and even recognized reason in religion. But above all, Kant offered not merely a refuge in which the idea of God could have been secured against radical Enlightenment critique. At this time there would still have been little occasion for this, at least in Germany. Explicit denial of the idea of God was not yet a force to be taken seriously; this is confirmed by the attitude adopted toward moral atheism. The actual gain lay in the fact that as well as merely saving the idea of God from what was not after all so serious a threat, the regrounding on a practical foundation seemed to offer a basis for reinstating the traditional theological corpus in virtually the same dimensions as previously—far more extensively than was ever to be hoped from the theoretical line of reasoning. The interest in putting the results in the practical field to theological use leapt unconcernedly, however, over the limits of postulation demarcated by Kant, regardless of the fact that in so doing it threatened the credibility of ethicotheology.

This consequence of the doctrine of postulates also involved what Kant had never intended, namely to reinstate the traditional doctrine of the attributes of God and produce a multitude of statements as to what God must do or may not or cannot do.[43] Orthodox thinkers were not in the wrong to be convinced that, if God's existence has to be assumed as a first step to safeguard morality, this assumption becomes truly fruitful only when it does not remain so abstract but acquires a concrete content, in the manner to which Fichte's *Critique of All Revelation* had largely pointed the way. All those who, with Kant, define the conditions of possibility of something for which there is no ground unless these conditions are presupposed, and the possibility of which could not in principle be conceived even if it were presumed to exist, may also feel themselves entitled to furnish the divine being disclosed in this way with all the predicates attributed to it by tradition. Moreover, the chance this gave for the practical rehabilitation of church doctrine opened up at the very time when the grounding of this doctrine in exegesis

43. See Fichte, *Attempt at a Critique of All Revelation*, pp. 125, 133.

and history was already under a markedly stronger threat than the crisis of philosophical theology had ever posed to the idea of God. Yet this tendency to restore the traditional theologoumena wholesale in their pristine form gave wings to the critique of ethicotheology and brought it to an unexpectedly speedy end. The main motive for the demolition of the moral argument does not lie either in the attempts made to correct it, which were of rather marginal importance, or in the coming to the fore of new approaches, but in vexation at the way in which it was extended and strained to the breaking point. By this means the moral argument itself is shortly driven to absurdity. We can illustrate this overextension of the practical argument by reference to three themes that were already touched on in the framework of the Kantian position: the concept of God as moral lawgiver, the concept of the highest good, and finally (abandoning completely the framework of Kant's position) the idea of God as him to whom the moral law is addressed.

(1) The assumption of God as moral lawgiver can, to be sure, find support in the actual text of the *Critique of Practical Reason.* In his *Critique of All Revelation,* however, it is only from the idea of God as creator of the world that Fichte derives the knowledge of God as moral lawgiver.[44] With this another mode of cognition takes precedence over the moral line of reasoning, obviously in order to bridge the gap which Kant left as to how the autonomy of moral reason was related to the assumption of a moral lawgiver. As a result, ethicotheology no longer confers the fundamental knowledge of God. It is then just this problem that reemerges in Fichte's position. This is not the only change, however, in the idea of God as moral lawgiver. For Kant the moral lawgiving of autonomous practical reason and the laws received from God are materially identical. This is presupposed by Fichte too. In regard to the moral possibility of such lawgiving he stresses that it is all the same whether regard for the moral law or for God as lawgiver (to the extent that he is defined purely as holy) provides the incentive for an action.[45] With Kant he too attributes considerably

44. Ibid., p. 78.
45. Ibid., p. 133.

greater effectiveness to the latter motive. Beyond Kant, he seeks
to bring the idea of lawgiving to completion by showing that God
actually does promulgate his law. To justify such an extension
he indicates that it does not come about with a theoretical aim
but solely on moral grounds.[46] He does not concern himself with
whether it does not perhaps, like theoretical knowledge, have an
adverse effect on morality. The demand for moral autonomy is
pushed into the background—to make heteronomy more effective.
Although this is already implied with Kant, the latter never so
plainly surrenders the tension between autonomy and divine lawgiving. But because Kant does not resolve the tension, it snaps a
short time later; and it is heteronomy that comes out best.

It is true that, in regard to the moral possibility of presupposing
God, Fichte restricts the scope by saying God can be represented
solely as law*giver,* irrespective of the promise of reward or threat
of punishment. But Gottlob Christian Storr and Friedrich Gottlieb
Süsskind quickly reveal this restriction to be meaningless.[47] A law-
giver who would not at the same time ensure that his law was kept
is an empty notion. For Kant's and Fichte's critics it is just God as
executor of the moral law that is central; and this is consistent, because this idea is a still more effective incentive than that of mere
divine lawgiving, which takes no heed of thoughts of requital, even
if only on the surface. If in the interests of morality it is allowed,
and even mandatory, to make theological assumptions, then this
applies also and above all to this assumption.

Admittedly such justifications fall away if one measures them
against Kant's strict concept of morality. But its fate since the
Critique of Practical Reason can be described as a progressive erosion of the opposition between morality and legality. The first signs
of such erosion are to be found in Kant himself—already in the use
made of the postulates to reinforce moral incentives and explicitly,
in *Religion within the Limits of Reason Alone,* with the notion of
requital. With Kant, however, such passages always remain an exception to the strict concept of morality. By contrast, Fichte's

46. Ibid., pp. 74–75.
47. Storr, *Bemerkungen,* pp. 41, 139.

Critique of All Revelation, notwithstanding all its verbal qualifications and provisos, levels from the very outset the tension between legality and morality. Those to whom revelation is addressed are the very ones who because of their prevailing, indeed dominant, sensuality are incapable of any moral actions. Revelation cannot therefore aim solely at reinforcement but must aim at replacement of moral incentives. But in this way we arrive indeed at legality. The stern demand for morality gives way to considerations of beneficent effect. Süsskind finally works in general with a concept of morality that is no longer defined by the opposition to legality. And where he takes the problem up, his solution can only be termed pettifogging: the sole incentive, he tells us, is respect for the moral law; the postulates, and above all the thought of requital, do no more than reduce to silence the objections of sensuous nature.[48] This negative function, however, makes them the decisive factor. Whatever could serve morality understood in this fashion is justified by the good end. As one such means Süsskind sees the revelation of a theoretical knowledge of God; this is understandable because there is no evident reason why this revelation should be more detrimental to morality, in his sense, than the notion of divine lawgiving. And even the hope of temporary advantages is viewed in the last resort as a legitimate means for promoting morality. With this the "practical" restitution of all traditionally ecclesiastical contents is accomplished and, in Schelling's words, "the triumph of these philosophical heroes" is consummated (*Br* 1:14). This development drives to absurdity the idea that theological propositions can be affirmed in addition to pure morality as a way of reinforcing moral incentives. It replaces Kant's concept of morality by sheer legality, and autonomy by the total heteronomy of practical reason.

In regard to the question why practical reason views God as lawgiver despite the fact that it itself delivers the law, reference should be made to one further argument of Fichte: "The idea of God as lawgiver, through the moral law in us, is thus based on an externalization [*Entäusserung*] of what is ours, on translating something subjective into a being outside us; and this externalization is the

48. Ibid., pp. 172–173.

real principle of religion, insofar as religion is to be used for determining the will."[49] Thus presented, the argument contains a surprising admission as to the reason for presupposing God and an insight into the essence of religion. But it occupies only a marginal position in Fichte's *Critique of All Revelation.*

(2) Fichte too postulates the existence of God from the idea of the highest good—but not without a considerable change of emphasis. The change is indeed along a path signaled by Kant, in that he too already justifies the necessity of presupposing God by the fact that otherwise the moral law would become self-contradictory and a figment of the brain—a sally that Storr repeats with gusto.[50] By surrendering the dominance of the moral will, of purely moral impulses, Fichte undermines the concept of the highest good. For him the primary determinant of will is the striving for happiness.[51] In view, however, of the more anthropological perspective of the third *Critique,* where the argument is in terms of the weakness of human nature, even this does not appear un-Kantian. But the actual impetus for extending the Kantian perspectives is the proposition that whoever wills the end must also will the means. For Kant too this is an analytical proposition.[52] Schleiermacher on the other hand already formulates reservations in this regard (*KGA* 1:90). Storr, however, makes exhaustive use of the possibilities offered by this proposition for his own purpose: whoever wills the highest good must also will the relevant means. Extenuation of the concept of morality permits extension of the means. Whoever is interested in reinstatement of the religious world of representation need merely extol it as a means to the prescribed end, and this presents no insuperable difficulties. Under this head it is easy to declare the plenitude of religious representations in their entirety as of service, indeed indispensable service, to morality and so demand them for morality's sake. In view of humanity's feeble moral constitution, the whole range of dogmatic content can be declared the instrument for overcoming sensible nature—even if it is only for the sake of

49. Fichte, *Critique of All Revelation,* p. 73 (translation revised slightly).
50. Storr, *Bemerkungen,* p. 33.
51. Ibid., pp. 31 ff.
52. Kant, *Fundamental Principles of the Metaphysic of Ethics,* p. 34.

the unity of religious doctrines and their freedom from contradiction.

On behalf of this religion—an anthropologically grounded religion inasmuch as it is based on moral weakness—the whole theoretical side of religion is now reinstated. For if the assumption of God is suited to subdue my sensual nature, then it can be assumed, contra Kant, that this function is enhanced in the same measure that I extend my knowledge of God. For morality's sake I am obliged to accept, at least subjectively, whatever could prove in any way conducive to weakening the resistance afforded by my sensual nature. Once the concept of morality is whittled away in this fashion, and once the watchword is given by Fichte for waiving the strict requirement for the sake of the beneficial effect, it becomes difficult to find convincing reasons why what perhaps conduces to morality should not be extended as far as one pleases. Even those divine commands that do not in the narrower sense belong to the moral law are legitimated by virtue of God's being assumed as lawgiver. If God is recognized as moral lawgiver, so argue Storr and Süsskind, then there is an evident need to keep his other laws too. The final outcome is also to justify doctrinal contents, the sacraments, and all the miracles as conducive to morality. The tone of this Tübingen dogmatism is very confident in this regard: if, so we are told, this is granted as a postulate, why not that too, since after all it too could serve morality?[53] In this way the historical aspect of religion also can be secured once again. For it cannot be utterly excluded that the historical too may not act beneficially on one or another human being. The boundless extension of the moral argument sometimes takes on, with Storr and Süsskind, an undertone that is positively scornful; they are amazed almost that some should still be so prudish when, after all, the rigorous requirement of autonomous practical reason has long since surrendered its innocence.

(3) Such an extension of the practical foundation to include even notions that cannot directly be regarded as morally relevant would in any case need an accompanying indication that their acceptance promotes my morality, and why it should do so. It is, so the reason-

53. Storr, *Bemerkungen*, p. 232.

ing might continue, morally necessary to show what could have determined God to act in this way and not another, to demand this and not that. The extension of the practical justification to the whole of traditional religion therefore calls for additional propositions concerning God's acting, accepted on practical grounds. This style of grounding again links up with Kant's idea that God alone can realize the highest good. At least according to the initial formulation, this function of God is limited to apportioning happiness in proportion to morality. Even the original doctrine of postulates does indeed contain pointers to something beyond this. Thus immortality could be interpreted as a divine institution for the perfecting of our morality: God keeps us in existence in order that we may come nearer to moral perfection. The creation and ordering of a world in which moral beings are able to act morally by virtue of their freedom can also be understood as an expression of divine concern for the promotion of morality itself, not simply the second component of the highest good.

The orthodox thinkers of the [old] Tübingen school give full rein to such assumptions. God is no longer thought of primarily as he who attributes the happiness appropriate in each case. He becomes himself the one to whom the moral law is addressed: it determines him to ensure the realization of the final end, to make particular arrangements that directly promote morality or at least eliminate obstacles to it. The sum total of these activities is the concept of revelation. The idea of revelation comes to the fore to the extent that God is recognized as having a function for promoting morality apart from merely creating conditions for responsible moral acting, and apart from making causality possible by means of freedom. It requires philosophy, however, to undertake a critique of revelation, such as Fichte set forth and, shortly after him, Maass. The first task of such a critique is to show that revelation is physically possible. This is already implied in the designation of God as lord of nature or as the one who realizes the highest good. It is a matter of no less importance whether such revelation—at least in the form of direct revelation—is also morally possible or whether it does not rather destroy morality. For Fichte and Maass this is still a problem, but no longer for Storr and Süsskind. Fichte affirms the moral possibility of direct revelation, but in regard only to the sort of person who would otherwise remain without morality, and not to genuinely moral persons or those in whom morality and sensuality are in constant conflict. Maass by contrast disputes the moral possibility of direct revelation because he regards as nonexistent the sort of person utterly untouched by the moral law; and for those caught up in moral conflict he deems natural, purely moral religion sufficient to reinforce moral incentives.

Maass's critique of revelation, like Fichte's, lands in this way in an impasse. For his concept of indirect revelation serves for the rehabilitation of physicotheology. Although he purports to keep wholly to Kant's terrain, unlike Fichte, this does not prevent him from inferring once again from the ordering of nature to the "infinite wisdom" of God.[54] This is logically consistent to the extent that the promotion of physicotheology to the level of indirect revelation with a view to furthering morality is designed to offset the shortcomings of ethicotheology: God is determined by the moral law to effect the particular arrangement consisting in indirect revelation. Fichte by contrast assumes direct revelation to be physically and morally possible. Maass objects to this, in much the same way as Hegel did later, that this is to open the floodgates to naive enthusiasm.[55] It is true that in his Critique of All Revelation Fichte makes, as Hegel says, only "moderate use" of this "mischief." Under his criteria it appears as nowhere given, and he adds that we are never entitled to judge that direct revelation is present: identification "of a certain appearance as divine revelation" is "based on nothing more than a wish."[56] Yet he makes on the whole so many concessions to "theological logic" that his ultimate hesitation about identifying direct revelation appears to be philosophical prudery. His Critique of All Revelation is a textbook example of the fact that departure from the rigorous idea of morality through constantly repeating the Kantian mode of reasoning (bringing to light the conditions of possibility of the highest good) is ultimately capable

54. Maass, Kritische Theorie der Offenbarung, p. 170.
55. Ibid., p. 162. Cf. Hegel, L 31 (Br 1:17), where he says that Fichte undoubtedly "opened the door" to the "mischief" that Schelling had deplored.
56. Fichte, Critique of All Revelation, p. 154.

of rehabilitating any religious representation one chooses (even the acceptance of fabulous beings) as being in the practical interest—even if it is only in order to keep religion free from contradiction. Once God is declared to be the guarantor of well-proportioned happiness and the reinforcer of moral incentives, then it is indeed philosophically venturesome but not inconsistent to follow the path leading to the orthodoxy of the old Tübingen school.

3.5. The Abandonment of the Moral Concept of Religion

The wholesale appropriation of Kant for the purposes of orthodoxy gave rise to an indignant reaction and in this way brought about, more than anything else, the rapid downfall of the practical idea of God and of religion. The resistance to such an amalgamation of critical philosophy and orthodoxy is nowhere more sharply expressed than in Schelling's letter to Hegel of 5 January 1795. The first of the *Philosophische Briefe über Dogmatismus und Kriticismus,*[57] which were published the same year, is also still wholly marked by this emotion. Schelling begins by laying bare the origin of the idea of a moral God, but then turns to theoretical considerations regarding the idea of God in general. He reproaches critical philosophy for having, by the "contraband traffic" of the doctrine of postulates, brought in again through the back door what it had ushered out through the front door.[58] Later we are told it assumed the existence of God only in order to bring moral ends into alignment with it (*GW* 4:270).

Schelling's turns of phrase show that already at this early stage he rejects the doctrine of postulates, even in its Kantian form. Hegel's criticism, by contrast, is first directed solely against the extension in the direction of orthodoxy. He himself adopts the standpoint of Kant's ethicotheology—even including the assumption that the existence of a personal God can in fact be postulated on moral grounds (*L* 32, *Br* 1:18). Fragments from the first half of 1795, in particular *Die transzendente Idee von Gott* (*J* 361–362), also show

---

57. Schelling, *Historisch-kritische Ausgabe* 3:50 ff.
58. Schelling, "Ueber Offenbarung und Volksunterricht," *Philosophisches Journal* 8,2:152.

that at that time Hegel still took a Kantian stand on this question. Even his criticism of the extension in the direction of orthodoxy seems to derive from the impulse furnished by Schelling's indignation rather than from motives of his own. But unlike his friend, who has in the meantime become a Fichtean, Hegel makes Fichte responsible for the extravagances of practical reason. This too shows that initially he does not yet seek the roots of the evil in Kant himself. It is not primarily irritation at the excessive theological interpretation of the moral proof that leads him to move on from criticizing orthodoxy's appropriation of Kant's results to revealing the root of the evil in Kant himself. Nor does he confine himself to merely bringing to its logical conclusion Schelling's criticism inspired in the first place by Fichte's *Science of Knowledge* and, since the time of the *Philosophische Briefe,* by Spinoza as well. Hegel discusses the extent to which the moral argument is appropriate to the phenomenon that it purports to be able to ground and to grasp. This is the path he takes between the spring of 1795 and the autumn of 1796, in other words until he moves to Frankfurt. It is only in this regard that the fragments from this period concern us. There is no intention of denying the presence of other themes, such as public education [*Volkserziehung*], enthusiasm for the beauties of Hellas, analysis of the contemporary scene; however, all that concerns us here is the changed foundation of the idea of God and of religion.

Hegel's Berne fragments from the spring of 1795 on can be interpreted as designed to test, not the conceptual consistency of Kant's practical foundation and its subsequent elaborations, but the function performed by ethicotheology in the purely moral view of religion. It is only later—from *Faith and Knowledge* down to the time of the Berlin lectures—that he comes to a systematic critique of the doctrine of the highest good and the postulates. The distinctive feature of his early approach lies, however, in the way in which the theory of religion undermines ethicotheology. The unmistakable character of the fragments from this period is only partly due to the fact that they investigate Christianity's suitability as a public religion [*Volksreligion*] or examine questions of positivity; it consists rather in testing the validity of the Kantian approach against historical material. While Hegel initially does not intend such an outcome, his attempt to encompass the actuality of religion with Kant's concepts ends with the insight that this is impossible.

Already in the Tübingen years, many elements of the Hegelian understanding of religion are not Kantian—for instance the prominence given to love as opposed to the conceptuality of morality and legality, or the protest against the separation of sensibility and fantasy (*TE* 30–58, *J* 3–29). This does not yet, however, decide the question of the ethicotheological concept of God. The Berne fragments even enhance the Kantian flavor still further. As long as Hegel links differing characteristics of the concept of religion in the Tübingen and early Berne fragments with the doctrine of incentives of the *Critique of Pure Reason,* no decision is reached as to the moral concept of religion. The first signs of such a decision appear when Hegel—probably reacting against the orthodox school's dilution of Kant—attempts a purely moral interpretation of the origins of Christianity in *The Life of Jesus* (*TE* 104–165, *J* 75–136). Doubtless his account of the life and teaching of Jesus does not aim to demonstrate the failure of the practical foundation. Rather this result imposes itself against his will. It does not yet find expression in the text itself. But that it did not remain concealed from the author can be inferred from the fact that the following fragments distance themselves from such an interpretation. The New Testament texts remain resistant to the attempt to interpret them from an exclusively ethicotheological standpoint, especially in the restrictive form this assumes in the doctrine of incentives of the *Critique of Practical Reason.* The life and teaching of Jesus too cannot be portrayed as purely moral in this sense. To be sure, this insight could also be turned against primitive Christianity and its founder. But it becomes an even stronger weapon against other religions. The acknowledgment that this criterion is insufficient is therefore more apposite.

The fragments following *The Life of Jesus,* known as *The Positivity of the Christian Religion* (*ETW* 67–181 *J* 139–239), also point in this direction. They reveal the difference between "good" morality and "bad" positivity as irrelevant for the understanding of religion: positivity does not first install itself after a purely moral beginning in the further course of a religion. It stands rather at its origin—as a constitutive moment, without which the religion would be mere morality but not actual religion. These fragments therefore seek to develop a concept by virtue of which religion is not exhausted in mere morality but at the same time does not have to be rejected as something merely positive. They distinguish the religious standpoint—the religion of Jesus—from the mere moral principle. In so doing they surrender in principle the ethicotheological grounding of religion. This does not, however, lead directly to a foundationally new type of approach to philosophy of religion. The fragments conclude rather with an ill-disguised admission of their failure. Hegel does not yet possess a conception wherewith to interpret the essence of religion. For him religion presents itself as a combination of positive and moral elements; hence it can be readily inferred that the enhanced positivity marking the subsequent history of Christianity stems from the fact that positivity originally occupied a greater place than morality. Since religion cannot be mere morality and must not be mere positivity, the philosophical quest for a new definition of religion is marked at the close of the Berne years by unresolved dilemmas. No definitive dispositions for future years are yet in place, other than the definitive abandonment of the ethicotheological interpretation. This abandonment becomes palpable in the fragment containing materials for a continuation of Part I of *Positivity* (*ETW* 145–167, *J* 214–231). And it also becomes clear that, strictly speaking, the history of religion, which Kant neglected, gives the lie to the vehicular function he imputed to historical religion: the positive elements make themselves independent. Nothing was less suited to act as a vehicle for pure religious belief than revealed religion. The moral concept of religion is therefore in a position neither to throw light on the origin of religion, nor to elucidate its current task, nor to conceptualize its history.

Hegel's historical investigation of the moral concept of religion has consequences that extend beyond the theory of religion in the narrower sense. They confirm the Kantian unity of theology and theory of religion, but with a critical intent. Precisely when one holds fast to a proper understanding of this unity, the failure of the analyses undertaken by the theory of religion for the sake of practical interpretation obliges one to reappraise ethicotheology. Whereas for Kant the latter functions as the basis, it is now called in question from the standpoint of what is alleged to be based on it. If religion is not supremely morality, then the unity of theology and religion implies that God too is not, or at least is not primarily, a moral God. The untenability of the moral concept of religion has repercussions on the moral concept of God, and thus it gives rise to the formulation of a new concept of God, though Hegel does not yet have such a concept at his disposal at the close of the Berne period. This gives the 1796 fragments an aporetic character that in some respects already points toward Feuerbach.

This is assuredly not the only form of criticism that can be leveled against the moral God and moral religion. Schelling's critique of the moral God already takes a different form. It does not, however, actually refute the moral argument. Indignant at the way in which the latter has been strained in the interests of orthodoxy, Schelling jumps off from it and thus lights upon a new mode of philosophical discourse about the absolute. And where the critical elaboration of Kant's ethicotheology does take place within the framework of pure philosophy—as for instance in Fichte's writings dating from the period of the atheism controversy—the moral argument is improved, not abandoned. The connection that Kant stresses between the idea of God and morality even becomes an identity: God is the moral world-order. We know no other God, but also need no other.[59] Compared with the path taken by Hegel this appears as a variant within the ethicotheological horizon, whereas Hegel's approach since the time when he left Berne aims at a final abandonment of ethicotheology. The results he attains in regard to philosophy of religion also make clear to him the deficiencies in the conceptual underpinning provided by ethicotheology. For his way of thinking it seems to have been necessary to undertake a historical critique of the moral concept of religion before going on to a critique of ethicotheology in principle. At the same

59. Fichte, "On the Foundation of Our Belief in a Divine Government of the Universe," pp. 24–25.

time that the lack of success attending his attempts at interpretation convinces him of the impossibility of a purely moral conception of religion, he is forced also to reject the moral God by the experiential evidence of the resistance of actual religion to being reduced to morals. Admittedly this may arouse doubts as to the demonstrative force of such an indirect argument. Empirical refutation of an a priori concept, distinguished as such by universality and necessity, would in any event be inconceivable. But, leaving this aside, the moral proof increasingly lost the status of a purely a priori argument, which Kant initially aimed at. In particular, anthropological considerations thrust themselves to the fore. There were even reasons why it was better no longer to deal with the topic within the framework of philosophy as a rigorous discipline.

3.6. God and Religion as a Topic of "Nonphilosophy"

Ethicotheology had represented itself as the sole remaining way to the philosophical grounding of the idea of God. It had also been widely understood as such. Its failure was consequently not the incidental lack of success of an extravagant foundational attempt but the failure of what was regarded as the only way available. It plunged the idea of God and the philosophy of religion into a deeper crisis than Kant's critique of all speculative theology because there was now no longer any alternative, at least in the traditional corpus of philosophy. This crisis confronting the idea of God and also the newly evolved philosophy of religion (for which the name had only just been found) did not, however, impinge so sharply on consciousness. In view of the multiplicity of new approaches, these years can be seen as an extraordinarily productive phase for the philosophy of religion. The demonstration of the conceptual inconsistency of ethicotheology, and the experience of the unsatisfactory nature of the moral approach, provided the criteria for a regrounding of philosophical discourse about God. Such regrounding could not be undertaken in either the practical or the theoretical sphere short of reconsidering Kant's critique of all speculative theology. The efforts aimed in this direction, for instance the recourse to physicotheology, remained initially unconvincing; this was because they did not overcome but simply disregarded the Kantian critique, and because they resurrected the idea of a God of whom it is said in Goethe's and Schiller's *Xenions*[60] that after he invented the bottle, he quickly made the cork tree too, so as to have stoppers.

(1) The field of philosophy as a whole necessarily seemed exhausted for purposes of grounding the idea of God insofar as no further field was discernible alongside the theoretical and the practical. This suggested the desirability of transposing the problem beyond the limits of philosophy in the strict sense—of making the *salto mortale,* the "mortal leap," into "nonphilosophy." When Friedrich Heinrich Jacobi first advocated this, in conversation with Lessing, the inevitability of the "leap" was not yet manifest; the ways of access to the idea of God did not yet seem blocked. At the time of publication of Jacobi's letters on Spinoza,[61] the theoretical grounding could already be said to have failed. But it was only now that the *salto mortale* must have seemed inescapable. It was no longer, as Friedrich Schlegel had still thought in 1797,[62] an individual option; it now had the character of an imperative. But the "elastic point" to which Jacobi had referred as the only one possible had of necessity still to be regarded as debatable as long as it could be assumed that the prescribed *salto mortale* could likewise be accomplished from other points, and that the place of reemergence was therefore not fixed—even if it was not to be expected that the number of such elastic points was unduly great. At all events it was a risky business after the failure of ethicotheology to caricature the seductive path that leads via morality to theology. The danger that without it one would no longer be capable of any kind of leap was all too plain.

Jacobi's solution was already sketched out in his letters on Spinoza. He formulated it once again in his *Open Letter to Fichte*

60. [*Tr.*] See *Xenien 1796,* edited from the manuscripts of the Goethe and Schiller Archives by Erich Schmidt and Bernard Suphan (Weimar, 1893); and *Goethe's and Schiller's Xenions,* selected and translated by Paul Carus (Chicago, 1896). In Greek a *xenion* is a gift to a guest.
61. [*Tr.*] Friedrich Heinrich Jacobi, *Briefe über die Lehre des Spinoza* (1785, 2d ed. 1789), in *JW* 4.
62. In his review of the second edition of Jacobi's novel *Woldemar* (1796). See *KSA* 2:69.

(1799),[63] as a program to replace philosophy's not-knowing [*Nicht-wissen der Philosophie*] of God by the knowing of nonphilosophy [*Wissen der Nicht-Philosophie*]. That God is not an object of cognitive thought had already been emphasized in the letters on Spinoza. Kant had shown that speculative reason was incapable of flying over the bounds of experience to knowledge of God since in so doing it gave birth only to figments of the brain. Jacobi had argued on the contrary that cognitive thought inevitably degraded God to a finite. This conclusion received its classic formulation in the *Open Letter*: "A God who could be *known* would be no God at all."[64] It was further elaborated and defended in the slightly later work *Über das Unternehmen des Kritizismus, die Vernunft zu Verstande zu bringen* (*JW* 3:59 ff.).

Jacobi sets the knowing of unphilosophy [*Unphilosophie*] in place of the philosophical knowing of nothing. What is true is not in knowing but outside the scientific knowledge of knowing, if indeed there is such a thing as what is true. If the true were humanly known, it would cease being the true.[65] This does not prevent Jacobi from holding fast to a changed version of the concept of reason: reason is, according to him, the in-tuiting or taking-for-true [*Wahr-Nehmen*] of the true that exists outside reason, outside knowing. But the mode of this becoming aware is no longer scientific knowledge; it is faith, presentiment of the true.[66] The question then arises, however, why I should trust such presentiment more than knowledge. According to Jacobi, reason teaches the idea of God with irresistible force. Reason itself is "not the perfection of life, not the fullness of the good and the true; and as surely as I do not *possess* the latter with it, and know it, so surely do I know that there *is* a higher being, and that I have my origin in it."[67] Even as-

---

63. *Open Letter to Fichte*, in *Philosophy of German Idealism*, ed. Ernst Behler (New York, 1987), pp. 119–141. [*Tr.* Quotations from this translation are modified slightly at the suggestion of the author.]

64. Ibid., p. 121.

65. Ibid., p. 130.

66. We cannot discuss here the relationship between Jacobi's conception and other contemporary approaches; cf. Jakob Friedrich Fries, *Wissen, Glaube und Ahndung* (Jena, 1805), esp. p. 176, also pp. 64, 178, 218, 233 ff., 326. [*Tr.* We have translated *Ahndung* as "presentiment."]

67. *Open Letter to Fichte*, in Behler, p. 132.

suming that one endorses the descriptive part of this proposition, one will see little basis for its conclusion unless one already has this certainty within oneself. Jacobi therefore sees himself obliged to adduce grounds for the assumption of God over and above the evidence of the heart. He maintains that human, merely in-tuitive reason is complemented by an independent form of reason, the fullness of the good and the true. The one "reason producing all truth out of itself alone . . . must certainly be present, or everywhere there would be nothing good or true; the root of nature and all beings would be a pure nothing."[68] Everything else that we call good, beautiful and sacred becomes "an absurdity merely destroying my mind . . . as soon as I accept that it is without any relationship to a higher true being."[69]

Such statements must be compared with the ambitious even though unsuccessful exposition of the transcendental ideal in order to gauge how much less they can lay claim to be a philosophical discourse about God. Thus Jacobi denotes it as a question of taste whether one prefers his philosophy of not-knowing or Fichte's philosophical knowing of nothing.[70] There would indeed no longer be any occasion for dispute in this regard. But if it is not to be a question of taste that is involved—and even for Jacobi this is ultimately not at all the case—then everything depends on whether the alternative presented by Jacobi is unavoidable: either goodness and beauty and God, or nothing; either God or the ego. The alternative would also be the same as that between God and nothing if the ego desired to conceal its nothingness from itself by making itself God: "God is, God is outside of me, a living self-subsisting being, or *I* am God. There is no third possibility."[71] It is only in order to implant the divine existence by means of suggestion that Jacobi lays out this supposed disjunction. For if God did not exist, I would not, in soaring up to the level of God, be in any sense a new, more actual God but a mere phantom. For Jacobi the real alternative

68. Ibid., p. 132.
69. Ibid., p. 133.
70. Ibid., p. 136.
71. Ibid., p. 138.

must therefore be: either God is a self-subsisting being outside me; or else human beings and the world they live in, truth, goodness, and beauty are all pure nothing. His unphilosophy does indeed acquire force of conviction if this disjunction is viewed as exhaustive, that is, if the opposite of his chimera is revealed with incontrovertible certainty to be not simply a chimera of equal value but loving surrender to the undisputed nothing.

Jacobi's vehement plea on behalf of the idea of God implies aporias in which anyone not assuming God's existence will become entangled. Kant's demonstration of the necessity of thinking the transcendental ideal, by contrast, rejected the inference to the givenness of this ideal. And moral atheism led to the insight that even the contradictory character of the reason that dispenses with the idea of God could not certify the idea. But Jacobi neglects to show the inevitability of his disjunction. His unphilosophy of notknowing does not lend itself to being brought into the form of a self-contained demonstration of the fallibility of each and every conceivable philosophy. The sole grounding it provides for the idea of God is by adducing reasons why this idea cannot be grounded and then by commending itself as the sole possible way through exhortation and the construction of frightening alternatives. Its attractiveness as the *ultima ratio* is due to a situation in which both the theoretical and practical knowledge of God could be regarded as having failed—both the knowledge that invokes the despotism of the moral God and that based on mere concepts (*JW* 3:188, 192). But that this situation had already arisen at this time could be disputed by referring to alternative forms of rational cognition. And in any event Jacobi's either-or of God and nothing has subsequently lost its terrors. The later history of thought shows that Jacobi here touched on a theme with much more serious implications than he himself recognized. The sole intention of the alternative he presented was to make the case for the God who exists outside me and who could provide a secure basis for everything true, beautiful, and good. What is really serious is not Jacobi's alternative but the inescapability of the nothing. Yet it was possible at that time in Jacobi's circle to argue in a way that made less far-reaching claims, to the effect that the assumption of God stemmed ultimately from a need and that nothing at all was "scientifically" demonstrated thereby[72]—and also that it did not need to be.

(2) Jacobi's surrender of the knowledge of God to nonphilosophy drew the consequences of his early assertion that all rigorous philosophy leads to atheism and fatalism. In other respects too the philosophical attractiveness of the talk of nonphilosophy caused the transition to nonphilosophy to be seen as a remedy following the collapse of speculative theology and ethicotheology.[73] But the alternative to grounding the philosophy of religion in a "rigorous" philosophy did not necessarily lie in nonphilosophy. In 1790 Karl Leonhard Reinhold had still contested the possibility of a philosophy of religion as such, on the ground that there were no recognized principles for it.[74] After the failure of both speculative and ethical theology, this could no longer be accepted as a conclusive objection: in order to legitimate the philosophy of religion it was now enough to observe that it was "only a testimony to the religion found in humanity" (*JW* 3:195). It is true that a little earlier, about the mid-1790s, the practical grounding still predominated. A comparatively faithful restatement of Kant's position was given by, among others, Jakob Salat, a later opponent of Schelling and Hegel.[75]

The first works to bear the name of philosophy of religion also are written by committed Kantians. Karl Heinrich Ludwig Pölitz

72. See Friedrich Köppen, *Ueber Offenbarung*, pp. 60–61.

73. See Carl August Eschenmayer, *Die Philosophie in ihrem Uebergang zur Nichtphilosophie* (Erlangen, 1803).

74. Karl Leonhard Reinhold, *Beyträge zur Berichtigung bisheriger Missverständnisse der Philosophie* (Jena, 1790), p. 376.

75. Jakob Salat, "Geht die Moral aus der Religion, oder diese aus jener hervor?" *Philosophisches Journal 5*, no. 3 (1797). He emphasizes (p. 231) that without religion morality cannot be complete. Also in the slightly later article "Noch ein Beitrag über die moralische Begründung der Religion," *Philosophisches Journal 8*, no. 4 (1798), Salat affirms (p. 218) that belief in God is necessary for virtue. In his later writings he rejects the moral grounding of religion because it leads to the "scientific monstrosity" of moral atheism. See *Die Religionsphilosophie* (Landshut, 1811), esp. pp. 53, 22, 394 ff.; and *Grundlinien der Religionsphilosophie* (Sulzbach, 1819), pp. 9 ff. In the latter work he turns against the new hyperidealism, which affirms an absolute independence of religion from morality (see p. 20).

in particular expressly took his stand in 1795 wholly on the practically grounded doctrine of God and religion. He dealt with the transformation of moral religion into universal religion or public religion—in the same way that Hegel did. Yet Pölitz demanded that philosophy of religion be grounded on human faculties and human nature.[76] Contrary to his own self-understanding, this program formed the exact antithesis to the ethicotheological grounding. What principally distinguished Kant was that religion lies beyond any anthropological considerations, in pure practical reason itself—in other words, that pure religious faith coincides with ethical concepts and has its seat and origin wholly a priori in reason.[77] In place of this grounding, reference was now being made to the factual side of religion as based on anthropological study.

This tendency is a sure pointer to the vanishing power of conviction provided by the moral grounding. It was carried on in accentuated fashion in Ludwig Heinrich Jakob's philosophical treatise on religion, where we find an adherence to the moral grounding alongside a reference to anthropological aspects.[78] This reveals not a bare misunderstanding of the Kantian approach but a pressing out beyond the restriction of religion to morality. It was even more marked in the preface to Jakob's slightly later work *Die allgemeine Religion* (1797). Within the framework of the anthropological approach the demand for religion to be treated psychologically also gained ground. To be sure, the problem of grounding was not simply left behind. Instead it switched away from the relationship between ethicotheology and philosophy of religion to the latter's relationship with anthropology, or, as Karl Heinrich Heydenreich put it, with the factors governing the faculty of imagining, desiring, and feeling. The science "which depicts human nature as the sum total of these faculties, in terms of the factors that originally govern them," includes among its tasks that of eliciting the representa-

76. Karl Heinrich Ludwig Pölitz, *Beitrag zur Kritik der Religionsphilosophie und Exegese unsers Zeitalters* (Leipzig, 1795), p. 115.
77. Kant, *Fundamental Principles of the Metaphysic of Ethics*, pp. 26–27.
78. Ludwig Heinrich Jakob, "Philosophische Abhandlung: Ueber die Religion," *Annalen der Philosophie und des philosophischen Geistes von einer Gesellschaft gelehrter Männer* 2 (1796): esp. 227.

tional mode proper to religion from its fundamental principles.[79] This new discipline's ambiguous attitude to ethicotheology was at least at first an advantage to philosophy of religion; for the anthropological orientation presented itself in association with the ethicotheological, passing tacitly over its lack of success. It had no qualms about using the concept of God without being too concerned about its anthropological grounding, and it also renewed its association with physicotheology. This shows, however, that there was no actual progress over Kant here, but rather a return to the position he had thought to leave behind. Kant's primary aim had in fact been to demonstrate that religion had to be studied not merely on the level of anthropology but on that of pure a priori reason. That had been the whole sense of the practical renewal of philosophical theology.

(3) Reflection on the implications of the anthropological grounding would have called not only for it to be unreservedly established in place of the ethicotheological grounding but also—in the light of the failure of theoretical and practical foundational studies—for its aim to be specified. To define human being in terms, for instance, of the capacity for cognizing and acting morally would have been of no use for solving the foundational crisis, at least as far as the idea of God was concerned. The atheism of theoretical or practical reason would have provided a poor foundation for the philosophy of religion. In recommending an anthropological approach as a remedy following the failure of previous attempts at grounding, one lets it be known that one does not regard human being as defined, at least not exclusively, by one of these two aspects or by both together.

Schleiermacher's *Speeches on Religion*[80] draw this conclusion: religion does not consist in thinking or in doing, nor is it made up of ill-compounded fragments of the two. Schleiermacher's polemic against the reduction of religion to metaphysics and morals is directed against an interpretation that is not only inappropriate but

79. Karl Heinrich Heydenreich, *Encyclopädische Einleitung in das Studium der Philosophie nach den Bedürfnissen unsers Zeitalters* (Leipzig, 1793), p. 45.

80. [Tr.] Friedrich Schleiermacher, *On Religion: Speeches to Its Cultured Despisers*, translation of the 1st ed. (1799) by Richard Crouter (Cambridge, 1988).

now also emptied of content, although shortly before it held almost unrestricted sway. It is not enough, however, to describe religion's relationship to metaphysics and morals merely in terms of its distinctness. It is true that religion is not reducible to them, yet it has the same object as they do—the universe and the human relationship to it—though in the form of feeling and intuition. Leaving aside the fascination exerted by these *Speeches,* the question arises as to the truth claim of such an "intuition of the universe" and the justification for designating it and the feeling corresponding to it as religion, properly speaking, and for radically depreciating historical religion by contrast. The answers to the first question place obstacles in the way of answering the second. To demand that the truth content of such intuition be laid bare reveals a misunderstanding of Schleiermacher's program. Far from wishing to bring individual intuitions back into a system and then scrutinize the system for its truth value, Schleiermacher takes the view that only the individual is true and necessary. This program involves a total subjectivism, which must account as equally justified in principle an infinite number of ways of intuiting the infinite. Nothing is said about criteria of appropriateness because they are utterly irrelevant to Schleiermacher's approach. It is for this reason that, in discussing the *Speeches,* Friedrich Schlegel speaks not only of a "purely negative view of divinity" but also of the "unportrayable character of religion" (*KSA* 2:281).

One may thus suppose that the individual ways of intuiting the infinite can be described as forms of an aesthetic relationship to the world. Credence is lent to this by the fact that Schleiermacher happily surrenders the whole array of features denoting the traditional religions—their individual traits, their respective definitions of human nature, their relationship to one another, and their differing images of God. The uncertainty in which Schleiermacher leaves these questions, which elsewhere stir up vigorous debate, goes to show that all this is of little account—whether one is speaking of God or of divinity or of gods. Yet his polemic is directed against identifying the religious intuition of the universe with the forms of an aesthetic relationship to the world no less than against reducing religion to metaphysics and morals. Clearly this delimitation does not anticipate a discussion that was yet to come. It is directed against a tendency of the time, following the decline of ethicotheology, which extended far beyond the circle of the early Romantic writers. The poetic character of religion is stressed both by Hölderlin[81] and by Johann Christian August Grohmann[82] or Friedrich Schlegel, and it is this that Schleiermacher has first and foremost in view in the distinction he draws. But there are also a number of other contemporary approaches that juxtapose religion and art and tend to equate philosophy of religion with aesthetics,[83] thus jeopardizing the separate position that has only just been established for religion over against metaphysics and morals. Schleiermacher therefore is emphatic that intuition and feeling of the universe, sense and taste for the infinite, are not to be viewed as aesthetic—whatever these expressions or the talk of "virtuosity" suggest to the contrary. As poetic, however, an intuition of the universe could not be scrutinized as to its philosophical justification. If it is not poetic, such scrutiny is unavoidable, even if the charm of the *Speeches* mostly disguises the fact. And the complete severance of all lines connecting with the historical religions deprives the *Speeches* of any justification for designating as "religion" what, in a skillful apologetic, they commend to its despisers. Religion, as Schleiermacher portrays it, is a fiction and assuredly a noteworthy fiction. It differs so greatly from what has previously been known under this name that it is necessary to inquire into the causes for so rapid and extensive a change both in the conceptual comprehension of religion and in religious experience, and also into the possible repercussions of new developments in the history of philosophy and

81. Friedrich Hölderlin, *Über Religion*, in *Sämtliche Werke*, vol. 4 (Stuttgart, 1961), pp. 275–281.

82. Johann Christian August Grohmann, *Ueber Offenbarung und Mythologie* (Berlin, 1799). Grohmann speaks of revelation as the poetry of the human race (p. 117) or as a work of providence in which humans poetize themselves and depict their portrait for eternity (p. 131).

83. See Jakob Friedrich Fries, who indeed assigns the philosophical doctrine of religion to practical philosophy and only on that basis goes on to aesthetics, but also combines both spheres under the title "religious-aesthetic worldview" (§§ 247 ff.), and says that "in the aesthetic worldview of religion all the contradictions of speculation are reconciled to a harmony of life"; see *Neue oder anthropologische Kritik der Vernunft*, 2d ed. (Heidelberg, 1831), 3:361, 364.

of theology as far as the character of religious piety is concerned. It is also necessary to inquire into the credibility of such a change.

Friedrich Schlegel depicted two possible effects of the *Speeches* on his contemporaries, but in so doing he tended to underestimate their apologetic character. Indeed, this is concealed by the fact that what first strikes their reader is the outright abandonment of all the traditional features of the religious. They have more the character of an indictment of positive religion. Their apologetic rhetoric emerges clearly only from the last of the *Speeches*. It is only after the cultured despisers have been won over to the new idea of religion that the traditional contents are rehabilitated, not by retracting what has previously been designated true religion but by defining it in such a way as to make it a generic concept, in fact an ideal. For the sake of this ideal, despite their imperfection, the religions are ultimately absolved from criticism, especially since the speaker attributes all their failings without further ado to philosophy or to the state. The gaps in argumentation are bridged by rhetorical sleight of hand. Indeed, the generic concept outlined in the *Speeches* lacks plausibility if only for the reason that the historical religions as a whole bear very little resemblance to it. It is also left vague what ground there is for affirming that religion is actually concerned with such a "universe" and, in this general sense, with the "infinite"—especially since these concepts remain wholly undefined, so that it is still today a matter of dispute what, for instance, Schleiermacher's "universe" means. If it denotes the One to which no understanding attains,[84] this concept could no longer, after Kant, be casually introduced into theoretical philosophy at least. Because all this remains open and the character of religion is presented in such vastly fictional terms, no inherent objection can be made to the possibility of this concept of religion—any more than a work of art can be refuted. But it is only Schleiermacher's concept of religion that may be considered a work of art. According to the critique Hegel leveled at it during his Jena period, religion

---

84. Thus Gunter Scholtz, *Die Philosophie Schleiermachers* (Darmstadt, 1984), p. 84. On the concept of the universe, see Eilert Herms, *Herkunft, Entfaltung und erste Gestalt des Systems der Wissenschaften bei Schleiermacher* (Gütersloh, 1974), p. 213.

itself as viewed by Schleiermacher succeeds only to perpetuate art but not to bring about the objectivity of the work of art, because it renounces all objectivity (*FK* 151, *GW* 4:386).

3.7. Grounds and Conditions of a Renewed Metaphysical Approach

Whether Schleiermacher's *Speeches* already influenced Hegel's last Frankfurt writings has been a matter of contention ever since Dilthey. The relationship between the *Speeches* and the Hegel of the Frankfurt period has been discussed since then primarily in regard to Schleiermacher's terms "intuition of the universe" and "sense and taste for the infinite" and Hegel's references in his *Fragment of a System* (1800) to rising from finite to infinite life. But the theme of the relationship of the one religion to the positive religions calls no less for attention. Strictly speaking, there is no literary evidence for Hegel's dependence here either. The basis of positivity and its assessment likewise forms the focus of the revised beginning to the 1800 text of *The Positivity of the Christian Religion*. In both cases positivity is regarded not as the result of a possibly unavoidable process of degradation but as an original and necessary feature of historical religion. Schleiermacher, however, thinks of the relationship of positive to true religion as one of individual to generic concept. Properly speaking, this requires each exemplar to be the concept's appropriate actualization. But this way of viewing the matter fuses with another, which builds on the concepts of finite and infinite. As something beyond the grasp of human understanding, religion has within itself, according to this view, the *principium individuationis,* and it individuates itself into an infinite number of finite forms. All historical individuation is thus an anthropological breaking down of the infinitude of true religion. It is true that anthropological elements also come into play when one considers the reasons for the multiplicity of religions. But they remain embedded in ontological questions. The relation of individual and genus does not provide a plausible explanation for the wide gulf between historical religion and generic concept, or for the way in which the pure content of religion is degraded in the individual appearances. The only plausible explanation lies in the mismatch between the infinite character of true religion and the finitude of *homo religiosus*. But if the difference between positive and true religion is to be viewed as the inevitable falsification of the infinite, then it cannot be maintained that in positive religion too, if one were only to seek it at its source and as it was originally constituted, "the dead slag was once the glowing outpouring of the inner fire"[85]—or that there is any historical point of origin where this fire can ever be found glowing in its original state.

The revised form of the beginning of *The Positivity of the Christian Religion* also does not take up the question of the subsequent lapse of an originally pure religion into positivity. It asks whether even the original form of the Christian religion attaches worship of the divine not only to what is accidental in general but to what is accidental as such (*ETW* 171, *J* 143). That the attachment to what is accidental in general is unavoidable, is no less clear for Hegel than for Schleiermacher, even if the reasons given are different, namely that the universal concept is one thing, actuality or living nature another. In actuality "what for the concept is a bare modification, a pure accident, a superfluity, becomes a necessity, something living, perhaps the only thing which is natural and beautiful" (*ETW* 169, *J* 141). Hegel sees here a relationship not of "true" religion to the "positive" religions but of configurations to concept. The concept is not the true, beautiful religion that can be opposed to the actual religions while also justifying them, the sacred fire that in them has degenerated to dead slag. Here—unlike later—it is an abstract concept. The fact that before it the "excess" of actuality seems only ice and stone (*ETW* 170, *J* 142) is not the fault of the configurations. It expresses an inappropriate way of viewing the matter, which begins by confusing concept and ideal, then makes unsuitable use of the concept, and consequently fails to recognize the reason that lies in religion. The concept, however, so we are told, is not the same as the ideal, which involves particularity, an "excess" over the concept. The difference between "true" and "positive" religion cannot therefore be described in terms of the model of genus and individual: an ideal is not a generic concept.

85. Schleiermacher, *On Religion*, p. 194.

Hegel's explanation of the plurality and changing forms of religions on the basis of the infinite modifications of human nature can be interpreted in two ways. According to one it is only the diversity of religions that can be attributed to human nature, while according to the other it is religion in general along with its historical diversification that can be so attributed. Hegel's attempt to explain the diversity and the imperfection of religion by linking them to the particularity of human nature leaves it unclear why there should be religion at all. Nor does he give an explicit account of the idea of God. As religion is in such large measure determined by human need, it seems an easy matter to assume a solely anthropological basis for the idea of God too, the need "to recognize a higher being who transcends our consciousness of human agency" (*ETW* 176, *J* 146). Philosophy would then spell out the modifiable structure of human need. Certainly God and religion would remain its subject matter, but solely from the point of view of human need. It would then be able to come to no conclusions in regard to God other than that he is an accidental or indispensable element in the nature of human need. Such a conception is, however, belied by the preceding Frankfurt fragments, which are devoted to the ideas of love and of life. The earliest materials relating to the concepts of love and unification still reflect the emergence of the new idea of God and religion from ethicotheology.[86] Hegel even designates love as the principle of morality (*J* 388) and also says that morality ensures the possibility of love (*J* 394). This, however, is to transpose the concept of morality to a new framework, and in the course of the inner consolidation of the new conceptualization the possibility of reverting to the old one disappears. Love becomes the power uniting nature and freedom, subject and object (*J* 376); where love is, the divine is. By this means the anthropological barriers are at the same time broken asunder. Nor are they reestablished when Hegel, in a manner foreshadowing Feuerbach, reverses the traditional statement that God is love into "love is God, there is no other deity than

---

86. A complete picture of Hegel's attitude to ethicotheology at that time would require reference to his commentary on Kant's *Metaphysic of Ethics,* to which Rosenkranz had access but which has since been lost; see *HL* 87.

118

love—only what is not divine, what does not love, must have divinity in the idea, outside itself" (*J* 391). Admittedly divinity is not relegated to what lies beyond human being, but it is also not categorically identified with it. The positive content of the new solution remains, however, imprecise.

There is one further piece of evidence that Hegel's approach during his last months in Frankfurt cannot be described as a consistently anthropological interpretation. One element in the definition of human nature is that of its relationship to God (*ETW* 167, 170; *J* 139, 142). The latter clearly belongs to the former, but without God's being thereby reduced to a mere element of human nature. Thus it is not a theoretical but solely a methodological abstraction to pay no regard to the task of elaborating the idea of God. Moreover there are two statements that go beyond such an abstraction. Hegel does not merely name the relationship of the human and the divine among a multitude of other questions that would have to be settled "elsewhere" (*ETW* 176, *J* 147). What he says rather is that its conceptual elucidation must "in the end [become] a metaphysical treatment of the relation between the finite and the infinite" (*ETW* 176, *J* 146). But neither here nor elsewhere—for instance in the *Fragment of a System*—does he explicitly elaborate this metaphysical character. The way in which Hegel refers to these questions in the two texts mentioned and also in the shorter fragments of the late Frankfurt period suggests that it is not merely as a matter of method that this aspect is excluded, because he does not yet have the necessary tools for a metaphysical treatment; in addition, his understanding of philosophy as mere reflection runs counter to the elucidation that would be needed.

Replacement of the concept of love by that of life also does not in principle lead beyond the inappropriate relationship between thought and its means of explication. From the perspective of philosophy of religion the concept of love—after the initial identification of religion and love (*J* 377)—is seen to be insufficient: there is no religion until love has been shaped by imagination into a God (*ETW* 248, *J* 297). In another respect too the concept of religion is superior to that of love: love is sublated by reflection, whereas religion is the union of love and reflection (*ETW* 253, *J* 302). It is even clearer that the concept of love is inferior to that of life. Love and unification presuppose something separate, whereas life involves both opposition and unification, association and nonassociation. The loftiest definition of the concepts of God and religion is therefore based on the concept of life: thinking life raises out of what is opposed to it an "all-living and all-powerful infinite life, and this life it calls God" (*ETW* 311, *J* 347). Religion is nothing other than this "raising" [*Erhebung*] from finite life to infinite life, which is God himself. The success or failure of this approach to a nonmoral concept of God and religion therefore depends on the intelligibility of the concept of life. To the extent that there was a consensus about these questions since the *Critique of Pure Reason*, it related to the fact that the possibility of such raising was disputed. And Hegel does indeed take this into account to the extent that he dismisses a mere raising from the finite to the infinite as a product of reflection. But his clarification to the effect that what is involved here is not that, but raising to infinite *life*,[87] does little to save his assertion from the possibility of criticism.

Our assessment of this raising is not helped by the fact that the fragments do not elaborate the concept of life in the breadth we would wish. Its philosophical context is clearer, and this is a context that links Hegel not with Schleiermacher's *Speeches* but with the circle of friends in Frankfurt and Hamburg. Hölderlin's fragment *Über Religion* also is based on a more infinite nexus of life. But his concept of life is confined to the spirit that reigns in a given sphere, to the relation in which each person stands to his or her world. It is not to be confused with Hegel's purely metaphysical concept of life. Hölderlin's fragment also aims in another direction: human beings learn from a more living relation to what surrounds them—a relation raised above the level of necessity—that a God exists. Assuredly this "proof" adduced "in a few words" is not of much help in the problematic situation confronting philosophical theology at that time. It distinguishes the religious from intellectual,

---

87. [*Tr.*] See *ETW* 311 (*J* 347): "This raising of the human, not from the finite to the infinite (for these terms are only products of mere reflection, and as such their separation is absolute), but from finite life to infinite life, is religion."

moral, and legal relationships on the one hand, and from physical, mechanical, and historical relationships on the other hand. But in terms of content the religious remains related to these two groups, especially since we are also told that religious conceptions are neither intellectual nor historical but intellectually historical, that is, mythical, containing neither mere ideas or concepts nor mere events. Delimited above all in this negative fashion, the character of the religious is not explained in more detail. The distinction then drawn between epic and dramatic myth leads to a theory of imaginative literature [*Dichtung*] from the standpoint of which all religion appears as essentially poetic. The wording of the *Ältestes Systemprogramm des Deutschen Idealismus*[88] also leads to an aesthetic interpretation of religion. There is no point in looking here for clarification as to the metaphysical status of "life" or the metaphysical treatment of the relation between finite and infinite that Hegel had previously called for.

By the end of the Frankfurt period Hegel is clear about the need for a metaphysical renewal of the doctrine of God and religion, but not about how it is to be accomplished. At least none of the sources justify the assumption that he had precise ideas in this regard, over and above his declarations of intent. This vagueness contrasts, however, with a very significant metaphysical stance. In explaining the necessity of a metaphysical treatment, Hegel implicitly points to a prior condition for a new interpretation of religion: the positive, he says, necessarily becomes "glaringly positive if human nature is absolutely severed from the divine, if no mediation between the two is conceded except in one isolated individual" (*ETW* 176, *J* 146). A renewal of philosophical theology and philosophy of religion thus presupposes that finite and infinite, divine and human nature, are not severed in this way. This is borne out by a reflection that is christological to the same degree that it amends traditional christology by means of Spinoza's metaphysics of substance—even though it is not as easy to point to the Spinozism in Hegel's Frankfurt fragments as it is in Schleiermacher's *Speeches*, for example, or even in Herder's *God: Some Conversations*. Here, however,

88. [*Tr.*] See chap. 2, n. 26.

Spinoza's thought acquires a preeminent and at the same time lasting importance for Hegel's philosophy: "There are not two independent wills, two substances; God and humanity must therefore
be one" (*J* 391; cf. 311 [*ETW* 264]). In the idea of this unity Hegel
sees the coincidence of Spinozism and the rightly understood content of christology—reason unfolded in philosophy and actualized
in religion.

CHAPTER II

THE FOUNDATION OF HEGEL'S SPECULATIVE PHILOSOPHY OF RELIGION IN THE WRITINGS OF THE JENA PERIOD

1. Background and Content of the New Conception

The few years between the *Critique of Pure Reason* and the final fragments from Hegel's Frankfurt period exhibit a rapid succession of diverse attempts to ground the philosophical doctrine of God and doctrine of religion. These differing lines of approach—ethicotheology, the not yet independent discipline of anthropology, and the spilling over of the problem of God into nonphilosophy, into feeling, faith, immediate knowing, prophetic utterance or poetry—spell out the conditions for the existence of these branches of philosophy, and form part of the history of philosophy itself. Alongside these approaches stand those of Schleiermacher and Hegel, which, despite isolated gestures in the direction of anthropology, in the last analysis base themselves on metaphysical concepts, but without attempting the conceptual clarification that is, properly speaking, called for.

Following Kant's critique of the metaphysical idea of God, what might provide the motive for an approach that would initially be implicitly metaphysical, but would ultimately see itself as explicitly so? At one extreme, a purely arbitrary decision to espouse such an approach might be imagined; at the other, the failure of ethicotheology could have driven the doctrine of God and of religion unavoidably back into metaphysics. Yet the renewed turning to metaphysics is in no way due to an abrupt change of course. It springs from many years of repeatedly unsuccessful attempts to deepen the philosophical understanding of religion. It follows on the downfall of ethicotheology, but not in strictly necessary fashion. For neither the fledgling anthropological approach nor Friedrich Heinrich Jacobi's attempt to transpose the problem of God to nonphilosophy could in any sense be regarded as refuted; they could, however, be rejected as insufficient. Certainly the content of philosophical statements about God can easily be limited to saying that it is just a requirement of human beings to worship a being that is higher than themselves. But then it would be necessary to proceed consistently and not overstep the anthropological restriction, at any rate without additional arguments. The withdrawal into nonphilosophy also cannot be refuted. But it can be argued that the reasons that seemed to necessitate it are insufficient, and above all that the thought dimension that remains to a nonphilosophy of God and of religion is all too impoverished.

The task of regenerating the doctrine of God and of religion as it presented itself at that time can therefore be formulated as follows. If one wanted to hold fast to the ideal of a rigorous philosophy, it was necessary to win back the concept of God for theoretical philosophy and on that basis ground the philosophy of religion anew—just a few years after this discipline had first constituted itself under that name and in a new guise. The concurrence of these two tasks was not merely by chance. It derived from the unity of ethicotheology and moral religion as well as of the critique directed against both. At the time it seemed a sensible principle to maintain this unity even under changed systematic conditions.

In holding fast to a rigorous concept of philosophy, Hegel was subscribing to a program that had last been carried out by Kant and, in a different form, by Fichte. At the end of his Frankfurt period he expressed this in the well-known statement that he had had to pass on from the more subordinate human needs to science; the ideal of his youth had had to take the form of reflection and become a system (*L* 64, *Br* 1:59). Such a system alone now seemed capable of grounding the philosophy of religion program too. What form this system might take, whether that of Schelling's *System of Transcendental Idealism* (1800) or of a different, metaphysical system, was probably still an open question at that time.

Of no less importance is a second consideration, concerning matters of content. Along with theoretical rigor, a new philosophical doctrine of God and of religion had to be able to attest to a concept of God who was not merely the abstract supreme being of Enlightenment philosophy, nor the preceptor and executor of the moral law, nor just a being outside me, standing over against me as I stand over against it in mutual independence. In Frankfurt, Hegel's thought had circled around the possibility of a unification; he had there defined the divine as the unification of nature and freedom, of subject and object. He could find similar, less elaborated ideas in romantic writers, from whom he doubtless gleaned a multitude of suggestions. What is decisive for his regrounding of a philosophical knowledge of God, however, is that he sought to strip romanticism's new experience of the divine, and particularly its idea of mediation, of its visionary form, and to introduce them both in their entirety into the framework of a demonstrability bordering on school philosophy, that is, into the form of reflection, as ingredients of the system. Had the natural and historical world not been drawn into the idea of God, Hegel's philosophy of religion would have become the same kind of "straw epistle" as the Enlightenment amputations of religion.

Unquestionably, the working out of a philosophy of religion under these two conditions was not achieved immediately, if indeed it was achieved at all. The forms in which it was initially conceived suffer from an evident disproportion between what they claim to do and the means of explication available to them. At the same time the development of the doctrine of God and of religion within the framework of the system can be regarded as a process of astonishing consistency for the most part[1]—even if the systematic means of

1. This development has not yet been investigated as it should, and it has not infrequently been entirely disregarded. A possible reason for this is the dispersed nature of the sources. Basically they fall into five groups:

(1) Occasional references to religion, as found in *The Difference between Fichte's and Schelling's System of Philosophy* and in the essays published in the *Kritisches Journal der Philosophie*, especially *Das Wesen der philosophischen Kritik* [a translation is found in *Independent Journal of Philosophy* 3 (1979): 37–45], *Faith and Knowledge*, and the essay on *Natural Law* (*GW 4*).

(2) Fragments from lectures delivered between 1801 and 1803 (*GW 5*), especially the natural-law lecture notes transmitted by Karl Rosenkranz and Rudolf Haym (*HL* 132–141, *JS*[1] 178–186).

its realization changed during this period. It is only in the Berlin *Lectures on the Philosophy of Religion* that the doctrine attains what is for Hegel its final form. But the two preceding decades did not remain empty as far as philosophy of religion was concerned. Specifically the Jena period contains a continuous development of the philosophy of religion within the elaboration of the system as a whole. The importance of this period for the development of Hegel's overall philosophy has become evident during the past two decades—its importance for the conception of the system as a whole, for speculative philosophy in the narrower sense, that is,

---

(3) The section "Kunst, Religion und Wissenschaft" at the end of *Natur-philosophie und Philosophie des Geistes* (1805–6) (*GW* 8).

(4) The discussions of religion in the *Phenomenology of Spirit,* especially in the chapter on religion (*GW* 9).

(5) The peculiar fragment *Vom göttlichen Dreieck* ("On the Divine Triangle") transmitted only by Rosenkranz, and the *Zeichnung mit Dreiecken und anderen Symbolen* ("Diagram with Triangles and Other Symbols") found among Hegel's literary remains (*GW* 5); these, however, occupy a special position. [A translation of *Vom göttlichen Dreieck* is found in H. S. Harris, *Hegel's Development: Night Thoughts (Jena 1801–1806)* (Oxford, 1983), pp. 186–188.] It is uncertain whether the triangle diagram is in Hegel's hand or whether much significance attaches to it and the accompanying comments. That Hegel's "speculation had initially a *theosophical* character," as Rosenkranz claims, can in no way be attested by these two pieces of evidence, even in conjunction with reports on excerpts Hegel made from Johannes Tauler and Meister Eckhart (*HL* 102). This could indeed be maintained as long as the chronology of the early writings was partly incorrect and partly incomplete. Rosenkranz assigns both the diagram and the fragment to the first half of the Frankfurt years, prior to the system draft now dated to the winter semester 1804–5. According to the new dating by Heinz Kimmerle, the "divine triangle" fragment originated in the spring of 1804, that is, between the first and second system drafts (see "Zur Chronologie von Hegels Jenaer Schriften," *Hegel-Studien* 4 [1967]: 144, 161–162; and "Die von Rosenkranz überlieferten Texte Hegels aus der Jenaer Zeit," *Hegel-Studien* 5 [1968]: 92). This refutes the assumption of a mystical-theosophical phase in Hegel's development. Nor can such an assumption be regarded as confirmed by Rosenkranz's report that "as late as the summer of 1806" Hegel called "the immanent dialectic of the absolute the career of God [*Lebenslauf Gottes*]" (*JS*[1] 264–265, *HL* 192), especially since this dating is questionable. The so-called "Boehme aphorism" (*HL* 547–548) also makes a theosophical phase rather improbable. The position it depicts comes very close to the ambivalent attitude that Hegel continues to adopt toward Boehme even later: "a dark halfway house" (*JS*[1] 257, *HL* 182). And as far as the triangle diagram is concerned, Helmut Schneider makes it clear that, regardless of which hand it stems from, it is not connected to trinitarian speculation (see "Zur Dreieckssymbolik bei Hegel," *Hegel-Studien* 8 [1973]: esp. 57, 76).

logic and metaphysics, and also for practical philosophy. With respect to philosophy of religion as well, it was during the Jena years that Hegel made the weightiest decisions. The relevant chapter of the *Phenomenology of Spirit* is already a late fruit of this development. It presupposes the working out of a conception of which it can justifiably be said—without contesting the possibility of criticism—that it combines within itself the two conflicting tendencies we have mentioned. On the one hand, and contrary to the prevailing tendency of the time, religion is once again placed in the context of a metaphysical system. This removes philosophy of religion from the sphere of the poetic, as well as from the "uncomprehending, prophetic manner of speech [of] an oracle" that Hegel's *Lectures on the History of Philosophy* attribute to Schleiermacher's *Speeches,* and not to them alone.[2] On the other hand, religion does not dissolve into logic and metaphysics, and neither is it a "ragged patchwork" of metaphysics and morals of the sort that Schleiermacher criticizes in his predecessors.[3] It is viewed in many different connections, for instance with art and ethical life, but it is not reduced to just one of these phenomena.

A philosophy of religion in the sense envisaged by the final Frankfurt fragments presupposes that, contrary to the *Critique of Pure Reason,* metaphysics is still possible as a science. This is what Hegel seeks to demonstrate from the time of his first writings from the Jena period. His repeated and constantly revised approaches to the problem form in their entirety the developmental history of the *Science of Logic.* With the latter Hegel believed that the demonstration he sought had been accomplished. The link between metaphysics and philosophy of religion acquires foundational importance because the task of explicating the concept of the absolute pertains only in part to philosophy of religion; it belongs also to metaphysics. Only when philosophy of religion is at the same time

2. *LHP* 509, W 15:643. This dictum forms part of a critique of contemporary approaches of which no trace has been found thus far in the transcripts of the Berlin lectures on the history of philosophy, and which therefore probably stems from Hegel's Jena lecture manuscript on this subject (1805–6).

3. Friedrich Schleiermacher, *On Religion: Speeches to Its Cultured Despisers,* ed. and trans. from the 1st ed. (1799) by Richard Crouter (Cambridge, 1988), p. 89 (translation altered slightly).

a science of the idea (see sec. 2 below) can it envisage undertaking those tasks without which it remains, in Hegel's view, a merely presumptive science of what, as he slightingly puts it, is called "human being" (FK 65, GW 4:323).

This prime condition for a regeneration of the philosophy of religion concerns only the possibility of a speculative theology and its relationship to philosophy of religion. It does not yet settle anything with respect to the systematic place or even the systematic form of philosophy of religion. At that time the more precise form to be taken by a philosophy of religion was a completely open question. The studies of Karl Heinrich Ludwig Pölitz and Ludwig Heinrich Jakob, the first to be conceived by their authors as philosophy of religion, bore the imprint of ethicotheology and physicotheology. This ruled them out as possible models, and there were no others. Hume's Dialogues or Natural History were as little suited to the purpose—even assuming Hegel was familiar with them—as the critiques of revelation of Fichte and Johann Gebhard Ehrenreich Maass. The early development of Hegel's philosophy of religion is therefore characterized by a wavering between different options that corresponds in part to changes in the conception of the system in general. Apart from its relationship to the actual science of the idea (sec. 2), it is primarily its proximity to aesthetics (sec. 3) and the philosophy of ethical life in the Hegelian sense (sec. 4) that influences its shape. Yet philosophy of religion breaks free from an undifferentiated linkage with other disciplines—but not in such a way as to break all ties. As it becomes gradually distinct from them it also becomes possible to see more clearly the interconnections that are indissolubly bound up with its systematic position. By the time he left Jena Hegel regarded these problems as basically solved. But hardly any answer had yet been given to the no less important question of the systematic form appropriate to a speculative philosophy of religion. This does not receive attention until the Berlin lectures.

2. Philosophy of Religion as Science of the Idea

(1) Kant's and Jacobi's critique had contested the possibility of a metaphysical knowledge of God—in general, the possibility of any

certain knowledge of what lay beyond the range of experience or the conditioned. Before grounding metaphysics anew it was necessary to dispose of these objections. Otherwise one would be merely harking back to a precritical stance, and perhaps, even prior to precritical metaphysics, to a form of philosophical atavism. If the attempt at regrounding was to be successful, it had to exhibit the possibility of metaphysical knowledge, or at least to lay bare the errors and absurdities of the critique of metaphysics, thus undermining its validity. Hegel's first published works are consistent in taking critical issue with the critique of metaphysics, especially in *Faith and Knowledge* (1802). If, as Jacobi thinks, the task of a philosophical theology consists in exhibiting the conditions of existence of the unconditioned [*die Bedingungen des Unbedingten*], it would indeed be utterly senseless. If, however, cognitive knowledge was not confined to the sphere of the understanding, this would not necessarily apply. For this reason Friedrich Schlegel, in his review of Jacobi's novel *Woldemar*, already attributes Jacobi's preoccupation with this supposed aporia to an "irreconcilable hatred for philosophizing reason" and calls for a process of reciprocal grounding to escape the infinite regress from one conditioning factor to another (*KSA* 199). And Hegel's objections to the *Critique of Pure Reason* extend from Kant's recourse to two streams or branches of knowledge to his critique of the proofs of God. By contrast, Hegel deems ethicotheology no longer worthy of critique: the postulate of immortality is quite incapable of philosophical portrayal (*FK* 94, 4:344–345). And he again transposes Kant's arguments for the postulate of the existence of God into theoretical philosophy in order to be able to derive from it aspects that are not completely outside the scope of philosophical discussion.[4]

Hegel's criticism is, to be sure, often confined to polemical rhetoric, such as that against Jacobi's "trail of nonsense and bombast" or the "chilly and insipid emotional effusion" of his popularizer Friedrich Köppen (*FK* 120, 135; *GW* 4:363, 374). But it does also relate to Kant's and Jacobi's premises. It could have been successful, however, only if it had shown that cognitive knowledge

---

4. On Hegel's discussion of the *Critique of Pure Reason,* see esp. Klaus Düsing, *Hegel und die Geschichte der Philosophie* (Darmstadt, 1983), pp. 216 ff., 231 ff.

does not merely move in finite oppositions but can pass beyond the standpoint of reflection to absolute identity, and that genuine knowing has to begin here. Hegel directs this objection explicitly against Fichte (*FK* 160, *GW* 4:392). But whether this is possible, and how it is possible, is left an open question in the Jena critical writings.[5] The somewhat awkward and continual references to the absolute identity of subject and object also give rise to the suspicion that the systematic explication of this identity still affords Hegel substantial difficulties at this time.

In his debate with reflective philosophy Hegel does not attempt to replace its concept of cognitive knowledge by another whose potential accomplishment would be limited to the restitution of ontology. A partial renewal of metaphysics would be fruitless because all of Hegel's objections depend on the concept of the absolute for their power of conviction: a restitution of ontology depends on the possibility of a restitution of philosophical theology. The plausibility of all the affirmative elements of Hegel's critique rests on the idea of God as absolute identity. It is therefore indeed consistent that Hegel should speak of the "concern of philosophy . . . to reestablish God from the very outset at the pinnacle of philosophy as the one and only ground of everything, as the sole *principium essendi* and *cognoscendi*" (*GW* 4:179); and in saying this he again takes issue sharply with the doctrine of postulates. But the critical writings provide no justification for philosophy to take this step. Instead of the self-evident explication of absolute identity that would in fact be necessary, Hegel finally points to another justification of his position, one invoking the history of philosophy. After the dogmatism of being or precritical philosophy, and the dogmatism of thinking or reflective philosophy (and the latter in the totality of its forms), "true philosophy," he suggests, arises out of the sum total of these formative stages. This historical recommendation for his own approach makes it plain that Hegel is in no way aiming at a mere restitution of precritical metaphysics. He even says of the last form this took, the one given it by Moses Mendelssohn,

5. [*Tr.*] These are collected in *GW* 4, *Jenaer Kritische Schriften*, and consist mostly of Hegel's contributions to the *Kritisches Journal der Philosophie*, edited by Schelling and himself, during 1802 and 1803.

that the world cannot be grateful enough to the gods, next to Kant, for deliverance from it (FK 97, GW 4:348). This is not only an apt sally but an appropriate way of expressing the unbridgeable gulf between the concept of God of the new philosophical theology and the metaphysics that had gone before it.

The justification deriving from the history of philosophy acquires connotations for the philosophy of religion in that it characterizes the present stage of "cultural refinement"[6] as one of infinite anguish and a "speculative Good Friday" (FK 189–191, GW 4:413–414)—and it does so on the basis of the Easter of speculation, the resurrection of the highest idea. It thus restricts the "speculative Good Friday" and the atheistic "religion of modernity" to the very short period since the appearance of the Critique of Pure Reason; and it claims to be able to conceive in appropriate manner the relative right of this speculative Good Friday as a moment of the highest idea. The possibility that the God who has been declared dead may achieve such a resurrection in the new philosophy is, however, in no way attested by the image used to legitimate it. Of more importance than Hegel's metaphor, to which too much significance is usually attached, is his largely ignored reference to the content of religion. He attributes a more correct insight to religion than to the philosophy of absolute subjectivity. Whereas the latter comprehends evil merely as the contingency and arbitrariness of an intrinsically finite nature, religion acknowledges it to be inherent in finite nature, certainly, but points to "a truly present and real redemption"—one embracing nature too—"not one that is put off into an infinite progress and hence never to be realized." Hegel illustrates the rupture of actuality by referring to the practical side of reflective philosophy, saying that alienation is overcome in the spirit as "the union of the subjective side [of God] with God become human," the union of the immanent and economic trinities. In this spirit "the world is in itself reconstructed and redeemed and hallowed in quite another way" than in the "ideal of the moral world order" (FK 180–181; GW 4:407).

6. [Tr.] "die Stufe der 'Bildung.'" Bildung has an ironic ring for Hegel: human culture in its highest and supposedly most refined development has issued in the death of God.

The peculiar fragment *Vom göttlichen Dreieck* ("The Divine Triangle") confirms, even if in a very incomplete way, the philosophical relevance of the doctrine of the Trinity. Here it resides in the mediation of God and "world" or "earth." In this fragment, in much the same way as in *Faith and Knowledge,* we are told: "For the consecrated earth this *self-consciousness of God* is *the Spirit,* which proceeds from God, and in which the earth is one with him and with the Son."[7] For the question of the superiority of this idea of reconciliation, it is of secondary importance whether or not it is conceived as specifically religious. In the same context Hegel refers to the designation of the world as a blessed god in the *Timaeus.* But whether the reference is conceived in Platonic or in Christian terms, no justification is given for this being not merely a superior but also a correct way of viewing the matter.

The latter could only be shown by genuine cognition. According to Hegel, such cognition must start from the absolute, but it cannot merely start from the absolute without returning to it again. The process of this knowing therefore coincides with the "self-construction of the absolute," the "self-construction of identity into totality." This process whereby the absolute becomes objective to itself in all its totality Hegel designates "the eternal human incarnation [*Menschwerdung*] of God" (*D* 170–171, *GW* 4:74–75). In religion, unlike the contemporary reflective philosophy, the unity of what is antithetical has already been thought. This reveals the conceptual content Hegel assigns to this doctrine, in opposition to the common religious view and, specifically, to more recent theological formulations. The only reason that he derives philosophical perspectives from the idea of the incarnation of God is that its meaning in no way resides for him in what a more recent theological interpretation believes to have found in it, namely that "God became human in Jesus Christ in order to distinguish definitively between God and humanity forever."[8] From Hegel's viewpoint this interpretation corresponds to reflective philosophy's image of religion: it

7. Karl Rosenkranz, "Hegel's ursprüngliches System, 1798–1806: Aus Hegel's Nachlass," *Literarhistorisches Taschenbuch* 2 (1844): 162 (see Harris, *Hegel's Development: Night Thoughts,* p. 187).

8. Eberhard Jüngel, *God as the Mystery of the World,* trans. Darrell L. Guder (Grand Rapids, Mich., 1983), p. 94.

extends limitation even into religion and places consummation in an otherworldly sphere. The only reason christology is of systematic importance for his philosophy is that he finds its content to lie in the precise opposite of this interpretation. But any meaningful talk of "the incarnation of God" requires knowledge of God. Since this presupposes, in the framework of religion, a knowledge of the God who is said to have become human, its metaphorical use in philosophy presupposes a philosophical theology; and the latter had already been shown to be desirable, to be sure, but not yet in any way possible.

(2) At the beginning of his years in Jena, Hegel has not yet found a way of recovering the concept of God for theoretical philosophy that satisfies him. His writings from this time form a rapid succession of approaches to the problem, each of which seeks to improve on the preceding; their sole common feature is their rejection of the differing representations of God of reflective philosophy. For the rest the concept of God, and even the definition of the organon of the knowledge of God, exhibit step by step a deepening insight into the way in which the problem presents itself. The prime element in this change comes from Hegel's attempts to establish the possibility of metaphysical knowledge. This was indeed an urgent matter if the renewed philosophical knowledge of God was to be neither the prophetic speech of an oracle nor a pious emotional effusion, but acquire conceptual form. But the way in which the idea of God is formulated on each succeeding occasion is not merely a result of the changed concept of knowledge—especially since Hegel stresses that all genuine knowledge begins from the absolute (*FK* 159, *GW* 4:392). What is of decisive importance, however, is not the priority of the one or the other, but their connection: recovery of the idea of God for theoretical knowledge is linked to a concept of the absolute that enables such knowledge to be understood as a mode of self-explication of the absolute.

Initially the most prominent feature in this regard is the antithesis of intuition and reflection.[9] There had already been talk

9. The brief indications that follow are based on an earlier treatment by the author, "Äusserliche Reflexion und immanente Reflexion," *Hegel-Studien* 13 (1978): 96 ff. Cf. Klaus Düsing, *Das Problem der Subjektivität in Hegels Logik* (Bonn, 1976), pp. 75 ff., although his main emphasis is somewhat different.

of "intuition" in Schleiermacher's *Speeches*. Hegel, however, fastens on Schelling's concept of intellectual intuition (*FK* 159, *GW* 4:392); "steady, clear intuiting" is, on this view, "the prime condition for philosophizing" (*GW* 5:264). It apprehends the "image of the absolute" that the absolute idea delineates of itself, and presents it to reflection (*GW* 5:262, 273). But although Hegel distinguishes intuition in this fashion, there is nothing he can say about it and its image of the absolute that could show the possibility of a philosophical theology. To be sure, the very fragmentary form in which this earliest conception has come down to us may not have preserved the passages devoted to intuition. Thus the start of the fragment *Die Idee des absoluten Wesens* (1801–2) refers to a section in which this idea is "portrayed as the speculative idea, and then as the *universum*" (*GW* 5:262). At the same time, however, these statements confirm doubts as to the role of intuition as organon, for they set the intuition of absolute being in opposition to the unfolding [*Entfaltung*] of the idea "for cognition." And when we are told that the place of cognition is "within philosophy itself" (*GW* 5:262), then the intuition of absolute being is prior to philosophy.

To this corresponds a further difference from Schelling: Hegel makes intuition in the first place a prime condition of logic, one that lies outside philosophy as such. Without it logic would have to establish antitheses without benefit of the guidance afforded by the idea of the absolute and would thus fail to get beyond the sphere of antithesis and reflective philosophy. But above all he does not assign philosophy in the proper sense—the construction and production of the absolute for consciousness—to intuition, but to reflection (*D* 100 ff., 120–121; *GW* 4:16 ff., 32), albeit reflection under the guidance afforded by the intuition of absolute identity. And intuition can in no way be sure of having even this function. For while it seems at one time as though reflection needs intuition to rise above the sphere of opposition, at another Hegel attributes this to reflection itself, rightly understood. Absolute cognition, he tells us, is "the form of reflection that splits into antithesis, but takes the antithesis back and destroys it absolutely" (*GW* 5:265). We find yet another formulation in the 1801–2 lecture fragment *Logica et Metaphysica* to the effect that the understanding is "secretly driven by reason" to imitate reason but only achieves a formal identity (*GW* 5:272). Thus already in the winter of 1801–2 —in other words, shortly after the essay on *The Difference between Fichte's and Schelling's System of Philosophy*, which lays so much stress on the indispensability for philosophizing of intuition (*D* 111, *GW* 4:27–28)—the latter is singularly bereft of any proper place or function. The fact that Hegel once again attributes greater importance to it in *Faith and Knowledge* might reside in the external circumstance that this contribution appeared in the *Kritisches Journal der Philosophie*, of which Hegel was joint editor with Schelling.

Reason or speculation is in any event regarded as the proper organon of true philosophy. But it too remains quite colorless. The *Difference* essay defines it as the identity of intuition and reflection (*D* 112, *GW* 4:29), but the slightly later demotion of intuition together with the enhancement of the concept of reflection to be the concept of absolute cognition blur the profile of speculation. The same is true of the field reserved for speculation, namely philosophy in the proper sense or metaphysics, which was still distinct from logic (*GW* 5:274). At least to judge from the fragmentary form in which the text of *Logica et Metaphysica* is transmitted, this preview gives a very much less colorful picture of metaphysics than of logic (*GW* 5:274–275). It makes no reference to a separate part devoted to *theologia naturalis*. Since the idea of God is viewed as the sole *principium essendi* and *cognoscendi*, it would be logical to abandon its treatment in isolation from ontology. There is, however, no trace in this metaphysics of any clear stamp of philosophical theology. Yet it is the science of reason, and this Hegel calls the universal and absolute, "which therefore neither needs nor can use anything other or alien for its production, because there is nothing external to the source of science, nothing external to reason" (*GW* 5:260). Rarely does the Spinozism of this earliest draft of a system[10] come so clearly to expression as in the phrase, "reason is the absolute substance." At the same time this contains the answer to Jacobi's ter-

---

10. [*Tr.*] Found in the 1801–2 lecture manuscript fragment, *Introductio in Philosophiam* (*GW* 5:257–265).

tium non datur—to the alternative of either God outside me or myself as God. By this means philosophical theology acquires considerably greater importance than it had in the precritical school philosophy, but it is not so tangible as, say, in the first part of Spinoza's *Ethics*. It would perhaps be tangible in the portrayal of the idea of absolute being as speculative idea and as *universum*—but this is at a level prior to actual philosophical cognition. Hegel himself seems to have experienced a certain deficiency here. He announces his intention of dictating propositions concerning the idea of the absolute, but at the same time dampens overly-high expectations. The idea, he says, will be presented in its utmost simplicity, and "because of this simplicity its portrayal will appear insignificant; it will seem to have no importance." Yet its "complete meaning" is "the whole of philosophy and life itself" (*GW* 5:264).

It is only at the close of the system that the general theological character becomes plain—in the "intuition of God," in the return to the pure idea in the philosophy of religion and of art.[11] This denotes a further insight for the construction of the system: the self-construction of the absolute would be incomplete if it did not also involve the return of the absolute idea into itself or, as it is put in a passage that has been deleted, "the resumption of the whole into one"—that is, if the absolute idea did not become self-referential in the intuition of God. In regard to the first part of the system, namely logic and metaphysics, it is stated, in the conceptuality of metaphysics, that absolute being is portrayed as speculative idea; in regard to the philosophy of art and religion, by contrast, Hegel speaks explicitly of the "intuition of God." It is only at the close of the system that the theological dimension of the absolute idea

11. *GW* 5:264. The editors of this volume here take "Anschauung G's" to stand for "Anschauung [des] Geistes" (intuition of spirit). It is more likely, however, that the text should read "Anschauung Gottes" (intuition of God). This brings out clearly the philosophico-theological dimension of the concluding section of the system. One argument for this reading is that it does not make it necessary to supply the supposedly missing article "des." Moreover, the manuscript for the Berlin lectures on the philosophy of religion shows that Hegel regularly uses "G" as an abbreviation for "Gott," but only rarely for "Geist," as in a phrase such as "PROCESS des Geistes" (see *GW* 17:284).

becomes manifest, in the return of absolute being into itself out of its unfolding.

From the fragmentary form in which the text has come down to us, it is unclear how Hegel portrayed this tension between the initial absolute being and the explicit idea of God. It is not even certain that he did so at any length since this system outline is found only in the context of the fragment *Introductio in Philosophiam* (1801–2). The systematic means that were available to him at the time can scarcely have been anything other than quite inadequate for such an explication. It is not until the Berlin lectures that this program is carried through. In this respect the systematic trajectory that Hegel here follows from the initial form of the speculative idea in logic and metaphysics to the philosophy of religion is at the same time the historical trajectory representing the development of his system.

Despite all the differences in the way this systematic framework is expounded, the link between philosophical theology and philosophy of religion, as it is perceived in the first Jena lectures, remains in force down through the later lectures. For Kant, religion limited to morals also requires a merely moral God. Hegel's insight into the nonmoral character of religion leads him to insight into the insufficiency of the merely moral God and to the attempt to win back the problem of God for theoretical philosophy. But the unity of philosophical theology and philosophy of religion is, since these earliest Jena lecture manuscripts, no longer an external concurrence of physico- or ethicotheology with a corresponding philosophy of religion. With the incorporation of philosophy of religion the system is to be conceived as philosophical theology in the broad sense. In this way the relationship of philosophy of religion and philosophical theology becomes a relationship *within* the latter: philosophy of religion is the culmination of philosophical theology, where the self-construction of the absolute returns into itself and becomes self-referential.

To be sure, Hegel already formulates this unity of philosophical theology and philosophy of religion in the first semester of his teaching activity in Jena. In the course of the substantial changes in the way he conceived his system, however, the conceptual elaboration of this unity was also subject to alterations that were initially still far-reaching. At the outset there are even two outlines that do not bear the mark of this self-referential activity of the absolute. Yet it is just they that confirm in negative fashion what is characteristic about Hegel's approach. For the very first outline of a system that he publishes, even before the *Introductio* lecture fragments, tells us little about his own concept. This outline is found in the *Difference* essay of 1801 (*D* 170–173, *GW* 4:75–76), in the section on the "Comparison of Schelling's Principle of Philosophy with Fichte's," and it belongs without doubt to Schelling's identity philosophy, even if it is found only somewhat later in Schelling's own work, in his *Philosophie der Kunst*. This outline of a system shows no sign of the tension between the science of the idea in the narrower sense and the philosophy of religion that embraces the system as a whole. To be sure, the polarity between the philosophy of nature and of intelligence ends only at their point of indifference. Intuition of the absolute appears partly as speculation, partly as art; on the side of art it subdivides into art in the narrower sense and religion. Thus on the one hand religion is subordinated to art in the broad sense and juxtaposed to art in the narrower sense. On the other hand, since Hegel denotes the entire sphere as "service of God" or "worship" [*Gottesdienst*], he establishes a dual concept of religion in parallel as it were to the dual concept of art. If intuition of the absolute can as a whole be termed service of God or intuition of God's eternal incarnation, this affords justification for classing it in its entirety under the heading "religion"—in much the same way as later in the *Encyclopedia* "religion" provides the heading for the whole sphere of absolute spirit. Even this evident modification, however, does not bring about the tension between the actual science of the idea and the philosophy of religion that characterizes Hegel's conception of his system only a few months later.

Hegel here calls the intuition of the absolute "a living intuition of the absolute life and hence a being at one with it." This unmistakably echoes turns of phrase found in the last Frankfurt fragments of 1800, in particular the *Fragment of a System* (*ETW* 309 ff., *J* 343 ff.). The program sketched in the revised preface to the essay on *The Positivity of the Christian Religion* is also carried out, since this intuition of the absolute life now stands in the context of metaphysics. The elaboration of this approach remains, however, highly nebulous. It is in fact only the presence of art and speculation that enables one to infer, for example, that the polarity of nature and intelligence is perpetuated into the point of indifference. The inadequacy of the conceptual apparatus is, moreover, clear from Hegel's recourse to the comparative: on the speculative side consciousness is "more" dominant, on the other side the unconscious is "predominant"—although it is stated in the same section that such predominance is "in any case something inessential." It also remains questionable to what extent the definition of art in the broader sense really characterizes religion: "intuition appears more concentrated in a point, and consciousness is stricken down." Furthermore not even identity philosophy's requirement for symmetry makes plausible why within art there should be a further distinction between art in the narrower sense and religion and this side as a whole should be termed art and not religion, or why they are not both classed under a third higher-order heading—especially as it is not clear why one of the two should have primacy within this intuition of the absolute. In any case, this outline of a system leaves open the question how art in the narrower sense as well as religion and speculation measure up to the task conceived for them, namely to be the "intuition of the self-shaping or objectively self-finding absolute" and, in this very form, of the "eternal incarnation of God." While Schelling's *Vorlesungen über die Philosophie der Kunst* can be regarded as carrying out this program in part, for religion the question remains entirely open.

A year later, in the essay on *Natural Law* of 1802–3, Hegel once again introduces a system outline based on the philosophy of substance (*NL* 73–74, *GW* 4:433). The difference between it and the earlier outline in the *Difference* essay is that its highest principle of classification does not lie in the traditional attributes of substance—being and thought, or spirit and nature—and that it does not construct any subject-object identities. Instead it conceives of the absolute with concepts of relation, such as the unity of indifference and the relationship in which plurality dominates, or the relationship in which unity dominates. The outline remains, however, molded by the doctrine of attributes of the philosophy of substance. The two forms taken by the unity of indifference and relationship are designated by Hegel, echoing Spinoza, as two attributes each of which expresses absolute and infinite substance and is itself absolute and infinite. He also explicitly calls them physical and ethical nature. It can therefore be assumed that these two forms do not constitute the whole of philosophy, and that beyond this treatment of the "appearance of the absolute" the idea of the absolute itself is developed in a preceding or subsequent part of the system.[12] Nor does the outline reveal where the philosophy of religion and of art might have its place—whether in a further part of the system, devoted to the explication of indifference, or within the philosophy of ethical nature. This can be presumed inasmuch as Hegel stresses that the genuine link between absolute form and absolute substance lies in the absolute ethical order (NL 110, GW 4:463). A further indication to the same effect is the fact that spirit is described as the form in which the absolute intuits itself—and not only in general, as in nature, but "as its very self" (NL 111, GW 4:464). The outline, however, leaves open all the questions that are of concern here—that of the actual science of the absolute idea as the part of the system that is in the eminent sense philosophical theology, and also that of where and how philosophy of religion comes in. Despite its laconic brevity, the information given in the Introductio lecture is much fuller than the outline of the system in the Natural Law essay, and it points forward to Hegel's later conception. But the outline in the Natural Law essay, based as it is on identity philosophy, remains isolated. The only similar draft, regarding the "appearance of the absolute" at least, namely the one in the Difference essay, stands obviously in the line of Schelling's conception of identity philosophy.

The distinctive character of the Introductio lecture is all the more evident by comparison with the Difference and Natural Law essays. Here there is no construction of subject-object identities or any talk of an absolute point of indifference or of attributes of sub-

---

12. See Rolf Peter Horstmann, "Jenaer Systemkonzeptionen," in Hegel: Einführung in seine Philosophie, ed. Otto Pöggeler (Freiburg and Munich, 1977), p. 49.

stance. The two identity-philosophy outlines, of which one directly reproduces Schelling's position while the other is based on him, form with the *System of Ethical Life* (1802–3) the texts in which the model drawn from the philosophy of substance dominates. In the *Natural Law* essay the concept of spirit already presses out beyond the philosophy of substance. In the fragments from lecture manuscripts of 1803—unlike the first system draft (1803–4)—there is already no longer any trace of this process. Here it is stated that spirit is "spirit only when it returns to itself out of this externalization and finds itself" (*GW* 5:371). This statement could be viewed in terms of a direct development from substance to subject. But to assume such a development runs up against the fragments of the *Introductio* lecture. The picture of the system it outlines is one far removed from a system based on the philosophy of substance. The idea of absolute being is not conceived as the indifference of nature and spirit; these are not characterized as attributes of substance. Nor is the collapse into unity of the unfolding of the idea to be understood as the sphere of indifference. The structure of the "resumption of the whole into one" competes with the system concept derived from the metaphysics of substance. This insight is more important than the much-discussed question on which attention tends to fasten first, whether the system at this time comprises three parts or four. For ultimately this concerns only the problem whether resumption is to be located within the sphere of spirit or in a part of the system belonging to it alone. Hegel can place it in a fourth part of the system but also say that absolute being "resumes itself as spirit, returns into itself and knows itself, and *is* the supreme being as this movement" (*GW* 5:262). "Resumption" thus describes the same movement that he later denotes as negation of negation. It is thematized in the reflection that "the whole unfolding of ethical and spiritual nature into the one idea" has "always remained encompassed in the one idea."[13] It is not by chance that Hegel does not here base himself upon the concept of substance but

13. The fragment *Die Idee des absoluten Wesens* speaks here of the encompassing of the whole "unfolding of ethical and spiritual nature in the one idea" (*GW* 5:262). The expression "ethical and spiritual," which is a peculiar one for Hegel, may be an error for "physical and spiritual."

that of spirit. The criterion for speaking of "substance" or "spirit" as it is precisely formulated later (*W* 17:9) also presents the structure of resumption as that whereby one passes beyond the philosophy of substance. The development of the Jena years therefore is not to be understood in terms of the model of the *Phenomenology of Spirit* as the advance from substance to subject, but as the evolution of the original approach in conjunction and contrast with conceptions drawn from the metaphysics of substance.

The chief obstacle to interpretation of the ensuing drafts as forms of elaboration of the first genuinely Hegelian conception of the system does not lie in the obscurity of these drafts or the fact that they bring in programmatic considerations that do not fuse together to form a unity—although these difficulties are also present. What is more troublesome is that the fragmentary form in which the texts have come down to us allows no precise information regarding the relationship of initial idea and philosophy of religion in the first Jena system draft (*Jenaer Systementwürfe I*, 1803–4 [*GW* 6, cf. *JS*¹]). Of it neither the section on logic and metaphysics nor the conclusion to the philosophy of spirit have been preserved. The link we are here concerned with is addressed directly on only one occasion. In a retrospective summary at the beginning of the section on the philosophy of spirit it is stated that the first part of philosophy construed spirit as idea and in the process arrived "at absolute self-identity, at absolute substance." In nature this idea had fallen apart, and in the philosophy of spirit unity existed by "taking itself back into absolute universality; it is really the absolute union as absolute becoming" (*JS*¹ 205–206, *GW* 6:268). This wording matches that in the *Introductio* lecture. Admittedly the concept of spirit does not mark the terminology in the dominant way it does later. But even at the beginning it is "spirit" that is construed as idea and as absolute substance. The fragments do not, however, throw light on the relationship between the concept of substance derived from metaphysics and that underlying the philosophy of spirit. The fragmentary state of the text also reveals nothing definite regarding the place occupied by the philosophy of religion. It may have formed the conclusion of the philosophy of spirit. As to the form it took we can only make guesses, which remain especially shaky because the draft of the following year affords no clarification either.

To be sure, this second Jena system draft (*Jenaer Systementwürfe II* [*GW* 7, cf. *JS*²]), the manuscript entitled *Logik, Metaphysik und Naturphilosophie* (1804–5), contains the first full metaphysics of Hegel that has been preserved in its entirety. At the same time it, too, is little suited to define the relationship between metaphysics and philosophy of religion; for reasons that are unknown, Hegel did not elaborate the part of the system concerned with a philosophy of spirit. This is not the place to interpret the relationship of logic and metaphysics or the novel method used in this system draft.[14] The sole concern here is to inquire into possible consequences of this change for the philosophy of religion.

Despite the passage of three years, the metaphysics of this system draft can be construed as a partial realization of the plans sketched in the *Introductio* and *Logica et Metaphysica* lectures of 1801–2. There it is said that logic—which itself is already metaphysics—will "destroy the false metaphysics of limited philosophical systems" (*GW* 5:263). These are still the object of concern: "cognition as a system of fundamental propositions," the "metaphysics of objectivity," and the "metaphysics of subjectivity." In *Faith and Knowledge* the latter two headings denote rationalistic metaphysics and reflective philosophy (*FK* 187, *GW* 4:412). While these are no longer treated historically here, their themes are: under "metaphysics of objectivity" the contents of *metaphysica specialis* are taken up, and under "metaphysics of subjectivity," the theoretical ego, the practical ego, and "absolute spirit." In particular the treatment of the highest concept of *theologia naturalis* shows the distance Hegel has come from precritical metaphysics. He presents the concept of the *summum ens* in relation to Spinoza's concept of substance,[15] but transposes it to the concept of the ego as the unity of the universal and the singular: "The theoretical ego discovers itself to be the highest being, . . . or that which the ego had posited as its absolute beyond" (*JS*² 179, *GW* 7:171). But this does not mean

14. See in this regard Düsing, *Das Problem der Subjektivität*, pp. 150 ff., and Jaeschke, "Äusserliche Reflexion," pp. 105 ff.
15. See Düsing, *Das Problem der Subjektivität*, p. 191.

that the theoretical ego has become God; on the contrary, the concept of the highest being reconstructed in accord with the theory of subjectivity loses its traditional theological connotations, and it loses them to the concept of absolute spirit as that which is self-identical and relates to itself in the other-being of itself (JS^2 180 ff., GW 7:173 ff.)—even though Hegel does not advertise the speculative theological dimension of this reconstructed concept. On the basis of it he inveighs against the idea of the infinite's going out to the finite, which has designated a fundamental issue since the time of Jacobi's letters on Spinoza: this problem, he says, consists in "expressions devoid of concept." Hegel's metaphysics offers no higher concept than that of the infinite as absolute spirit; this is not because cognitive knowledge is limited but rather because it is inwardly complete in the sense that it knows what stands over against it *as itself*. At the same time this metaphysics points beyond itself to a sphere to which it is itself inferior. To be sure, metaphysics is for us the coming to be of absolute spirit, "and is spirit as idea": this paves the way for the terminological replacement of "absolute spirit" by "absolute idea." In metaphysics, however, absolute spirit is not absolute spirit on its own account; it does not yet know itself as absolute spirit (JS^2 184–185, GW 7:177). Such cognitive knowledge, according to Hegel, arises only when one has gone through the entire system of philosophy from beginning to end—that is, through the philosophy of spirit that is missing here, and presumably through a philosophy of art and of religion, similar to that of the next system draft.

The philosophy of religion of the third Jena system draft (*Jenaer Systementwürfe III*, 1805–6 [GW 8]) does not attain the conceptual level of the previous year's metaphysics. The two drafts are a long way from being fully comparable. Unlike the previous draft, the new one includes a philosophy of spirit but no metaphysics. It is true that apart from the nearly contemporary *Phenomenology* the new draft contains the fullest account of religion. But the relation between what it says about religion and its metaphysical grounding in the concept of absolute spirit is much less close than might have been expected from the 1804–5 metaphysics and even the *Introductio* lecture. This does not, however, permit the conclusion that the metaphysical grounding is of no importance for the philosophy of religion. A more obvious explanation is that, in these years when Hegel was continuously moving toward a deeper conception of his system, he did not succeed in shaping the novel discipline of "philosophy of religion" in such a way that it ever did justice to the demands made on it by metaphysics and the other adjacent disciplines of the system. This failure to resolve the problem may have been the cause for the subsequent extensive transformation of the philosophy of religion. Even so, metaphysics and philosophy of religion are not at this juncture simply juxtaposed in unrelated fashion. This is shown by the general definition of religion, as indeed distinct from art: religion is "the self-knowing of *absolute* spirit as absolute *spirit*" (*GW* 8:280, cf. 265). It is precisely to such knowledge that the 1804–5 metaphysics points the way. Philosophy of religion is thus at the same time science of the idea, since this idea is absolute spirit that does not yet know itself as itself and realizes this knowledge only in religion and ultimately in philosophy. And even the most pregnant definition of this philosophy of religion harmonizes with the metaphysics of the previous year: "Absolute religion is the knowledge that God is the depth of spirit that is certain of itself; this is what makes God the self of all." Hegel also makes clear the sense in which he speaks of "spirit": "Absolute religion is the depth that has come to light; this depth is the ego—it is the concept, the absolute and pure power" (*GW* 8:280–281). In thus naming the "concept" Hegel brings into the approach of the preceding metaphysics, based on the theory of subjectivity, a new aspect that becomes important for the further elaboration of the philosophy of religion.

3. Philosophy of Religion as Aesthetics

(1) The statements just quoted establish a close connection between religion and metaphysics. Hegel conceives religion as a complement to metaphysics: religion is the self-knowing of absolute spirit *as* absolute spirit, which in metaphysics remains a desideratum. This concept of religion presupposes the lengthy development of the Jena years. One of its conditions is, however, already formulated

by Hegel at the start of this period: religion could not be related to metaphysics in the manner stated if it were grasped only as something positive, and not idealistically (*FK* 55, *GW* 4:315). It is only because reason is in it that religion contributes to the consummation of metaphysical, rational knowledge. By virtue of this alone, in Hegel's view, is there philosophy of religion. If religion were merely something positive, it would not be knowing spirit's self-relation to itself. In that case it would not only fail to achieve the task assigned to it at the end of the Jena years; it would not be an object of philosophy at all. Despite all the criticism leveled at ethicotheology, Hegel later gives Kant credit for having also sought, unlike the Enlightenment critics of religion, to know reason in religion, even if it was merely practical reason (see p. 15 above)

Contrary to a widespread assumption, the metaphysical concept of religion does not give rise to the dilemma that one destroys religion by an unbalanced normative definition. It does, to be sure, impute to it an understanding it does not share, but it does not exclude its other aspects—its interweaving with art, with ethical life in the Hegelian sense, with history, in other words with the "spirit of a people"[16] in general. Reflection on the similarities and difference between religion and these other spheres is ushered in, not by the outline of the system in the *Difference* essay (*D* 172–173, *GW* 4:75–76), but in the lecture notes on natural law transmitted only by Karl Rosenkranz (*JS*¹ 178–180, *HL* 133–134; see below, pp. 180–181). Here Hegel combines the points of reference needed for his task—art, scientific knowledge, and ethical life—no longer in the schema derived from identity philosophy but in a form that already points to the subsequent solution. In religion, he tells us, spirit has for the individual initially "the shape of an objective power that lives and moves in the people as its spirit and is alive in all of them." The same spirit is also the object of "scientific knowledge" [*Wissenschaft*]. At least in the form in which it has come down to us, the text does not make wholly clear the dividing line between such knowledge and religion. But Hegel does already

16. [*Tr.*] "Geist eines Volkes." Generally we translate the term more commonly used by Hegel, *Volksgeist*, as "spirit of a people" or "spirit of the people."

stress here that, although "in respect of its subject matter" knowledge has no particular primacy over religion, indeed, "in religion spirit is not in the ideality of science, but is in connection with reality." Consequently religion "necessarily has a *delimited* shape, which, when fixated for its own sake, makes up the *positive* side of every religion." The "speculative idea," as the intuition of which art and religion are likewise already defined in the *Introductio* lectures, is coupled with a "limitation derived from the empirical existence of the people." This limitation is distinct from the "limitation of the idea in the way that art must employ such limitation in general." Hegel does not indeed say explicitly what the latter consists in.[17] He does, however, name yet another distinction: religion is "an activity that complements art and science"; it is "the cultus that raises subjectivity and freedom to their highest enjoyment." This practical aspect provides the basis from which he goes on to define the "basic idea of religion," namely reconciliation, which he conceives in a way clearly influenced by the early romantics: it is "*irony* directed toward the mortal and profitable activity of humans." What distinguishes religion from art and scientific knowledge, according to Hegel, is not a particular form of subjective spirit—for example, representation as opposed to intuition and knowledge; rather it is its objectivity, its being tied to the life of a people, and its reconciliation of individuality and universality by the destruction of a part of individuality in sacrifice.

Hegel does not at first say much about the interweaving, to which he here points, of religion with art, ethical life, and philosophy, and thus also of the philosophy of religion with the philosophies of art and ethical life. The subsequent development can be described as a process of differentiating out an independent discipline called "philosophy of religion." Such a discipline must satisfy three conditions. It must comprehend religion in such a way that the connection with metaphysics is not lost, that religion does not now dissolve into art after being previously reduced to morals, and finally that its locus in the ethical life of a people is not con-

17. See below, p. 174. On further aspects of this delineation of art from religion, see Walter Jaeschke, "Kunst und Religion," in *Die Flucht in den Begriff,* eds. F. W. Graf and F. Wagner (Stuttgart, 1982), esp. pp. 166 ff.

cealed while due recognition is also given to those aspects of religion that lead beyond the framework of ethical life so conceived. Fragmentary as they are, the sources do reveal a progressive approximation to these criteria. But even the last text of the Jena period does not yet recognize the systematic independence of religion within the system of philosophy. At least in a formal sense, the philosophy of religion remains in Jena encompassed in the ethical sphere and ultimately in the *Phenomenology of Spirit*.

(2) The rudimentary definition of the relationship of religion to art, scientific knowledge, and ethical life quoted above sees the character of religion primarily in the practical sphere—not, however, in the sense of ethicotheology but of the religious cultus and the relation to the spirit of a people. In terms of its content the new discipline of philosophy of religion was at first molded by another discipline that had already developed further, namely the philosophy of art. The latter had already elaborated an armory of methods and of questions—one of which concerned the relationship between the art of the ancients and that of the moderns. So there were good reasons for visualizing the problems posed by the philosophy of religion also from the standpoint of questions posed in aesthetics, especially in view of the close connection in which art and religion stood to one another for Schelling, as well as for the system outline found in Hegel's *Difference* essay. Nowhere does collaboration between Hegel and Schelling show itself more closely than in the coupling of aesthetics and philosophy of religion. Their conceptions seem so similar that in the 1830s a vehement dispute broke out regarding the authorship of the essay entitled *Ueber das Verhältniss der Naturphilosophie zur Philosophie überhaupt.*[18] Ultimately the dispute turned on whether Hegel had at that time an independent conception of the philosophy of religion. The dispute was in fact

18. The author was actually Friedrich Wilhelm Joseph Schelling, but the essay is published in the collected works of both Hegel (*GW* 4:265–276) and Schelling (*SW* 5:106–124). See also Schelling's lectures on *Philosophie der Kunst* (1802–3, *SW* 5:353–736), and *On University Studies* (1803), trans. E. S. Morgan (Athens, Ohio, 1966), esp. chap. 8, "On the Historical Construction of Christianity." Hegel's views are set forth in his lecture notes on natural law transmitted by Rosenkranz (*JS*[1] 178–186, *HL* 132–141), and in the introduction to *Faith and Knowledge* (*FK* 55–66, *GW* 4:315–324). [Note emended by the translators.]

conducted on the false premise that Hegel's position was identical with that of the essay in question. The substantial and highly significant difference between Hegel's position and that of the essay can be seen if one interprets them both in light of the topic with which Schelling's essay is mainly concerned, namely the so-called quarrel of the ancients and moderns.[19]

Considerable research has been done on this quarrel as far as it concerns the theory of the graphic arts and poetics.[20] Little is known, however, about the extension of the debate to the field of philosophy of religion. As far as subject matter and personalities were concerned, the extension started from the point attained in Schiller's essay *Über naive und sentimentalische Dichtung* and in Friedrich Schlegel's essay *Über das Studium der griechischen Poesie*.[21] In terms of history of philosophy the corresponding point is to be found in the links between the early romanticism of Jena, centering on the early works of Schlegel, and early German idealism, represented by Schelling and Hegel. All three were contemporaries in Jena and were in personal contact—at least Schlegel with Schelling, and Schelling with Hegel.

With the scope of the quarrel extended to include religion, it becomes possible to compare the various religions—in regard to both their knowledge of the absolute and their interpretation of their own times—in a manner devoid of apologetic or polemical intentions. The history of religion too is viewed in a different fashion than, for instance, in Hegel's *Early Theological Writings,* where it is seen solely as a falling away from a possibly pure, not yet positive origin. The introduction of religion into the quarrel does, how-

19. The following comparison of the positions of Schelling and Hegel forms a revised and expanded version of a previous study by the author, "Early German Idealist Reinterpretation of the Quarrel of the Ancients and Moderns," *Clio* 12 (1983): 85–117. On further aspects of this matter, see Annemarie Gethmann-Siefert, *Die Funktion der Kunst in der Geschichte* (Bonn, 1984), pp. 159 ff.

20. Cf. among others Peter Szondi, *Poetik und Geschichtsphilosophie I,* eds. S. Metz and H.-H. Hildebrandt (Frankfurt am Main, 1974); Hans Robert Jauss, "Literarische Tradition und gegenwärtiges Bewusstsein der Modernität," and "Schlegels und Schillers Replik auf die 'Querelle des Anciens et des Modernes,'" in *Literaturgeschichte als Provokation* (Frankfurt am Main, 1970).

21. See Friedrich Schiller, *Werke: Nationalausgabe,* vol. 20 (Weimar, 1962); and Friedrich Schlegel, *KSA* 184 ff.

ever, necessitate a reconsideration of the results achieved in the field of poetics. The question pertaining to the theory of art—whether modern art is so radically different from classical art as to make imitation quite impossible even if, aesthetically, it seems desirable—cannot be repeated in this form within the context of philosophy of religion. A religious imitation would be even less credible than artistic imitation. The problem of classicism arises only in the sphere of art, not that of religion. But the question as to the superiority of ancient or modern religion poses itself as insistently as ever. It becomes more explosive because it was not possible within the framework of philosophy of religion to rest content with the answer that proved fruitful for aesthetics, namely that the two were fundamentally different, and that though it might therefore be possible to compare them, the one could not justifiably be regarded as of less value than the other. Religion's truth-claim precludes so ambivalent a result. If one became convinced of the superiority of ancient religion, one would not even be able to invoke the necessity of imitating antiquity in order to make the admission of one's own inferiority more tolerable. The only course open would be to point the way, or at any rate the direction, whereby the form of religion prevalent in modernity might be superseded by some future form that could bear comparison with antiquity.

An interpretation of the philosophy of religion of early German idealism in relation to the quarrel of the ancients and moderns seems relevant only to a subsidiary aspect, for the philosophy of religion is found primarily in the context of a new type of theoretical knowledge of the absolute. But the comparison of the religion of classical times and the present day in no way touches on a merely subordinate point of view in Schelling's account, and Hegel's natural-law lecture notes also conceive philosophy of religion primarily as history of religion for the purpose of making modernity intelligible to itself. Despite the little that was known about non-Christian religions at that time, Schelling's contrasting of paganism and Christianity could not be justified if his aim had been a comprehensive grasp of the history of religion. Only a short time before, in the *System of Transcendental Idealism,* he divides the history of religion into the ages of fate, nature, and providence.[22] The subsequent exclusion of all other religions—of the Far and Middle East and also of Judaism—through the dichotomy of ancient and modern is in the interests of the "quarrel" and thus of achieving an understanding of the present. Also this does not conflict with identity philosophy: as an explication of absolute identity, philosophy of religion conceives the differing forms of knowledge of the absolute as actualized conjointly in antiquity and in modernity. Admittedly the historical polarization is not the necessary result of approaching the matter from the standpoint of identity philosophy, any more than it is only the introduction of the contrast between ancients and moderns into the context of identity philosophy that provides the basis for the idea of a historicality of the absolute; it does, however, favor it. Systematic religiophilosophical explications of the absolute cannot, therefore, be played off against religiohistorical connotations. The goal is cognitive knowledge of the absolute under the conditions of the modern world, which requires at the same time a theory of the modern world. This would be a contradiction only if the absolute were to be conceived as unhistorical. But that this is not the case, Schelling and Hegel each seek to show in their different ways.

Schelling's historicizing of the absolute combines the current state of discussion in the theory of art with his own approach, which conceives art as the highest form of portrayal [*Darstellung*] of the absolute. If, toward the close of the eighteenth century, the forms of art, and in particular the different types of poetry, are recognized as epoch-specific, then one must also assign a history to knowledge of the absolute, to the extent that it occurs in the medium of art. But the conception of a historical process of knowing the absolute destroyed the *idea* of the absolute unless it were at the same time to be conceived as the *self*-portrayal of the absolute, falling within, and indeed itself constituting, history. Yet if one intends to go beyond a general insight into the historicality of the absolute, and to understand its history by means of the opposition

---

22. Friedrich Wilhelm Joseph Schelling, *System of Transcendental Idealism,* trans. Peter Heath (Charlottesville, Va., 1978), pp. 211–212.

of antiquity and modernity as history of religion, this has onerous consequences for the concept of the modern. While the demarcation of the epochs of antiquity remains unchanged in philosophy of religion, or at all events is limited to the epoch of Greek religion, the range and with it the character of modernity is basically altered. Applied to the history of religion, the concept of modernity undergoes an extension that sharply distinguishes it from its meaning in aesthetics. The quarrel opposes "modern" post-Renaissance art to Graeco-Roman antiquity, leaving Christian antiquity and the Middle Ages aside. But when the concept of "modern" is used in philosophy of religion, the effect of equating "modernity" and "Christianity" is to extend its range to the point where it includes the age commonly referred to as "antiquity" or at least "late antiquity." Schelling therefore extends the concept of "modern," formally speaking, to its original scope: initially it denoted Christian late antiquity, in contrast to pagan antiquity. Although the limited scope originally predestined this word to the concept of epochs, this usage is precluded at the time of Schelling, after nearly two thousand years of "modernity." To interpret the contrast of ancient and modern in terms of philosophy of religion inevitably results in emptying the concept of "modern" of all content, especially since Schelling does not historically differentiate modernity extended in this way—for example, by limiting "modernity" to the last epoch of the Christian era. Such differentiation would, however, destroy the rigor of the antiquity/modernity contrast. To be sure, Schelling mentions the opposition of Catholicism and Protestantism in regard to their differing attitudes to mythology, but he does not make use of this opposition to define the specific character of the modern world.

To interpret the contrast between antiquity and modernity in terms of history of religion is thus to make the term "modernity," though not "antiquity," unsuited to function as a concept denoting epochs. To be sure, the result of contrasting historical epochs is to introduce the concept of history into the subject matter of identity philosophy. But this interpretation is itself neutral in regard to the grounding or at least favoring of historical thought: it can either promote historical thought or destroy it.

In addition to characterizing the Greek and the modern world in terms of the opposition of "nature" and "art," Schelling uses the explanatory means afforded by his identity system of 1801. Ancient and modern art and religion are understood as two sides of absolute identity: the ancient form as infusion [*Einbildung*] of the universal into the particular, of the infinite into the finite, the Christian form as infusion of the finite into the infinite. Antiquity portrays the infinite in the form of the finite, modernity the finite in its idealization, its transfiguration into the infinite. This kind of schematic definition, however, leaves in doubt whether the specific character of the ancient and the modern world can be grasped in this way as the unifying of finite and infinite from one side or the other respectively, and whether this distinction applies to Christianity, which has a key role in this schema. Indeed, Christ is viewed in the first place as an infusion of the infinite into the finite, as are the Greek gods, even if in him, otherwise than in antiquity, this movement from infinite to finite in turn leads beyond this to its sublation. As for Hölderlin, Christ is the last of the Greek gods, the brother of Hercules, but at the same time the hero of the new, "modern" world, to the extent that his fate marks the beginning of the infusion of the finite into the infinite.

It is, moreover, not clear what law—other than "absolute necessity," which is invoked on more than one occasion but not expounded—determines such a historical sequence. Above all it is not clear by what means and when the "diremption"[23] that is said to characterize modernity comes into the world. The different character of the two worlds confronts an identity-philosophy interpretation, unlike art theory, with the task not only of recognizing the two worlds as given and comprehending their relationship, but of exhibiting the ground of these differences in the very essence of the

---

23. [*Tr.*] *Entzweiung.* This term, which means literally "division into two" (*Entzwei-ung*), is used frequently by both Schelling and Hegel in a special sense to refer to that separation or division which is intrinsic to the developmental process of spirit. Sometimes the word carries as well the overtones of "estrangement" (*Entfremdung*), and it is clear that diremption can issue in a sense of estrangement or alienation, but strictly speaking these terms, while closely related, are distinct. Reconciliation can overcome estrangement but not, for Hegel at least, diremption. See below, pp. 166–167.

absolute, which is supposed to manifest itself in their historical sequence. The talk of "infusion" already presupposes the diremption of finite and infinite. But then the Greek and the Christian world would not be related as nature and diremption, but as two distinct forms of diremption. Schelling therefore declares as unsuitable the use of the word "infusion" in regard to the Greek world. He places the beginning of the rupture of finite and infinite in the Christian era, but when the Christian era itself begins remains inexplicable.

Behind the dichotomous schema of the reciprocal infusion of universal and particular we can discern a triadic schema—original identity succeeded by diremption, and diremption by the reconstruction of identity. This throws light on the difference between the Greek and the Christian images of divinity. The Greek intuition of the infinite within the finite permits, Schelling argues, an inner cross-permeation of universal and particular, in which the universal does not only signify a particular, as in schematic thought, and a particular does not only signify a universal, as in allegory. Rather both would stand in complete harmony in symbolic portrayal. Christianity by contrast sublates finitude into the infinite. Its idea of God can only be expressed allegorically and is thus subject to the conditions of a diremption that cannot be sublated. By means of this argument the grounding of the reciprocal infusions in identity philosophy is in fact surrendered for the sake of a critique of Christian modernity. The inferiority of modernity is also plain from the fact that in it mythology is necessarily the work of an individual. Owing to this deficiency of modernity it needs indeed a new mythology.

The relationship between the complete interpenetration of the universal and the particular in Greek symbolism and Christian allegory, and between the temporal simultaneity of antiquity and the modern sense of temporal sequence, is conceived by Schelling moreover as a relationship of nature and history, with Greek religion intuiting the universe as nature and Christian religion as history.[24] This once again breaks through the framework of recip-

24. On the systematic aspects of this, see Werner Becker, "Über Schellings Konstruktion des Christentums," in *Subjektivität und Metaphysik,* eds. D. Henrich and H. Wagner (Frankfurt am Main, 1966), pp. 1–20.

rocal infusion based on identity philosophy. Schelling is obviously introducing into the "quarrel" Schleiermacher's conception of religion as intuition of the universe. By reverting, however, to "nature" to characterize the ancient world, he returns to a position predating the insight gained in art theory, that what we view as "nature" in the Greek world is nonetheless "art." In the framework of aesthetics it would no longer have been permissible to contrast antiquity and modernity as nature and art. But even if one replaces the antithesis "nature and art" by "nature and history," this cannot relegitimate the concept of nature as a means of denoting the Greek world.

In thus abandoning the narrower poetic framework of the opposition of art and nature in order to include problems relating to the history of religion and general philosophy of history, and in placing an apparently unhistorical nature at the start of history, Schelling is not interpreting the concept of nature historically. For a genuine historicization, it would not be enough merely to make "nature" temporally prior to "history." Schelling understands the primordial state of nature as a state of perfect culture, from which only an inexplicable falling away causes humankind to sink into barbarism. History does not for him invalidate the concept of nature, it does not reduce the "natural" state to a variation of history. History and along with it modernity, as what are other to the original unity of nature, are logically simply the contra-natural. History is convicted of being what ought not to be since it offends against nature. Because history is defined solely in opposition to nature, as the phase of diremption, instead of being defined in terms of its intrinsic content, it remains subject to the normative force of the concept of nature. Contrary to the approach based on identity philosophy, but consistent with his concept of nature, Schelling thus arrives at the vision of a renewed simultaneity of nature instead of the sequentiality of history. Missing from his conception is an aspect that already motivated Schiller's polemic against Rousseau, namely that modernity was not nature, to be sure, but rather what the ancients obtained from nature and the moderns from freedom; therefore, however inferior to antiquity modernity might be, antiquity likewise could not equal modernity at the point of its greatness.

The consequences of Schelling's religiophilosophical reinterpretation of the quarrel are far more threatening for the sake of modernity's self-understanding than the call to imitate antiquity by classicist aesthetics. Because of the conceptual difference between antiquity and modernity, any imitation of antiquity would be impossible. Under the conditions of diremption the original identity cannot be actualized by means of imitation. Yet, as diremption, modernity remains subject to the normative judgment of antiquity as nature. And the interpretation of this opposition as a relationship of nature and history approximates the mythical contrast between a pure origin and an inexplicable falling away, to be overcome as soon as possible.

Schelling uses the differing function of mythology in ancient and modern times to throw light on the antithesis between them. His concept of myth is closely linked to that of Herder and, above all, the Jena romantics. For him myth is not, as it is for the radical Enlightenment's critique of religion, sheer nonsense or even priestly deception; but neither is it, as it is for the mythical school, the expression of a childhood stage of humanity, now left behind; nor is it the pictorial clothing of originally rational truth. It is a form of divine portrayal [*Gottesdarstellung*] that can be made use of in the present as well. In its consummate form, as the complete interpenetration of universal and particular, of finite and infinite, mythology is not something that can be evoked at will. It belongs to the immediate unity that Schelling conceives as "nature." In classical mythology he finds already present all the elements he encounters in the course of the rational construction of the concept of art. It is the highest archetype [*Urbild*] of the poetic world; on it depend both art and religion. Its binding character derives from the fact that it is the work of all—the work of the human race, to the extent that the race takes the form of a single person. The founding relationship that applies in the modern world is the converse: here the task is to elaborate a new mythology on the basis of religion. The new mythology, however, differs from Greek mythology in no longer having binding force. It is not the work of the race but of individuals, who must produce their world themselves since it is no longer given to them in advance. It is the world-historical task of modernity to found a new mythology in order to establish the basis for a new art and a new ethical order. This call for a new mythology also stands at the center of Friedrich Schlegel's *Rede über die Mythologie*. Elsewhere Schlegel stresses that his sole aim is to found a new morality—and this is not in any way to be understood as a reversion to ethicotheology. It means, rather, to write a new Bible, to become what Jesus and Muhammad were.[25]

Modernity, Schelling argues, is distinguished from antiquity by the loss of a binding mythology. It is separated from a perhaps not-so-distant future by the fact that it has not succeeded in reestablishing such a mythology. As well as stretching its temporal range to the breaking point, Schelling's model thus results in depleting the concept of modernity: it is the age of mythological deficiency. He does not attempt to demarcate, by means of a philosophy of history, the present from Christian antiquity or from the Middle Ages. Like other mythical models, his too leaves the present notably devoid of content between primal time and end time. All that remains to modernity is that in place of the lost mythology the individual may sketch one of his own. As with Friedrich Schlegel, the individual's greatness is measured according to the success of such an individual mythology. Logically, therefore, the greatest individual of the modern world is neither Napoleon nor Shakespeare but Dante.

The identification of the Christian with the modern world has consequences for the fate that Schelling predicts for Christianity. Christianity is not a form of reconciliation but an expression of diremption. What is called for, therefore, is a philosophical alternative to Christianity—either a complement to the one-sidedness of earlier Christianity or its replacement. The idea of a complement links up with the concept provided by identity philosophy, that antiquity and modernity each have their opposite inherent in themselves. Christianity is complemented primarily by a renewed turning to nature, whose loss stamps the concept of modernity.

25. Friedrich Schlegel, letter to Schleiermacher, summer 1798, in *Aus Schleiermachers Leben: In Briefen*, eds. L. Jonas and W. Dilthey, 3 vols. (Berlin, 1860–1863), 3:80; letter to Novalis, 20 October 1798, in *Friedrich Schlegel und Novalis*, ed. Max Preitz (Darmstadt, 1957), p. 130.

Complementation forms the reverse process to the rise of the idea of the infinite—the rise of "idealism"—since the time of Plato. This rise Schelling understands as the intrusion of proto-Christian elements (as a complement to the orientation to nature) through the attention that was beginning to be paid to history, in which the seeds of diremption are already operative. Christianity's preoccupation with history would have to be corrected in similar fashion by the return to nature. This return to nature does not, however, stop at the complement, but presses on beyond Christianity. Schelling interprets modernity as a transitional phase in the process of eternal necessity, from the original unity of infinite and finite through the phase of diremption to a unity reestablished by speculation at a higher potency [*Potenz*]. This provides, perhaps intentionally, no clear answer to the question as to the fate of Christianity. But Schelling's tendency is clear: Christianity must be transcended because it grasps the finite not as a symbol but only as an allegory of the infinite, and the simultaneity of the absolute only as a historical sequence. The future mythology must rest on a new symbolism. It can, to be sure, take as its point of departure a movement that has not infrequently been suspected of heretical tendencies and that (in contrast with the allegorical representation of orthodox Christianity) has already produced a new symbolism, namely mysticism. The symbolism of mysticism, however, remains subjective, while the future symbolism must be objective. To outline it is, in Schelling's view, the task of the speculative philosophy of nature, a task on which he believes a start has already been made in his *Ideen zu einer Philosophie der Natur* (1797). It forms for him the content of the "eternal gospel," of which he speaks in alluding to Lessing and earlier traditions. It was again Friedrich Schlegel who had previously suggested the use that could be made of this old idea, whose content in fact has been different each time it has been formulated. In his *Athenaeum* fragments Schlegel already links the eternal gospel to the philosophy of nature (*KSA* 2:265–266). The aim of this speculative physics is, as Schelling expresses it, the creation of a new mythology, a binding symbolism of the absolute; it is the reconversion of the Christian-modern sequentiality of history into the ancient simultaneity of nature, the dismissal of Christian modernity in favor of the "serenity and purity of the Greek intuition of nature" (GW 4:275).

(3) Hegel too speaks of the eternal gospel, of original harmony and of reconstruction (JS^1 184–186, HL 139–141). Even the call for a new mythology is first to be found, though in another form, in Hegel's handwriting, in the *Ältestes Systemprogramm des Deutschen Idealismus* (1796).[26] It has escaped the notice of scholars that a place belongs to Hegel in this debate since, apart from the *Systemprogramm,* they have taken into account only his later texts, not those written in Jena. Indeed in Jena he found early romantic and early idealist ideas already coupled together. But despite the assumed identity between Schelling's project and its appropriation by Hegel, the consequences drawn by Hegel run strictly counter to Schelling's intention. In the early Jena years, however, Hegel's conception lacks stringent formulation. Several inconsistencies derive from the fact that, despite the irreconcilability of their conceptions, he employs Schelling's conceptuality. It is only in the course of the Jena years that Hegel eliminates this disharmony. In so doing he lays the basis for an interpretation of art and religion in the context of modernity to which he will remain essentially faithful down to the Berlin lectures.

An outward sign of the differing conceptions of the two writers is afforded by the lesser prominence Hegel gives to the contrast between antiquity and modernity, although he was already familiar with this instrument for self-understanding of the present in his student essays. To be sure, the basic interpretative model remains initially the contrast between undifferentiated harmony and diremption, between identity and the reconstruction of identity. Hegel no longer conceives the contrast, however, as the opposition of antiquity and modernity, and he softens it by inserting several intermediate links. Above all he does not flatly equate modernity with the age of diremption. This opens the door to a historically concrete understanding of modernity: it is not the Christian world

26. [Tr.] Published in *Hegel-Studien*, Beiheft 9 (Bonn, 1973), pp. 261–265, together with several critical studies; translated in H. S. Harris, *Hegel's Development: Toward the Sunlight, 1770–1801* (Oxford, 1972), pp. 510–512. At one time authorship of this essay was attributed to Schelling or to Schelling and Hölderlin.

in general but its most recent, Protestant phase—though there is no trace here of the confessional narrow-mindedness that might seem necessarily linked to this concept. Later too Hegel sees the beginning of modernity not only in the Reformation but in Descartes's principle of subjectivity. The form in which Protestantism appeared, molded by the Enlightenment, is more important for this understanding than any contemporary definition of its formal and material principles or any differences in the doctrine of justification and the scripture principle. Protestant too, in this sense, is the call for a new Luther to save from the yoke of the letter.[27] The difference between the Reformation with its Lutheran imprint and humanism becomes less marked.[28] It could be said, alluding to Troeltsch's later interpretation, that Hegel's perspective was based on neo-Protestantism and its significance for the modern world.

Thanks to the replacement of Schelling's traditional, philosophy-of-art pattern by one based on the history of the confessions, the concept of modernity once again becomes suited to the concept of epochs. At the same time this is not to be found in those fragments by Hegel that have been preserved. Its relegation to the background can probably be seen as an indication that it would have reinforced the dichotomous schema of the "quarrel" in the philosophy of art and so jeopardized the self-understanding of the present. Only by avoiding a religiophilosophical interpretation of the quarrel can there be any hope of achieving a more appropriate interpretation of the present. The model by means of which the discussion in poetics succeeds in understanding the relationship of ancient and modern literature distorts a historical understanding if it is carried over into the philosophy of religion or is even raised to the category of a concept applicable to the philosophy of history in general. A differentiated comprehension of modernity entails renunciation of this schema of periodization.

The mere act of replacing the concept of modernity by the Christian age of diremption does not in itself involve abandoning

27. Gotthold Ephraim Lessing, *Eine Parabel* (1778), in *Sämtliche Schriften*, ed. K. Lachmann, 3d ed., vol. 13 (Leipzig, 1897), p. 102.

28. See Ernst Cassirer, *The Philosophy of the Enlightenment*, trans. Fritz Koelln and James Pettegrove (Princeton, 1951), pp. 137 ff., 160.

Schelling's mythological schema, especially since Hegel continues to interpret the decisive break between periods in terms of the opposition between identity and diremption.[29] In the first place, history begins also for him with the original reconciledness of spirit and its reality in the beautiful individuality of the Greek world. The concrete content both of the initial harmony and of the ensuing diremption is, however, fundamentally changed. Identity does not lie, as for Schelling, in the possibility of a symbolism of the world of the gods but in the fact that subjectivity has not yet set itself over against the world. Thus unity is itself the expression of a deficiency. The "religion of nature," as Hellenic religion is still called here, constitutes only the one form of the ideality of spirit, namely art. The "form of ideas" must be added to it for the new religion to constitute "the highest ideas of speculation expressed not just as a mythology" (*JS*[1] *184, HL* 139). Over against Schlegel's and Schelling's call for a new mythology, what is needed for the reconstruction of undifferentiated harmony is not a new mythology but reconciliation in thought, along with a significant socio-therapeutic component. An aesthetic mythology of modernity would be insufficient—not because it could not symbolize the interpenetration of finitude and infinitude but because the present age rests on a different attitude of the subject to actuality, namely on the antithesis of ideal and real. The undifferentiated unity of thought and reality cannot be recaptured; it is therefore not possible to recapture or repeat antiquity as such. This insight at the same time disposes of the normative character of antiquity that encumbers Schelling's interpretation of modernity. The ages of unity and diremption are not related as nature and history, but as two stages of history. "Nature" cannot be conceived of as preceding history. While this conclusion is implicit in the natural-law lecture notes, it is explicitly drawn for the first time one year later in the fragment *Das Wesen des Geistes* (*GW* 5:370 ff.). The historical relativization of the

29. In the fifth of his *Hymnen an die Nacht* Novalis seeks to resolve this break. His reference to the experience of death, however, hardly carries the necessary weight to afford an understanding of the end of the ancient world. But see Hermann Timm, *Die heilige Revolution: Das religiöse Totalitätskonzept der Frühromantik* (Frankfurt am Main, 1978), pp. 108–109.

mythical periods, the historicization of the concept of myth, integrates the concept of nature into history and relativizes the normative character of the ancient world. The lament for the lost world of beauty is coupled with the affirmation of the subject's relationship to the world that is constitutive for modernity, in the way in which that relationship has developed through the differing forms of Christianity.

A dual experience marks, according to Hegel, the start of Christianity. It shares with the Roman world the insight into "the desacralization [Entgötterung] of nature, hence contempt for the world." With the separation of the ideal from the real principle, nature is left behind as a desecrated corpse. Christianity differs from Rome, however, by its belief "that in this infinite division one man still bore within himself the confidence of being one with the absolute" (JS[1] 182, HL 137). This certainty is itself conditional on there having been diremption; spirit has to *return* into itself. In Christianity the contrast is repeated between beautiful religion and desacralization of the world, the cycle that leads from undifferentiated harmony via the experience of diremption to a new reconciliation. In order to be assured of unity with God, the first form of Christianity, by which Hegel means Catholicism, revoked the radical desacralization of the world and imparted to everything secular a new religious sanctity. By analogy with Greek mythology, Hegel calls Catholicism a "beautiful religion," which moreover went some way toward establishing a mythology. But this term in no way denotes unqualified approval: because Catholicism seeks to reinstate identity without regard for the altered conditions, it constitutes a reversion to the past shape of the world. The historical process accordingly does not yet find an end here. With the new sanctification is coupled the renewal of anguish in the cultic reenactment of anguish and reconciliation.

The link between diremption and the reconstruction of undifferentiated harmony does not only characterize the origin of Christianity—it forms the basic structure of its history. Its present shape, Protestantism, changes the cycle of anguish and reconciliation into the infinite longing of the subject. As in the Roman world spirit's original unity with its reality broke asunder and nature was desacralized, so Protestantism destroys the sanctification of the world imparted by Catholicism. The Protestant culture of the understanding reiterates the negative Christian presupposition, its original contempt for the world. Subjectivity draws back within itself and surrenders the world to profanity. But the specifically new element of Christianity is present in Protestantism too, namely, the moment of reconciliation. The act of turning to this desacralized world results in being reconciled directly with empirical reality, which becomes the material on which the inwardly infinite subject acts.

The two variants of Protestantism seem mutually exclusive. The beautiful soul, fashioned beyond this reality by infinite longing and the poetry of anguish, seems to have no connection with reconciliation in empirical actuality and the prose of understanding. Despite the apparent opposition, Hegel points to not merely a logical but also a historical connection between them. Basic to Protestantism, in his view, is the emphasis laid on pure subjectivity. It finds its expression in the longing to rise above this world. A necessary complement to this pure inwardness is pure externality: the world sinks into indifference for the subject that in its longing only rises above the world and does not find where it can be reconciled in it. Such a world could be characterized by Hegel's pronouncement on Roman religion, namely that nature is left a desecrated corpse. The sacred grove is reduced to mere timber, beauty again becomes a mere thing (*FK* 57, *GW* 4:317). The religious sanctification by means of which Catholicism has sought to reinstate the undifferentiated harmony is thus surrendered again. What is not surrendered is the certainty of oneness with God, the original Christian experience.

What is less clear is how this conjunction of elements can again turn into a reconciliation with empirical actuality. Both moments, that of fleeing from, and that of losing oneself to, finitude are deduced by Hegel, although in fairly cursory fashion, from the persistence of subjectivity (*FK* 58, *GW* 4:317). The first answer is that the renewed reconciliation occurred "when the time had come" (*FK* 58, *GW* 4:318). This at all events shows that the reason is to be sought in terms of the philosophy of history. The second answer does, to be sure, explain the reconciliation with empirical actuality as having been facilitated by the fact that the cultus no longer involves the renewal of anguish. But this does not render the persistence of the subject's infinite longing comprehensible. Hegel resolves the antithesis between infinite longing and renewed reconciliation in empirical reality by recourse to history: Protestantism, he tells us, changes the cycle of anguish and reconciliation into longing, and then longing into the thinking and knowing of reconciliation. It therefore declines into empirical reconciliation with the commonality of empirical existence and everyday necessity, and it ends by losing hold of religious elevation and the sanctification of empirical existence: life has become a commonplace, unhallowed workday.

Hegel's conception at this time thus seems close to the theory of secularization. At all events these texts stress the connection between Protestantism and the desacralization of the world or, as we have said since Max Weber, its "demystification." Alongside the apparent similarity, however, there are considerable differences. According to Hegel, it is not Christianity that desacralizes the world. This had already happened in the Roman world—though how and when he does not tell us. Initially Christianity even resanctifies the world. Modern secularity could, however, be understood as a consequence of Protestantism, which here becomes a term to designate the present epoch. Desacralization is indeed a "sign" of Protestantism in both its varieties, although there is no saying why this should be. The most obvious explanation is in terms of a "principle of the North," which already for Novalis forms a mediating moment of "genuine Catholicism."[30] Direct recourse to such a "principle," however, explains nothing. An explanation could be offered by a history of subjectivity. This would necessitate an overall outline of the philosophy of history and of the history of philosophy, such as Hegel did not yet possess in these early Jena years.

There is yet another respect in which Hegel's interpretation dif-

---

30. *FK* 57, *GW* 4:316. Novalis speaks of "the cold, dead Spitzbergen of constricted understanding," which raises poetry to splendor "like an India adorned." See Novalis, "Die Christenheit oder Europa," in *Schriften*, vol. 3, ed. R. Samuel et al., 3d rev. ed. (Darmstadt, 1983), p. 520.

fers from the secularization theorem. Thus described, the shape of the world is clearly evaluated in a pejorative way. Neither the alien, religious sanctification of the world by Catholicism nor the immediate reconciliation of Protestantism succeeds in transcending the opposition. The radical desacralization of the world is, to be sure, the hallmark of the present epoch; it is, however, characterized in derogatory fashion, and as a passing phenomenon. It is regarded as a precondition, to be fulfilled before "the spirit can venture to sanctify itself as spirit in its own shape, and reestablish the original reconciliation with itself in a new religion," consecrating the world no longer in alien fashion but its own. But this will come about only "when there is a free people and reason has found once more its reality as an ethical spirit, a spirit which is bold enough to assume its pure shape on its own soil and in its own majesty" (JS^1 185, *HL* 141). It is not the founding of a new mythology or the demand for one that characterizes the modern world, but the end of all mythology and the knowledge of a reconciliation which Hegel designates as a new religion but which at the same time he assigns to philosophy.

Discussions of theory of poetry around the turn of the century were molded by the growing insight into the illusory character of the hope for a return of the world of beauty—the insight that it is not possible to renew either the contents of classical mythology or the poetic forms in which the content was once living. Meanwhile, at least in Hegel's view, the endeavor on which romanticism had embarked with such high hopes to establish a new mythology had also come to nought. Certainly Hegel shares the view held by Schelling and the romantics, that a compelling art needs a compelling mythology. But he acknowledges that to found such a mythology precisely at this time proves to be illusory: under the conditions of modern diremption it is not possible to bring back antiquity. Art and mythology are incapable of attending to their previous function on the soil of contemporary diremption. Nor can they, as had been supposed, overcome diremption. Art has not the power of unification. It is itself only the highest expression of complete unification, the loss of which leaves art with no soil in which to grow. All that is left then is to renounce all romantic adjurations directed to renewing mythology and using art to treat the ills of the present. Faced with the loss of the beautiful world of the gods, the artist can, to be sure, conjure up his dream of a world, but this is then only a dream world, not the actual world.

If ancient art is pronounced to be unattainable and inimitable, present-day art remains saddled with a deficient status that can be seen as expressing its general deficiency. Hegel's solution relates in particular to the contemporary insight into the historicity of poetic forms such as the naive and the sentimental. It goes beyond the historicizing of art forms, however, to the historicizing of art as such. Irrespective of its particular contents and forms, art as such belongs to a past epoch. The same considerations with respect to the philosophy of history and of art that free the present from subjection to the normativity of antiquity lead during these years to the thesis of the end of art. This thesis and the release from the demand to imitate antiquity and its norms are linked together in compelling fashion, the former being the latter's price.

The fact that art is denied the power to reconcile modern diremption leads one to expect that this task will be assigned to religion. Religion, however, is equally unsuited in Hegel's eyes for the purpose. Certainly it aims at reconstructing the undifferentiated harmony, but it remains in the sphere of diremption. At best, therefore, it attains relative forms of identity. While Catholicism, as the religion of beauty, gives the false impression of passing beyond this level, Protestantism, by repeating the original profanization, renews the gulf between the subject and actuality. In doing so, however, it opens the road to genuine reconciliation. This lies in cognitive insight [*Einsicht*] into the necessity of spirit's development, and "this insight only philosophy can give" (*JS*[1] 186, *HL* 141). The young Hegelians were not the first to have understood Hegel's thesis concerning the end of art as a paradigm for the thesis concerning the end of religion in the modern world.

Admittedly this reconciliation is regarded as a reconstruction of the undifferentiated harmony. But for all its Schellingian overtones, this terminology does not conceal any mythical return to the pure origin. Reconciliation is not first achieved under future, wholly altered conditions. It does not reach back behind diremption, behind the development of life, which is always accomplished in antitheses. It mediates subjectivity and actuality within diremption, within a desacralized world. For this very reason it sanctifies anew the world—or, to use the terminology of the triangle fragment, the "earth." Modernity is not the epoch marked by a loss of mythology resulting from the allegorical Christian representation of God. Its character is therefore not to be formulated by reference to art or to religion, since that could only be to define it negatively. The character of modernity shows itself—as one could formulate it on the basis of the Berlin texts—in the free unfolding of subjectivity. But because Hegel in these Jena years still takes a pejorative view of the concept of subjectivity, he regards the modern world, determined as it is by subjectivity, as a shape that must be transcended in order to achieve genuine reconciliation.

This conception presupposes Hegel's historicizing of the concept of nature. Any normative designation of a past condition as "nature," as found for example in Schelling, makes the present and all other ages more or less depraved, makes them subordinate to a shape that is past but still lays claim to normative status. By bringing within the framework of history Schelling's reinterpretation of the poetic opposition of nature and art in terms of the antithesis of nature and history seen as historical stages, Hegel introduces the concept of nature into that of history. What appeared as nature in antiquity is just as much historical as the actualization of subjectivity within the framework of history is subjectivity's own nature. Hegel's concept of spirit downgrades the concept of nature viewed as an original state. This original nature, not brought about by freedom, is *not* nature, precisely because the nature of spirit is its freedom to overcome the nature that served only as a beginning. This conception relating to the philosophy of history, which also determines the philosophy of art and of religion, forms Hegel's answer to the controversy over the normative character of antiquity or the independent status of modernity. To move on from this is indispensable if modernity is to be defined in terms of epochs, once one is no longer considering aesthetic questions but questions relating to philosophy of religion. Otherwise, as is the case with Schelling, the recourse to philosophy of history tends to result in the interpretation of modernity in the context of the mythical schema of origin, loss, and return. Hegel's solution saves modernity from this danger, without devaluing antiquity by comparison with modernity, and also without taking refuge in the historical ambivalence of a multitude of distinct, not properly comparable epochs.

The few mythical features that initially enter into Hegel's conception along with Schelling's terminology are revised by him while he is still in Jena. Thus the fragment *seiner Form,* written only one year later, explicitly denies that the beautiful Greek mythology reflects an original undifferentiated harmony; it is preceded, he says, by archaic mythology (JS^1 254–256, *GW* 5:374–375). The discovery of the historical character of the Greek world could have been explained away in mythical terms, by shifting the original perfection that was no longer to be found in Greece to an even remoter, still less known past. If Hegel does not place the world of Iran or India in the position formerly occupied by Greece, as several of the romantics did, this could be because it appeared frivolous to his historically concerned mind to affirm that the pure origin was to be found just where it could not for lack of historical knowledge be disproved. Another factor, however, probably played a greater part in bringing about the revision of the mythical schema, namely a change in the relationship of concept and history. The original unity, which along with all mythical conceptions Schelling believes to be present from the outset in history, pertains solely to philosophical cognition. It must not be misinterpreted as an initial historical shape. The beginning is marked, not by consummation, but by a first immediacy—in logic the poorest category, in history the poorest epoch. All historical shapes constitute forms of diremption, in which the unity of the concept realizes itself, and this is true of modernity as well. This is a fundamental objection to the retrogressive socioromantic desire to pass beyond a comprehension of this structure and find an immediate reconciliation that does not rest on diremption. But this insight into the illusory character of the ideal of a unity free from difference, of an escapism based on myth, needed a further systematic account of the connection between religion and the ethical life of a people.

4. Philosophy of Religion as Philosophy of Ethical Life

(1) It is particularly in the early Jena years that the kinship of the philosophy of religion to the philosophy of art influences the former discipline in its still meager development. From midway through the Jena period, from the time of Schelling's departure, its importance declines. This is not to say, however, that philosophy of religion becomes an independent discipline. Hegel continues to conceive of it within the framework of "ethical life" [*Sittlichkeit*]—not, to be sure, as in the sketch in the *Difference* essay, inspired as it is by identity philosophy, but as already formulated in the *Introductio* and *Naturrecht* lectures. At least formally speaking, this remains the case down to the final Jena system drafts. At the same time it would be erroneously one-sided to take the view that Hegel's conception of religion in Jena is wholly contained within the horizon of ethical life. For the development of his philosophy of religion takes the form of a progressive emancipation from the context of the philosophy of ethical life. In this respect the initial dominance of ethical life is an obstacle. The philosophy of religion finds its conceptual shape to the degree that it transcends the sphere of ethical life.

According to Rosenkranz, whenever Hegel lectured on his system in the course of these years, he "treated art and religion, without entering into particular detail, as the closing section of his discussion of ethics" (*HL* 124). What he says tallies with what we are told in the fragment *Die Idee des absoluten Wesens* (*GW* 5: 264). The fact that philosophy of religion is placed at the end of the system confirms the importance of the function that was already assigned to it during these years, that of concluding the system. The lack of detailed exposition does not therefore point to a lessened interest in these themes but rather to difficulties of presentation. The reference to "ethics" unquestionably relates to the philosophy of "ethical life," which means for Hegel something other than "ethics" in the traditional sense and especially the sense in which it is used by critical philosophy. It treats "that form of practical spirit in which, as in the objective freedom of a people, legality and morality are posited as immediately identical" (*HL* 173). The relationship of this "ethical life" to religion is also quite different from that of Kantian morality. How it is to be defined, however, is problematic. The delimitation and relation of these two fields gives rise to difficulties—difficulties that extend to the final Berlin texts, which are devoted to this relationship. One of the difficulties lies in the fact that Hegel tries to apprehend the relationship from two sides: from his conception of the system, and from his insight into connections relating to constitutional law and constitutional history.

(2) In regard to the political relationship of religion to the state, the fragments comprising *The German Constitution*[31] arrive at two equally pertinent statements, which at the same time cannot be combined. The one formulates the traditional understanding of religion and its relationship to the state. In religion the innermost being of humanity expresses itself; it is the stable center in which human beings coalesce (*PW* 158, *GW* 5:171). With the split among confessions, religion has not cut itself adrift from the state. Rather it has carried the rift into the state and "completely rent the state asunder" (*PW* 193, *GW* 5:99). This seems to call for a renewal of the old unity of religion and state. But Hegel emphatically adopts the opposite position. It is only the tearing apart of the state by religion that "has afforded an inkling in a remarkable way of certain principles on which a state can rest." The confessional split has torn human beings apart in their "innermost being." But in place of the old unity there is now an external linkage, and this is "the principle of modern states" (*PW* 193, *GW* 5:99). State authority severs itself from religious authority and no longer needs the church in order to exist (*PW* 159, *GW* 5:172). From this Hegel draws far-reaching consequences: "Simply for a state to be possible, the separation of religion and politics is necessary; a power over religion does not have to be demanded for the supreme authority, God forbid!" (*GW* 5:56). That conversely power over the state does not have to be

31. [*Tr.*] The so-called *Verfassungsschrift*, composed between 1799 and 1803 (*GW* 5:1–219). The translation contained in *PW* 143–242 is from an abbreviated text contained in *Schriften zur Politik und Rechtsphilosophie*, ed. G. Lasson, 2d ed. (Leipzig, 1923).

demanded for religion is so evident to Hegel that he does not explicitly mention it.

Certainly Hegel is not the first to voice this insight into the political aspects of the confessional split—although he does so at a time when it runs counter, not to political trends, but to political philosophy imbued with romantic ideas. This insight must have been in tension, however, not merely with competing viewpoints but also with Hegel's own conception. For he sees the link between religion and ethical life to be so close that it could only be achieved in a premodern state (to use Hegel's own image). This mismatch between the insight based on political history and the requirements of the system is not resolved simply by pointing out that the highest concept of "ethical life" for Hegel was at the time not that of the state but of the people. For the events which are said to have torn the state apart also split the people. In any event the fragments give no indication that Hegel posed in explicit terms the problem as to how the systematically close connection between religion and ethical life is to be preserved if the modern state—whose advocate Hegel makes himself—is no longer defined by the meaning-constituting medium of religion but by the principle of voluntary association. Yet this difficulty must have been an impelling motive for the new conception of the relationship between religion and ethical life.

(3) There is another point of unclarity, which has already been mentioned, namely whether religion falls within the sphere of ethical life itself or only stands in a very close relation to it. Until recently it was possible to avoid ambiguity by contesting the reliability of the *Introductio* lectures transmitted by Rosenkranz.[32] The rediscovery of the sources has shown this to be a false path. Already in the winter of 1801–2 Hegel outlines the conclusion of the system as the return to the pure idea and to the intuition of God in the "philosophy of religion and art"—a sphere that lies above and beyond ethical life (*GW* 5:264).

---

32. Thus Johann Heinrich Trede, "Mythologie und Idee: Die systematische Stellung der 'Volksreligion' in Hegels Jenaer Philosophie der Sittlichkeit (1801–1803)," in *Hegel-Studien*, Beiheft 9, esp. p. 175 n. 9, and pp. 198–199 n. 24 (contesting Rosenkranz's description of the text as a continuation of the *System der Sittlichkeit*).

This is contradicted by the *System of Ethical Life* written one year later and the *Natural Law* essay of summer 1802.[33] They concern us at this point solely with respect to the position of religion vis-à-vis ethical life and especially the share religion has in the task that here falls to ethical life, that of concluding the system. According to the *Natural Law* essay and the *Introductio* lectures, what concludes the system is that the absolute intuits itself as itself in its reality—in the spirit, which is therefore higher than nature (*NL* 111, *GW* 4:464). This structure still leaves open where such self-intuition is actualized, whether in religion or in ethical life or in the religion that is only to be conceived within the horizon of ethical life. According to the *System of Ethical Life,* the system is brought to completion once there is a perfect adequacy between intuition and concept, people and individual, in the idea of absolute ethical life. In the people, individuals intuit themselves as themselves in each and every other individual; the individual "reaches supreme subject-objectivity," "recognizes in its opposite, i.e., its object, absolutely the same thing that the subject is."[34] In this intuiting the individual "is as a particular consciousness plainly equal to the universal, and this universality which has flatly united the particular with itself is the divinity of the people; this universal, intuited in the ideal form of particularity, is the God of the people. He is an ideal way of intuiting it."[35] Why, in addition to the actual divinity of the people, there should also be such an intuition of the universal in the ideal form of particularity, is not in fact explained.

It is only at the end of the following section, dealing with the forms of the state, that Hegel reverts to the question of religion. In monarchy, he tells us, there must be a religion in addition to the monarch: "the more empirical he is and the more barbaric the

33. See Hegel, *System der Sittlichkeit,* ed. G. Lasson, 2d ed. (1923; reprint, Hamburg, 1967), pp. 52 ff. (*JS*[1] 142 ff.); and *Ueber die wissenschaftlichen Behandlungsarten des Naturrechts* (*GW* 4:415–485, *NL* 55–133). On the interpretation of these works, see Trede, "Mythologie und Idee."

34. *System der Sittlichkeit,* pp. 54–55 (*JS*[1] 144–145). The penultimate word should read "subject" and not (as in Lasson's edition, from which the translation is made) "object."

35. Ibid. (*JS*[1] 144).

people is"—these two are equated—then "the more the monarchy has authority and the more independently it constitutes itself." To the extent that a people becomes one with itself, with nature and ethical life, "all the more does it take the divine into itself and get rid of this religion that stands over against it."[36] In aristocracy there is "little imagination or religion," while in democracy "absolute religion does exist, but unstably, or rather it is a religion of nature." The function of concluding the system does not therefore belong to religion as the intuition of the universal in the form of the ideal. Such religion does not ground the actual divinity of the people or the supreme intuition of subject-objectivity. While it is marginally related to the forms of the state, it does not come within the doctrine of classes or estates [*Stände*] broadly conceived.

(4) It is just this that happens in the *Natural Law* essay, written slightly earlier; and it does so in a form that reconciles us to the omission of this theme from the *System of Ethical Life*. Religion here plays a constitutive role in concluding the system: in it the absolute intuits itself—"and indeed as itself" (*NL* 111, *GW* 4:464). What is constitutive for it is the difference between the classes made up of the unfree and the free. The latter class becomes what is properly divine: ". . . the very first thing is that the absolutely pure and indifferent shape and absolute ethical consciousness shall *be*" (*NL* 108, *GW* 4:462). The relationship of the unfree to this would be only as its empirical consciousness. This is corroborated by the reference to the difference between the "absolute work of art" and the onlooker (*NL* 108, *GW* 4:462). On the side of the real the relationship of the unfree to the free is characterized by fear, trust, and obedience; on the side of the ideal—that of the intuition of the communal God—the necessarily separate classes are one. To ground this ideal side we are told that ideality as such must "be given a pure absolute shape, and so must be intuited and worshiped as God of the people, and this intuition must in turn have

36. [*Tr.*] ". . . und verliert an dieser ihm widerstehenden Religion" (ibid., p. 91). The English translation reads ". . . and suffer loss [lose faith?] in this religion that resists it" (*JS*[1] 177). The change of translation has been made at the suggestion of the author.

its own vivacity and joyful movement in a cultus" (*NL* 116, *GW* 4:470).

This answers the question that was left open above (p. 147) concerning the nature of the "limitation derived from the empirical existence of the people." Thus two considerations are relevant. The first concerns the relationship of religion to the structure of the self-intuition of the absolute, based as it is on the classes. As a relationship to the ideal God of the people, religion is, to be sure, bound up with the particularity of a people in general. But it is independent of the speculative deduction of a Brahman ruling caste, which coincides more especially (since it is supposedly at the same time the class of valor) with the military caste of the Kshatriyas and ultimately also embraces the philosophers, because the task of genuinely working off particularity is one for philosophy itself (Hegel adds this, not on his own authority, but by invoking Plato and Aristotle: *NL* 100, *GW* 4:455). Hegel apparently attaches more weight to this idea than to the thought that justifies the superiority of spirit over nature, namely that "in intelligence alone is individualization carried to the absolute extreme, i.e. to the absolute concept," and that intelligence alone is the "supreme identity of reality and ideality" (*NL* 111, *GW* 4:464). Here again, for this later version of the identity of absolute individuality and absolute universality, the doctrine of classes is not constitutive.

The second consideration concerns the content of ideal divinity. The formal definition of the idea of God propounded here leaves it open how the limitation derived from the life of the people is to become important for the development of religion. It is, however, primarily corresponding passages in the natural-law lecture notes that lead us to the insight that this is far from exhausting the content of religion. It is said there that religion expresses "two things at once: on one side the speculative idea of the spirit, and on the other the limitation derived from the empirical existence of the people" (*JS*[1] 180, *HL* 134); the first of these is common to religion and "science," and it is the object of logic and metaphysics. Religion necessarily goes beyond ethical life because it holds to the intuition of the absolute as a metaphysical intuition. Without this reference back to its pure shape, the self-intuition of the absolute would be quite impossible. The fragment *Die Idee des absoluten Wesens* expresses this by affirming that the people "reverts to the pure idea in the philosophy of religion and art" (*GW* 5:264).

(5) If it seems that in the early Jena years Hegel conceives religion exclusively in the context of ethical life, this is due to the *Natural Law* essay and the *System of Ethical Life*. Both tend to delimit religion, with consequences that are evident particularly at the conclusion of the *Natural Law* essay. Despite the "incongruity between absolute spirit and its shape" (*NL* 132, *GW* 4:484), Hegel does not allow himself to transcend the sphere of ethical life, tied as it is to the people, so as to attain "the shapelessness of cosmopolitanism" or "the void of the rights of humanity, or the like void of a league of nations [*Völkerstaat*] or a world republic." Nor does he allow himself what the above-mentioned fragment had envisioned as the consummation of the system of philosophy, namely the return to the idea (*NL* 132–133, *GW* 4:484). The abstruse political theology of the state based on classes does not owe its existence to an excess of metaphysics but to the fact that the return to the pure idea has been renounced. It does, however, ascribe an excess of metaphysical dignity to the people. But this position is an isolated one. It is not only the *Introductio* lectures that it contradicts. The ensuing system drafts are characterized by a continuous decline in the importance of the concept of the people and the progressive elaboration of a "philosophy of absolute spirit" out of the philosophy of ethical life. Soon religion is no longer restricted to ethical life. The lost conclusion of the philosophy of spirit and hence of the system as a whole, which Rosenkranz places at the end of the *System of Ethical Life*,[37] explicitly controverts the view expressed

37. Rosenkranz, *HL* 132–133 (*JS*[1] 178 [the translation of the last sentence of the quotation that follows has been modified at the suggestion of the author]). Trede, in "Mythologie und Idee," pp. 198–199 n. 24, contests the view that this brief text belongs here chronologically precisely because it leads beyond the ethical realm. But as a result of the discovery of the *Introductio* lectures, it can be shown that it was quite possible for Hegel at this time to transcend the ethical realm in this way by means of religion. In this text, moreover, Hegel calls philosophy the "ideal complement of war." This notably odd expression does not recur in later years, but it is reminiscent of the view expressed in the *Natural Law* essay (*NL* 100, *GW* 4:455), referred to above (p. 174) [associating philosophy with political rule]. This is a further indication of an early date for the text transmitted by Rosenkranz.

in the *Natural Law* essay: "The absolute consciousness of the individuals of the people, the living spirit of the same, must be pure, absolute consciousness, absolute spirit, both in respect of form and in respect of content; and the spirit of the people [*Volksgeist*] becomes spirit of the natural and ethical universe. Only then has the spirit returned absolutely into its absolute self-equality, into the aether of its simple idea, and the end of philosophy has returned to its beginning." And even this conclusion, so Rosenkranz tells us, no longer satisfied Hegel when he came to communicate it orally in Jena, and it was replaced by those passages in the natural-law lectures to which we have referred above (pp. 146 ff.) in relation to aesthetics.

There are three reasons for not restricting religion to the sphere of ethical life. In the first place, Hegel explicitly acknowledges the "incongruity" between absolute spirit and its shape. Secondly, consideration of the function of religion in modern political history could also have facilitated insight into the unsatisfactory nature of the position taken in the *Natural Law* essay. For this function is utterly remote from what this essay assigns to religion. In modern times religion does not bring about the integration of a people or a state but their dissolution. Finally, consideration of the historical forms of religion also reveals a picture that is at variance with its being restricted to ethical life. Christianity in particular resists being brought into the *Volksgeist* schema. Christ is not a people's intuition of the absolute in the ideal form of particularity. The shape of Christ "expresses in its history the whole history of the empirical existence of the human race." "The history of God is the history of the whole race, and every individual human being goes through the whole history of the race." The natural-law lectures see religion no longer as limited to the ethical life of a people but from the point of view of world history and the history of the human race. Admittedly they retain the term "religion of the people" [*Volksreligion*], but it acquires a new, dissonant ring: Christ is not the God of a single people, but the "national God of the human race" (*JS*¹ 183, HL 137–138).

(6) The fragmentary state in which the texts have come down to us does not permit tracing in its entirety the course by which a

philosophy of religion that lies beyond the sphere of ethical life developed. For no part of the system are the source materials so insufficient as for its concluding section. From the first system draft (1803–4) the concluding section of the philosophy of spirit at least has been lost, and though the second system draft of the following year (1804–5) has a metaphysics, it lacks a philosophy of spirit. Not until the third system draft (1805–6) is it again possible to assess the relationship of religion and ethical life.[38]

All that can be used to determine this relationship, therefore, are a few references in the first system draft and in two contemporary fragments. We are not here concerned to describe the character of this draft in general—the transformation of the philosophy of ethical life into the philosophy of spirit and the emergence of the concept of consciousness. Despite having overcome the *Volksgeist* concept in the natural-law lectures, Hegel still seems to have viewed religion in its light in this draft, just as he did language, understanding, and reason. This is supported by the fragment *seiner Form* (*JS*[1] 254–256, GW 5:375), which reads in part like a reminiscence of parallel passages in the *Early Theological Writings* (*J* 377). It is evident here too, however, that the *Volksgeist* concept precludes any but a very limited concept of religion, and indeed one into which Christianity does not fit.

The preconditions for the emergence of the spirit of the people or absolute consciousness are named here more precisely than before. They consist in the struggle for recognition and the formative process to which it gives rise whereby absolute consciousness becomes absolute substance.[39] In a way similar to those parts of the fragment *ist nur die Form* (*JS*[1] 251–253, GW 6:330–331) where

38. [Tr.] *Jenaer Systementwürfe I* (GW 6) lacks a section on logic and metaphysics but has a full philosophy of nature and portions of a philosophy of spirit, which breaks off with a section on "the people" (only the philosophy of spirit is translated in *JS*[1]). *Jenaer Systementwürfe II* (GW 7) contains a logic and metaphysics (which is translated in *JS*[2]) and a philosophy of nature but no philosophy of spirit. *Jenaer Systementwürfe III* (GW 8) contains a philosophy of nature and a more complete philosophy of spirit, with a brief concluding section on "art, religion, and science" (no translations are yet available).

39. On the relationship between the concepts "absolute consciousness," "absolute substance," "spirit of the people," and "recognition," see *JS*[1] 212–213, 240–243; GW 6:273–274, 312–316.

Hegel reflects on the philosophy of art, religion would probably have to be defined here as the "relation . . . of the single consciousness to absolute consciousness." This definition offers an approach to the critique of religion as well as of art. For Hegel distinguishes two forms of such a relation: the living relation would be "that a people as consciousness in the form of individuality brought forth a universal work in which they intuited their absolute consciousness as shape." The fragment gives no information, however, about the realization of this living relation. It can therefore be assumed that art and religion are forms of the other—that is, nonliving—relation: "this absolute consciousness . . . does not become a self-fulfilling, here-and-now vital, work; and it is an absolute beyond, in the face of which the individual consciousness can only nullify itself." Moreover Hegel denies art the power through its form to "remove the essential [quality] of such content, the fact that it has no presence, but has only absolute yearning." This echoes what already in the *Early Theological Writings* provided the dominant motive, namely the critique of eschatology: "The content in which the absolute consciousness appears must free itself from its yearning, from its individuality that has a beyond in the past and the future." The critique of eschatology becomes the trigger for passing to speculation: "The mere concept of absolute self-enjoyment must [be] elevated out of the reality in which it has submerged itself as concept, and as it [gives] itself *the form* of concept, it reconstructs the reality of its existence and becomes absolute universality." A few lines earlier, in a sentence that is later deleted, Hegel establishes the link between self-enjoyment and speculation: "absolute self-enjoyment is a purely speculative enjoyment." Thus, it is clear from the sources, incomplete though they are, that regardless of the probable incorporation of religion into ethical life, the conclusion of the system can no longer be formulated in the concepts of the ethical sphere. It is only in philosophical speculation that the self-enjoyment of the idea first attains absolute universality.

(7) It is only in the third system draft, in the manuscript entitled *Naturphilosophie und Philosophie des Geistes,* that we have a philosophy of religion. Even it does not finally release philosophy of religion from the sphere of ethical life. The section "Art, Religion,

and Science" [*Kunst, Religion und Wissenschaft*] forms the third part of the account of "Constitution" [*Constitution*], and it concludes the system as a whole. In so doing it follows, formally speaking, on the doctrine of classes or estates [*Stände*]. The fact that it comes under ethical life, however, is here due solely to external considerations relating to the architecture of the system. As far as content is concerned, the exposition of religion involves neither the doctrine of classes nor the concept of the people. The very first sentence of the new section marks the difference: "The absolutely free spirit . . . brings forth another world, a world that has the shape of itself, where its work is accomplished within itself, and it attains the intuition of *itself* as *itself*" (*GW* 8:277). To be sure, ethical life, the "spirit that has certain knowledge of *itself*," forms the presupposition for this concluding sphere. Hegel stresses now, too, that the eternal has its existence or determinate being [*Dasein*] in the spirit of the people (*GW* 8:284). But it is no longer the absolute ethical life of a people that achieves intuition in religion. "Determinate spirit" progressively develops "from primitive trust and toil to the knowledge that absolute spirit has of itself. It is at first the life of a people in general"—but now comes the laconic statement: "from which it has to free itself" (*GW* 8:265). As spirit that knows itself as spirit, religion is distinct from the "existing spirit" of ethical life. This is not to deny all "knowing" to ethical life. The limited self knows of itself as a being; the "government" is "the spirit that knows itself as universal being and universal actuality—the absolute self." But it is only in religion that "each self raises itself to this intuition of itself as a universal self," to "knowing itself as spirit." Such raising presupposes the general externalization or divestment [*Entäusserung*] "of all actuality" (*GW* 8:281). Hegel contrasts religious externalization with the merely ethical: "a higher abstraction is necessary, a greater antithesis and cultural refinement, a more profound spirit." The higher diremption consists in the fact that "each self returns completely into itself, knows itself as such, as [absolute] being, attains the peculiarity of being separate from the existing universal, yet of being absolute—of possessing its absolute directly in its knowing" (*GW* 8:262).

This difference is not only structural or even a matter of chance:

"individuality's knowing itself as absolute, this absolute self-containedness," has come about as "the higher principle of modern times, unknown to the ancients, to Plato" (GW 8:263). Here Hegel still links it to a "Nordic mode of being." Later he will term it the principle of Christianity. The insight afforded by philosophy of history into the difference between antiquity and modernity compels the systematic severance of the sphere of religion from ethical life. The emancipation of absolute spirit from ethical life is therefore no indication of an increasing conceptual esotericism. Such a criticism does not take account of the historical difference between the Greek world and the modern spirit expressed in the Christian religion. The specific features of political history that separate the ancient *polis* from modern politics systematically necessitate the emancipation of absolute spirit from the realm of ethical life. And by this means are eliminated also the abstruse thinking and reactionary politics that characterize the early Jena doctrine of classes with its apotheosis of a universal class.

The external framework for the emancipation of philosophy of religion from the philosophy of ethical life is constituted by the transformation of the latter into the philosophy of spirit. How such a transformation is to come about is already evident in the first system draft of 1803–4. The larger whole composed of a philosophy of spirit following on the philosophy of nature provides a context in which the spheres of subjective, objective, and absolute spirit can be treated in uniform fashion but also delineated sufficiently from one another. They do not, however, occur here under these names. Hegel distinguishes the spirit of the people as subsisting absolute spirit from religion as thinking spirit (GW 8:286). Already "religion" can denote this latter sphere as a whole (GW 8:265). Within it "art, religion, and science" together constitute the spirit that knows itself as absolute. Here for the first time the triad of forms of absolute spirit is clearly expressed, of which there are already intimations in the natural-law lectures (see pp. 146–147 above). And now for the first time Hegel distinguishes religion primarily by its theoretical form: it has its object neither in the form of intuition, as in art, nor in that of conceptual knowing, as in science, but in the form of representation [*Vorstellung*]. This categorization does not mean, however, that the systematic schema of subjective spirit becomes the paradigm of absolute spirit. For Hegel at this time is still quite without a "philosophy of subjective spirit," with its subdivision into intuition, representation, and conceptual thought. The place subsequently taken by subjective spirit is here occupied by "intelligence," which is not, however, built up out of the three above-mentioned forms. At least in point of time, the delineation of the forms of absolute spirit precedes the differentiation of subjective spirit based on the theory of faculties. Presumably for this reason this differentiation is also carried out in more pointed fashion in later versions of the philosophy of absolute spirit than in the corresponding philosophy of subjective spirit.

In any event "intuition" still had, shortly before, another conceptual meaning: in the *Introductio* lectures or the *Difference* essay it denotes the undifferentiated unity, not mediated by reflection, in which the "image" of the idea is grasped in nondiscursive fashion. And up to that point "representation" was still quite without any defined meaning. Schelling later reproached Hegel for having taken over the concept of representation from Karl Leonhard Reinhold, alleging that the "antithesis between representation and thought" remained obscure with him, "like so much else" (*SW* 13:172–173). But no evidence can be found to support this. What is more important is that the philosophy of spirit of 1805–6 enables us to see to some extent the genesis of the concept of representation, how Hegel introduces it into the context of philosophy of religion. Particularly telling is the addition of the word "representation" in a marginal note (*GW* 8:282). Subsequently, however, the word also occurs in the main text, so that the date when it was first used can be fixed with certainty. Thereafter it is first introduced into the philosophy of subjective spirit. The Nuremberg *Encyclopedia* of 1808 and the following years already distinguishes "intuition" and "representation," even if still as a subdivision of the section "recollection" (*W* 18:180). It is clear from these passages that they were written not without regard to the relationship between art and religion.

Already the 1805–6 philosophy of spirit does not simply juxtapose the three forms of absolute spirit. They form the stages of ever more adequate self-knowledge of the absolute. But this hierarchical structure does not become evident solely on the basis of classification in terms of the theory of faculties, for the faculties themselves do not stand in a fixed order within subjective spirit. The subordinate position of art is attested by the split that occurs between the self of the artist and the selflessness of enjoyment as well as between form and matter. The material aspect of the art work always remains, in Hegel's view, something inadequate for spirit. Nor can intuition comprehend the infinite; it remains "only *meant* infinitude"—devoid of necessity, not having the "shape of thought in it."[40] With only a little modification, however, this objection also applies to religion. It is not itself the consummate unity of knowing and truth, but the act of "*representing* the unity of knowing and truth." In religion the existent, actual spirit has "become an object to itself as spirit—but in the shape of representation and faith." Although, properly speaking, spirit is inherent in it, it "flees . . . beyond itself, far away from it." The content of religion is "the object of speech only, not of insight—not concept, not self" (*GW* 8:284). It "is indeed *true*; but this being true is an assurance—devoid of insight" (*GW* 8:286).

This account of religion is influenced in large measure by the delineation of religion from art and philosophy. A second point of view, namely the historical, has only a marginal role. In the first Jena "philosophy of religion"—the lecture notes on natural law—the history of religion provides the structural principle. It is less important here, yet the short historical sketch is already akin to the later conception. The natural-law lectures only distinguish classical mythology as the "religion of nature" from the reconstruction of undifferentiated harmony. Now, on the contrary, the development heralded in the fragment *seiner Form* is accomplished: prior to classical mythology Hegel inserts a phase that represents the divine being as "what is awesome in the power of nature, wherein the self is of no account" (*GW* 8:280). This basically alters the conception of the religion of nature. And Christianity, which here brings the

---

40. *GW* 8:279. On the consequences of this limitation, see Jaeschke, "Kunst und Religion," pp. 168–169.

history of religion to completion, is for the first time regarded as the "absolute religion."

Its absoluteness is manifest not only in the fact that, as in the natural-law lectures, it depicts the history of the human race in terms of the fate of one individual. Hegel defines religion in general as "*absolute* spirit's knowing of itself as absolute *spirit*" (*GW* 8:280). This conception of religion corresponds to the concluding section of the metaphysics of the second system draft (see p. 143 above). It points toward the self-knowing of absolute spirit as such. This definition of the concept of religion establishes the closest link between religion and metaphysics. At least insofar as it encompasses the entire sphere of absolute spirit (*GW* 8:265), religion can be comprehended as the consummation of metaphysics and at the same time of the system of philosophy: "In religion, however, spirit becomes object to itself as absolutely universal, as the essence of all nature, [of all] being and doing, and it does so in the shape of the immediate self—the self is universal knowing and by this means the return into self" (*GW* 8:280). Hegel does not substantiate this metaphysical concept of religion by reference to the religion of the "power of nature" or to the "religion of beauty." About them he says little more than that they are imperfect. The demonstration that reason is present in religion rests solely on the traditional components of Christian dogma—the doctrine of the trinity, christology, and ecclesiology. To be sure, it is only as interpreted by Hegel that they are suited for this purpose. This is less clear of the doctrine of the trinity, regarding which Hegel here mentions the immanent and the economic trinity, as he had already done in the divine triangle fragment. The metaphysical interpretation attaches in particular to christology, which is viewed as a representational expression for the "inner idea" of the absolute religion, for the "speculative idea that the self, or what is actual, is thought—essence and being [are] one and the same." This idea is expressed as follows: "that God, the otherworldly absolute being, [has] taken human form, [has] become this *actual* human being" (*GW* 8:282).

This interpretation could be criticized as incorrect. While it does not run utterly counter to traditional teaching, one consequence of the speculative reinterpretation of christology does. As the "depth of spirit that has certain knowledge of itself," God is "the self of all, he is essence, pure thought; but, divested [*entaüssert*] of this abstraction, he is actual self, he is a human being who has common spatial and temporal existence—and *this* individual human being is *all* individual human beings" (*GW* 8:280). Otherwise God would not be the "self of all" nor the "depth of spirit that has certain knowledge of itself"—the pure "ego," "the concept, the absolute, pure power" (*GW* 8:281). Only this interpretation of individuality as universality enables Hegel to say even more pointedly: "divine nature is none other than human nature" (*GW* 8:280). The *Early Theological Writings* justify this basic premise of philosophical christology by the Spinozistic idea of the unity of substance (see p. 121 above). Here it follows from the identity of universality and individuality. In metaphysical terms christology transcends not only the difference between divine and human nature but equally the antithesis of God and nature: "the being that subsists in itself, that is, God, comes on stage in nature as *actual*; everything other-worldly, every beyond, has vanished."[41]

The absolute religion is thus characterized by a threefold negation: by the surrender of the "abstract otherworldly being"; by the negation of the actuality of the God-man [through his death]; and finally by the community's renunciation of its being-for-self and its immediate nature, such that it "gives itself the consciousness of unity with [the divine] being" (*GW* 8:283). This movement of negation makes explicit in its entirety what is involved in God's being "spirit." And only to the extent that Christianity grasps the absolute being as spirit is it the "true religion" (*GW* 8:282). Here, at the end of the Jena period, Hegel arrives at the basic idea of his metaphysics of Christianity, which he no longer revises even at a later date. He likewise anticipates his subsequent critique of the representational character of religious doctrine: in religion the moments of spirit have only "the form of immediacy and of event; they are not the object of conceptualization or insight" (*GW* 8:286).

41. "... das *ansichseyende* Wesen; d.h. GOTT TRITT IN der Natur auf—*als wirkliches*; alles Jenseits ist entflohen." This is in all probability how the sentence should read; in *GW* 8:283 the sense is distorted by the addition of a bracketed "ist" following "Wesen."

The medium of representation does not do justice to the content of religion as it is manifest for speculation. From now on this tension molds the concept of religion: It "is for the represented spirit, the self that does not integrate its pure and its actual consciousness, that the content of pure consciousness appears in actual consciousness as an other over against it" (GW 8:282). For this reason the idea that is nonetheless religion's inmost idea escapes it, the idea of reconciliation—the reconciliation of God and humanity, of nature and spirit, and indeed of God with himself. Here as later, as well as already in parts of the *Early Theological Writings* and in the fragment *ist nur die Form* (*JS*[1] 253, GW 6:330–331), eschatology is regarded as the prime example of the failure of religion. The metaphysical meaning of christology is that "everything otherworldly, every beyond [*alles Jenseits*] has vanished." But the spirit that is actualized in the community—whose concept it is to achieve for itself in the cultus the consciousness of unity with the divine being—this spirit flees "beyond itself, far away from it." The "enjoyment and existence" of reconciliation are for it something "beyond and in the future" (GW 8:286); it separates the kingdoms of heaven and of actuality instead of acknowledging their identity.

This very densely written sketch of a philosophy of religion finally breaks away from the early Jena conception. Formally incorporated though it still is in ethical spirit, it carries out the project outlined in the fragment *Die Idee des absoluten Wesens* at the beginning of the Jena period, namely that after being realized in nature and in spirit the absolute idea should, in religion and art, revert to itself, to the intuition of God. By this means the special connection that was already at an early stage said to exist between metaphysics and philosophy of religion is realized. The subsequent development can be interpreted as a continuous elaboration of the concept of religion arrived at here. The later restructuring of the philosophy of spirit only draws out the consequences of the independence of religion vis-à-vis ethical life that had already been substantially achieved. Nor does the ambivalent status of religion change from now on: religion is absolute spirit's knowledge of itself as absolute spirit—but in the form of representation, without insight. It is the truth of art—but it finds its own truth in philosophy, which *comprehends* the idea of which religion provides only an assurance. It proclaims the reconciliation of God and nature, of this world and the beyond—but in such a way that the kingdoms of heaven and of earth remain separate and spirit regards its reconciliation as attainable only in what lies beyond it.

5. Philosophy of Religion as an Element in the Phenomenology of Spirit

(1) The chapter of the *Phenomenology of Spirit* devoted to religion (Chap. VII) throws up a multitude of problems, especially in regard to the history of the work and the function the chapter has within the system. Here we are concerned with it solely as it relates to the state of development of the philosophy of religion. Allowance must be made, however, for the possibility of differences between the portrayal of philosophy of religion in the context of the *Phenomenology* and in that of the system to which the *Phenomenology* forms an introduction. Thus we have no way of telling what shape the philosophy of religion might have assumed as part of the system at that time—especially since the 1805–6 philosophy of spirit, written only a few months earlier, is much shorter.

The chapter on religion completes the development of the philosophy of religion in Jena, not in the merely chronological sense that the *Phenomenology of Spirit* is the last testimony of the Jena years, nor in the merely quantitative sense that this chapter contains the fullest exposition to date—and for a considerable time to come. It shows rather the complete realization of the four tendencies that characterize the development of the philosophy of religion in Jena: the emancipation of religion from the context of ethical life; the systematic differentiation of religion from art and philosophical science; the elaboration of history of religion into an aspect of the philosophy of religion; and the coalescing of the metaphysical and the specific approaches to grounding the philosophy of religion. The latter tendency remains understandably concealed in the *Phenomenology* because it does not treat religion in the context of the system but of a "science of the experience of consciousness" (as the original subtitle has it[42]) or a science of spirit in its appearing.

The conception of the work is, however, determined by the first three tendencies. The history of religion again occupies a much more prominent place than in the 1805–6 philosophy of spirit. It even forms the basic outline for the treatment of religion.[43] The systematic differentiation of religion does correspond to the preceding philosophy of spirit, but only as far as the delineation of religion from conceptual thought is concerned. It follows from the overall design of the *Phenomenology* that this is not equally true for the relation between religion and art. For it treats art only as a moment in the history of religion, as "religion in the form of art" [*Kunstreligion*]. The fact that it is only in curtailed form that art is introduced into the process of substance becoming subject is a defect only partly attributable to the lack of further development in Hegel's aesthetics. In the 1805–6 philosophy of spirit as well, Hegel does not sketch an independent history of art or a theory of the connection between art history and art forms. That he does not treat these in their own terms (as he does in the philosophy of spirit) but solely as reduced to the distinction between the abstract, the living, and the spiritual work of art within *Kunstreligion* is probably due to the difficulty of introducing this differentiation of aesthetics into the course of the *Phenomenology*. Striking, finally, is the emancipation of religion from ethical life. In this the *Phenomenology* is simply drawing the consequences of the separation that had already been materially brought about by the philosophy

42. [Tr.] The original title was *System der Wissenschaft. Erster Theil, Wissenschaft der Erfahrung des Bewusstseyns.* See *GW* 9:444, 469 ff.

43. [Tr.] Chapter VII of the *Phenomenology* is arranged as follows:
A. Natural Religion
   a. Luminous Being (the religion of Israel [see sec. (5) below])
   b. Plant and Animal
   c. The Artificer (the religion of Egypt)
B. The Religion of Art (the religion of Greece)
   a. The Abstract Work of Art
   b. The Living Work of Art
   c. The Spiritual Work of Art
C. The Revelatory Religion (the Christian religion)

of spirit. The basis for spelling out the content of religion is not the self-consciousness of a people, let alone the way it is organized in classes. The content has to be explicated as the self-knowledge of absolute spirit, as the expression of the inwardly differentiated unity of self-consciousness and the absolute being.

(2) In the introductory remarks to the chapter on religion, Hegel does not present the speculative concept of religion—religion as the self-consciousness of absolute spirit—as fully as its novelty and its systematic importance required. It is expounded in a brief though important passage preceding the historical review of the religions. The exposition takes place as a definition rather than as a further logical determination of the development of the concept attained before the start of the chapter on religion. To be sure, the transition from "self-certain spirit" [*seiner selbst gewisser Geist*] to religion appears as one of those transitions in the *Phenomenology* that can be more easily accomplished a posteriori. To make it plausible, however, it would be necessary to show how the concept of religion derives from self-certain spirit, why the difference between consciousness [of an object[44]] and self-consciousness should break forth in religion as the pure self-certainty of spirit, and why religion, as the self-consciousness of spirit, should have alongside it the aspect of consciousness, that is, existent, actual spirit. In all three respects we have to consider whether Hegel provides sufficient justification for his radically new conception of the concept of religion.

The introduction of religion follows upon the final shape of "spirit that is certain of itself" (*Phen* Chap. VI.C): "the actual I, the universal knowledge of itself in its absolute opposite, in the knowledge which remains internal, and which, on account of the purity of its separated being-within-self, is itself completely universal." This does not yet make the transition to religion comprehen-

44. [*Tr.*] Consciousness for Hegel is always consciousness *of* something; it has something standing over against it, a *Gegenstand* or "object." To bring out this aspect of consciousness, especially as contrasted with *self*-consciousness, we occasionally add in brackets the words "of an object." The problem of religion as portrayed in the *Phenomenology* is to work out the tension between the consciousness of God as an object, a "supreme" or "absolute being," or so-called "God-consciousness," and the self-consciousness of spirit, which is the self-knowing of absolute spirit in and through the self-certainty of finite spirit.

sible. Hegel achieves it by interpreting the "reconciling 'yes,'" in which the two I's let go their antithetical existence," as "God appearing in the midst of those who know themselves in the form of pure knowledge" (*Phen* 409, *GW* 9:362).[45] Shortly before, he defines absolute spirit as "a reciprocal recognition" that comes about because existent spirit "beholds the pure knowledge of itself as universal being in its opposite, in the pure knowledge of itself as absolutely self-contained individuality" (*Phen* 408, *GW* 9:361). This determinacy of absolute spirit is not religious, at least in the sense of explicit religion. Hegel effects the transition into this sphere solely by means of biblical allusion and the express mention of God. This transition from the "existence of the I that has expanded into a duality" (*Phen* 409, *GW* 9:362) to the idea of God is convincing only if the latter is not located beyond the self-certainty of the pure I. The link becomes clearer in the following passage. In conscience, in the self-consciousness that is present to itself, spirit has "for itself, represented as an object, the significance of being the universal spirit that contains within itself all being and all actuality." To be sure, it has "*shape* or the form of being in that it is the object of its consciousness," but in religion this remains "posited essentially in the determination of *self*-consciousness"; its actuality is therefore "universal actuality as *thought*" (*Phen* 411–412, *GW* 9:364).

Hegel emphasizes that the relationship of religion to the moments of spirit that precede it is not to be conceived as historical. At the same time, by having recourse to historical shapes [*Gestalten*] such as the religion of the Enlightenment or of morality, he sets the introduction of religion in a historical perspective. This is not to be understood as though Hegel holds the nonsensical view that there was no religion prior to the Enlightenment. It is, however, only after the shapes referred to have been traversed that

45. [*Tr.*] Our translations of passages from the *Phenomenology* frequently differ from Miller's version, to which page references are given along with references to *GW* 9. Miller's translation is based on the Hoffmeister edition of 1952 rather than the critical edition, but more importantly, our rendering of several commonly recurring technical terms differs from Miller's usage. We have also dropped Hegel's frequent emphasis of words except where it helps to bring out meaning.

the concept of religion can be adequately grasped, as the *self-consciousness* of spirit, "which is conscious of being all truth and contains all actuality within that truth" (*Phen* 415, *GW* 9:367). This concept of religion could not be grasped before self-certainty was achieved in the shapes referred to. Neither before nor later did Hegel express in such a categorical way the difference between the pre-Enlightenment and post-Enlightenment concepts of religion. The distinction here drawn shows, moreover, how far Hegel has come to diverge from Schelling's approach to religion during the same period.[46]

In order to show, however, that this definition of the concept of religion is also appropriate, it is necessary for the concepts of pure knowledge and, in particular, absolute spirit to be explicated within the system to which the *Phenomenology* is first and foremost designed as an introduction. Since there is no metaphysics in the roughly contemporary third system draft, the only source to which to turn for this purpose is the metaphysics of the second system draft, which has already been briefly discussed above (pp. 143–144). It defines for the first time the relationship between metaphysics and religion as that between the self-knowing of absolute spirit and the self-knowing of absolute spirit *as* absolute spirit. This provides the only security against the self-certainty of pure knowledge being misunderstood in psychological or anthropological terms. To be sure, Hegel decisively refashions his metaphysics in these years, as is shown by the sketch of the system in the 1805–6 philosophy of spirit. But there too "spirit's self-knowledge" is regarded as the consummation of metaphysics (*GW* 8:286).

This knowledge is a presupposition for the plausibility of the phenomenological concept of religion. It does not, however, make comprehensible the split that is constitutive for religion between self-consciousness and consciousness [of an object]. Hegel does not substantiate the necessity of such an externalization or divest-

46. See Schelling, *Philosophie und Religion* (*SW* 6:11–70); and *Of Human Freedom*, trans. James Gutmann (Chicago, 1936). Nothing is said here by way of comparing Hegel's approach to religion with Schelling's since these writings of Schelling no longer are of significance for the genesis and development of Hegel's philosophy of religion.

ment [*Entäusserung*] of the pure I, of moving from the pure self-consciousness of self-knowing spirit to the representation of this spirit as an object with the "significance of being the universal spirit that contains within itself all being and all actuality" (*Phen* 411, *GW* 9:364). Admittedly he gives the assurance that the shape of this object remains "perfectly transparent" to itself because in religion consciousness "is posited essentially in the determination of self-consciousness." But this only guards against relapsing into a relationship based merely on consciousness. A theory of religion that understands religion as pure self-consciousness, "which is conscious of being all truth and contains all actuality within that truth" (*Phen* 415, *GW* 9:367), would not have merely to affirm that the idea of God is tied to self-consciousness but would above all have to show the constitution of this consciousness: to use a later turn of phrase that is textually akin to the *Phenomenology*, it would have to show by virtue of what necessity there should be a renewed emergence out of the night of self-consciousness into the day of consciousness.[47] Above all it would be necessary to make clear what truth-value attaches to this object of consciousness as differentiated from self-consciousness. At the very least there is the objection that this relationship-of-consciousness [*Bewusstseinsverhältnis*[48]] is based solely on a misunderstanding of pure self-certainty—that it is perhaps a hangover from the time when this concept of religion was unknown, or that religion in principle does not correspond to its concept. Furthermore it is difficult, in terms of the traditional self-understanding of religion, to establish the speculative element of the pure self-consciousness of spirit in addition to the relationship-of-consciousness. For religious consciousness, the concept of religion as the pure self-consciousness of spirit is no less daunting

---

47. Hegel, *Einleitung in die Geschichte der Philosophie*, ed. J. Hoffmeister, 3d, abridged ed. of 1959, prepared by F. Nicolin (Hamburg, 1966), p. 61; *Introduction to the Lectures on the History of Philosophy*, trans. T. M. Knox and A. V. Miller (Oxford, 1985), p. 42. Cf. *Phen* 492, *GW* 9:433.

48. [*Tr.*] As consciousness of an object (see n. 44), consciousness entails or constitutes a relationship: it is what Hegel calls a *Bewusstseinsverhältnis*. This term, which occurs with some frequency in the following pages, we translate as "relationship-of-consciousness," using hyphens to bring out its special meaning.

a proposition than is the call for the sublation of representation in concept (as the later conceptuality has it).

The speculative concept of religion does not lay stress on doctrine but on cultus—not on the knowledge of God established in the relationship-of-consciousness but on the self-certainty of the community. At least according to the later lectures, it is Hegel's view that the moment of consciousness, the concrete representation of God, is "sublated" in the self-certainty of the community. Yet the dominant role assigned to self-consciousness in the concept of religion does not accord with the phenomenon of religion. Hegel does indeed make it a point of criticism that the community does not conceive of itself as the actual self-consciousness of the divine. Its understanding of itself corresponds rather to the relationship-of-consciousness. For this reason reconciliation appears to it as something remote in the past and future (*Phen* 478, *GW* 9:420–421). Here too eschatology is again made the prime object of attack: in it the community's misunderstanding of its own concept finds its highest expression.

This criticism is directed primarily against the Christian idea of reconciliation. It can, however, also be formulated, *mutatis mutandis,* for other religions. For the problem lies in the concept of religion itself, in the relationship between self-consciousness and self-consciousness in the form of God-consciousness. This relationship cannot be dissolved into the pure unity of the self-certainty of spirit. Nor is the conflict between the relationship-of-consciousness (the representation of God and also of reconciliation) and the self-certainty within which this relationship-of-consciousness is nonetheless "enclosed" (*Phen* 412, *GW* 9:364) resolved by the fact that God is represented as a self-consciousness. For the "represented self is not the actual self" (*Phen* 417, *GW* 9:369). Because the relationship-of-consciousness is constitutive for religion, it belongs to the concept of religion not to have consciousness of what it is in itself. What Hegel says here about the Christian community is true for religion as a whole: "it is the spiritual self-consciousness that is not an object to itself as this self-consciousness, or that does not unfold itself to a consciousness of itself" (*Phen* 477, *GW* 9:420).

His interpretation does not, to be sure, answer the obvious question as to the origin of a self-consciousness of spirit whose concept it is not to know itself but an other. Yet on the basis of the speculative concept of religion, it is clear that religion necessarily has the impression that it is not thought about adequately in speculative terms. For it belongs to the concept of religion to be the self-consciousness of spirit in the form of consciousness [of an object]. The reason that inheres in religion remains hidden from it and is visible solely to philosophy. In this lies the possibility of a philosophy of religion: religion is not to be conceived as the relation of human beings to a divine being that subsists outside them. This does not, however, as in the alternative presented by Jacobi, make human beings God. As self-consciousness of spirit, religion is the same as philosophy of religion. The sole difference between them is that in philosophy of religion self-conscious spirit itself—and not a representation—becomes the object of its consciousness. Thus there is a unique link between the possibility of philosophy of religion on the one hand, and the speculative concept of religion and of the God-idea on the other. To alter this link would entail finding new grounds for the possibility of a philosophy of religion.

The concept of religion precludes the possibility of religion's convincingly refuting the speculative interpretation. Any protest on the part of religion is deemed as expressing its own lack of an adequate consciousness of itself. The concept of religion in the *Phenomenology* is therefore not ambiguous, though it may be two-edged. It stresses the lofty status of religion, speculatively understood. Were religion, on the contrary, to be what it appears to be to religious consciousness, were the relationship-of-consciousness to be its truth, it would stand at a subordinate level and would, as religion, be quite impossible. For at the level of consciousness the concept of an object of consciousness, and perhaps of a thing, may be possible, but not an adequate concept of God. Where religious consciousness holds up the relationship-of-consciousness as an objection to speculation, one can counter it by insisting that that relationship pertains to an idea of God that is not only incorrect but obsolete.

The fact that no valid objection can be made from the side of religion does not, however, legitimate the speculative concept. The *Phenomenology* attains this concept by analyzing, not religion as such, but the spiritual history of the Enlightenment. It seeks to show the adequacy of such a concept in historical fashion. The history of religion does not display merely a static disproportion between pure self-consciousness, which religion in itself is, and the consciousness of an object, which is the way it understands itself. The dynamic of its history resides in the harmonization of the consciousness and the self-consciousness of spirit, to the point where "the shape in which it appears for its consciousness will be perfectly harmonious with its essence, and it will behold itself as it is" (*Phen* 414, *GW* 9:366). This interpretation of the history of religion does indeed support the speculative interpretation—even if the tension is not completely resolved and the relationship-of-consciousness never completely overcome in religion. The consummation of the history of religion and the actuality of absolute spirit are attained when the truth of spirit becomes identical with the certainty of itself (*Phen* 415, *GW* 9:368)—when the self "beholds the determination of the object as its *own,* consequently beholds *itself* in the object" (*Phen* 417, *GW* 9:369). But even the Christian religion does not take the relationship-of-consciousness in its entirety back into pure self-consciousness: the self does not behold itself as itself, and reconciliation remains something represented.

But that religion should have any history at all is not comprehensible solely from the split between consciousness and self-consciousness. The mediation between them is not the sole paradigm in the history of religion. Not only the consciousness but also the existence of spirit is distinct from its self-consciousness, because "in religion the determination of the consciousness proper to spirit does not have the form of free otherness" (*Phen* 412, *GW* 9:364). The shapes that precede religion constitute "spirit as it has come to exist [*daseyender Geist*]," which is "their totality, *taken together,*" whereas religion is "their *simple* totality or absolute self." From this point of view "the perfection of religion consists in the two becoming identical with each other: not only that religion concerns itself with spirit's actuality but, conversely, that spirit, as self-conscious spirit, becomes actual to itself and an object of its consciousness" (*Phen* 412, *GW* 9:365). But it is only when it frees itself from its representational objects [*Vorstellungen*] that it can, as self-conscious, become an object to itself—and this happens in philosophy.

On the basis of the second paradigm Hegel seeks to understand why there should be any such thing as a history of religion. Only the whole of spirit is in time: only its shapes have displayed themselves "in a temporal succession; for only the whole has true actuality and therefore the form of pure freedom in the face of an other, a form that expresses itself as time" (*Phen* 413, *GW* 9:365). And the individual shapes of the moments of spirit also differentiate themselves in time. Yet all that is plausible to immediate observation is that the moments of spirit—consciousness, self-consciousness, reason, and immediate spirit—have no history. Why nonetheless both the individual shapes and the whole of spirit have a history does not become sufficiently clear. It is not until the chapter on absolute knowing that Hegel adds a fuller justification (*Phen* 487 ff., *GW* 9:429 ff.). Spirit is in time as long as it has not grasped its concept. This gives rise to the tendency to transfer more and more of the contents of consciousness into the form of spirit's self-knowledge—a movement away from the immediacy of the contents of consciousness to the actualization of the self-certainty that is implicitly present. This argument justifies not only mere being-in-time, which indeed applies no less to nature, but also the dynamic of history: spirit is the process of becoming what it implicitly is. Behind this idea lies the old argument, dating back two thousand years, for the necessity of a historical development of spirit—the argument that perfection cannot be immediately actual, cannot stand at the beginning of a process, because then it would not be brought about by freedom, which nonetheless is an indispensable component of perfection. But even this somewhat more precise indication of the reasons for the historicality of spirit provides no adequate determinacy. It presupposes a theory concerning the connection between spirit and time that is not developed in the *Phenomenology* and would indeed be systematically out of place there. Possibly the first series of lectures on the history of philosophy, which were delivered shortly before, in 1805, but have not been preserved, had more to say about the relationship of spirit and history. Nonetheless the *Phenomenology* confines itself to elaborating the history of religion itself and not the conditions for a history of spirit in general and of religion in particular.

(3) Unlike the 1805–6 philosophy of spirit, the *Phenomenology* contains no separate treatment of the concept of religion. It outlines the philosophy of religion exclusively as history of religion, and indeed in a way different from both the later philosophy-of-religion lectures and the earlier natural law lecture notes. The natural law notes understand Christianity, in the wake of Greek mythology and the Roman desacralization of the world, as opening the way to the reconstruction of undifferentiated harmony, while the Berlin lectures distinguish a history of religion, which is normally structured triadically, from the consummate religion. By contrast the *Phenomenology* distinguishes between nature religion, Greek mythology, and revelatory religion. True, the Roman world forms a transition to Christianity, but more in the context of the history of actual spirit—especially because of its concept of person, but also because it assembles the gods in a pantheon, which is then replaced by the true pantheon of the Christian religion. And the principle determining the structure of the history of religion lies in the dialectic of consciousness and self-consciousness[49]—not in the gradual taking-back of the object of consciousness into the self, but in the transition from the epoch of consciousness to that of self-consciousness and to the unity of the two modes of consciousness, in which, however, the element of "shapedness" [*Gestalthaftigkeit*] continues to be operative. This necessitates spirit's ultimate passing beyond religion.[50]

49. Günter Wohlfart, *Der spekulative Satz* (Berlin and New York, 1981), interprets the *Phenomenology's* conception of the history of religion in terms of the model of the speculative proposition (see *Phen* 454, *GW* 9:400). The two models here coincide because in the proposition, "The absolute being is the self," it is in fact the relationship of consciousness and self-consciousness with which Hegel is concerned.

50. [*Tr.*] Just as religious knowledge is necessarily representational, in Hegel's view, so also religious practices necessarily appear in historically determinate shapes, including Christianity as the "consummate" or "revelatory" shape of religion. Spirit *appears* only in shapes of consciousness (*Gestalten des Bewusstseins*) and shapes of

While Hegel's method here is different from what it will be in the Berlin lectures, the results he arrives at are similar. Let us therefore already at this point indicate a number of objections. Although Hegel knows about the inner history of the individual religions, he pays no attention to it and expresses the view that the character of each can be defined "by the particular unity of consciousness and self-consciousness [in that religion]" (*Phen* 418, *GW* 9:370). It is only the abstract, the living, and the spiritual work of art that could be interpreted as historical stages of the religion of art. Moreover, the absence of a historical development is concealed by the choice and arrangement of religiohistorical types, these being guided by what it is desired to demonstrate. Unless the existence of a historical connection linking the individual religions to the unity of religious history could be established, even a chronologically accurate ordering of the types would, however, remain of no account. For unless the higher forms of religion can be interpreted as resulting from a process of development, their emergence remains a matter of chance. The typologization is here carried out in an even more comprehensive and rigid fashion than later, so much so that in the case of the nature religions the historical references are partly concealed, partly lost altogether.

(4) These references are lost in the section portraying "plant and animal" religion (*Phen* 420–421, *GW* 9:372–373). Its inclusion is doubtless due in particular to the methodological constraint Hegel imposed on himself, namely the decision to model the structure of the sphere of nature religion on the first three chapters of the *Phenomenology*—sense certainty, perception, and understanding—without giving consideration to the conditions of applicability of this model. Attempts to identify these "religions" historically have so far remained tentative. In the case of the "artificer" (*Phen* 421–424, *GW* 9:373–375) the references are clear, even if surely only

---

a world (*Gestalten einer Welt*) (*Phen* 265, *GW* 9:240). Everything historical is "shaped" or "configured," and the *Gestalthaftigkeit* of *Geist* is overcome, so Hegel claims, only in the absolute self-knowing of philosophy, which in the strict sense lies beyond a "phenomenology" of spirit, which is the science of spirit in its *appearing*.

one aspect of Egyptian culture is encompassed. But insufficient light is thrown on what lies behind this talk of the "artificer" [*Werkmeister*]. The word can be found several times in the Old Testament, but without express reference to the monuments of Egypt. The "artificer" does, however, occur in Novalis's *Lehrlinge zu Sais* ("The Acolytes of Sais"). The reference there is to old tales and poems in which "human beings, gods, and animals" appear "as artificers in common." An allusion to Egypt is provided by the title and theme of the poem.[51] Seen from this point of view, the "artificer" reveals behind him the figure of the *archaeus*—in all probability not only the figure personified by Helmont and Novalis as *archaeus faber*, to whose workshop reference is made in the paralipomena to the *Lehrlinge zu Sais*, but the *archaeus* as *anima mundi* and "vital principle" in general.[52] This is borne out by Hegel's mention that the artificer's mode of operating is "instinctive" (*Phen* 421, *GW* 9:373).

(5) The background to the expression "luminous being" [*Lichtwesen*][53] (*Phen* 418–420, *GW* 9:370–372) is still obscure. Hegel could have taken it from Schelling's philosophy of nature—for example, from his *Von der Weltseele*.[54] But the references to "luminous being" occur there in quite a different context. In the case of this first shape of nature religion, however, the historical references seem ambiguous. Hegel's mention of the "luminous being" has been taken as evidence that, in the debate then under way among the romantics as to whether the pure origin of all history was to be found in India or Iran, Hegel came down on the side of the "Iranists"—even if the earlier materials from the Jena period

51. See Novalis, *Schriften* 1:83.
52. Ibid., p. 111. See the explanation of the editor, p. 78. [*Tr.*: According to the sixteenth-century Paracelsians, the *archeus* was the vital principle that directs and maintains the growth and preservation of living beings.]
53. [*Tr.*] This term has been translated variously in *Phen* and *LPR* as "light-essence," "essential light," "God as light," and simply "light." Since what Hegel intends is a living divine being whose essence is that of pure light, the best translation is the one suggested to us by the author, namely, "luminous being."
54. *SW* 2:368 ff. Schelling refers, e.g., on p. 368 to "that omnipresent luminous being in which the totality of things is dissolved," "the Jupiter with which everything is filled." "Luminous being" functions as the counter-concept to "heaviness."

do not mention the religion of ancient Iran. For example, the natural-law lectures take the classical mythology of Greece as marking the beginning of history, while the fragments of 1803 and the philosophy of spirit of 1805–6 give classical mythology a predecessor in the form of the archaic religion of Greece. The *Phenomenology*, on the contrary, for the first time broadens the history of religion to include the oriental religions, and this change remains permanent. The first series of Berlin lectures also seems to adhere to starting with Iran.[55] But the identification of the religion of the "luminous being" with that of Iran needs to be scrutinized. This necessitates comparison of the *Phenomenology* with the analogous texts that stand closest to it in time. In the absence of any other Jena materials for the purpose, the texts that come closest in time are the Berlin lectures, in particular the 1821 and 1824 series. From them it becomes clear that another interpretation is the correct one.[56]

The view that Hegel's 1821 lecture manuscript regards the history of religion as beginning with Iranian religion is untenable.[57] To be sure, the manuscript does refer in passing to several of the nature religions that are later presented in a more differentiated way, but it does not treat them historically.[58] This would still be no argument against the accuracy of the identification in the *Phenomenology*—if the latter contained conclusive pointers to Iranian religion. But the sole evidence in favor of an Iranian interpretation

55. See Ernst Schulin, *Die weltgeschichtliche Erfassung des Orients bei Hegel und Ranke* (Göttingen, 1958), pp. 29, 35. On the *Phenomenology of Spirit*, see Thomas Vance Yates, "Hegel and the Natural Religion of Modern Philosophy" (Diss., Freiburg, 1975).

56. For the following, see *LPR* 2:124–125, 134 ff. (the lecture manuscript of 1821); and *LPR* 2:423 ff. (the lectures of 1824). Hegel's allusions to biblical texts are identified in the footnotes to *LPR* 2 and the annotations to *V* 4, and are not repeated here.

57. This view goes back to G. Lasson's edition of the *Vorlesungen über die Philosophie der Religion*, 4 parts in 2 vols. (Leipzig, 1925–1929; reprint, Hamburg, 1966), part 2/1, *Die Naturreligion*, pp. 237–238.

58. See *LPR* 2:104–109. Section "b. Concrete Representation," where the various nature religions are discussed in their historical concreteness, does not treat the religion of Iran. Scattered references occur for the first time in the section on the cultus (*LPR* 2:114 ff.), but these do not amount to a discussion of Iranian religion.

would be the one occasion where Hegel contrasts light and darkness by saying that the otherness of light is "the equally simple negative, darkness" (*Phen* 419, *GW* 9:371). Moreover, there is no trace here of the central concept for the later portrayal of the religion of Iran, the concept of the good, nor of the other elements included in the subsequent portrayals.

The theme of "lordship and power" and the actual metaphors used in regard to light are apt subjects for comparison. Spirit beholds itself in the form of being that is filled with spirit; this includes "the form of lord and master over against the self-consciousness of spirit that retreats from its object" (*Phen* 419, *GW* 9:371). This theme is lacking from Hegel's later conception of the religion of Iran. It is, however, bound up with the religion of Israel. There it is even central (*LPR* 2:124 ff.), as it is in the following three lecture series.

The relation of "luminous being" to the world is not, however, defined by Hegel solely as lordship. The *Phenomenology* also speaks of "creations" (*Phen* 419, *GW* 9:371). It is said of natural things that they are only attributes of substance, without "self-substance" and remaining "merely names of the many-named One." This One is "clothed with the manifold powers of existence and with the shapes of actuality as with an adornment that lacks a self"; "they are merely messengers, having no will of their own, messengers of its might, visions of its glory, voices in its praise" (*Phen* 419–420, *GW* 9:371). This is repeated in the philosophy-of-religion lecture manuscript—but with reference to the God of Israel: "Natural things are only attributes, accidentals, its adornment, its servants and messengers" (*LPR* 2:136). Still another factor points to the religion of Israel, namely the reference to "sublimity" (*Phen* 419, *GW* 9:371). Indeed, the later title for Jewish religion is "religion of sublimity." Subsequently Hegel does, to be sure, draw an explicit distinction between the sublimity of the measureless with its ridiculous distortions and grotesque exaggerations, and "true" sublimity, or elevation above nature and above the world so that the latter is represented as swallowed up in power (*LPR* 2:136). In the *Phenomenology* the two forms that are later distinguished are still linked together: the sublimity of thought moves aimlessly about in nature and "enlarges its bounds to the measureless, and its beauty, heightened to splendor [*Pracht*], is dissolved in its sublimity." The manuscript too speaks of splendor or excellency in this connection—the "excellency [*Pracht*] of the beasts" (*LPR* 2:140)—and also of the fact that this excellency does not suffice to comprehend the essence of God. For God is the abstract substance of nature, which cannot be adequately defined by the beauty, heightened to splendor, of the forms of nature (*LPR* 2:142). While according to the *Phenomenology* the beauty heightened to splendor is dissolved in sublimity, the manuscript notes laconically, as if this slogan were all that Hegel wished to retain from the *Phenomenology* for the lectures: "To sublimity [belongs all] pomp" (*LPR* 2:136). This encapsulates in the barest terms the idea developed in the *Phenomenology*. The concurrence between the religion of "luminous being" and Jewish religion as treated in the manuscript can thus be traced in several cases down to the actual wording. By contrast, the subsequent portrayal of the religion of Iran offers no analogies of any kind.

It seems to be otherwise as far as Hegel's use of the metaphor of light is concerned. Undoubtedly the religion of Iran is for him, even if only secondarily, the religion of light. And the *Phenomenology* speaks of light in a variety of ways—not only of "luminous being" but also of darkness as the otherness of light. It describes the creations of light as "torrents of light" and also "streams of fire destructive of structured form" (*Phen* 419, *GW* 9:371). This in itself, however, does not guarantee that the use of the metaphor of light in the *Phenomenology* relates to Iran; for "light" is one of the outstanding characteristics of the God of Israel (*LPR* 2:136, 433). In the *Phenomenology*, God's luminosity is coupled with his shapelessness. Thanks to the "shape of shapelessness," the simple relation of spirit to itself is "the luminous being . . . which preserves itself in its formless substantiality" (*Phen* 419, *GW* 9:371). The lectures, too, stress that the God of Israel is "shapeless" (*LPR* 2:424, 671). Admittedly the 1824 lectures specify that, in virtue of the shapelessness of the God of Israel, nothing particular is worthy of him—not even the attribute of light that pertains to nature religion (*LPR* 2:426). But this does not belie the luminosity of the Old Testament God because luminosity is not a natural attribute in the sense of nature religion. This is why here too Hegel still stresses the characteristic of light. Following in the wake of Herder,[59] he establishes a link between the creation of light at the beginning of Genesis and Psalm 104:2: "Thou coverest thyself with light as with a garment." The shapeless being clad with the garment of light is none other than the "luminous being." Its creative activity, too, is expressed by reference to light. Thus the *Phenomenology* speaks of "torrents of light," while in the 1824 lectures we are told that God creates by his word: let there be a mere breath, and "this breath [of God] is here light as well, the world of light, the infinite outpouring of light" (*LPR* 2:433).

Thus an impressive weight of evidence speaks in favor of the view that by the term "luminous being" the *Phenomenology* is speaking of the God of Israel. "Luminous being" is the cipher not for Ormazd but for the shapeless shape, veiled in the garment of light, of the God of the Old Testament. Apart from the *Phenomenology*, however, this understanding of the religion of Israel is confined to the Berlin manuscript and the 1824 lectures. In the later lectures, use of the light metaphor recedes wholly into the background. The other two aspects, however, the shapelessness of God and his lordship, remain determinative later as well. They are supplemented and dominated, at least in the 1827 lectures, by the concept of purpose. It is therefore only by separating out the four lecture series that a full picture can be obtained of the meaning of the light terminology in the first two series and, with it, of the concordance that exists with the *Phenomenology*.

Conversely, the arguments in favor of the Iranian interpretation remain weak. Even in the manuscript the religion of Iran is mentioned only in passing, in the course of portraying the cultus of the religion of nature. Moreover, there is in the *Phenomenology* no trace of the elements that characterize the content of Iranian religion in the three later lecture series—not even the central concept of the good. Indeed, it is only in a secondary sense that the religion

59. See Johann Gottfried Herder, *Aelteste Urkunde des Menschengeschlechts* (1774–1776), in *Sämtliche Werke*, ed. B. Suphan, vol. 6 (Berlin, 1883), pp. 219–220.

of Iran is for Hegel the religion of light. Apart from the lack of analogies between Iranian religion and that of the "luminous being," there is a further piece of evidence for the view that the *Phenomenology* is not speaking of the religion of Iran. Characteristic for the latter is the struggle between the powers of light and darkness. But of this there is no word in the *Phenomenology*. For the darkness it designates as the "otherness" of light does not stand opposed to light as a hostile power: the otherness of light is the sphere of its externalization, its creation by means of "torrents of light." These come about "in the *unresisting* element of its otherness" (*Phen* 419, *GW* 9:371, emphasis ours). Light and darkness are therefore understood not in the sense of Iranian dualism but in that of the beginning of Genesis. The light is separated from the darkness, and the darkness—contrary to the light, which is located in the firmament of heaven (Gen. 1:14)—has its place in the earthly world, into which the light is poured out. Thus the portrayal of the "luminous being" is quite unrelated to Iranian religion. It concerns solely the religion of Israel, even if surely only one special aspect of it.[60]

The section on the "luminous being" thus solves a problem that weighed upon Hegel's religiohistorical conception since the early Jena years, namely the difficulty of finding a locus and a systematic role for Old Testament religion. Schelling's conception in terms of identity philosophy bypasses Israel. Hegel's natural-law lecture notes assign to the religions of Israel and Rome a place at the break between classical mythology and the reconstruction of undifferentiated harmony. After the collapse of this conception (itself still mythical) of the history of religion, there is again no place for the religion of Israel, and the 1805–6 philosophy of spirit passes over it in silence. The *Phenomenology*, on the contrary, places it at the beginning of religious history. Viewed chronologically this is not inappropriate, especially since under the heading "artificer" it is only more recent strata of Egyptian religion that are addressed. The

60. Suppositions in this direction have previously been voiced by David Friedrich Strauss (see Jörg F. Sandberger, *D. F. Strauss als theologischer Hegelianer* [Göttingen, 1972], pp. 166–168, 178–180), and also by Emil L. Fackenheim, *The Religious Dimension in Hegel's Thought* (Bloomington, Ind., 1967), p. 250.

pride of place now assigned to Judaism does, however, result in its being placed among the religions of nature. As will be shown later (p. 275) in another context, this is for Hegel in no way inconceivable.

(6) At least since the *Fragment of a System* of 1800, Hegel has viewed Christianity as the irreversible concluding stage in the history of religion. The natural-law lectures too discuss at length the place in world history occupied by Christianity and the confessional forms in which it appears. While the incorporation of religion into ethical life does not directly affect the treatment of the historical religions, one gains the impression that it continues to reflect the religion of the *polis*. Just for this reason Hegel rejects this conception as unsuited to the modern world. The 1805–6 philosophy of spirit again sees the crown and consummation of religious history in Christianity as the "absolute religion"; and the standpoint of the *Phenomenology* is very similar, even if it speaks of the Christian religion primarily as the "revelatory religion." It is "revelatory," not because it is revealed,[61] but because the object of consciousness "essentially and directly has the shape of self-consciousness" (*Phen* 459, *GW* 9:405). The process that leads to this stage is described by Hegel as the externalization or divestment [*Entäusserung*] of substance, its growth into self-consciousness, and the externalization or divestment of self-consciousness, its growth into the universal self (*Phen* 457, *GW* 9:403).

More clearly than in the later lectures, the religiohistorical conception of the *Phenomenology* is that of an incarnation of God in human form. Hegel accordingly links the unfolding of the content of the revelatory religion to the shape of the incarnate God, the very shape in which spirit recognizes the absolute being to be a self-consciousness. For self-consciousness is only the God who "is sensuously and directly beheld as a self, as an actual individual human being" (*Phen* 459, *GW* 9:405). So the history of religion leads up to the christological idea that has been central ever since the *Early*

---

61. [*Tr.*] Unfortunately the English translations of the *Phenomenology of Spirit* have blurred this distinction by translating *offenbar* ("revelatory") as though it were *geoffenbart* ("revealed").

Theological Writings,[62] namely that "the divine nature is the same as the human, and it is this unity that is beheld [*angeschaut*]" (*Phen* 460, *GW* 9:406).

Already in the *Early Theological Writings* this christology stands in the context of an ontology. And as in the 1805–6 philosophy of spirit (*GW* 8:280), Hegel passes over directly from this definition of the content of the revelatory religion to the conceptualization of this idea. The absolute being is "a subsisting object" [*seyender Gegenstand*], but it "likewise immediately has the significance of pure thought." It is known as thought and likewise as a subsisting self-consciousness. This identity of thought and being is in fact what self-consciousness is; "or the *thought* unity has at the same time this [subsistent] shape of what it is" (*Phen* 461, *GW* 9:406).[63] It is only by this insight that the idea of the revelatory nature of God and of the "spirit that knows itself as spirit" is attainable. And because Hegel sees this idea as the central point of Christianity, he is consistent in denoting the "knowledge of the revelatory religion" as "speculative knowledge" (*Phen* 461, *GW* 9:407). The idea of the identity of thought and being is thus attained otherwise than in the ontological proof. What this proof undertakes to demonstrate—the identity of thought and being—is regarded as already actualized in Christianity and as having entered into actual self-consciousness: the absolute being is beheld as immediately existing self-consciousness and only so is it known as spirit (*Phen* 460, *GW* 9:407).

For all its apparent completeness, this concept of the self-consciousness of spirit is, however, once again restricted by the discussion that follows. Hegel distinguishes three stages of revelatory being: sensible intuition, representation, and the self-consciousness of the community (*Phen* 461–463, *GW* 9:407–408). He links these stages with the three elements of pure thought, representation, and self-consciousness (*Phen* 464, *GW* 9:409), which already herald the

---

62. See *ETW* 176, *J* 146; also *GW* 8:280. See above, pp. 121–122, 184.

63. [*Tr.*] "oder die *gedachte* Einheit hat zugleich diese Gestalt dessen, was sie ist." The Miller translation adds the word "existential" in brackets, but "subsistent" (*seiende*) or "existent" (*daseiende*) would seem more suitable if a term is to be added at all.

later articulation of the "Consummate Religion." The way in which they are elaborated will have therefore to be considered in the context of the Berlin lectures. But even in the third element the representational structure is not totally dissolved. The implicitly available unity of consciousness and self-consciousness does not, therefore, yet exist for the community, although it is the community's concept to actualize this unity.

The fact that the interpretation of the Christian religion in many ways heralds the content and the architectonics of the later lectures indicates that the emergent phase of the philosophy of religion must be regarded as completed. In the *Phenomenology* the plan adumbrated in the fragment *Die Idee des absoluten Wesens* takes concrete shape: in the philosophy of religion (and of art) spirit takes itself back into itself, returns to the pure idea, and provides an organon for intuiting God. The systematic conditions for such a return are undoubtedly radically changed, which is why Hegel now no longer speaks of "intuition" but of spirit's knowing itself as absolute spirit.

During his time in Jena, Hegel not only raises his system from the pregnant but still ill-developed formulae of the *Introductio* lectures to the argumentative heights of the *Phenomenology*. In the course of this development he also attains an affirmative relationship to Christianity. The natural-law lectures, while they see in Christianity the conclusion of the history of religion, for that very reason still see the need to transcend at least the traditionally confessional forms in which it appears. By contrast, the 1805–6 philosophy of spirit, and to a still greater extent the *Phenomenology*, find metaphysical aspects in Christian dogma. From the viewpoint of the metaphysical and at the same time historical significance of Christianity for the shaping of the modern world, Christianity acquires added interest for Hegel's philosophy. The fact that the exposition of the main features of his philosophical system was contemporaneous with the adoption of an affirmative attitude toward Christianity is not, therefore, merely a chance coincidence. But the question whether Christian dogma also plays a determining role for Hegel in elaborating his systematic positions must be answered in the negative, at least with the source material currently available. Measured by the overall development of the system, the sections dealing with the theory of religion occupy a fairly modest space, however important they may be in their different ways for concluding the system. And as for the question of priority, it is as Hegel later expresses it: one must already have the concept in order to discover its determinations in actuality—in order to be able to read the hieroglyphics of reason in religion too.

CHAPTER III

THE FOUNDATION AND DEVELOPMENT OF THE SPECULATIVE PHILOSOPHY OF RELIGION IN HEGEL'S BERLIN LECTURES

1. Preliminary Questions of Interpretation

(1) In a letter to Immanuel Niethammer dated 20 May 1808, Hegel says that in Jena he had "hardly laid the foundation" for the logic (*L* 175, *Br* 1:230). This phrase could likewise indicate the status of his work on the philosophy of religion. On this topic too no more had been done in Jena than to lay its foundation by liberating religion from a context that was inappropriate to it and defining it as the self-cognition of absolute spirit, the nature of which was explicated primarily in the metaphysics. But that is not to say that the philosophy of religion had thereby assumed systematic form. The concurrences between the *Phenomenology* and the Berlin lectures concern only the part treating the Christian religion (important though that is) and the decision in principle to accord to the history of religion a major influence on the systematic form of the philosophy of religion.

Hegel did not, however, make use of the years in Bamberg and Nuremberg, as he did for the *Logic*, to elaborate the philosophy of religion. The few relevant texts from this period point to a standstill in the development of the philosophy of religion rather than progress. The only evidence that he continued to work on the philosophy of religion comes from the chapter on religion in the Heidelberg *Encyclopedia* and the related *Notizen zum absoluten Geist* a decade after publication of the *Phenomenology*. Their subject matter, however, is too limited for these texts to throw any light on the systematic form of the philosophy of religion. This emerges clearly only from the Berlin lectures of 1821, 1824, 1827, and 1831. They for the first time develop the philosophy of religion of the system in the full sense—that is, both at the level of the system and in a form of argumentation corresponding to it. In the sense of being at the level of the system, the "philosophy of religion of the system" includes, in addition to the lectures, the chapter on religion in the three versions of the *Encyclopedia* and a few occasional writings; in the sense of having an appropriate form of argumentation, it includes only the lectures.

(2) But even the "philosophy of religion of the system" is not all of one piece—not even the portrayal of the Christian religion. This can be seen by examining the three editions of the *Encyclopedia* and the four series of lectures. The conception underlying the lectures seems opposed to that expressed in the *Encyclopedia*. Which version is authoritative appears to be an easy matter to decide in view of the differing status of the two groups, since texts published by an author generally take precedence over material published posthumously and more especially from transcripts—although the *Early Theological Writings* are a prime instance of this rule being honored more in the breach than in the observance. It appears especially plausible to give primacy to the printed texts in this case because we are not basically concerned with the conflict between published works and posthumous material but between published works and auditors' transcripts or notebooks [*Nachschriften*], which can hardly be regarded as possessing the same authenticity as manuscripts found among the author's effects. But only on two conditions would printed material enjoy a wholesale priority over transcripts: they must represent an identical stage of development, and the subject matter must coincide. Neither of these conditions is fulfilled here, however. The most detailed published material on the philosophy of religion—Chapter VII of the *Phenomenology*—belongs to another stage of development than that of the Berlin lectures. As is well known, Hegel later modifies both the concept of religion and the way he conceives history. Moreover the argument that the lectures supposedly merit less confidence owing to their lesser degree of authenticity is not valid, at least not any longer. For purposes of exact wording, works from

the same period of development that were published by the author doubtless enjoy precedence. But this is not equally so for the overall conception of the lectures. To the extent that the conception is attested by several independent witnesses, no less certainty attaches to it than to that of a single published work or posthumous fragment. This is assuredly only true of the new edition of the lectures, which for the first time affords an insight into the conception underlying each series. It must be added, however, without prejudice to this gain in authenticity, that the lectures are not as finished a product, intellectually speaking, as would be a published work on philosophy of religion from Hegel's own pen.

By contrast, the chapters dealing with religion in the three versions of the *Encyclopedia* belong to the same developmental stage as the lectures. Indisputably they must be accorded a high rank, especially as there are only minor divergences between the three versions. This unchanged character, however, is not the result of the lectures giving a less authoritative picture (one presented perchance solely as a pedagogical exercise) but is due to the fact that the version in the *Encyclopedia* offers only a section of the overall conception of the philosophy of religion. Moreover it adheres to such a high degree of abstractness that it is little affected by the system's subsequent development. Only if the version in the *Encyclopedia* as well as the lectures encompassed the entire philosophy of religion—albeit in differing form—could authenticity be made the basis for deciding between them. But this is not the case. It is not only by comparison with the lectures that the presentation in the *Encyclopedia* is exceedingly compressed. Although Hegel portrays the philosophy of right in a relatively detailed way in the *Grundlinien der Philosophie des Rechts,* he devotes seventy paragraphs of the *Encyclopedia* to it but only eleven to the philosophy of religion—whereas the lectures on the philosophy of religion are much longer than those on the philosophy of right. Even so it would be possible for the *Encyclopedia* to contain the whole of the philosophy of religion in outline. Yet it offers only a small section of the subject matter of the lectures, a section, moreover, whose place within the system can be identified only by comparison with the philosophy-of-religion manuscript. It is therefore only the manuscript that makes comprehensible the basic scheme of presentation adopted in the *Encyclopedia,* although certainly not that of the philosophy of absolute spirit as a whole. It is accordingly the lectures that have priority—not on the grounds of greater authenticity or authoritative presentation, but because they for the first time make it possible to determine the place of the *Encyclopedia*'s chapter on religion within the whole of the philosophy of religion. For purposes of interpretation it is not, therefore, a matter of discretion what use to make of the lectures. They are also indispensable if one seeks to determine the content intended in the *Encyclopedia* text. Only a reference to the lectures holds in check the otherwise free play of associations. To aid interpretation, recourse is often had to elements from other parts of the Hegelian corpus which are here out of place. Furthermore the lectures are in fact used to elucidate the text of the *Encyclopedia* even where such elucidation is rejected on the basis of methodological considerations. For the majority of problems cannot be resolved, cannot even be formulated, using the form of presentation in the *Encyclopedia.* Use of the lectures to interpret the *Encyclopedia* remains uncritical, however, unless one is clear about their conception and the changes in the definition of individual concepts.

(3) Reference to the lectures does indeed allow the question as to which version is authoritative to come up again in altered form, namely as a choice between Hegel's lecture manuscript and the transcripts or notebooks of his students. And the answer is similar to what it was before, namely that the greater authenticity of the manuscript applies only to the wording, not to the underlying conception insofar as this conception evolves in the course of time. Research has now reached the stage of being able and indeed having to take account not only of the primary differences that separate the lectures from the early theological writings and the Jena drafts, but also of the distinction between the four series of lectures given in Berlin, which differ considerably in approach and execution. Developmental analysis also promotes systematic understanding, if only because it excludes a series of false problems and makes it possible to see the individual conceptions in their specific form. Especially for the first and second parts of the lectures, the later series

furnish evidence both of a more mature conception and of a greater wealth of material. The same does not apply, however, to the third part, for which the *Phenomenology* paved the way.

(4) There is another reason why the question is posed falsely by asking in wholesale fashion whether the lectures or the *Encyclopedia* are the more authoritative. For, apart from the broad tripartite division between concept, history, and actualized concept, the lectures do not display any uniformity of conception. For the "Consummate Religion"—and it is only here that the lectures and the *Encyclopedia* can be compared at all—the essential difference is between the manuscript and the text of the *Encyclopedia* on the one hand and the later lectures on the other. Here as in other aspects the answer to the question as to the authoritative structure of the philosophy of religion presupposes an analysis of its successive conceptions, and this is made possible only by the new edition of the philosophy-of-religion lectures (unless one were to go back to the sources themselves). On the basis of the previous editions, it was impossible even to pose the question which conception is authoritative. Yet a developmental analysis of the "Consummate Religion" shows that a developmental interpretation is quite inappropriate as a means of explaining the difference between the *Encyclopedia* and the subsequent lectures. Our prime purpose in referring here to these involved relationships has only been to challenge the supposed superiority of the *Encyclopedia* version and to emphasize the indispensability of the lectures.

(5) It is not our intention in what follows to undertake any overall presentation or commentary on the philosophy of religion of the system. Our aim is merely to inquire into the ground of its claim to conceive religion as self-consciousness of the absolute. This claim embraces on the one hand the relationship of philosophy of religion to metaphysical logic, and on the other the place it occupies as an independent discipline in the framework of the philosophy of spirit. Here too the distinctive character of Hegel's conception of his system and the methodological concept it entails rules out any prior decision on these problems. The foundation of the philosophy of religion becomes clear only from the way it is constructed, not by means of a prior epistemological critique. But if it is only the actual

execution of the lectures that can demonstrate the possibility of the philosophy of religion, then it follows, in the first place, that the philosophy of religion in its entirety has to be studied from this point of view, and, in the second place, that the lectures have to be studied in the totality of their four forms. For these drafts do not constitute mere variations that one can take or leave as one chooses. They are the result of an ever-renewed, if perhaps not ever more appropriate, grounding of the speculative philosophy of religion. To modify Hegel's remark about Schelling, it might be said that Hegel constructed his philosophy of religion before the ears of his audience.

The following interpretation does not argue for a wholesale, revolutionary alteration in Hegel's understanding of religion, such as a sweeping reevaluation of the relationship of philosophy and religion or a new attitude on Hegel's part toward Christianity—in other words his conversion from right- to left-Hegelianism or vice versa. If one seeks to determine the *fabula docet* from the lectures in this abstract fashion, they do indeed appear a unity. The view that they supposedly afford no evidence of any (or at least any major) development is then only a logical result of the question's having been falsely posed. What we must do, however, is not merely to trace the history of single concepts or show the differing approaches to be self-legitimating variations on a theme. Rather, the four lecture series have to be interpreted as four different approaches to the task of demonstrating that philosophy of religion— to use a Kantian formulation—is possible as a science.

Our interpretation is consequently confined to an analysis of those developmental differences that affect the systematic form of the lectures. This form is of surpassing importance for the demonstrative force of Hegel's philosophy. There are few philosophies for which this is equally true. Hegel is well aware of this, and he therefore works on this form from series to series. Its particular significance derives from the way in which he conceives the method his philosophy is to adopt, namely, its claim to explicate the content in a frame of reference furnished in advance by the concept. Admittedly this claim cannot be formulated for those parts of the system devoted to the philosophies of nature and spirit in the same way that it can be, for example, for the *Logic*. Yet the philosophy of religion develops its subject matter according to the necessity that is immanent within this subject—even if it is subsequently coupled with references to matters of history and geography. Only in such fashion can the expositions offered by the philosophies of nature and spirit lay claim, in Hegel's eyes, to truth. The shape of the philosophy of religion is therefore relevant to the question whether it fulfills the task that falls to it within the context of the system, that of recovering the concept of God for theoretical philosophy. Unquestionably this task does not fall to the philosophy of religion alone. The entire system is dedicated to it; the system is the explication of God, and nothing else. It is for this very reason that the philosophy of religion, as the final discipline of the system, enjoys so preeminent a rank. It must give evidence that such an explication was the constant concern of the preceding disciplines as well, and it must demonstrate within itself the unity of theology and philosophy of religion—namely, that a philosophical theology is possible only as philosophy of religion, and conversely that the philosophy of religion is possible only as philosophical theology. Over and beyond all questions as to its concordance with Christianity, the central problem of the philosophy of religion is therefore whether its systematic form is such as to enable this claim to appear justified. Unless the differences between the lecture series throw light on this question, a historical, developmental analysis will have only marginal importance. But the converse is also true: any interpretation is inadequate unless it takes this developmental character into account. It cannot be disregarded as something merely historical.

A historical analysis does, however, involve risks. These are comparable to those that arise in the relationship between philosophy and history in general. How can philosophy claim to explicate the truth when it has a history made up of countless systems that agree solely in the claim of each to be true? And how can the systematic form of the Hegelian philosophy vouch for the truth of its results and yet change from one lecture series to another? Undoubtedly the truth-claim of this system is jeopardized if one assumes a history of development in the strict sense. When they came to edit the lectures, Hegel's pupils had good reason to reject the developmental perspective as incompatible with the claim to truth. Such considerations demand an at least negative consensus as to the systematic character of the philosophy of religion. This character might be seen in terms of a direct correspondence to the discipline that is rightly regarded as the absolute basis of the system, namely the logic. The development of the philosophy of religion, like that of the *Phenomenology*, would then be linked to the development of the logic: if its shapes correspond to logical categories, then a change in the conception of logic must entail a change on their part too. In view of the fact that it was elaborated at a late date, however, long after completion of the *Logic*, no such development can be assumed to have occurred for the philosophy of religion. But this does not mean that it did not develop at all. This would be the case only if the systematic character of philosophy of religion consisted in its being strictly modeled on detailed logical structures. Any attempt to show the consistency of Hegel's arguments in the philosophy of religion by matching them with specific forms of judgment or inference is doomed to failure. Even if such correspondences could be shown to exist in a few places, this would be of significance in assessing the philosophy of religion only if it could be shown why a specific passage has one particular logical structure rather than another.

By disentangling several strands of reasoning in Hegel's philosophy of religion, developmental analysis throws light on hitherto unresolved problems. To this extent it may appear to run counter to the demonstration of the unity of philosophical and theological reasoning. Once such differences are spelled out, they can no longer be disregarded. But this is not mandatory. For it is, in any event, not the sometimes rather indiscriminate amplification of traditional contents that makes Hegel's philosophy of religion worthy of interpretation, but the constantly renewed endeavor to demonstrate the possibility of a speculative philosophy of religion.

(6) The variances between the four lecture series arise on an invariant background. Leaving aside the "Introduction," Hegel divides the lectures on each occasion into the "Concept of Religion," "Determinate Religion," and the "Consummate Religion." In the

architectonics of the philosophy-of-religion lectures there is, apart from this broad tripartite structure, only a single further detail that remains unchanged throughout all reworkings. The basic triadic structure is developed by Hegel for the first time in the introduction to the lecture manuscript. It diverges in twofold fashion from the chapter of the *Phenomenology* dealing with religion. There is no "Concept of Religion" either in the *Phenomenology* or in the 1805–6 *Philosophy of Spirit*. And the *Phenomenology* deals with the reality of religion in a threefold history of religion, whereas the lectures treat the "Consummate Religion" separately from the shapes of "Determinate Religion" as the adequate realization of the "Concept of Religion." The decision to treat the "Concept of Religion" separately and to remove the "Consummate Religion" from the history of religion may be viewed as two aspects of one and the same change in conception. The Christian religion cannot be opposed to the history of religion as the consummate realization of the "Concept of Religion" until this "Concept" itself is also elaborated as the opposite pole to the historical development.

Nothing commonly appears more self-evident to interpreters of the philosophy of religion than this triadic arrangement, the more so as Hegel lends support to this impression. This is, he says, "always the pattern in scientific knowledge: first the concept; then the particularity of the concept—reality, objectivity; and finally the stage in which the original concept is an object in itself, is for itself, becomes objective to itself, is related to itself" (*LPR* 3:249). Yet neither the system itself nor any of its disciplines other than the philosophy of religion is structured in this way. Unless we are to assume that all other disciplines lacked the necessary systematization—and this would be true also for the *Logic*—we must acknowledge that this pronouncement affords no adequate justification for the way the philosophy of religion is structured.

Nor does Hegel ever justify the distinctive and yet conceptually congruent threefold division of the philosophy of religion. The summary in each series setting out the "division of the subject" merely looks ahead to what is to follow. These summaries are "only of historical value"—in the sense in which that expression is used in the introduction to the *Science of Logic* (*SL* 54, *GW* 11:25); they have no justificatory character. But the fact that he does not formulate a clear justification anywhere else either is not because the scientific explication of this discipline requires no justification; it is because the philosophy of religion is presented in lecture form. To be sure, those parts of the system published by Hegel in more detailed form also show the difficulty of a conceptual justification of the principle of construction adopted in each case.

The problem of the triadic structure of the philosophy of religion is not, properly speaking, that it does not speak for itself or is not in accordance with the concept. It lies in the fact that it is to be met with only here. The summary setting out the division of the subject in the 1827 lectures cites an argument that helps to throw light on the specific difference in structure between the philosophy of religion and other disciplines. The systematic form of the philosophy of religion accords more fully with the nature of spirit than that of the other disciplines, since the concept that is to be divided is none other than that of spirit itself. From this concept Hegel deduces the necessity for its manifestation in "Determinate Religion" and also for its being taken back out of externalization, the coincidence of being-in-self and being-for-self and, along with it, the freedom of the concept—its presence-to-self in being-an-other, as actualized in the "Consummate Religion" (*LPR* 1:176–177). One can conclude from this argument that it is the concept of spirit—the idea—that shapes the peculiar relationship between concept and realization in the philosophy of religion, unlike, for instance, the *Logic,* which does not involve the difference between the concept and its realization in history. It is also plain to see that the philosophy of nature knows nothing of a distinction between a concept of nature, a historical realization, and a consummate shape. But it is more difficult, in the case of other disciplines of the philosophy of spirit, to explain why the philosophy of right for example does not likewise develop first the concept of right, then its historical realization, and finally its consummate shape in the modern state.

For Hegel's explanation to be satisfactory, it would at least have to apply to the way in which art and philosophy, and perhaps even absolute spirit as a whole, are conceived, and to render minor differences between them comprehensible. Although the present situation, editorially speaking, precludes any categorical statements as to the way these disciplines are conceived, it is at least plain that this condition is not fulfilled. Attempts to furnish a justification for the difference in structure of even the most closely related parts of the system have up to now provided at best only an accurate description of the differences.[1] Thus at least for the present one must acknowledge the failure of attempts to go any further. Only the publication of further materials relating to the lectures on philosophy of art and history of philosophy and a consensus as to their conception could bring us closer to a solution.

2. The Introduction and the Concept of Religion[2]

2.1. The Conception of the Manuscript

(1) In all probability it was a rapid decision on Hegel's part to treat the philosophy of religion in the summer of 1821 for the first time in a separate lectures series.[3] His lecture manuscript shows signs of having been composed in haste. Some parts seem to have been written shortly before the start of the semester, and other, especially

---

1. This applies also to the discussion of Hegel's differing conceptions of phenomenology, aesthetics, philosophy of religion, and history of philosophy by Reinhard Heede in "Die göttliche Idee und ihre Erscheinung in der Religion" (Diss., Münster, 1972), pp. 115–122. Heede's conclusion, that three structural models occur, each of them twice, does not in any event simply iron out the differences that are present. However, this conclusion is not reached without a degree of harmonization—for example in regard to the supposed agreement between the structure of the *Encyclopedia* and the philosophy of religion. For in fact the third part of the system, the philosophy of spirit, does not correspond to the shape that represents the consummation of the history of religion. There would indeed be an analogy if the *Encyclopedia* were divided into A. Logic, B. Incomplete Reality of the Concept in Nature and in Spirit, and C. Consummation of the Concept in Absolute Spirit. But even then the relation between the logic on the one hand, and the philosophies of nature and spirit on the other, would be quite different from the relation between the "Concept of Religion" and "Determinate Religion."

2. [*Tr.*] See the tables providing a comparative analysis of the structure of the "Introduction" and the "Concept of Religion" in *LPR* 1:66–67, 78–79.

3. Elsewhere the author has advanced a hypothesis as to the reasons. See *V* 3:x–xii [cf. *LPR* 1:2–3]; and "Paralipomena Hegeliana zur Wirkungsgeschichte Schleiermachers," in *Internationaler Schleiermacher-Kongress, Berlin, 1984,* ed. K.-V. Selge (Berlin and New York, 1985), pp. 1157–1169.

later, parts during the course of lecturing. Under these circumstances it would not be surprising if the conception of the manuscript was not yet highly refined—at least in those sections for which Hegel could not draw upon work done in previous years, namely the "Concept of Religion" and also "Determinate Religion." Moreover in the "Concept of Religion" there was neither a historical nor a dogmatic guiding thread by which Hegel could find his way.

(2) The manuscript defines the ultimate goal of the philosophy of religion as "to know and comprehend the religion that already *exists*" (*LPR* 1:91). Philosophy can presuppose religion, however, only in the sense that it is not its task to produce religion and piety; therefore it is not to be gauged by the success or failure of the attempt to promote religiousness. But it cannot presuppose religion in the sense of making it unnecessary to ground it. Its task is indeed to know and comprehend religion, and this means "to develop and represent the necessity of religion in and for itself"—and so comprehend it as rational (*LPR* 1:90).

(3) The success of this demonstration provides the criterion for the success of the philosophy of religion. A first line of approach, consisting in a diagnosis of the present age, is explored in the "Introduction." It distinguishes two forms of the relationship of religion to thought and to actuality: on the one hand, the attitude of naive piety, which expressly acknowledges everything to be created by God, without opposing a merely secular realm to this God-given one; and on the other hand, the merely formal recognition that everything is created by God, to be sure, but which in fact ignores this dependence and opposes to the divine a merely secular realm. Piety, so we are told, remains free from this opposition only as long as it accepts all content wholesale as God-given. But in this way it does not attain determinate knowledge, and therefore becomes "very boring" (*LPR* 1:96). Where the relationship does become determinate, the specific natural or historical content is subordinated to divine purposes—and in Hegel's eyes this teleological way of viewing things leads to an inconsistency or an antithesis. The contents that point to God's acting are no "absolute content" but finite. They are therefore incongruous with the divine mode of act-

ing and also mutually antithetical. Thought, on the contrary, demands consistency. Its goal is to grasp cognitively the necessity of the multifarious content; thus it "encloses within itself the world of finitude, to [constitute] a *system of the universe*," and indeed a universe "that does not need God and lies outside religion." Religion, by contrast, does, to be sure, unfold the absolute content, "but without any cognition according to this concept of cognition." It therefore "shrivels up into simple feeling, into a contentless elevation of spirit into the eternal, etc., of which, however, it knows nothing and has nothing to say" (*LPR* 1:101–103).

The elevation of spirit above pious boredom thus leads initially to rupture, cleavage, or estrangement.[4] Though Hegel describes this process in historically neutral terms, it is clear that he has in mind recent religious history, in particular the end of the Enlightenment. Thus for instance he denotes the situation he portrays as "the discord of our times" (*LPR* 1:107). Linguistic allusions reveal that he pictures this discord in the form in which the work of Friedrich Heinrich Jacobi epitomizes it for him: over and against the self-enclosed world of the understanding constituted by *les sciences exactes,* with no mediation between them, stands the absolute content. Hegel's continuity with, and divergence from, the Enlightenment and also from Jacobi are evident in the fact that he takes this discord seriously but does not characterize it as something that cannot be sublated. There seem to be two ways of going further. The first consists in pointing to the fact that cleavage is nothing alien to Christianity. It too begins with "absolute cleavage," but leads beyond it. The cleavage that is constitutive for Christianity is, to be sure, defined by Hegel in other terms than as the "discord of our times"; he defines it as the cleavage of nature and spirit, on the one hand, and of the "I" and the infinite, absolute being, on the other (*LPR* 1:105). For this reason the reconciliation to which religion points is unsuited to heal the ills of the time. While the Christian religion certainly begins with cleavage, in it reconciliation has the form of faith and the "form of revelation as opposed to reason,

4. [*Tr.*] These three terms all translate *Entzweiung*; see chap. 2, n. 23. The term *Zwiespalt* ("discord," "splitting into two"), used below, is etymologically related.

and more recently, to cognition" (ibid.). It is thus in the sphere of Christianity that this "discord of our times" first developed. Once the cleavage has broken out in its most extreme form, once the absolute and the finite content split asunder, religion's healing power is forfeited. This is shown by Hegel's examples for the failure of the mediation that is required: the religion of feeling, mere religious yearning, indifference toward religion, and historical preoccupation with it (*LPR* 1:107–108). These remained one-sided, for religion itself "has stimulated cognition to develop in all its consistency as form, a world of form, and at the same time to oppose itself to the form in which the Christian content exists as a given truth, only for representation and feeling" (*LPR* 1:107).

This indicates why philosophy of religion is needed and what its task is. Only philosophical cognition, according to Hegel, has the power to resolve the conflict between insight and religion (ibid.). If the discord of our times is between the absolute and the finite content, and if the reason why the latter's domain is so firmly entrenched is that it is the domain of cognition as absolute form, then mediation can only be thought of as mediation of the absolute content—the divine—with the absolute form. The credibility of this solution rests on two previously unexpressed premises. The first is Hegel's assumption of the "absolute" justification of cognition. Not to take it seriously would be to undermine the discord instead of mediating it—as in the above-mentioned four forms. Hegel's recognition of the right pertaining to cognition again reveals the heritage of the Enlightenment. The second premise, by contrast, points to the heritage of the Western history of religion as a whole. The required mediation of absolute form and absolute content is indeed in no sense an external joining together of the two. It is possible only if the religious content is *accessible* to thinking cognition— that is, if there is indeed reason in religion. Philosophy could not posit the absolute substantial content and the absolute form as "identical" (*LPR* 1:109) unless they were identical in themselves. It is, however, only in the philosophy of religion that the correctness of this premise can be demonstrated.

This takes the philosophy of religion far beyond the usual framework of the tasks that arise within philosophy. To it alone Hegel assigns the task of overcoming the cleavage between absolute form and absolute content that is the hallmark of the times. But the problems to which this gives rise also now come into sharper focus. For the philosophy of religion cannot simply lay hold of religion as something that already exists and analyze, for instance, its social function. In so doing it would be failing in its task. The advance of spirit "from the other modes of its willing, imagining, and feeling to this its absolute mode," that is, to cognition (*LPR* 1:90), has to be thought of precisely as demonstrating the identity of absolute content and absolute form. But the "Introduction" leaves it still uncertain how the philosophy of religion can accomplish this task.

(4) The summary outline and the beginning of the "Concept of Religion" are in agreement in indicating a two-part plan for the "Concept of Religion." The first part will take up the concept of religion on the basis of representation, while the second will develop the necessity of this concept, and it will do so in relation to the cosmological proof. In carrying out this project Hegel gives the second part the title "Scientific Conception of the Religious Standpoint." The stress laid on its scientific character obviously underlines the contrast with the first part. And the very first sentence makes it clear that Hegel's initial aim is nothing other than what he has announced, namely "the portrayal of the *necessity* of the religious standpoint" (*LPR* 1:199). For this purpose he reverts to the distinction between external and internal necessity. Although he broadly illustrates the former, it goes without saying that the necessity of the religious standpoint cannot be an external necessity in the sense of the physicotheological proof. But after expounding the concept of internal necessity Hegel breaks off the argument in order first to characterize more precisely the philosophical concept of religion: "However, [we must] come to an understanding of the pure concept [of religion] more precisely in its simple abstract moments, . . . in order to apprehend more definitely the thing whose necessity we have to grasp" (*LPR* 1:204).

A second stage in the argument supplies this more precise understanding. Religion is "the consciousness of the true in and for itself" (ibid.). Admittedly, this is what has to be demonstrated—but taken first in the manner of a definition. This addendum[5] closes with the statement that "this [is] the more precise understanding of the definition of religion that we are acquainted with initially from representation" (*LPR* 1:207). But the ensuing third stage also does not take up again the theme of "necessity." It elucidates "the determinate standpoint and concept of religion" (*LPR* 1:220–221). This demonstration of the speculative concept of religion and of what "speculative" can mean in the sphere of religion—namely the identity of the universal ego and the individual ego—does not pass beyond assurances that are akin to definitions. It does not demonstrate the identity either of absolute and finite content or of absolute content and absolute form. This is admitted in the remark that concludes this section: "The next point concerns the cognition of the *necessity* of this standpoint and its proof—the cognition of its truth, of the fact that it is the true and the veracious [*das Wahre und Wahrhafte*]" (*LPR* 1:221).

This proof accordingly seems to fall within an originally unforeseen Section C. But it is clear from its very first sentence that the necessity can "not here be treated in detail." The sole concern is "to understand it and its procedure" (*LPR* 1:221). The reason for this curtailment of scope is given in the special material from the second edition of the *Werke*: to demonstrate the necessity would involve retracing "the whole sphere of the philosophical sciences" (*LPR* 1:225 n. 106). While it maintains that the religious standpoint can be proved, this statement affirms that it is only in the actual course of the system that this can be done. As it cannot be the task of the philosophy of religion to retrace the system, this implies that the original project of conceptualizing this necessity cannot be carried out. The assertion that the announced proof has rather already come about gives rise to the suspicion that it forms part of a defensive strategy. At the very least the conception elaborated in the manuscript becomes open to doubt. Indeed, it cannot be an element in the systematic exposition of the concept of religion

---

5. [*Tr.*] This section is contained on a special sheet intended for insertion into the manuscript at this point (see *LPR* 1:204 nn. 56, 57).

to indicate that the expected proof cannot be undertaken in the framework of the philosophy of religion.

There is another respect too in which Hegel modifies his procedure. While his original design included only the establishment of the concept from representation and the demonstration of its necessity, he now says it is not a matter of demonstrating the correctness of a presupposed representation; scientific development has nothing whatever to do with a presupposed representational image of God or of religion. This implies a barely concealed abandonment of the original plan. A marginal notation to the manuscript makes the point in pungent fashion: instead of proving the necessity of the presupposed representational image—of God, or of religion—such an image has to be reduced to what has been developed as true in and for itself; in other words, these images are to be discarded (*LPR* 1:222 n. 102). In this case scientific explication replaces representation—as though the two had nothing in common. On the contrary, the process of reduction has potentially critical consequences for religion. The extent to which they strike at its roots will depend on the relation between such representation and the scientific form.

Here too, however, Hegel only cites, without taking due account of, the presupposition for rejecting representation in this way, namely the proof that the content is true in and for itself. To be sure, he spells out what the philosophy of religion will have to do in demonstrating necessity. The religious standpoint contains the objective side, "the natural and spiritual world in its full expanse and in the endless articulation of its actuality," and likewise the subjective side "in the full expanse of its self-consciousness." Both sides are totalities, each having incorporated what was its other into itself (*LPR* 1:221). A few lines later he calls the content of the objective side "*the true,* which has being in and for itself, and which we call *God.*" And he cites as the content of the subjective side "the fact that religiousness is the *true actuality of self-consciousness,* its true life" (*LPR* 1:222). In this further definition of the two sides Hegel in each case already presupposes the proof that, properly speaking, it is the business of philosophy of religion to provide.

It seems that the opposition between the two sides must be sublated prior to the philosophy of religion. After all, the logical realm is already the identity of nature and spirit. But Hegel rejects the reduction of the opposites to a preexisting identity. A unity achieved by reduction would eliminate the difference between nature and spirit and replace it by an undifferentiated unity within the logic. Hegel's criticism is not directed against some conjectural fancy; it is aimed at Spinozism, both at Spinoza himself—who has the attributes merely disappearing into substance without sublating themselves in themselves—and also at Schelling's system of identity. In contrast with these, Hegel's program for demonstrating the unity of cognition and objectivity, of nature and spirit, seeks to sublate the antithesis by traversing the two sides of the totality and making this sublation intelligible in the philosophy of religion. This explains the latter's metaphysical significance. At the highest level the identity of the objective and subjective sides consists in the fact that the being-in-and-for-self of spirit becomes consciousness, and its consciousness becomes being-in-and-for-self. This is religion as "the self-consciousness of the idea itself, or . . . the idea . . . as self-consciousness."[6]

The crux of the problem raised by this outline of the "Concept of Religion" lies in the fact that it does not seem capable of any systematic explication. It depends entirely on the reference back to the course of the system and on the assurance that everything needful has already been done—despite the fact that in the course of the system itself little prominence is given for the most part to references to the philosophy of religion. Difficulties also stem from the transition from the concept of the "universe" [*Universum*] as the totality of the objective side to the idea of God (*LPR* 1:221–222)— at least if such a transition is not viewed as already accomplished. To be sure, it would not be identical with the transition effected in

6. *LPR* 1:228. At this point the manuscript has a marginal notation reading "*Phenomenology of Spirit*" (*LPR* 1:229 n. 119). This has led Reinhard Heede to argue that according to the conception of the manuscript "the absolute religious standpoint results from the self-ascent of the phenomenological experience of consciousness" ("Hegel-Bilanz: Hegels Religionsphilosophie als Aufgabe und Problem der Forschung," in *Hegel-Bilanz,* ed. R. Heede and J. Ritter [Frankfurt, 1973], pp. 58 ff.). But this interpretation of different ways of conceiving the concept of religion is not borne out by the special material from the lectures of 1821 (*LPR* 1:229–230 n. 120).

the cosmological proof to the first, all-conditioning cause, but it presents comparable difficulties. This may well be the reason for the frequent references to this proof. A passage from a secondary source (LPR 1:231 n. 124) distinguishes between the appearance of the divine life in the mode of finitude and the religious standpoint, where God as object of consciousness is "the absolute power and substance into which the whole wealth of the natural and spiritual world has returned." This circumlocution conceals the problem of the transition from the philosophy of objective spirit to the philosophy of religion. What is at issue here is in no sense merely whether it is legitimate to use the words "God" and "religion." Rather it is whether philosophy is justified in going beyond nature and subjective and objective spirit as the two totalities within which the development of the system takes place. At issue too is the status of the religious vocabulary if it were the case that Hegel did not work out this transition on his own account because he regarded it as accomplished in immediate fashion. For an immediate fusion of the absolute and the finite content would reduce God to the universe [das All].

Hegel distinguishes, however, the development of the content [Stoff] within God himself and in the field of finitude, the latter of which yields only "finite configurations and spheres." He also does not simply identify the world with the Son of God, but calls the Son "the truth of this finite world" (LPR 1:230–232). This transition from the world to its truth leads beyond pantheism. But Hegel only assumes it, without explicating it systematically. Although he makes the differentiation in verbal terms, he does not shrink from expressing clearly an unavoidable consequence of his approach. If the path that leads to the religious standpoint by demonstrating the necessary development of the system is to be understood as the self-development of the absolute—and the concept of the absolute cannot be attained in any other way—then there is no escaping a consequence that has from time immemorial been regarded as theologically questionable: "God's internal self-development has thus the same logical necessity as the development of the universe" (LPR 1:231). But initially it seems as though Hegel wishes to attenuate this consequence. He first stresses that this necessity is only one according to form—a necessity by means of which conceptual thought brings its content under its sway. As in the "Introduction" he divides this content into finite and absolute substance [*Stoff*], but has at least to modify this distinction. Absolute substance that merely stood over against the finite would itself be finite, and finitude would thus be made the absolute. For this reason Hegel stresses emphatically that the identity is not only one of logical necessity but also one of substance: "these two sorts of material [*Stoff*]—the internal self-development of God and the development of the universe—are not so absolutely different" (*LPR* 1:232). But even now Hegel does not simply identify the two. He denies the finite substance independence and presents it as merely the appearance of God.

The fact that some phrases are couched in future terms might be taken to mean that the transition to the religious standpoint is reserved for a later section of the "Concept of Religion" (*LPR* 1:231). In all probability, however, they relate to the further course of the philosophy of religion as a whole and not to its first part. For Hegel affirms that "the portrayal of the absolute as the absolute power and concrete encompassment of this wealth [of a world] lies behind us" (*LPR* 1:230). That "the true acquires this signification of the absolutely universal . . . and that this is the absolutely true" is "the starting point of the philosophy of religion, and the necessity of this truth is the [philosophical] science that precedes it." But the necessity also emerges "as the development of the idea and of the material in its element" (*LPR* 1:233). In this ultimate form, however, the necessity is not explicated in the "Concept of Religion" to any greater extent than is the transition to the religious standpoint.

(5) This deficiency ought not to be seen as due to mere chance or lack of time. For after these remarks on the demonstration of the necessity, Hegel goes on to discuss the relationship of religion to art and philosophy, a topic that had no place in his original program. Evidently he considers the theme "Necessity of the Religious Standpoint" to be exhausted. Thus he appends only the description of the forms of absolute spirit. And though he emphasizes that this "is part of the definition of the concept of religion," doubt is in-

directly cast on this by the later lecture series, which do not attribute to the relationship to art and philosophy any constitutive significance for the "Concept of Religion."

Hegel's account is based on the distinction drawn in the 1805–6 *Philosophy of Spirit* in terms of the theory of faculties. Intuition is attributed to art, representation to religion, and conceptual thought to philosophy.[7] In addition Hegel also mentions the practical moment, the cultus, as a distinguishing feature. This account differs from the *Phenomenology* in that here it is the incongruity of representation and the absolute content that drives spirit beyond religion. This eliminates the immediate contradiction that religion is the self-consciousness of spirit, but a self-consciousness that never attains actual self-knowledge. This change, however, is more a matter of shift of emphasis than a radical revision. The *Phenomenology* also can express the mutual estrangement of self-consciousness and consciousness with reference to the concept of representation, and the concept of religion in the manuscript can likewise be formulated in the terminology of the difference between self-consciousness and consciousness. For the manuscript too deems adequate knowledge of the truth to be achieved only when I have in the absolute content "the consciousness of the concept." Only then do I have truth "*as* truth *in the form* of truth—in the form of the absolutely concrete and of that which harmonizes within itself purely and simply." And according to the manuscript too, this knowledge belongs no longer to religion but to philosophy (*LPR* 1:250).

With this Hegel returns at the end of the "Concept of Religion" to the theme that according to the "Introduction" seems central but in Part I of the lectures is given less prominence than the proof of the necessity of the religious standpoint. Hegel's claim to have furnished this proof cannot, however, be regarded as justified, inasmuch as the necessity in question has to be sought in those configurations of the system that precede religion. The necessity can indeed be demonstrated there, but not in the transition to the religious

7. *LPR* 1:234; cf. pp. 181–182 above. This is not the place to enter into the content of this section in detail. See the author's "Kunst und Religion," esp. pp. 172–173.

standpoint—nor in the development of the idea of God itself, for the very reason that Hegel does not explicate it further. The last quotation does, however, bear on the identity of absolute form and absolute content in rational knowledge. Nowhere else is this identity defined in such pregnant terms: "All that is meant by the indeterminate word 'reason,' 'rational insight,' is, not that within me there is anything that is certain and stands fast, but that there is within me that which stands fast for itself, objective in and for itself, established within me, i.e., it is grounded within itself, is determined in and for itself. Such, however, is the pure concept" (*LPR* 1:249–250). This also suffices to show what it means that human beings have their freedom in religion, yet in Hegel's view do not have it entirely. For this identity of absolute content and absolute form no longer belongs to the religious standpoint in the narrower sense. It is a characteristic "that is added by the *philosophical cognition of truth*," and indeed only by "wholly *speculative philosophy*" (*LPR* 1:250–251).[8] It is the characteristic defect of the manuscript that while it formulates this idea in the "Introduction" and at the conclusion of Part I, it does not explicate it systematically. It thus remains a mere assurance that philosophy has good reason to express the relationship of knowing to the religious content in this way.

2.2. The Conception of the Lectures of 1824

(1) Hegel's second lecture series replaces the many uncertainties of execution in the "Concept of Religion" by a wholly new conception. It is related to the earlier draft only in the solemn opening words—which also figure in the third series—and in the demonstration of the necessity of the religious standpoint. It is not Hegel's understanding of religion and the tasks confronting the philosophy of religion in general that has changed, but the systematic explication. And yet it is on this that the burden of proof falls for his refounding of philosophical discourse about God and religion.

(2) Hegel's further work on the systematic form of the philos-

8. [*Tr.*] Translation corrected slightly; see V 3:159.

ophy of religion also affected the "Introduction." The 1824 "Introduction" no longer argues with seemingly timeless forms of piety but develops the concept of the philosophy of religion, taking as its starting point the "needs of our time," namely the cleavage mirrored in the contemporary philosophical and theological situation. The relationship of philosophy of religion to *theologia naturalis* is already touched on in the manuscript, where it is stated that natural theology has been inconsistent in that it had not grasped God as spirit (*LPR* 1:190–191). The 1824 lectures assign much greater weight to this idea. Seen from the outside, the two disciplines differ in their subject matter: in one case God, in the other religion. They have the appearance of two sciences between which a relationship is only established a posteriori. But two related arguments run counter to this view. According to the one, this view is based on the incorrect presupposition that *theologia naturalis* is a still available option; it disregards the demonstration of the failure of natural theology. Hegel is no less convinced of this failure, even if in general he avoids expressly endorsing this criticism directed against natural theology, adducing instead other arguments against it. His main objection relates to the fact that it is misdirected. Even if there were no objections to its traditional mode of proof, its idea of God would in any event be inadequate. For it comprehends God as a most perfect or necessary being, at all events as a supreme being, and consequently as "hollow, empty, and impoverished" (*LPR* 1:124 n. 31). In Hegel's eyes, this idea of God is the complement to talk of God's unknowability, which expresses what is contained in the metaphysical idea of the supreme being. He contests only the view (for instance that of Kant or Jacobi) that an appropriate mode of speculative theology simply does not exist. But whether the supreme being is designated as "substance" or "absolute subject," or as spirit as in Christianity, is in his view unimportant. For what matters is not the empty word one uses to denote God but that God should be conceived as spirit. The conditions for this are briefly summarized by Hegel as follows: "It will be evident that God can only be genuinely understood in the mode of his being as *spirit,* by means of which he makes himself into the counterpart of a community and brings about the activity of a community in relation to him; thus it will be evident that the doctrine of God is to be grasped and taught only as the doctrine of *religion*" (*LPR* 1:116). This sentence contains in a nutshell the program of the speculative philosophy of religion. The objection to *theologia naturalis* is not so much that it is incapable of conceiving its idea of God but that its idea is inadequate.

Herein lies the decisive argument why the philosophy of religion cannot simply refer to a presupposed religion and explicate the form in which it appears. It is not merely an alternative (perhaps a preferable alternative) to philosophical theology but the genuine carrying out of speculative theology. A philosophy of religion that abstracted from its theological character would be guilty of the reverse one-sidedness to that of *theologia naturalis*. It is true to its task only if it grasps religion as the self-consciousness of absolute spirit. This means that it does not abstract from what spirit implicitly is, namely "essence grasped in the concept," the meaning of which is "coincident with the logical idea" (*LPR* 1:119). "Philosophy of religion" is thus in no way merely a popular expression for onto-theo-logic,[9] nor is it the successor discipline to *theologia naturalis*, but its complement in the broader framework of philosophical theology. It has the same subject matter as speculative theology and philosophy in general, namely God. But it has this subject matter in a different, and for the first time an appropriate, form: as self-knowing in self-consciousness.

This account affords us very precise insights into Hegel's conception of the philosophy of religion. Initially, however, in line with its position at the beginning of the "Introduction," it has the status of a declaration of intent. Hegel implies here that the concept of God is identical "with the logical idea" (*LPR* 1:119). To this extent it is not philosophy of religion but metaphysical logic that replaces the former *theologia naturalis*. Moreover Hegel's conceptual apparatus reflects a change as compared with the 1805–6 *Philosophy of Spirit*. Now it is no longer the "absolute spirit" but the "absolute idea" whose self-knowing as the idea first arises within the frame-

9. See Karl Löwith, "Hegels Aufhebung der christlichen Religion," in *Hegel-Tage, 1962*, ed. H.-G. Gadamer (Bonn, 1964), p. 194.

work of the discipline with which the philosophical system concludes. The apportionment of areas of competence between logic and religion also makes clear the distinctive task of the philosophy of religion. Its responsibility is to demonstrate that religion is to be conceived as the form of manifestation of the divine being who in logic remains merely abstract—to demonstrate the identity of the concept and the reality of God in the self-knowing spirit.

(3) The second and third sections of the "Introduction" do not have the philosophical dignity of the first. But they too relate to the foundational questions concerning the philosophy of religion since they discuss its relationship to two contemporary theological approaches, the so-called "rational theology" and orthodoxy. Hegel accepts the term "rational theology" [*Vernunfttheologie*] despite the fact that it is, in his view, mere theology of the understanding [*Verstandestheologie*] in the form of rationalistic exegesis or theology based on argumentation or reasoning. The latter makes God into the supreme being, a "hollow abstraction," instead of grasping God as triune, that is, as the process of inwardly differentiating in which God "loves himself, i.e., remains identical with himself" (*LPR* 1:126–127).

Hegel does not, however, indicate how this self-communion in otherness [*Beisichsein im Anderssein*] also becomes a "matter of the concept." His intention is here directed to defining his position vis-à-vis the above-mentioned theological currents. He shares the fear that rationalistic exegesis may discredit the Bible and rob religion of its content, but he does not agree with orthodoxy's demand for a return to the traditional interpretation, since this ignores the link between exegesis and its time. Yet historical theology—which he proclaims a "plague" (*LPR* 1:128)—appears to him no more suited to recapturing the absolute content. From this he draws conclusions for exegesis as a whole: "if the interpretation that emerges is supposed to be in accordance with reason, then we can here claim the right to develop religion freely and openly out of reason" (*LPR* 1:124). This program rests on a very skeptical assessment of exegesis, one that views interpretation as a matter of substituting, at minimum, one word for another and, properly speaking, one thought for another. Interpretation, on this view, necessarily goes beyond the text; because it cannot leave reason out of account, it is necessary to improve the conceptual framework within which interpretation operates by basing it on an appropriate concept of reason (*LPR* 1:122 ff.).

Thus Hegel's critique of rational and historical theology commends the speculative philosophy of religion as alone suited to the task of recapturing the absolute content. The stress laid on theology's inability to secure this content serves at one and the same time to immunize the philosophy of religion against objections on the part of theology and to establish the genuine theology of reason, which develops the nature of God and of religion "freely and openly out of reason, without taking as our starting point the specific word [of scripture]" (*LPR* 1:124). This assumes that in religion itself there should *be* reason, with which this rational development can converge. This assumption also provides the justification for Hegel's assertion that the philosophy of religion has more in common with "positive religion" than with the so-called rational theology. These are no mere words of ingratiation; they follow logically from the proposition that, while religion has indeed the absolute content, it does not have it in the absolute form, whereas the theology of the understanding has forfeited both alike. The conclusive character of this affirmation of identity rests on the idea that there cannot be several kinds of reason—not "two kinds of reason and two kinds of spirit, a divine and a human reason or a divine and a human spirit that would be strictly distinct from one another" (*LPR* 1:130).

The principle of the unity of reason is well suited to reinforce the unity of content of religion and philosophy. For religion cannot protest that its content is after all merely positive; if it did, it would be acknowledging the criticism leveled against it by the Enlightenment as conducive to its own better self-understanding, and would thus fall victim to such criticism. Admittedly it is open to religion to "ridicule" the assertion of its rationality "with proud irony" as a Trojan horse presented to it by philosophy. But even so, it cannot defy the call for rationality. Once the need for cognition, and for cognition's break with religion, has been awakened, "insight has its rights which can no longer be in any way denied" (*LPR* 1:131

n. 43). In the following section, dealing with "Preliminary Questions," Hegel puts the matter even more bluntly: "There is no ground for supposing that faith in the content or in the doctrine of positive religion can still persist when reason has convinced itself of the contrary" (LPR 1:134).

The assumption that there is reason in religion could, however, be an error. Initially no grounds are given for it. The assurance that human spirit is not "the sort of divided thing in which the two sides of a contradiction could subsist," namely faith and reason (LPR 1:134), is not of itself to be regarded as a sufficient argument. It is, however, only in the course of developing the philosophy of religion in its entirety that the rationality of religion is demonstrated. Hegel therefore pushes "to one side" (LPR 1:138) the objections to the possibility of a philosophy of religion that have been formulated in the four "Preliminary Questions"—or, properly speaking, he leaves them to be dealt with in the actual course of its development. He does not reject the demand for proof as such, but only the call for philosophy to "get this over first"—"to secure a being for its objects in advance, before it begins" (LPR 1:137–139). Philosophical proof is not surrendered but transferred to the philosophical science of religion; the determination of God as what has being in and for itself falls within the philosophy of religion itself (LPR 1:140).

(4) The survey describing the different moments of the concept at the end of the "Introduction" points to a conception that is totally changed from that of the manuscript. Here too Hegel introduces the concept of religion—"taken in its speculative, absolute sense"—in definitional terms as the "concept of the spirit that is conscious of its essence or of itself," and is so in the form of representation. This concept comprises three moments: the pure thought, the relationship-of-consciousness[10] of the finite subject to the object, and the "uniting of both sides," the "return to the first, substantial standpoint" in the cultus (LPR 1:142). This tripartite division is not wholly new. Already in the manuscript it forms the structural principle for the treatment of "Determinate Religion"

10. [Tr.] Bewusstseinsverhältnis. See chap. 2, n. 45.

and also the "Consummate Religion." This structural similarity has to be seen against the background of the statement that in the two latter parts the concept of religion becomes objective. Its basic logical pattern is obviously that of concept [*Begriff*], judgment or division [*Urteil*¹¹], and conclusion or syllogism [*Schluss*]. But here Hegel designates it as the triad of abstract concept, realization, and the identity of the two (*LPR* 1:142). However, this paradigm does not seem to be that of the "Concept of Religion" but of the whole conception of the lectures. This raises the question of the conceptual specificity and foundational function of the "operational triads."¹²

(5) The characteristic problem of this conception does not, however, lie in the indeterminateness of the logical paradigm. It lies in the fact that the "Concept of Religion" adheres to it so little that it could be assumed that the survey of the subject and the way in which it is actually presented belong to different lecture series. This divergence is of prime importance specifically for the foundational problem. For it is now stated that there is not only one path to attainment of the concept of religion but two, an empirical and a speculative (*LPR* 1:257). Both, according to Hegel, rest on presuppositions, the empirical approach on existent religion and on consciousness, and the speculative approach on the course that philosophical science has already traversed. This duality is reflected in the two parts into which the "Concept of Religion" is divided.

In the process of traversing the first path Hegel develops the

11. [*Tr.*] The normal translation of *Urteil* is "judgment," but in Hegel's usage one hears the root sense of "division" (*teilen, Teil*), or more literally "primal division" (*Ur-teil*). In *LPR* we translated *Urteil* as both "judgment" and "primal division." Here we have avoided "judgment" and simply used "division" as the best choice for capturing the several senses of *Urteil,* logical, philosophical, and theological.

12. Reinhard Heede expresses the view that these triads are "of significance in the role of metacategories only in their identical structure," and that "categories that occupy the same relative position within the triads" have "a homologous function" (see "Die göttliche Idee," p. 111). It would then be a matter of indifference whether the structure of the "Concept of Religion" was to be understood in terms of the model *Begriff-Urteil-Schluss* or *Begriff-Realität-Identität.* But the logical categories would not then make it possible to comprehend even the difference in structure between Part I and the lectures as a whole.

forms of religious relationship: immediate knowledge, feeling, and "consciousness in more determinate form." He rejects the first two as inadequate. All immediate knowledge can say is that the universal *is* (*LPR* 1:266). This criticism still points to the disagreements with Jacobi in particular more strongly than the criticism of feeling points to the disagreement with Schleiermacher. Certainly the disagreement with Schleiermacher will be seen as the reason why Hegel here explicitly opposes feeling, and not, as in the manuscript, sensibility, as an appropriate foundation for the religious content. The section on feeling does not, however, contain any polemic aimed directly at Schleiermacher. It is only in the ensuing section that we find the remark that animals too would have religion if it rested on the feeling of dependence.[13] The critique of feeling is not even linked to Hegel's systematic presuppositions. Essentially it switches between two lines of argument: (a) Feeling is a mere form, capable of assuming but not legitimating any content one cares to mention. (b) Even as form, feeling is inadequate, since God does not have in it "free absolute independence" (*LPR* 1:276). It is difficult to dispute either statement.

The next form of religious relationship Hegel terms "Consciousness in More Determinate Form." This terminological embarrassment is only a pointer to the difficulty of defining this consciousness in terms of content. Its specific characteristic lies in the fact that finitude and infinitude are at one and the same time related and opposed. This is why, after portraying this consciousness, Hegel treats the relationship between finitude and infinitude, in order presumably to achieve the transition to the concept of religion on the basis of a genuine definition of this relationship.

It remains to be seen, however, to what extent this "empirical path of observation" enables the relationship of finite and infinite

13. *LPR* 1:279–280. On some aspects of Hegel's critique of Schleiermacher to which little attention has been directed elsewhere, see the author's "Paralipomena Hegeliana." No proof is needed of the fact that Hegel's critique misses the sense of Schleiermacher's concept of feeling. But what Schleiermacher probably meant—the precise conceptual content of which is still a matter of investigation today—would also have been rejected by Hegel as not providing a suitable starting point for the philosophy of religion or dogmatics. [*Tr.* See also the editorial note in *LPR* 1:279 n. 37.]

to be adequately developed, and how one is to pass over from here to the concept of religion. When he comes to discuss the relationship of finite and infinite, if not beforehand, Hegel abandons the path of "empirical observation." No other section of the lectures is so closely based on the *Logic* as this one. Apart from this, the result Hegel arrives at is that observation has as its ultimate object the antithesis between finite and infinite (*LPR* 1:310–311). In part he gives the impression that some more adequate relationship of finite to infinite can still be observed—such as the elevation found in devotion. But he ends with the broad insight that observation remains confined to the sphere of finitude because it is itself an external, finite relationship. This insight throws into question the division of the "Concept of Religion" into two parts, and casts doubt on the assumption of an empirical and a speculative path to the concept of religion, and hence of two modes of grounding. Hegel does not mince his words in formulating this result: "It follows, then, that in order to find the ground of religion we must abandon the abstract relationship of observation; we must renounce this empirical standpoint" (*LPR* 1:313). The supposed path of observation is not only a detour but a false trail. Yet it is the path taken by "the prevalent views that purport to be philosophical in the general culture of our time" (*LPR* 1:258). It is to its refutation that the lengthy discussion of observation is addressed. This discussion has only a negative function for grounding the speculative philosophy of religion. The demonstration of failure does not concern a mere exercise in thinking; it serves to commend the sole remaining path, that of speculation. The possibility of this path remains, to be sure, an open question.[14]

(6) The new approach involving the "speculative concept" of religion also does not realize the plan outlined in the survey of the

14. The relationship between the two parts is obscured in Lasson's edition by the fact that he places Hegel's résumé of the impracticability of the empirical path (*LPR* 1:313–314) in an earlier section of this path itself (see *Vorlesungen über die Philosophie der Religion,* ed. Georg Lasson [Leipzig, 1925–1929], part I, *Begriff der Religion,* p. 129). In so doing he gives the impression that the empirical path can yield an insight into the genuine relationship between finitude and infinitude and provide a means of passing over to the speculative concept of religion—as though there were a twofold grounding of the concept of religion.

subject. Admittedly it does not, as in the manuscript, derive the concept of religion from representation, but it only introduces it in the manner of a definition: religion is "the affirmative relation of consciousness, . . . [the affirmation] that the truth with which consciousness is actively related embraces all content within itself." But it immediately goes on to confirm that what has to be done is "to show that the content is necessary in itself and in principle" (*LPR* 1:315–316). In accordance with this requirement Hegel starts by formulating a more profound definition: religion, he says, is "the idea of spirit that relates itself to itself, the self-consciousness of absolute spirit." In the "highest idea" it is "essentially the highest determination of the absolute idea itself" (*LPR* 1:318). At the start of the section describing the necessity of the religious standpoint, Hegel once again spells out what this definition means: the content of religion is "the absolute truth, simply the whole truth." And he goes on to tell us that "the absolute idea alone [is] this truth" and that "all things have their truth only in it" (*LPR* 1:319). While the formulations cited previously stand closer to the *Phenomenology,* Hegel is unmistakably referring here to the end of the *Science of Logic,* where it is stated that the absolute idea alone is "*being,* imperishable *life, self-knowing truth,* and . . . all *truth*" (*SL* 824, *GW* 12:236). No other passage in the lectures presents the concept of religion so insistently. This section also provides renewed evidence of the structural links between the *Philosophy of Religion* and the *Logic.* The 1804–5 *Metaphysics* already assigns the self-knowing of absolute spirit as such to the discipline with which the system comes to a close. Similarly it is here for the first time that the logical designation of the absolute idea as all truth acquires the significance attested to it in the concrete content.

This concept of the religious standpoint embraces the entire sphere of absolute spirit, whose absoluteness consists in the very fact that it thinks itself. In this alone resides the concept of absolute spirit. The question therefore arises whether religion in the narrower sense does itself actualize this concept of absolute spirit—whether in religion spirit in fact already knows itself as object in such a way that self-consciousness and consciousness, absolute content and absolute form, are in perfect identity. This would be the case only if religion did not have its object in the form of representation. But there is no doubt that Hegel continues to regard religion in the narrower sense as characterized by the representational form. The moment of separation does not belong solely to the ethnic religions, of which it is an easy matter to acknowledge that they do not yet genuinely actualize the self-consciousness of absolute spirit; it is inherent in the concept of religion itself. To be sure, religion recognizes that what is other to knowing spirit[15] is also spirit, but it does not know the former as identical with the latter.

(7) Thus the sole restriction to be placed on the proclaimed identity of absolute spirit is that in religion knowing spirit does not yet have the absolute form of conceptual knowledge. This identity remains problematical with respect to the further definition of the object of nature and the ethical realm as "the absolutely universal object" (LPR 1:317). This problem is dealt with in the section on the necessity of the religious standpoint. Hegel is aware of the definitional character attaching to his introduction of the concept of religion: "These assertions that this content of religion is the absolute truth—this [is] what is to be proved." But here too as in the manuscript it is stated: "This deduction lies outside our science" (LPR 1:319). It is solely in regard to this topic of the demonstration of necessity that an affinity is evident between the second lecture series and the manuscript. The affinity is so close that it can be traced to individual turns of phrase.[16] The consequence of this is that the later expositions are little more satisfying than the earlier ones. For the transition from the manifold objects of spirit to "the absolutely universal object" is problematical in the manuscript in the same way that it leaves something to be desired in the *Encyclopedia*. Regardless of possible objections to the way the question is developed in the *Encyclopedia*, it can easily be seen that inasmuch as spirit has not only nature but spirit for object, what it implicitly is exists for it; it is the nature of spirit "that it is, like

15. [Tr.] Here and elsewhere we translate *erkennende Geist* as "knowing spirit." In order to maintain a distinction between *erkennen* and *wissen*, we would need a less familiar rendering such as "cognizing spirit."

16. Compare the subsequent revision of the manuscript (LPR 1:224 lines 5 ff.) with the 1824 text (LPR 1:319 lines 24 ff.).

nature, idea implicitly," but also "that what it is in itself also appears to it, i.e., the idea exists in its appearance" (*LPR* 1:321).[17] Both the manuscript and the special materials in the *Werke* formulate this idea as the equivalence of consciousness and substantial being (*LPR* 1:228–229). The transition to knowledge of the "absolutely universal object" requires, however, that this object "is exhibited as necessary, as the truth of all things, as the absolute truth into which, precisely through itself, all this other content returns" (*LPR* 1:321); or, as it is expressed in the first Jena lectures, it requires "the resumption of the whole into one" (see p. 136 above). The only way in which it can be conceived here is that knowing spirit comprehends both nature and subjective and objective spirit as the appearance of the absolute idea and by this means attains to the idea of all truth. The Heidelberg *Encyclopedia,* § 454, assigns to "ethical substance" in particular "the significance of absolute power and absolute soul as well as of the essence of both nature and spirit."[18]

(8) In the manuscript the topic "Necessity of the Religious Standpoint" concludes the "Concept of Religion," except for the section clarifying the relationship of religion to art and philosophy. In the 1824 lectures, on the contrary, it is only here that there begins what could be called a systematic exposition of the concept of religion. From now on Hegel describes the further determination of the concept of religion as its own realization. He takes as his point of departure the definition of religion as the self-consciousness of absolute spirit. "In common speech this means that God is the unity of the natural and the spiritual" (*LPR* 1:325). And for what follows this "common" way of defining it becomes more important than the actual definition. The concept of God is the concept of the idea, "and the exposition of the philosophy of religion

17. [*Tr.*] The translation has been modified slightly; cf. *V* 3:224.
18. [*Tr.*] Translations of passages from the *Encyclopedia* are essentially our own. Frequently the author quotes from the 1st (Heidelberg, 1817) or 2d (Berlin, 1827) editions, which are not translated; but even when passages from the 3d edition (Berlin, 1830) are cited, we have generally found Wallace's renderings too idiosyncratic to follow. Section or paragraph numbers (§) are identical in the 3d German edition and the English translation, and those of the 2d German edition are similar to those of the 3d.

displays nothing but this development of the concept of the idea" (*LPR* 1:326). As the absolute unity of the spiritual and the natural, the idea contains the moments of substantial unity, differentiation, and absolute affirmation. But a God who does not appear is an abstraction. The substantial unity is therefore not distinct from differentiation and itself forms part of it. This corresponds to § 455 of the Heidelberg *Encyclopedia*, where it is stated that the diremption of the universal substance of spirit is "the division [*Urteil*] *into itself* and *into a mode of knowing* for which it exists as such." This only covers the relationship of the first two moments. The lectures by contrast reduce the above-mentioned three moments to two relationships: the relationship of differentiation or consciousness, which is the representational side or the theoretical relationship; and the sublation of the rupture, which is the side pertaining to the cultus or the practical relationship (*LPR* 1:327).

The stringency of this development hinges on the aspect to which least attention is paid, namely the determination of the idea as the absolute unity of both moments: "the solid, substantial unity of the idea—God as having being, the God that has being as a self-relating unity" (*LPR* 1:327). The later editions of the *Encyclopedia* comprehend absolute spirit as the "*identity* that is self-contained as well as returning and having returned into itself," as "the one and universal *substance* as spiritual" (§ 554). It is an easy matter to interpret this living identity of the first moment as God in his immanent-trinitarian life, and likewise the "division" as the act of creation of the world.[19] But the standpoint of the "Concept of Religion" precludes any interpretation of this identity except as "absolute unity of the spiritual and the natural" (*LPR* 1:326). An explicitly theological interpretation would accomplish a leap that would rob the conceptual development of its power of conviction. And the course of the system is such that "division" can mean only that of spirit, which at the standpoint of ethical life reaches the position of having itself as object. This way of viewing the matter is confirmed by § 455 of the Heidelberg *Encyclopedia*.

19. See esp. Michael Theunissen, *Hegels Lehre vom absoluten Geist als theologisch-politischer Traktat* (Berlin, 1970), pp. 120, 125.

It might be argued that the philosophy of religion embraces solely the theoretical and the practical relationship—and the idea of God only to the extent that it arises in regard to them. But the necessity of the "division" and, with it, of the two relationships is incomprehensible without a metaphysical exposition of the idea of God, namely the abstract concept and the appearance of God. Since Hegel does not enter into such an exposition, for the further development of the concept of religion he has no alternative but to turn to the "historical" form which elsewhere he rightly rejects; all he can do is inform us that "this idea comprises the following moments" (LPR 1:326). Yet at the end of the "Concept of Religion" he still distinguishes, as the "two aspects" of the reality of spirit in religion, "spirit in its objectivity, preeminently God," and "spirit in its subjectivity." And the text transmitted by the *Werke* stresses that God, "as the absolute unity of these his two moments, is absolute spirit" (LPR 1:363–364)—and obviously is so only as such unity.

The lack of clarity in the way the idea of God and its role in grounding the theoretical and the practical relationships are formulated carries over into these relationships themselves. Hegel does not specify God's appearance in terms of the differing forms included within the relationship-of-consciousness. They are already dealt with by "empirical observation." Hegel follows the second of the paradigms referred to in the "Survey of the Stages of Our Discussion," that of concept, realization, and the identity of the two (LPR 1:142). In so doing he anticipates the historical realization of the concept of religion, which in fact has its proper place only in Parts II and III of the lectures. The treatment of the cultus also shows the same mixture of conceptual and historical modes of discussion. Its justification lies in the fact that the forms of religious action and knowledge are affected by the course of history. This is particularly true for the definition of faith as the witness of spirit to spirit.

With the concept of spiritual witness, the 1824 lectures express the consummation of the concept of religion. The witness spirit gives of absolute spirit is "the unity of pure self-consciousness and of consciousness. Or it is the infinite form of knowledge as such and of the absolute content. The unity of the two is the absolute content, which is the form of self, i.e., it is knowledge of itself, and hence defines itself as universal as opposed to singular, so that the latter exists simply and solely as semblance" (*LPR* 1:343). Hegel denotes this concept as "what is innermost, what is at the heart of speculation"; it is a point "that can only be apprehended speculatively." Terminologically it combines elements of the *Phenomenology* and of the manuscript: the identity of self-consciousness and consciousness is the identity of absolute content and absolute form. For this very reason it is questionable whether it is actualized in religion itself. For the object that is known in the form of representation can never be dissolved in the "unity of pure self-consciousness and consciousness," and the self-consciousness of absolute spirit cannot therefore be consummated on the soil of religion. This could be why Hegel treats this "deepest point" in the framework not of representation but of the cultus, as the sublation of rupture or estrangement.

2.3. The Conception of the Lectures of 1827

(1) In the "Introduction" and Part I of the lectures of 1824, Hegel is seeking a conceptual form for the philosophy of religion. This search is successful insofar as his "Survey of the Stages of Our Discussion" points to a conception that fulfills this purpose. But it fails to the extent that Hegel does not succeed in carrying this conception out. The numerous departures from his own program thus give rise to an impression of uncertainty, in fact of the absence of a conception—above all in the juxtaposition of the two irreconcilable paradigms presented in the survey as well as in those passages that still follow the lines of the manuscript, and in the broad treatment of "empirical observation," which is of no significance for the systematic development of the concept of religion.

By contrast, the lectures of 1827 do carry out the conception that had already been outlined in the 1824 survey. The lectures of 1831 still adhere to this form and, as far as can be judged from the inadequate sources for this last series, depart from it only in minor details. This does not imply that Hegel arbitrarily precludes any further revision; he has now succeeded in developing the concept of religion in a form that he regards as appropriate to the "life of the concept." For the interpretation of the "Concept of Religion" primacy therefore goes to the 1827 series.

(2) The clearest agreement between the 1824 and 1827 lectures is shown in the two "Introductions," even in regard to the topics that in the 1827 lectures are not the subject of separate sections, such as the "Preliminary Questions." Despite this far-reaching material congruence, there is a major shift in the way Hegel assesses the relationship of the philosophy of religion to contemporary viewpoints. His attitude to them in the 1824 lectures can be termed one of wholesale rejection. But although there has been no change in the positions impugned, Hegel now also finds in them elements that to some extent reflect the program of the philosophy of religion.

This more positive attitude is unconvincing as far as the content is concerned. Contemporary theology, according to Hegel, has surrendered the religious content instead of preserving it, as did the medieval unity of philosophy and theology which he often invokes but without fully elaborating. The new situation is more favorable in that one serious obstacle to the philosophical treatment of the absolute content has been eliminated, namely theology's fear that the content of religion is jeopardized by philosophy. It is true that, in its attempt to recover the absolute content, philosophy is in no way spared from the critique of theology. It can, however, now "operate without constraint" vis-à-vis church doctrines in view of the fact that they are held in such low esteem (*LPR* 1:158). The more favorable situation is thus limited to philosophy's possession of a few tactical advantages, which are in fact only the obverse of a grave deficiency.

By contrast, the formal change in philosophy's attitude to the principles of the time is a matter of importance. In the 1824 lectures Hegel's treatment of immediate knowledge is still exclusively polemical. Now, in contrast, he speaks of it as a "preconception" "that the highest or religious content discloses itself to the human being in the spirit itself, that spirit manifests itself in spirit, in this my own spirit, that faith has its root in the inner self or in what is most my own, that my inmost core is inseparable from it" (*LPR*

1:160). The effect is to remove "all external authority, all alien con-firmation," and "all objective determinateness has collapsed into the inwardness of subjectivity" (*LPR* 1:159–161). This relationship of subject and content also constitutes a "basic determination" in philosophy. It is therefore "to be regarded as a gain, as a kind of good fortune, that basic principles of philosophy itself are active as general preconceptions in the universal [i.e., popular] mode of representation" (*LPR* 1:161). This interpretation is endorsed in the 1831 lectures (*LPR* 1:462). And it alone corresponds to the tenor of what Hegel says regarding the attitude of a philosophy to its age: it is only because of the reevaluation of immediate knowledge that the basic concepts of the philosophy of religion can be linked to the general convictions of the age (*LPR* 1:164–165). All that Hegel now opposes is the false belief that philosophy is incapable of tran-scending the bare inseparability of myself and the absolute content, and of raising the absolute content into the form of conceptual thought. Thus the standpoint of immediate knowledge now be-comes the main ally of the speculative philosophy of religion in its controversy with orthodoxy, which, to be sure, retains the content but as external to self-consciousness. Hegel, by contrast, seeks to unite the principle of the age, the principle of immediate knowl-edge, with the traditional maintenance of the content; he seeks to show that even if subjectivity is recognized as constituting all truth, it is necessary to hold fast to the objectivity of the absolute con-tent—in a changed form, to be sure, which it is the task of the philosophy of religion to explicate.

There is yet another perspective for specifying the relationship of the philosophy of religion to the convictions of the age. The manuscript and the 1824 lectures establish the distinction between *theologia naturalis* and philosophy of religion in terms of the for-mer having as its object God, and the latter religion; but in any event the concept of God is seen as leading necessarily to religion as the self-consciousness of God. Now by contrast Hegel laments the fact that in modern times people speak only of religion: the na-ture of God is no longer made an object of theology (*LPR* 1:162–163). This complaint could be misunderstood as seeking to resusci-tate *theologia naturalis*, whereas it only corrects the false impression that the approach linked to immediate knowledge and religion makes it superfluous to reflect on the idea of God or to ground the philosophy of religion in a philosophical theology. For in Hegel's view this makes religion a matter of drawing lines into empty space (*LPR* 1:191–192).

As opposed to the traditional idea of God as something external to self-consciousness, the principle of immediate knowledge makes it possible to hold fast to the idea of God. If religion is understood, on the basis of the concept of immediate knowledge, as knowledge of the inseparability of God and self-consciousness, then it is the task of the philosophy of religion to make the nature of God its object—albeit in a new form. Similarly in the 1831 lectures Hegel mentions that in the Middle Ages it was not only required that human beings should have religion, but also "God's essence was given more consideration and definition." The change in the principles of the age does not, however, give him cause for complaint: "We have to acknowledge the truth implicit in the [modern practice] of not considering God in isolation from the subjective spirit. But we do so not for the reason that God is something unknown, but only because God is essentially spirit, is [God] as knowing [spirit]" (*LPR* 1:383 n. 47). Thus the altered assessment of immediate knowledge does not affect the fact that speculative theology has to be worked out as philosophy of religion and vice versa. The two disciplines do not thereby coincide in undifferentiated fashion, nor is one only the philosophical or the popular expression of the other. Hegel's conception of their unity is to be seen rather as an attempt to articulate the conditions governing theoretical comprehension of the post-Enlightenment idea of God. It is his conviction, additionally, that the new conception is truer to Christian religion than the traditional view of the subjective side of religion as a relationship-of-consciousness.

(3) In the 1827 lectures as well, the "Introduction" does not represent a rising to the systematic standpoint. The manuscript gets around this deficiency by deriving the concept from representation and then seeking to demonstrate the necessity of the religious standpoint; the 1824 lectures, by introducing the concept of religion in the form of a definition and then again going on to demonstrate the

necessity of religion. Hegel was quite aware of the weaknesses of both procedures. In the 1827 lectures he forgoes the supposed demonstration of necessity, which in any event consists solely in referring to the course of development of the system. His new attempt to solve the problem of securing a beginning draws the consequences from the foregoing unsuccessful procedures. The foundation of the philosophy of religion is, he tells us, the result of the development of the system hitherto; the standpoint of religion has to be taken as proved. It is "a lemma or subsidiary proposition . . . that the content with which we begin is genuine content" (*LPR* 1:366). This is the sole "demonstration of necessity" that matches the system, unless the system is to be traversed all over again. Hegel does, to be sure, mention yet another way, that of turning to one's own consciousness. But the result of this could not be something "demonstrated" but only "conceded." To invoke the religious consciousness merely reinforces the "assurance" that the idea of God is the result of philosophy (*LPR* 1:368). It does not replace scientific proof.

Elevation to the absolute standpoint corresponds formally to the cosmological proof. Compared with this, a second line of argument passes over from the concept to the reality of God, thus corresponding to the ontological proof. The two lines of argument are related to one another—in the same way that in Christian Wolff's *Theologia naturalis* the first part corresponds to the cosmological argument and thus proves the *existentia et attributa Dei* a posteriori, while the second conducts the proof of God *ex notione entis perfectissimi.*[20]

This solution offered by the 1827 lectures is the only one that does justice to the position the philosophy of religion occupies within the system. For it does not seek to make the proof an element in the systematic exposition of the concept of religion; after

---

20. See the titles of the two parts: Christian Wolff, *Theologia naturalis. . . . Pars prior . . . qua existentia et attributa Dei a posteriori demonstrantur. Pars posterior, qua existentia et attributa Dei ex notione entis perfectissimi et natura animae demonstrantur* (Frankfurt and Leipzig, 1739, 1741). On the connection between the two forms, see Dieter Henrich, *Der ontologische Gottesbeweis*, 2d ed. (Tübingen, 1967), pp. 55–56.

all, such a demonstration "lies already behind" the philosophy of religion. A further argument in favor of this conception is that the 1831 lectures take it over apparently unchanged.[21] Since, however, the logical result of this approach is to refer to the course of development of the system, the previous objections to the transition to the sphere of absolute spirit also remain valid.

To clarify the problem, let us refer to the two passages where Hegel passes over from objective to absolute spirit: § 552 of the *Encyclopedia* and §§ 358–360 of the *Philosophy of Right*. The latter paragraphs simply sketch the preconditions for the world-historical emergence of Christianity and the main epochs in its history. Here we find the illuminating remark that in the modern world truth has "abandoned the world of beyond and its arbitrary force (shape?[22])" and that self-consciousness finds in religion "the feeling and the representation of this its own truth as an ideal essentiality." The "division" into object and self-consciousness is thus already accomplished, and it remains an open question why and how knowledge of the truth as ideal essentiality is arrived at and what status such essentiality has. This is *not* the elevation to the concept of religion that matches the system and is required by it. The main text of § 552 in the second edition of the *Encyclopedia* also makes the transition from the sphere of objective spirit to that of absolute spirit in primarily historical fashion—with the remark that the thinking spirit of world history abandons its own worldliness, "in such a way that this knowledge raises itself inwardly to the *knowledge of absolute spirit,* as the eternally actual truth." The fact that the emergence of religion is here said to presuppose that the restricted character of the "spirit of the people" has been transcended is probably due to the architectonics of the *Encyclopedia.* Taken at face value, all this remark does is to assign to cosmopolitanism the place that had otherwise been withheld from it in the system, but without securing a foundation for religion. The corollary is couched somewhat more precisely: the point of depar-

21. See *LPR* 1:384–385 n. 47. This special material is confirmed by Strauss's excerpts; see *LPR* 1:464–465.

22. [*Tr.*] The author suggests that the word *Gewalt,* here rendered as "force," may be a mistake for *Gestalt,* "shape," in the text of *PR* § 360.

248

ture in each case is said to contain the "material that constitutes the content of the concept of God." But the genuine material is "spirit, . . . whose absolute determination is effective reason, i.e., the self-determining, self-realizing concept itself—freedom." Hegel is here attempting to do belated justice to Kant's practical grounding of theology, even if in the process he totally changes Kant's manner of thought; his concept of freedom and Kant's are utterly irreconcilable. For this reason the genesis and the tenor of the concept of the "divine universality" of spirit, spirit "wholly in its indeterminate universality" (*LPR* 1:380), remain indeterminate here too. This concept of God as "the absolutely universal in-and-for-itself" (*LPR* 1:385) is most reminiscent of the absolute idea at the end of the *Logic*. This would indeed make it impossible to understand why the philosophy of religion is located at the end of the system, and it would be less than just to its approach inasmuch as it takes as its starting point the concept of spirit.

The crux of this question can be broken in two extreme ways, either by assuming that Hegel's system is quite incapable of displaying the elevation to the idea of God—any more than earlier metaphysics could display the elevation to the concept of first cause or of necessary being—or by assuming on the contrary that no metaphysical proof at all is needed for this purpose and that philosophy of religion need have no qualms about making the idea of God its starting point. Neither answer takes Hegel's way of thinking into account. Despite a few obscurities the latter does grasp the transition sufficiently clearly for it to be possible to derive conclusions from it as far as the concept of religion is concerned.

The transition to absolute spirit is to be made not from the end of objective spirit but from the concept of spirit in general. Hegel terms spirit the idea that "has attained to its being-for-self" from nature, the idea "whose *object* no less than *subject* is *the concept*" (*Enc* 2d ed. § 381). It is absolute as "in *an implicit as well as explicit unity* of the objectivity of spirit with its ideality or concept" (*Enc* 2d ed. § 385). This concept of absolute spirit is in no sense a mystification. All it says is that knowing spirit, which in the sphere of objective spirit knows spirit as an appearance of the idea, as the truth of nature and as a world "which it has to produce, and

which it has produced"[23]—this knowing spirit transcends the re-
strictions of this sphere and knows spirit as its own self and its object as thought. This means knowing the absolute as spirit. It is not
just at the end of the *Encyclopedia* but already in the corollary to
§ 563 (2d ed.)—whose appropriate place is in § 552 (3d ed.), in
the transition from objective to absolute spirit—that Hegel elucidates this self-thinking of spirit by the concept of *noēsis tēs noēseōs*.
There is a difference between this and the Aristotelian use of the
term in that for Hegel thought does not think itself in isolation but
knows itself as all truth—as the thought that recognizes itself in actuality and returns into itself from actuality. Only then is substantiality identical with subjectivity.

The actual obstacle is thus seen to be, not the transition to absolute spirit, but the entire course of the system—from the beginning in logic, through nature as externalization of the idea, on
to objective spirit. Whoever understands the absolute idea as self-
thinking thought and the sphere of reality as appearance of the idea
has, to use a Hegelian phrase, "already accomplished" the transition to absolute spirit. The advance to absolute spirit then no longer
conceals any special problems. To what has gone before it adds
only the moment of identity of knowing spirit with spirit as object. The concept of spirit as such already involves the resumption that is the precondition for thinking the universal. Individual
subjectivity, by contrast, is abstract unless the concept of spirit is
grounded metaphysically. The attempt to secure the transition to
religion from the sublation of individual subjectivity in objective
spirit would at best lead to an ideology with religious trimmings.

This interpretation of religion and of the idea of God is doubtless
open to critical objections. The proper answer to them is, as Hegel
would put it, that however full one's heart may be, philosophy is
not concerned with what is in the heart but what is developed and
demonstrated. And there is no other concept of absolute spirit that

23. See *Enc* § 385. On the concept of the other "world" produced by spirit, see
already *GW* 8:277. Transcripts of Hegel's Encyclopedia lectures might contain
further clues to the transition from objective to absolute spirit, but there are no extant sources that relate to this subject.

Hegel developed. For him the "task of philosophy" is to know this concept cognitively—to grasp what in the Christian religion "is *given* to representation and what being [*Wesen*] is *in itself,* in its own element, that of the concept" (*Enc* 2d ed. § 384)—in other words, to grasp infinite content in infinite form. Hegel regards this as attained in his conception. Indisputably it is open to criticism in many respects, precisely because it is embedded in the system. But the initial result of subjecting it to criticism is not another philosophy of religion, but none at all. For the task Hegel set himself was, following the demise of the traditional school philosophy and also the moral interpretation of religion, to win back the concept of God and of religion for philosophy. This reminder of the contemporary theoretical situation is in no way designed to exclude alternatives. It simply draws attention to the fact that other approaches to philosophical theology—or to a philosophy of religion that does not lay its claim to legitimacy on the mere fact of religion—would require a renewed search for a foundation. But for Hegel the search for an alternative is of no current interest. In reply to the demand for a more appropriate idea of God and a better grounding, he would cite the words Fichte used to defend himself in the atheism controversy: "We need no other God, nor can we conceive any other."[24]

(4) This interpretation of the transition from objective to absolute spirit in the framework of the third lecture series is also applicable, mutatis mutandis, to the two preceding series. The difference between them and the third series does not reside here but in the consistent fashion in which Hegel carries out in 1827 the conception of the "Concept of Religion" he had already outlined in 1824. This consistency is already evident at the beginning of the "Survey of the Treatment of Our Subject." Hegel stresses here that in all science there can be just one method, the self-explicating concept. From this concept he develops the structure of the "Concept of

---

24. Johann Gottlieb Fichte, *Gesamtausgabe,* ed. R. Lauth et al., part 1 (Stuttgart–Bad Canstatt, 1964 ff.), 5:354. Cf. "On the Foundation of Our Belief in a Divine Government of the Universe," in *Nineteenth-Century Philosophy,* ed. P. L. Gardiner (New York, 1969), p. 25.

Religion." This can be read as a criticism directed both at the 1821 conception with its duality of representation and proof of necessity, and at the supposed duality between the empirical and the speculative grounding of the philosophy of religion in the 1824 lectures.

The preview of Part I corroborates what Hegel has already said concerning the concept of absolute spirit: religion is "spirit conscious of its own essence, conscious of itself. Spirit is conscious, and that of which it is conscious is the true, essential spirit." The identity of the spirit that is conscious and the spirit that is known is expressed by Hegel in an almost provocative manner: "True spirit is *its* essence, not the essence of an other" (*LPR* 1:178). Because of this identity he defines religion as idea. In it the side of the concept of spirit is identical with the side of its reality, and the first moment of the idea is that of "substantial unity"—"the universal in and for itself, the purely spiritual without further determination" (*LPR* 1:178). Religion proper does not therefore belong to this first moment, but only to the breaking up of the substantial unity in the relationship-of-consciousness and in knowing oneself in unity with God, in the cultus.

For Hegel this conception reflects "the rhythm or the pure eternal life of spirit." But the logical paradigm lying behind this metaphor cannot be determined in exact fashion. On the one hand it seems to reside in the moments of universality, particularity, and individuality, and on the other in the nexus of concept, judgment (or division), and conclusion (or syllogism). Hegel seems unaware of any impediment arising from this discrepancy. He even links the differing paradigms by an "or"—though to be sure in a text that is based only on secondary sources (*LPR* 1:177 n. 68). Moreover he denotes even the realization of the concept in "Determinate Religion" as a mode of "division" of the concept (*LPR* 1:181). He does not attempt to articulate with logical definitions the major difference in the ways the concept "divides" into the relationship-of-consciousness on the one hand and into the historical religions on the other. This suggests that the logical definitions play only a small constitutive role in the architectonics of the philosophy of religion. As Hegel obviously pays little attention to this topic, it seems right to refrain here too from seeking to interpret the structure of the philosophy of religion in a consistent, logical manner.[25]

(5) In 1827 Hegel does not, as he did in 1824, reduce the moments of "substantial unity," "difference," and "reestablished unity" to two relationships in such a way as to dispense with separate discussion of the first moment, that of substantial identity. Even now Hegel does not really do justice to the key position this moment occupies for the unfolding of the "Concept of Religion"— presumably because the actual systematic derivation of this concept of substantial identity precedes the philosophy of religion, and its concrete exposition does not pertain to the first moment but the second and third. Yet categories that only belong there do in fact intrude into the treatment of the first moment. The question indeed arises whether this is not also true of the concept of God. Hegel acknowledges that at the start of the philosophy of absolute spirit "God" is initially an abstract name "that has not yet received any genuine import" (*LPR* 1:367). The only thing that is systematically developed is the concept of what is in and for itself universal, containing absolutely everything within itself (*LPR* 1:367), the one true actuality. At this standpoint "an actuality that we call thinking has as yet no proper place"; thinking as the locus of the universal is "absorbed" in the One that has actual being in and for itself. The distinction between thinking and the universal belongs "in the first instance to our reflection" (*LPR* 1:373). By analogy the question arises whether the expression "God" ought not to be reserved for the universal that is the object of religious knowledge.

The universal "in which there is no limitation, finitude, or particularity" is also termed "absolute substance" (*LPR* 1:369). Misunderstandings arise here because although Hegel makes it clear that the references to "absolute substance" do not imply Spinozism

25. The present tendency to seek parallels between even the finest ramifications of structure in the philosophy of religion and logical paradigms leads to results that verge on the laughable, especially when this effort is not based on a developmental analysis of the previous lecture compilations. But it is in no way our intention to dispute the possibility that an interpretation along these lines but based on reliable editions will also yield better results, although it will have to adopt a critical approach to Hegel's texts as a whole.

or pantheism, it remains a mere assurance that their result is not to exclude subjectivity—especially since Hegel hardly carries out his stated intention of showing at once how the substance in question is related to subjectivity (*LPR* 1:369). The obvious misinterpretation is excluded only if one's understanding of "absolute substance" is based on the concept of spirit in the *Encyclopedia*. Moreover, there it is expressly stated that substantiality is henceforth equated with subjectivity (2d ed. § 563 cor.). In similar fashion David Friedrich Strauss's excerpts affirm that "God is not merely substance in general but self-knowing substance or subject" (*LPR* 1:465). It is only because "absolute substance" is conceived as the "substantial identity" of spirit and as subjectivity, as thinking, that it is possible to apply here the category of "division"—the distinction between what knows and what is known and between the individual forms of this knowing.

The concept of the substantial unity of absolute spirit is the speculative core of Hegel's philosophy of religion in its mature form. It comes into being through the process of elevation above the sphere of objective spirit. This process also provides the systematic justification for an axiom that can be traced back to the *Early Theological Writings,* that of the consubstantiality of divine and finite spirit. If the idea of God is the idea of spirit as what is utterly universal, the essence of finite spirit, and if finite spirit is a moment of the universal, then substantive diversity is precluded, although not difference as such. This also makes clear Hegel's reasons for disputing the call for a prior demonstration of the possibility of cognitive knowledge of God. A philosophical theology that understands "God" as an otherworldly "supreme being," or in general as abstract, necessary being, unquestionably falls into difficulties in seeking to secure the existence of its object. The problems with Hegel's conception, by contrast, lie in showing that the development of the logical determinations proceeds in a consistent manner and that these determinations form the inner structure of nature and of spirit. If spirit is the resumption of the system, then the individual spirit's self-knowing within spirit as the universal does not present a problem. The demonstration that is required in Hegel's system may ultimately be no less problematical than the unsuccessful demonstration provided in the framework of traditional philosophical theology. But its course is totally different. This explains Hegel's vehement polemic directed at the assertion that God is unknowable: if religion is nothing other than the individual spirit's knowledge of spirit as the universal, then surely it is hard to understand where there could be difficulties of principle.

(6) The definition of this unity forms the actual content of the "Concept of Religion." The basis for advancing further is indicated by Hegel only laconically: "The second [moment] after this absolute foundation is distinction in general, and only with distinction does religion as such begin." He even rejects the idea of explaining the absolute division more precisely and refers instead to the *Logic*: from it we must take over the fact "that this absolute universality proceeds to the internal distinction of itself, it proceeds to the primal division" (*LPR* 1:380–381). This reference to the *Logic* would be of little avail if the advance could not be made intelligible on the basis of the concept of spirit. To the extent that the substantial identity is to be conceived as knowing oneself in the spirit, differentiation is already posited as forming part of identity. Finite spirit knows spirit as its essence, so knows itself to be sublated in spirit and yet stands over against spirit as something distinct from it. This is precisely what is meant by saying that in the "absolute division" God exists as spirit for spirit; the same thing is said in § 554 of the *Encyclopedia*. To this extent the third lecture series corresponds to the second (see above, p. 241). Yet it differs from it at two points concerning the way in which the "division" is concretely specified.

In the first place Hegel now seems to accord the division cosmological significance as well: expressed concretely, it is the "creation of the world." But he at once goes on to explain that this means creation "of the subjective spirit for which God is object." He also defines the concept of manifestation, of spirit's self-revealing, in terms of the creating "of subjective spirit for which the absolute is" (*LPR* 1:381). Although what is said here seems to reduce the significance of speaking of "creation of the world" to the question of the relationship-of-consciousness and how it is to be grounded, it points at the same time beyond that question, in a dimension that again becomes evident only from the general concept of spirit. The revealing of the abstract idea is, we are told, the transition, the becoming of nature. But as the revealing of free spirit it is the "*positing* of nature as *its* world—a positing that, as reflection, is at the same time the *presupposing* of the world as self-subsistent nature" (*Enc* 2d ed. § 384). Only to this extent is it possible to speak here of the division as having a cosmological significance, or to speak of a "creation of the world."

In the second place, the further definition of the division follows a different path from that of the preceding lectures. In 1824 the key word *Urteil* includes the historical realization of the religious relationship; in 1827, by contrast, it includes the entire range of its forms, but not as historical forms. Spirit's self-knowing encompasses all forms of consciousness. Hegel reduces the multiplicity of religious forms to immediate knowledge, feeling, representation, and thought. He regards the first two as subjective and the last two as objective (*LPR* 1:385–386). This distinction would seem not to do them justice. For even religious representation is not, in Hegel's eyes, an external mode of representation, like the representation of any sort of mental or sense-content. It remains constantly embraced by religious certainty. This again finds its most pregnant expression in the concept of spirit's witness to spirit, that is, in the knowledge "that this content conforms to the nature of my spirit and satisfies the needs of my spirit. My spirit knows itself, it knows its essence— that . . . is the absolute verification of the eternally true" (*LPR* 1:389).

It is not for us here to comment in detail on the broad portrayal of the forms of religious knowledge. Even in the three later lecture series Hegel defines the central concepts of this religious relationship in such differing fashion that a developmental-historical comparison would be needed in order to describe them. For example, he treats the concept of faith in the 1824 lectures as the concept of the cultus; in 1827 he understands it as the first form of immediate certainty (*LPR* 1:387); and in 1831 he treats it as the third form, following feeling and representation (*LPR* 1:466–467)—as he had already done in one of the enumerations of the forms of religion in the corollary to § 270 of the *Philosophy of Right* (*PR* 166,

W 8:335). The change of place in the system expresses a changed definition of the forms of religious relationship. Admittedly they are in each case arranged in hierarchical manner. But it cannot be said that Hegel passes over "dialectically" from one to the other. The only sense in which representation is "sublated" is that the succeeding form, thought, is introduced. The philosophy of religion speaks of thought, however, only in the framework of the way in which the proofs of God are conceived by the understanding. Despite this, Hegel is of the view that the explication of the proofs of God is "the explication of religion itself" (LPR 1:416). Yet it is only in 1827 that he treats the proofs as a form of the religious relationship. The other lectures assign them to individual religions or stages in the history of religion. Nor do they, in Hegel's eyes, actually function as proofs; rather they are forms of the "elevation to God"—though this applies only to the cosmological and the physicotheological proofs. For Hegel makes no mention at all of the ethicotheological proof, in which Kant sees the sole basis for a philosophical foundation of the idea of God; and the ontological proof does not depict an elevation to God. It is rather in the development of the system as a whole that the idea of God is, properly speaking, demonstrated.

(7) As the sphere of "division" [Urteil], the phenomenology of religious consciousness forms only the middle section of the "Concept of Religion," and ought rightly to be followed by a sphere consisting of "conclusion" or "syllogism" [Schluss]. This in itself affords grounds for suspecting that the religious knowledge of God is ultimately inadequate and has to be replaced by a more appropriate knowledge, or that the forms of knowledge are, as such, inappropriate to their object. Both presumptions are correct. The unsatisfactory nature of religious knowledge is made sufficiently plain in Hegel's discussion of representation and of thought based on the understanding, where he says that, unlike conceptual thought, representation takes mental and sense-content as "isolated in its determinacy," whereas the form of thought is "universality" (LPR 1:404). But though universality can also enter into religion, its proper place is in philosophy. To this extent it would be an easy matter to pass over at this point from the treatment of the

religious consciousness to philosophy. But this would be to leave the territory of the philosophy of religion.

It is in any event open to doubt whether anything is achieved by such a transition if it is correct that the theoretical form as such falls short of its goal, namely the cognitive knowledge of God. Hegel himself seems doubtful in this regard. In the theoretical relationship, he tells us, consciousness is immersed in its object and knows nothing of itself. "But this knowledge, this connection without relationship, is not the whole of what is in fact present." "The true . . . is the relationship of myself and this object" (LPR 1:442). And, he goes on, this kind of connection no longer belongs to the theoretical but to the practical relationship.

The differentiation of these relationships, those of knowledge and of the cultus, is the only factor common to the 1824, 1827, and 1831 lectures—even if in 1824 it does not have the same significance as in the later lectures for the architectonics of the "Concept of Religion." The concrete shape of its content changes, however, between 1824 and 1827 in a way that casts doubt on whether the two relationships can be appropriately described as those of knowledge and cultus. The 1824 lectures define the theoretical and the practical relationship as that of differentiating and of sublating the rupture (LPR 1:327–328). Similarly the "Introduction" to the 1827 lectures also still denotes the cultus as "the sublating of this antithesis of the subject and God, of the separation, this remoteness of the subject from God" (LPR 1:180). In the "Concept of Religion" itself, however, Hegel does not describe the theoretical relationship as rupture or separation but as "connection without relationship," as forgetting myself and immersing myself in the object, in fact as "immediate unity." It is only in the will, and thus in the practical relationship, that the separation between me and the object, between subjectivity and objectivity, begins—and likewise begins the overcoming of this antithesis.

Hegel does not call the first form of the cultus "faith" here, but "devotion" [Andacht]: "it is subjectivity that possesses itself therein, that prays, speaks, passes through [and beyond] representations, knows itself and the object itself, and is concerned with its elevation." An important aspect of the cultus is "the mystical" (*LPR* 1:445), and the "innermost feature of the cultus" is "the consciousness of my union and reconciliation with God." The "external form"—sacraments, sacrifice—Hegel cites in second place, while he denotes as "the most genuine cultus" ethical life, the purification of one's heart to attain the universal. Philosophy in particular is viewed as a "continual cultus; it has as its object the true, and the true in its highest shape as absolute spirit, as God" (*LPR* 1:446). And finally he explicitly distinguishes the theoretical and the practical relationship as, respectively, the elevation that is itself knowledge, and as the knowing of this elevation.[26]

The two relationships ought not therefore to be designated primarily as those of knowledge and cultus, but of consciousness and self-consciousness. Then the distinction between the 1824 and 1827 lectures disappears. In the relationship-of-consciousness, the knowing subject and the object are separated, but this separation is not reflected upon. It is only reflection on this knowing that thematizes the finite subject as a constitutive moment. Once the two relationships are defined in this way, it becomes clear why the theoretical relationship, as one of mere consciousness, is necessarily insufficient for the cognitive knowledge of God: its orientation to something objective makes it impossible to conceive God as spirit. For this latter requires the inclusion of the knowing subject—and hence the relationship of self-consciousness. The suggestion that the two relationships should be viewed primarily as those of consciousness and self-consciousness does, to be sure, seem to conflict with the 1827 lectures' association of the witness of the spirit with the witness "of one's own spirit, [the witness] that this content conforms to the nature of my spirit and satisfies the needs of my spirit" (*LPR* 1:389). But this concept is portrayed in broader fashion in the 1824 lectures, indeed in the context of the second relation-

---

26. *LPR* 1:449. The textual situation is unclear here. Hegel seems to want to distinguish three stages: elevation, which is itself a mode of knowing (the theoretical relationship); the knowing of this elevation made explicit (the practical relationship); and the knowing of this knowing. It is possible, however, that the abbreviated version transmitted by the Berlin anonymous transcript (*An*) is the correct one.

ship, where it would hardly have an appropriate place if it were designated as a practical relationship and not as a relationship of self-consciousness.

But even if the primary definition of the relationships as those of consciousness and self-consciousness were correct, it would still be open to doubt whether they could justifiably be developed in this separate fashion. In any case the differentiation of knowledge and cultus could be appropriate, but simply not yet realized. As far as can be seen from Strauss's excerpts, Hegel does indeed define the cultus in the 1831 lectures as consciousness of "having been taken up into God" and as "consciousness of union with absolute spirit as the universal spirit of a people" (*LPR* 1:469–470). Yet the emphasis lies on the establishment and enjoyment of this unity, so that there seems to be justification rather for distinguishing the "single forms"[27] of religion, as forms of knowing, from the "forms of the cultus."

(8) In the 1824 and 1827 lectures the portrayal of the cultus concludes the "Concept of Religion." This is convincing especially if such a portrayal is understood primarily as an explication of self-consciousness. Although the standpoint of the 1831 lectures is broadly in accord with that of 1827, Hegel does in addition discuss here the relationship of religion to the state. The other series also mention this theme in passing, but it has no separate place in the overall system of the philosophy of religion. By contrast the different versions of the philosophy of right show that Hegel is constantly led to speak of this relationship, even if the context differs somewhat from case to case. Religion is a theme in the philosophy of the state, but the state is not a theme in the philosophy of religion. It is true that the second edition of the *Encyclopedia* furnishes an example to the contrary. It deals with the relationship of religion to the state in the corollary to § 563, in other words in the framework, not of the philosophy of religion properly speaking, to be sure, but of absolute spirit. In the third edition, however, Hegel places this corollary at the end of "Objective Spirit," as a bridge

27. [*Tr.*] These "single forms" (*einfache Formen*) are feeling, representation, and faith.

to the philosophy of absolute spirit. Thus in this respect the evidence of the *Encyclopedia* agrees with that of the lectures. We could more readily assume that the discussion of the relationship to art and to philosophy is a constitutive moment in the "Concept of Religion," as the manuscript still maintains (*LPR* 1:233). But the later lecture series tacitly revise this way of viewing the matter.

In the 1831 lectures current affairs provide an evident occasion for appending the theme "Religion and State" to the "Concept of Religion," namely the July 1830 Revolution,[28] which Hegel views primarily in religiopolitical terms. Nevertheless, for the foundational problems of philosophy of religion such considerations remain irrelevant, unlike the case in the Jena period, during which the philosophy of religion only gradually emerged out of the philosophy of ethical life. But the religiopolitical aspects do gain in importance during the course of the Berlin years. From the mid-1820s on, Hegel also again accords to the confessional factor[29] a greater impact on political relationships; this is not due to any inner logic in his approach but is triggered by the political situation and reinforced by personal experiences. Central to the standpoint of the Berlin years is the idea of the unity of religion and state, which is not to be confused with a unity of church and state, or with a theocratic ideal of the state. This latter form of unity he regards as the hallmark of despotism. Since *The German Constitution* (see above, pp. 170–171) Hegel regarded separation from the church as a necessary condition for the rise of the modern state. The call for the unity of state and religion rather stems logically from the systematic linkage between the philosophy of objective spirit and that of absolute spirit. State and religion are both forms, though differing from one another, of the self-knowledge of spirit and its freedom: "There is *one* concept of freedom in religion and state" (*LPR* 1:452).

28. On Hegel's assessment of the July Revolution, see the author's "Hegel's Last Year in Berlin," in *Hegel's Philosophy of Action*, ed. L. S. Stepelevich and D. Lamb (Atlantic Highlands, N.J., 1983), esp. pp. 32–40. On the relationship of religion, church, and state, see his "Christianity and Secularity in Hegel's Concept of the State," *Journal of Religion* 61 (1981): 127–145.

29. [Tr.] That is, the rivalry among the major Christian confessions, Catholic, Lutheran, and Reformed.

But Hegel's historical reflection and diagnosis of the contemporary scene also furnish arguments for the unity of religion and state. For he sees the modern idea of the state as resulting from the world-historical actualization of the "Christian principle." This is in no way to be understood as meaning that the state is organized through direct application of biblical principles. It is shaped, in Hegel's view, by the principle of freedom and subjectivity that has become dominant in the Christian world—a principle linked to biblical teaching but not to be understood, or justified, solely on a scriptural basis. For the principle in question had already come on the scene in the ancient world, but without becoming a world-historical force. In Christianity too it was not something complete from the start. It had needed a long time to develop, through the forms of Christianity of late antiquity and the Middle Ages down to the present day. Hegel's insight into the necessity of differing configurations of realization guards him against labeling some of these forms as "decline" or "loss of origin." As already in *The German Constitution,* even the confessional split is not viewed by him here as a world-historical misfortune but as an indispensable event for the establishment of the modern state. In the context of this world-historical realization of the "Christian principle," the confessional schism also acquires, in Hegel's eyes, a new function. What is decisive for him is not differences in sacramental doctrine or in the attitude to scripture or in the doctrine of justification, but differences in the idea of freedom. His understanding of Protestantism in the Berlin years is no longer based on the idea of the Protestant "demystification" of the world that marked the Jena years nor the idea of Protestantism as a "cultured" religion characteristic of the Nuremberg period. Central now is the Protestant sublation of the gulf between holiness and worldliness in order to develop ethical, rational institutions. Herein lies, he believes, the political relevance of Protestantism. This ethical life is to be termed Christian insofar as it is mediated with the principle of subjectivity, which acquires a shape for the first time in the Christian world. In this and nothing else, in Hegel's view, does the Christian character of the modern state reside. This conception forms his definitive answer to the problem, which was a particularly pressing one in his day, of the relationship of religion and state. The answer is *not* furnished by the concluding remarks in the manuscript, where Hegel saw no alternative to that of ending with the "discord" that he found present in the actuality of his time.

3. Determinate Religion[30]

Hegel's treatment of "Determinate Religion" is characterized by an assumption and a claim—his assumption that there is such a thing as a single history of religion, and his claim to be able to supply it with a logical grounding. It is this claim that alone makes the history of religion a genuine theme of philosophy—something it in no way was in Hegel's day, nor is today. This claim has hardly ever been endorsed by anyone. And today the assumption that there is a universal history of religion is also almost equally open to question. Most likely it is not merely a coincidental link that exists between the rejection of assumption and claim alike.

The "Concept of Religion" discloses what it can mean that there is reason in religion. But the concrete substantiation of this hypothesis is afforded only in Parts II and III of the lectures, which are devoted to actual religion—"Determinate Religion" and the "Consummate Religion" respectively. We have already referred briefly (see above, pp. 215 ff.) to the reasons for this threefold division. But even if one accepts the argument that religion is idea and that it is therefore necessary to develop first the concept, then the reality, and lastly the unity of the two, it remains initially unclear why the reality should not only pertain to time as such but have to be conceived as *history* of religion. To understand this one must go back to Hegel's general views on the "nature of spirit," namely that the reality of spirit is always historical and not mere nature. For it belongs to the essence of spirit to be at first immediate, merely natu-

---

30. This section is a revision of a lecture given by the author, "Zur Logik der Bestimmten Religion," published in *Hegels Logik der Philosophie,* eds. D. Henrich and R. P. Horstmann (Stuttgart, 1984), pp. 172–188. The most detailed previous treatment of the compositional problems of Part II of the lectures is found in Heede, "Die göttliche Idee und ihre Erscheinung," pp. 147–181. [*Tr.* See the table providing a comparative analysis of the structure of "Determinate Religion" in *LPR* 2:88–89.]

ral, and only through freedom to become what it implicitly is—and this means, in the present case, to achieve the shape wherein the concept of religion finds its own appropriate mode of reality.

These general considerations do, to be sure, fix the terminus a quo and the terminus ad quem of a history of religion. They also imply the multiplicity of religions and at the same time a unitary history of religion. They give no information, however, regarding the principles of this history, its periodization, the number of shapes the history of religion has to traverse until its consummation, or even the historical identity of these shapes. And it is not only these questions that they leave open, but also the more general question to what extent the history of religion can at all be determined more concretely through principles of reason. Hegel claims such rationality for the history of religion in general as well as for the individual religions. It is, to be sure, primarily the external side that is shown by the history of religion. It is therefore "one of the most difficult tasks" to study it in such a way as "to apprehend . . . its *rationality*"; "it is human beings who have lighted upon such religions, so there must be *reason* in them." But alongside the demand for such cognitive knowledge stands the insight that "contingency and locality pervade all these forms" (*LPR* 1: 198–199). This is what causes the difficulties when it comes to systematizing the history of religion, and in each lecture series Hegel adumbrates new principles with a view to resolving these difficulties.

The four series can therefore be interpreted as so many attempts to ground a philosophy of the history of religion. Thus it is necessary here too to discuss the conception of each series separately, and at any rate not in the manner that Hegel's expositions are sometimes analyzed, in their entirety. The question of reason in religion must be limited to the principles governing the structure of the history of religion in each series. In this connection we shall also have occasion to speak of other aspects of the religion under discussion. We cannot, however, enter into Hegel's treatment of the individual religions as such. For this purpose it would in any event be a more appropriate procedure to study not primarily the four conceptions as a whole but how the treatment of a particular religion changed over the four lecture series.

3.1. The Structural Principles of the History of Religion

(1) What Hegel affirms is that the history of religion constitutes an ordering of the logical moments directed toward an end, an ordering determined by the concept itself. This implies first of all that, to be able to attest their ordering function, these moments have themselves to come before us as ordered. The "Division of the Subject" in the manuscript does, it is true, describe the sphere of "Determinate Religion" in general terms as the development of the concept, as "the *positing* of what is contained in the concept," and, in such positing, as elevation to the idea (*LPR* 1:110–111). It does not, however, name any specific principles of construction. It is only the short introduction to "Determinate Religion" that adopts the *Logic*'s division into the doctrines of being, essence, and concept as paradigmatic for the history of religion too. By this means a principle seems to have been found that is legitimated by the speculative logic itself. This threefold division, however, conceals within itself more problems than are initially apparent from Hegel's text.

An obvious course would be to relate these three spheres of logical determination to the tripartite division of the religions to be found in the previous editions of the *Philosophy of Religion*: to assign nature religion to "being," the religions of spiritual individuality to "essence," and the Christian religion to "the concept." But this is not at all how the logical structuring is intended. Hegel has a quite different conception, of which we have been unaware until recently. With a single modification, to which we shall return, he consistently articulates "Determinate Religion" into three sections, primarily as follows: nature religion, the religions of sublimity and beauty, and lastly the religion of expediency. By this means "being" is attributed to nature religion, "essence" to the religions of Israel and Greece, and the "concept" to Roman religion. So the tripartite division of "Determinate Religion" for which Eduard Zeller, for example, seeks in vain is actually realized. By contrast, it is less easy to follow Christian Hermann Weisse in treating the Christian religion as a third following on the two spheres of "Determinate Religion."[31] The insight gained into the actual conception does, to be sure, eliminate such seeming problems. But it does not solve the real difficulty, namely that a strict threefold division does not leave any logical sphere to be attributed to the Christian religion. Hegel therefore acknowledges that it is not the concept as such but only the finite concept that corresponds to the religion of Rome. By this means the strict parallel drawn between logic and history of religion is undermined, especially since Rome is assigned the concept of expediency or purposiveness [*Zweckmässigkeit*], whose place in the system does *not* come at the beginning of the logic of concept.

This is not the place to consider in detail to what extent the correlation of being with nature religion and essence with the religions of Greece and Israel is justified or even compelling. The category of being may appear appropriate for nature religion because the latter is the immediate form of religion, and the logical expression of immediacy as undifferentiated relation to self is "being." Immediacy, however, is not defined by the fact of being found to be historically first, but by the "absolute, undivided unity" of the two sides—God and self-consciousness (*LPR* 2:99). Similar arguments are introduced by Hegel for designating the second stage as that of essence. Even the duality of the religions treated at this stage must be seen as related to the concept of essence. Admittedly the way in which these questions are discussed in the survey setting out the division of "Determinate Religion" (*LPR* 2:95–97) does not provide a sufficient basis for interpreting Jewish and Greek religion in their own terms and in their relationship to each other as religions of essence. But at the beginning of the section devoted to these religions Hegel also indicates that the designation highlights the duality between universal thought and immediacy downgraded to

31. Eduard Zeller, "Hegel's *Vorlesungen über die Philosophie der Religion*" (1841), reprinted in *Die Flucht in den Begriff*, eds. F. W. Graf and F. Wagner (Stuttgart, 1982); see p. 128. Christian Hermann Weisse, "Über die eigentliche Grenze des Pantheismus und des philosophischen Theismus" (1833), reprinted in *Die Flucht in den Begriff*; see p. 69.

inessentiality. Essence is "the universal as absolute power" that manifests itself, and "its reality is the totality of its show [*Schein*]" (*LPR* 2:124). The category of necessity also fits the designation of this sphere as that of essence. It is another question whether it is appropriate to identify the religions of Israel and Greece as religions of essence, especially since the relationship between the idea of God and finitude is defined quite differently in each of them. And even from an external point of view it is striking that the concept of the One, to which Hegel gives prominence in the religion of Israel, pertains not so much to the logic of essence as to that of being, as does the dialectic of the one and the many. Even more problematic is the analogy between the "concept" and Roman religion. At the beginning of this section Hegel explains what he means by the concept, namely freedom, the truth of necessity (*LPR* 2:191). The concept freely posited for itself is initially confronted by reality, which "is determined as a negative opposed to it. [Later on] in the absolute concept or the pure idea, this reality, this hostile element, melts into unity . . . with the concept" (*LPR* 2:193–194). But what we are here principally concerned with is not such questions but methodological points of view.

Hegel provides no further justification for assigning the stages of logic to the history of religion. He simply assigns them without our being told why they should form the paradigm of the history of religion. This tempts us to ask whether it is not better to structure the history of religion by the three moments of the concept—universality, particularity, and individuality—or according to the model of concept, division, and conclusion, or some other model of choice. The history of art, for example, which exhibits at least a number of points of contact with the history of religion, obviously does not follow the model of the logic, nor does the history of philosophy. In regard to the latter Hegel proceeds differently inasmuch as he affirms a correspondence between individual logical categories and configurations of the history of philosophy. It might be advisable, therefore, to make the attribution of logical categories to contents in the field of the philosophies of nature and spirit subject to the following criterion: every such attribution must be justified vis-à-vis the application of other models in similar cases.

Interpretations that do not satisfy this criterion, rather than providing the supposed logical precision, tend to become an exercise in, at best, logical schematics or, at worst, sheer interpretative caprice. And all that the latter accomplishes is to nourish the objections constantly raised against Hegel for allegedly having enveloped the riches of historical reality within an arid logical schema. The way in which the search for logical principles of construction has recently been carried out also in other areas of Hegel's philosophy is all too conducive to this manner of viewing him. And in the special case of the logical structuring of the history of religion, it must be acknowledged not only that Hegel did nothing to justify his assignment of categories, but also that research to date has provided no subsequent justification either—if only because no effort has been made to do so.

The objections to establishing a parallel between the history of religion and the logic are not a merely external response to the text. In all probability Hegel entertained them too. For it is only in the first lecture series that the logical structuring is to be found. Never again did he draw parallels in such wholesale fashion. He did not merely correct the initial attribution historically, without departing from the logical paradigm, but chose another principle for structuring the history of religion. Alongside the logical paradigm the 1821 lectures already also employ a structuring of religions in terms of the proofs of God. But this is relegated to marginal importance by the parallel with the logic, and it is not carried out very consistently. As is well known, Hegel always uses in his argumentation the three proofs of God's existence dealt with in the *Critique of Pure Reason*. Since he always correlates the ontological proof with Christianity, only two proofs remain for the structuring of the history of religion; and since each of the three stages in the history of religion is supposed to have a proof, he treats the cosmological proof as the metaphysical concept both of nature religion and of the religions of Israel and Greece, while assigning the teleological proof to Roman religion. The sole variation is in the way Hegel formulates the reflective form of the cosmological proof. For nature religion he regards as the starting point "this colorful world of multiplicity, multiformity, and manyness," and as the goal of elevation "pure being . . . , the simple, the universal" (*LPR* 2:101). For Jewish and Greek religion he does not lay the emphasis on multiplicity and unity but on contingency and necessity (*LPR* 2:132).

(2) By contrast, the second lecture series apportions to the proofs of God a greater influence on the conception. In summarizing his program Hegel states that the succession of religions is contained in the succession of proofs (*LPR* 1:145). Initially his plan is again for a tripartite division of "Determinate Religion." The second stage would be "the religion of spiritual individuality or subjectivity"—Greek and Jewish religion. Roman religion is announced only as the third form—as the religion of external purposiveness or expediency (*LPR* 2:234 ff.). While lecturing on the ethnic religions, however, Hegel modifies his plan, reducing the announced three forms to two, nature religion and the religion of spiritual individuality, possibly because of the correspondence between three nature religions and three religions of spiritual individuality (*LPR* 2:388–390). This too once again confirms the strongly experimental character of the 1824 lectures.

The announcement that the proofs of God are the principle of construction of the history of religion thereby loses its persuasiveness. For now only one proof—the teleological—is available for the three distinct religions. But Hegel has to assign to each of the three, to the extent that they are independent, its own metaphysical concept. In accord with his plan he relates the metaphysical concepts in each case to the proofs of God. But with the first of these, the metaphysical concept of the religion of Israel, he acknowledges that the concept of the One "is not suited" to the proof of God (*LPR* 2:394). And with the second, the concept of necessity in Greek religion, he harks back in modified fashion in 1824 to the cosmological proof, despite already having cited it as the principle of nature religion (*LPR* 2:262). It is only the third metaphysical concept, that of external purposiveness, that corresponds to one of the proofs of God, the physicotheological. The assertion that the history of religion is structured by the proofs of God is thereby undermined. And the confusion is not lessened by the fact that the "concrete definition" of Jewish and Greek religion also is governed by the concept of purposiveness.

By contrast the teleological proof is assigned only to Roman religion, that is, to the last in the sphere of determinate religions and not the sphere as a whole, whereas the cosmological proof corresponds to the concept of nature religion as such. The proofs therefore do not furnish a sufficient principle of construction for the history of religion, especially when it is kept in mind that from 1824 on Hegel no longer treats nature religion as a unity but divides it into the religion of magic, Hinduism, and Iranian and Egyptian religion. A history of religion that distinguishes in any event eight religions cannot be adequately structured by means of only two proofs of the existence of God. With increasing historical differentiation the metaphysical concepts of the single religions thus gain in importance. They express the forms of elevation in general terms, whereas the proofs formulate the elevation to God for the reflective consciousness, thereby becoming the special case of the metaphysical concepts.

The tripartite portrayal of each of the religions—metaphysical concept, concrete representation, and cultus—is carried out especially strictly in the first lecture series, although it is only while composing his manuscript that Hegel conceives the idea. At the outset he announces a dual analysis only, the metaphysical concept and the aspect of subjectivity (*LPR* 2:94). While the metaphysical concepts initially coincide essentially with the proofs of God, the increasing differentiation of the history of religion necessitates additional metaphysical concepts. They form, especially in 1824 and 1831, the points of linkage between the categories of logic and the shapes of the history of religion; they are the principles that govern the logical determination and also the typologization of the religions, illuminating what makes them different and what the history of each consists in. But the series of metaphysical concepts is in no way suited to validate Hegel's claim that the sequence of the historical religions is "ruled and determined by the concept" (*LPR* 1:146). For this to be the case the sequence of metaphysical concepts would have to correspond to the series of logical categories. Hegel does of course demand this also for the history of philosophy. We may suppose that his claim is made good to an even lesser extent in the history of religion than in the history of philosophy.

Thus the concept of the good, which pertains to Iranian religion as one of the nature religions, occurs in the *Logic* only after that of purposiveness, which pertains to the last of the determinate religions. We have already expressed doubts concerning the systematic place of the concept of the One. And even if the sequence of the logical categories did not run counter to the course of religious history, it would remain unclear why these and not any of a dozen other categories should assume the role of metaphysical concepts. Given a plurality of historical religions, it is true that such concepts can suitably express the logical, rational nucleus of each, but they do not form a structural principle for the history of religion as such.

(3) Even this relatively flexible systematization according to metaphysical concepts is abandoned by Hegel in the third lecture series—and also in the fourth, as far as can be judged at present. The 1827 lectures, at least, treat the proofs of God all together in the "Concept of Religion," and their place is not taken by the metaphysical categories. The link between the history of religion and the logic thus appears especially loose. Certainly the course of the religions is supposed here, too, to follow the "life of the concept." But how this is defined in individual cases remains unclear. In the 1831 lectures Hegel does, to be sure, again assign the proofs of God to the stages of the history of religion. But they do not function as a principle of construction. The cosmological proof is here assigned by Hegel to the second stage, and the teleological to Greek religion, which now constitutes the content of the third stage, while Roman religion seems limited to the role of a transition to Christianity.

(4) Hegel's final approach to the structuring of the history of religion was not previously known on the basis of the sources. It uses the schema of unity, rupture, and reconciliation. It is true that this schema could also be discerned from the previous published editions, but it was there superimposed on an alien content and so contributed more to confusion than to knowledge. Indeed, this schema does not seem especially original. It does not set out a succession of categories of thought in the narrower sense but describes the general "life of the concept." But this does not mean that it is also suitable for the purpose of systematizing the history of religion. At any

rate it is insufficient since Hegel now distinguishes ten religions in addition to Christianity. As far as can be judged, the way in which they are apportioned within the triadic schema is not determined either by the "concept" or by any other principle. Rather it follows the way in which the material relating to the history of religion is interpreted.

3.2. The Lack of Conceptual Grounding

The insight into the actual relationship of the structural principles to the history of religion entails consequences as far as assessment of this part of the lectures is concerned. A well-known reproach directed against Hegel's way of proceeding is that his "scholasticism of the concept," his dialectical, ideal-genetic[32] method, is incapable of encompassing the actual course of the history of religion and must be replaced by a genetico-psychological procedure. In fact Hegel's method is neither genetic nor psychological. It establishes types, or even typologies; the types are then ordered as a system, partly according to external criteria pertaining to a correspondence of spheres, and partly according to criteria relating to content, such as a progression from indeterminacy to determinateness, or the relationship of substance and accidents. The course of the history of religion could for instance be described as a progression from substance as sheer power to a substance that posits ends and then posits ends within itself—a substance that not only determines what is other, but ultimately determines itself as the other of itself. The attempt to systematize these types is not open to objection in principle. There would indeed be justification for the sharp criticism usually leveled at Hegel if he had in fact tried (assuming a correlation between metaphysical concept, representation of God, and cultus) to derive the series of metaphysical concepts from the *Logic* without further examination. But this is not the case. He does not cast a net of a priori categories over the history of religion, but rather, starting from the religiohistorical material and interpretative keys already at his disposal, projects an ordered system whose beginning and end points—the immediate and the consummate

32. [*Tr.*] See below, n. 36.

concepts of religion—are, to be sure, fixed. In other respects he varies not only the principles on which the history of religion is presumed to be constructed but also the historical succession of the religions. These variations are due in part to differing principles of systematization, in part to the fact that the religiohistorical materials are being permeated by thought. Such increasing knowledge of the history of religion on Hegel's part is evident in regard to all the Eastern religions.

The religion of China gets no mention in the manuscript. The fact that it is brought into the history of religion in the 1824 lectures is probably related to Hegel's treatment of it in the lectures on world history and the history of philosophy. But in 1824 as well, Chinese religion is not yet regarded as an independent religion but as a particularly striking variant of the religion of magic. The 1827 lectures, by contrast, characterize it more as the religion of heaven. At the same time it still remains, formally speaking, a special form of magic. The 1831 lectures see it from the point of view of order, of substantial relationships, which is why here for the first time it is given the title "religion of measure." For the first time too it is now given formal independence. These changes show an increasing insight into the distinctive character of Chinese religions. There is no ground for assuming that considerations relating to the logic of the system contributed to this process. It can be explained as due solely to the sources to which Hegel gave preference on each occasion.

Buddhism too first comes into the picture in the 1824 lectures—again as a special form of the religion of magic and even as an appendix to Chinese religion. In 1827 it already acquires formal independence, but in point of content Hegel's portrayal of it remains tied to the link with the religion of China. It is only in the 1831 lectures that Buddhism is recognized to be a religious creation of India and placed after the treatment of Hinduism, albeit along with Lamaism.

More important, however, for Hegel's conception of the history of religion as a whole is the change affecting immediate or nature religion. Hegel equates its conceptual basis, not without polemical ends in view, with the natural religion of the Enlightenment (*LPR*

2:238, 517). In the manuscript the sphere of immediate religion is not yet historically differentiated. There are only scattered allusions to Indian, Iranian, and Egyptian religion. The 1824 series treats the Eastern religions, other than the religion of Israel, in full: they perceive the unity of the natural and the spiritual in a shape that was itself natural. As more and more concrete historical data are amassed, this concept is indeed seen to be inappropriate. This probably explains the change of emphasis in the 1827 lectures: "Hence nature religion is not a religion in which external, physical objects are taken to be God and are revered as God; instead it is a religion in which the noblest element for human beings is what is spiritual, but the spiritual [recognized] first in its immediate and natural mode. The initial and natural mode is the human being, this existing human being" (*LPR* 2:531). Elevation above the natural is first achieved, for 1827 too, in Greek and Jewish religion.

The last lecture series, by contrast, takes an entirely different view of the concept of nature religion. It is true that here too the original period of an undifferentiated unity of the spiritual and the natural is again regarded as the age of nature religion. But now it no longer coincides with the Eastern religions. For these no longer constitute forms of the still insufficiently differentiated unity of natural and spiritual. Hegel now places them at the second stage of the history of religion—as forms of elevation above the natural, a process that, according to the first three lecture series, begins only after the Eastern religions. He is therefore not inconsistent in now assigning to them the cosmological proof. All that remains as nature religion is the sphere of magic. Since the differentiation of spiritual and natural is not actually accomplished in the religion of magic, it is only with reservations numbered among the religions, and logically it has no proof of God assigned to it just because it still lacks the elevation above the finite. Hegel's conception of nature religion has thus become very narrow, by contrast with Ferdinand Christian Baur's later call for all pagan religions to be assigned to the stage of nature religion. It is possible that in 1831 Hegel was following Karl Rosenkranz, whose *Naturreligion* appeared the same year—especially since the year previously Rosenkranz had already sketched out a similar outline in a review of

Schleiermacher's *Glaubenslehre*. The removal of Eastern religions from nature religion can also be understood, however, as internally motivated—as denoting a greater permeation of the religiohistorical material by thought.

The above-mentioned changes in conception derive at least in large part from a thorough study of the sources and not from a change in the principles on which the history of religion is constructed. Indeed, the changes in conception can also lead to reformulation of the principle underlying the history of religion. This becomes especially clear in the last lecture series. The separation of the Eastern religions from nature religion cuts across the previous conception of the history of religion. But since Hegel holds fast to the threefold division of religious history, he now presents the religions of the Near East and Egypt as "transitional forms" of Greek religion, which he combines with Roman religion to form the "religion of freedom" or of "reconciliation" (*LPR* 2:748, 722). He thus chooses for them the same titles that in the first two series characterize the Christian religion. This final conception thus completes an astonishing change in the assessment of Greek religion. Whereas in the Jena lecture notes on natural law it is seen as the stage of undifferentiated harmony, it would now have to be conceived, in the terminology of the lecture notes, as the reconstruction of undifferentiated harmony—admittedly as still imperfect, in a state of rupture, but even so a stage where the divine is related to the subject in affirmative fashion.

The most telling alteration, however, concerns the religion of Israel. It also is now placed in the transition from the Eastern religions to the religion of reconciliation and freedom, at the first stage of this transition, forming, together with Iranian religion, the religion of the good. Next come Syrian and Egyptian religion as the religions of anguish and the enigma, respectively. Jewish religion thus belongs among those that in previous years were regarded as nature religions—and it becomes complementary to the religion with which it is commonly confused in the *Phenomenology*. Its ties to Christianity are thereby made even looser than in the other lecture series.

The 1831 lectures are distinguished by a number of individual insights. The above-mentioned problems mean, however, that we must not see in this part of the lectures, as we do in the "Concept of Religion," the gradual elaboration of a valid form of the system.[33] And even apart from the historical and conceptual problems, this second part shows a singular variation in the succession of religions. If one takes as guiding principle the extent to which the idea of God achieves definite shape, as in the 1827 lectures, the religion of Israel is placed above Greek religion: it is only in Jewish religion that an idea of God is attained which *we* too can acknowledge (*LPR* 2:669). If by contrast stress is laid on the mediation of the infinite and the finite—on God's assumption of human shape [*Menschwerdung Gottes*], understood both as incarnation [*Inkarnation*] and as apotheosis—then Greek religion counts as superior to Jewish. But it is not logical, or in the broader sense conceptual, principles that determine even such changes as these, but rather the endeavor to interpret the inner content of the religions in an appropriate way. A final principle of ordering, which is also the most profound, is cited in the 1831 lectures: the religions "differ according to the degree to which this concept of the freedom of spirit has come to consciousness within them" (*LPR* 1:472).

Developmental-historical analysis of this second part of the lectures admittedly does not lead to as clear results as is the case with the first part. At the same time such analysis remains indispensable for the purpose of interpreting the individual religions as well as grasping and criticizing Hegel's conception. For, out of the confusion that typifies all previous editions, developmental analysis elaborates conceptual units that can be interpreted and principles that can be criticized. To take the imaginary products of previous editors as representing Hegel's conception is a waste of scholarly effort. And even for the purpose of interpreting just one of the

33. The only evidence for this final conception comes from Strauss's excerpts. It might therefore be supposed that some divergences from the earlier lectures are attributable to him and not to Hegel, especially the position in which the excerpts place the religion of Israel. But comparison with the two editions of the *Werke* shows that Strauss's version is very faithful. On the basis of his excerpts it is possible, above all, to spot the 1831 conception in the two editions of the *Werke*. The excerpts even enable us to recognize that it was the introduction of this conception that was responsible for discordances and breaks in these two editions.

conceptions actually formulated by Hegel, disregard of its developmental history tends to make us underestimate the flexibility he shows in (for example) the correlation of logical categories and historical shapes. The petrifaction commonly attributed to Hegel's conception is only the result of unwillingness to engage in developmental analysis. Instead of being subject to the supposedly rigid compulsion of logical principles of construction, his treatment of the history of religion forms an experimental field in which virtually everything is tried out. In the four lecture series only a single structural element remained unchanged, namely what commonly counts as a favorite example of Hegel's caprice and faulty method: the transition from Roman religion to Christianity.

The insight gleaned into Hegel's way of proceeding entails a reconsideration of the generally accepted criticism of his work, which is based on an uncritical study of uncritical editions. What has to be criticized is not his a priori harnessing of actuality but his holding fast to a program that requires a conceptual derivation of the principle on which the history of religion is constructed, despite the fact that each successive series of lectures made it clearer that this aim was unattainable; and pertinent arguments can even be adduced why it runs counter to Hegel's own premises. It would have been entirely appropriate to his program to treat the religions using the concept as a guideline if this had been done solely for purposes of scientific exposition and not also to establish a historical sequence.

3.3. The Historicality of the History of Religion

The arguments that rescue Hegel's conception from familiar criticism make it appear, however, no less questionable as a philosophical theory of the history of religion. The only reason it escapes the charge of imprisoning actuality in the straitjacket of the concept is, in essence, that doubt is cast on its conceptual foundation as such. Such considerations have not been advanced here against the conceptual content of the individual religions as portrayed by Hegel but solely against his assertion that the religions occur in a sequence that is ordered by the concept and is at the same time historical. It is not only the demonstrated multiplicity of structural principles that casts doubt on this thesis. Nowhere does Hegel expound a foundational principle for the history of religion as such; nowhere does he explain why the concept should have ordered the plurality of religions into a history. There is, to be sure, no lack of individual pointers, but they remain confusing and, not being brought together, insufficient. The manuscript speaks of a development of the concept, a positing of what is contained in the concept. This positing constitutes the reality of the concept, and perfects it into the idea (*LPR* 1:110–111). These remarks suggest the model of the transition from the logic of subjectivity to the logic of objectivity and the doctrine of ideas. In the 1824 lectures, however, Hegel uses this model to describe the relationship of concept, knowledge, and cultus as the three sections of the "Concept of Religion." Yet he does not carry out this triadic ordering in the 1824 lectures, but only in 1827. The 1824 lectures conceive the transition to "Determinate Religion" rather as a "self-resolving" (*Sichentschliessen*) of the concept (*LPR* 1:142), which is reminiscent of the transition from the idea to nature. The 1827 lectures by contrast characterize this transition, at least in the initial survey, as a "division" [*Urteil*] of the concept (*LPR* 1:181). Yet in his actual execution Hegel follows the paradigm of concept-division-conclusion in dividing the "Concept of Religion" into the concept of God, knowledge, and cultus (*LPR* 1:381–382), whereas the "Introduction" suggested that this latter relationship was to be conceived according to the model of universality-particularity-individuality (*LPR* 1:178 ff.). Thus it is not possible to indicate a precise logical paradigm for the transition from the "Concept of Religion" to "Determinate Religion" and finally to the "Consummate Religion." Such a paradigm is lacking both for the internal differentiation of the "Concept of Religion" and for the transition to "Determinate Religion." The only feature common to all models is that the middle part of the lectures forms a sphere of differentiation in which the moments making up the concept are set out separately as they constitute actuality.

Even if it is assumed that a transition from the "Concept" to "Determinate Religion" can be made comprehensible, it is not immediately clear why this positing of the determinations, this "division" or "self-release"[34] of the concept, should result not in a mere multiplicity but in a history of religions. How does what exists in juxtaposition become temporally connected? How does the mere multiplicity of realizations of the moments of the concept of religion become one universal history of religion? The texts are even less forthcoming in providing explicit answers to these questions than to that of the systematic form of the transition. Historicality cannot be inferred from the principles Hegel adduces for the realization of the concept of religion. Recourse might be had to the argument of the *Phenomenology*, that it is not just the moments but only the shapes of spirit in its entirety that exist in time. But this answer does not suffice either if one is asking, in the strict sense, for the principles on which the history of religion is constituted. The fact that the religions are understood as shapes of spirit in time does not suffice to convince us that they form a history. They would also exist in time if they occurred alongside each other or one after another, but without a historical link. Even if all the other missing presuppositions were deemed to be present, this justification for the historicality of the determinate religions would still be lacking.

It is possible, in fact, to point to statements in Hegel's work that throw doubt on the historicality of the religions: "What spirit does is no history [*Historie*]" (*LPR* 3:232). Or in the last lectures we are told that religion is the genus, and the individual religions are related to it as species (*LPR* 2:513, 721). This model shows rather that these species are not related to one another historically. In any

---

34. [*Tr.*] *Sichentlassen*. At the end of Part I of the *Encyclopedia*, Hegel states that the idea "resolves to let the moment of its particularity . . . go forth freely from itself as nature [*sich als Natur frei aus sich zu entlassen*]" (*Enc* § 244), this self-release being what constitutes the "absolute freedom" and "absolute truth" of the idea. The same image is repeated in the *Lectures on the Philosophy of Religion:* "It belongs to the absolute freedom of the idea that in its act of determining and dividing, it releases [*entlässt*] the other to exist as a free and independent being" (*LPR* 3:292). It is worth noting that *ent-lassen* is the Germanic equivalent of the Latin *ab-solvere*, which means to "loosen from" or "release." Hegel's "absolute" is not something independent or isolated, cut off from everything finite, but rather is precisely that which divides and releases itself, thus giving rise to what is other than itself, namely finite things. These finite things exist apart from the absolute yet in profound communion with it, a communion that is also the self-communion of the absolute.

case a nonhistorical relationship seems better suited to Hegel's presentation, which resembles a *geography* of religion more than a *history* of religion. At the very least a conceptual grounding of the *history* of religion presupposes steps in argumentation that are not clearly discernible in the texts and would have to be inserted by analogy or supplied only subsequently. It might therefore be supposed that the references to "history" are not meant to be taken seriously—that all Hegel is concerned with is the multiplicity of religions in history, and that this does not have to be pursued in such a way as to yield a theory of history. But although he does not actually substantiate the historical character of the plurality of religions, he does not assume that they simply emerge in the course of world history but that they are historically connected. He explicitly calls the determinate religions "necessary conditions for the emergence of the true religion" (*LPR* 2:517), and among these religions the later ones are said to presuppose the earlier ones.

The sole argument for the historicality of the religions lies in the fact that Hegel refers several times, somewhat paradoxically, to the "nature of spirit," saying that for spirit perfection is not to be found at the beginning. It is the result not of an organic process, so to speak, but of a development determined by freedom. This idea, which is central to historical thinking in general, already in Jena weaned Hegel from following the mythical yearning for totality that was rife among his contemporaries, and from seeking the consummation of history before its beginning. Only in this way is it possible to conceive of a history in general, as well as a history of religion, which, in harmony with the *Logic,* sees the beginning characterized by the most impoverished shapes. This would provide a possible basis for going on to argue that the temporally later stages in fact presuppose the earlier ones.

One could use this argument to describe partial correlations between individual religions that can be ascribed to one shape of consciousness. It would also be fruitful if applied to the internal development of a religion, which is an aspect that Hegel always introduces only peripherally into his treatment of the history of religion, centered as it is on the establishment of types. But a universal history of religion presupposes not only the identical nature of a substrate such as spirit but also the continuity of a consciousness. However, this could not be accepted as an argument for the unity of the history of religion unless one's starting point was the unity of subjective spirit as the substrate of this history—unless, for example, history of religion was conceived along the lines of a universal history of education. But the broadening of outlook precisely in Hegel's day, and also in his philosophy, means that such attempts could not be taken seriously. At the same time the historicality of spirit would also be safeguarded if not just a single form of immediacy were assumed to be original, or indeed if not just a single shape of consummation were accepted, or if doubt were cast on the possibility of such exclusive shapes of consummation as such. The "nature of spirit" may, then, serve as a basis for the historicality but not the unity of the history of religion, at least not directly.

Comparison with the other forms of absolute spirit brings us no nearer to the goal. To gain an insight into the logical grounding and structuring of the history of religion, it would be necessary to take account also of the differences between art, religion, and philosophy. This is indeed not presently possible, but at the same time another line of approach lies open along this path. It is not only the history of religion that is based on the concept but also the histories of art and philosophy as well as world history. It does not therefore make sense to suppose that each of these histories possesses principles of its own. There are clearly points of contact between them; in part they are identical, as is stated to be the case at least for the history of religion and world history (*Enc* § 562 Cor.). A multiplicity of principles would mean that all these principles would have to be fused into a single historical process; this would be an extremely delicate matter, and would of necessity immeasurably increase the abundant problems that already exist. In any case it would not help to make such a construct any more credible. Moreover, Hegel too uses another argument, to the effect that the philosophy, art, and religion of each epoch are permeated by a single principle.[35] It is perfectly sensible to assume this, especially

35. Hegel, *Introduction to the Lectures on the History of Philosophy*, trans. T. M. Knox and A. V. Miller (Oxford, 1985), p. 111.

as all the forms of absolute spirit are constituted by the inward reflection of ethical spirit. But then it is also impossible to find any principles that would determine the separate histories generally. The historical course of the religions has therefore to be related to the historical course of this one substantial principle in its respective configurations. It is from this alone that "Determinate Religion" in its plurality derives its historicality.

This is a possible answer to the question of the unity of the history of religion without departing from the Hegelian model. The claim advanced by the philosophy-of-religion lectures has therefore to be modified at least to the extent of bringing into play the shapes of objective and of absolute spirit. The problem then shifts to the question of the constitutive principles of the partial histories of absolute spirit and of history in general. For a detailed analysis it will be necessary to await critical editions of the lectures on the philosophy of art as well as of the lectures on world history and history of philosophy. The history-of-philosophy lectures at any rate present more than one conception. The decisive factor in any event is indeed likely to be the unity of the history of religion and world history—particularly in the light of the 1831 lectures' affirmation that the sequence of religions is ordered according to the degree to which the concept of freedom has attained consciousness in it (*LPR* 1:472). For the states that make up world history are also ordered according to this criterion—according to progress in the consciousness of freedom. The question of the historicality of the history of religion cannot therefore be separated from that of world history.

For this very reason, however, it may be doubted that a higher-level examination of this kind will enable one to come any closer than previous attempts to the goal of demonstrating a history of religion—at least not in such a way as could be regarded as making good Hegel's claim that his conception encompasses the history of religion and encompasses it as a unity. This is already excluded if only because the assumption underlying Hegel's claim to ground the history of religion on the logic—the assumption that the history of religion forms a unity—is false.

For this reason the criticism leveled against Hegel for the most part also misses the mark. Under the influence of the previous editions, Hegel's critics have rejected, or even sometimes poured ridicule on, his claim to place the history of religion on a logical foundation. The evident inconsistencies in the way the history of religion is structured, and the no less patent deficiencies in grounding it, have at least initially fostered the view that the failure of Hegel's approach is due solely to his erroneous ideal-genetic method—as though another method could yield the goal of a universal history of religion. Apart from isolated correlations, however, an empirico-genetic method is no more capable of yielding a universal history of religion than an ideal-genetic one.[36]

Hegel's claim to found the history of religion on the concept is doomed in advance because he is mistaken in assuming that there is such a thing as a single history of religion. He may be excused in view of the fact that, despite the difficulties in which all talk of such a single history has become entangled, the illusion has even now not entirely disappeared that such a history may still be conceivable, using other means. His claim to provide a conceptual grounding for the history of religion does at least lend plausibility to the assumption that such a history exists. Once the claim was forfeited, the assumption lost much of its plausibility.

While the difficulties standing in the way of Hegel's program reside, it is true, in his method, they reside no less in the content of the program itself. Even the assumption of a temporal succession of religions cannot be sustained—nor is this the case with Hegel alone. There are, for instance, no temporal differences worth mentioning between the so-called higher religions, nor is there any identity worth mentioning such as would substantiate the unity of the history of religion. And the time is probably past even for a unity to be constituted on the basis of the end or goal of religious history. The geography of religion that Hegel actually gives us fits the facts better than the kind of universal history of religion he aimed at.

Beyond this it is noteworthy that his theory of religion does not need a unitary history of religion of this kind. Because of its concept of spirit it does, to be sure, need the idea of development. Without

36. [Tr.] An "ideal-genetic" (*idealgenetisch*) method is one that understands genesis or origination to take place on a conceptual level, while an "empirico-genetic" (*realgenetisch*) method understands genesis to take place on a factual level.

a preceding history of philosophy and religion, it would be difficult to imagine that the thorny metaphysical problems Hegel sees as inherent in Christianity could be solved. His conception does not, however, require that the unity and unidimensionality of this development should be demonstrated. For the absoluteness of the "Consummate Religion" is not defined by the complete course of "Determinate Religion." Hegel's conception could not yield an exclusive totality of this kind for the very reason that he provides no rigorous logical grounding. The absoluteness of the "Consummate Religion" is determined rather by the fact that in it the moments that make up the "Concept of Religion" themselves become the content of religion. Part III of the lectures serves to demonstrate that this has happened in one of the historical shapes of religion.

4. The Consummate Religion[37]

Hegel does not treat the Christian religion solely as the last and highest of the manifold configurations of the history of religion. As the consummation transcending time, as the mode of reality that corresponds to the concept, he releases it from the course of history. Despite the special position to which he assigns it, his philosophical treatment of the Christian religion has been criticized for attempting the impossible by seeking to comprehend Christianity, which is above all reason, with the same methods as those used to grasp the content of the ethnic religions, which are beneath all reason. But the striking feature about Hegel's philosophy of religion is that these assertions are equally untrue: reason is the same in the history of the religions as it is in Christianity and also in philosophy.

The introductory words to Part III of the lectures characterize the Christian religion as the religion of revelation, of truth, of reconciliation, and of freedom (LPR 3:63–65). These predicates are not independent of one another: because it is the religion of revelation, it is also the religion of truth and freedom—and this dependence also obtains in reverse order (LPR 3:170–171). The ultimate ground of all these epithets lies in the fact that Christian-

37. [Tr.] See the table providing a comparative analysis of the "Consummate Religion" in LPR 3:54–55.

ity is for Hegel the absolute or, to use the term he most commonly employs, the consummate religion.

Hegel does not define this consummateness in relation to the preceding history of religion. For this would imply a dubious comparison such as is expressed in Schleiermacher's assertion that "Christianity may be more perfect than any of the configurations we would otherwise find reason to place on the same level with it." And even the superlative is, properly speaking, only a comparative: "Indeed, by mere comparison," Schleiermacher tells us, Christianity appears "as the most perfect of the religions that have attained the same level of development" (*KGA* 7/1:49, 52). In contrast, for Hegel the reference to consummation is determined by referring back to the concept of religion. In Christianity this concept is objective to itself. So the references to consummation cannot be legitimated by saying, for example, that only in Christianity is God conceived in appropriate fashion. The criterion of appropriateness is the concept of religion—the self-consciousness of absolute spirit. But all religions are forms of this self-consciousness. To call Christianity consummate can be justified only by showing that in it God is known as God is in himself, in other words by comparing the idea of God developed in the "Concept of Religion" with that developed in Christianity.

Already the manuscript lists "the more precise determinations" of the concept of religion, "which directly constitute its content": "the determination of absolute unity," of the substantial unity between the object and subjective spirit; then "the moment of separation, of difference"; and lastly the "subjective moment"—"the fact that spiritual self-consciousness is itself an eternal, absolute element." This means, and not in a merely formal way, that none of the three may be forgotten: they constitute in their totality the appropriate cognitive knowledge of the absolute. So the only appropriate form for the "Concept of Religion" to take within the system is that which does not simply refer to these three moments in passing but is altogether guided by them, in other words the form of the last two lecture series. The manuscript, however, initially draws another consequence, namely "that the consummation of religion itself brings forth its concept and makes it objective to itself. Once it has been thus objectified, it is developed, and the totality of its determinate characteristics is posited in it." Hegel alludes already here to the fact that these characteristics "emerge in this revelatory religion as essential moments of the content, together with the consciousness of the content and with the determination of being the truth" (*LPR* 1:194–196). They form the content of the "concrete representation" of the Christian religion alone, as it is portrayed both in the middle section of the lectures dealing with the Christian religion (*LPR* 3:73 ff.) and in §§ 567–570 of the *Encyclopedia*. The moments making up the concept of religion form, as it were, the object of Christian dogmatics—even if the knowledge that this is so is not a matter for religion itself. This alone means that the concept of religion has become an object to itself, that the Christian religion has for its object what religion as such is (*LPR* 1:317). And this alone is what makes it the consummate religion.

4.1. Theological and Philosophical Interpretation

For the purpose of interpreting Part III of the lectures, theology has long viewed itself as competent. In light of the theme, this is in no way surprising. By contrast it is noteworthy that, since the period of intensive reception in the Hegel School, philosophical interpretation of the lectures has fastened on a whole range of themes both important and marginal, but has only seldom really become engaged with the philosophy of religion, despite the elevated position it occupies in the system. A greater engagement on the part of philosophy would in no way have led to mere duplication. The methods of theological and philosophical interpretation differ too widely for this to be the case. In saying this we in no way wish to reopen in an inappropriate context the gulf that it was one of the main aims of Hegel's philosophy of religion to bridge. In any event this gulf has for a long time again been unmistakably evident. Above all, in affirming the identity of content shared by religion and philosophy, it was in no sense Hegel's aim to deny that the two disciplines differed in the way they approached this identical content.

By "theological" we do not mean here any possible interpretation undertaken from the theological side, but an interpretation that is primarily interested in whether Hegel's philosophy is in harmony or discord with Christianity, or that even, in sweeping fashion, regards the answer to this question as a sufficient criterion for assessing his philosophy. By way of legitimating itself, such an interpretation makes frequent reference to the fact that Hegel's philosophy grew up on the soil of Christianity and in dialogue with it. If this philosophy is nurtured on Christian substance, it is understandable that theology should claim the right to guard the integrity of this substance in its idealistic metamorphosis too. But this stipulation does not go uncontested. It would need to be demonstrated from a developmental point of view, and it is by no means certain that such a demonstration will corroborate it. Admittedly in his *Early Theological Writings* Hegel makes religion, and in particular the Christian religion, the object to an extent that few others have done. But the form and contents of his treatment vary from occasion to occasion depending on the philosophical premises with which he is studying Christianity, and the contents give no reason to infer the changing nature of these premises themselves. This is all the more the case for the Jena years during which the foundations of the system were laid. They show that Christianity is on each occasion of interest to Hegel to the extent that he can interpret its doctrines in the context of his philosophy. The Christian religion does not, however, afford a basis for understanding either the terms in which the fundamental principles are formulated or the way in which they are developed in the system. It could be called a necessary but not a sufficient condition of Hegel's philosophy.

Even if it were to be conceded that Christianity exerts a greater influence on the genesis of Hegel's philosophy as a whole than is the case with his philosophy of religion, the possible consequences of this affirmation would remain an open question. The fact that the roots of Hegel's philosophy lay in theology would afford no better a philosophical argument for it than against it. It would not even confer the right, not simply to diagnose lines of argument that diverge from the Christian religion, but for that very reason to reject them—even if Hegel's own program seems to imply that his philosophy does nothing other than to conceive the idea of Christianity. In this latter way his philosophy seems to subject itself to the criterion of a purely theological interpretation. Admittedly his program means that we cannot, like Feuerbach, sweep aside the question of the concordance of Hegelian philosophy with Christianity as an absolutely stupid question (see below, p. 283). But even Feuerbach grants that we are wholly entitled to ask whether there is a correspondence between Christianity and what Hegel presents as Christian.

"To conceive the idea of Christianity" is an ambiguous expression, however, unless one spells out what one means by the "idea of Christianity." This only emerges from the third part of the philosophy-of-religion lectures, as does what it can mean to conceive this idea. The call to conceive it implies that it is something conceivable. And the references to an "idea of Christianity" suggest at least that this means something more specific than the prevalent understanding of Christianity (and even the latter is by no means an object of unanimity). Hegel's formulation of his program is not therefore to be understood as readily submitting to the verdict of a purely theological interpretation. All that finally matters for it, too, is what is conceived.

The guiding point of view for our presentation of Part III of the lectures does not lie in its concurrence with the Christian religion as generally understood. It lies in the question whether this part can be regarded as a convincing conclusion to the philosophy of religion—convincing, at any rate, on the basis of the premises and method of Hegel's interpretation of religion in general. Only in this way is Hegel's philosophy taken seriously as philosophy. Mere agreement with Christian doctrines would not entitle it to rank as philosophy. Such agreement would be evident only to the extent that Hegel had confined himself to unaltered repetitions of dogmatic contents (in the wider sense) or credal statements. The question of agreement conjures up an ever-present danger of viewing the philosophy of religion as theological dogmatics. But from the latter perspective virtually the only verdict that can be passed on it is that it is a form of dogmatics that has been incompletely thought through—a weak and moreover frequently distorted echo of a great tradition. If it is misunderstood as dogmatics, the demonstration of its nonagreement with Christianity is not surprising, but also irrelevant. Then the assertion that it is in accord with Christianity may even give rise to the suspicion that the sole aim is to present Hegel as an ally for dogmatics in its sore plight or even to give theology a means of defense against possible objections—to make orthodox concepts of divinity palatable once again by affirming their harmony with philosophy. The sole interest of Hegel's philosophy of religion, for philosophy and theology alike, can only be if it is understood as philosophy—as a supreme attempt to give fresh life to the philosophical doctrine of God and of religion by reappraising the Enlightenment critique and assimilating it in a productive fashion. Only then could the philosophy of religion make good its promise to enable the threatened content of religion to take refuge in the concept.

The notion that it is the task of the system in general and of the philosophy of religion in particular to conceive the idea of Christianity refers philosophy to something prior to it. But the formulation of the "idea of Christianity" already belongs to philosophy, and "conceiving" too is the task peculiar to it. What it involves, to use the terminology of the manuscript, is to raise the absolute content into the absolute form, to raise the truth into the form of truth (*LPR* 1:250). Only what can be thought in the form of the concept can be an appropriate object of thought. Philosophy can indeed take as its starting point contents with which it is presented historically or on the basis of authority. It must, however, change these contents into the form of the concept: it must develop the absolute content according to necessity and know and acknowledge it as objective content; it must produce the truth but recognize it "as at the same time not produced, as the truth that subsists in and for itself" (*LPR* 3:345). This conception of Hegel's, who was "Lessing's intimate" (*L* 32, *Br* 1:21), could also be formulated in terms of § 72 of Lessing's *Education of the Human Race*: We can marvel at the truths of religion as revelations only until such time as reason teaches us to deduce them from "its other established truths" and combine them with them. However much it may differ in execution, this is precisely what Hegel's interpretation of Christianity seeks to achieve. Lessing's interpretation of the trinity in § 73 would no more incur Hegel's opposition than the interpretation of original sin in § 74, or the claim that, in order to be of any service to the human race, revealed truths have as a matter of sheer necessity to be developed into truths of reason (§ 76). What is involved, however, is not merely to envelop the religious content in a cloak of speculation nor to reduce it rationalistically to sound common sense. The program is less pertinently described as one of "modifying" or "transposing" than it is by Hegel's reference to the production of truth from the concept. It is only because this "development" involves a production according to criteria and laws all its own that the results can lay claim to an evidential value that owes nothing to religion and provide a conceptual foundation for it.

It follows from this, on the one hand, that a methodologically consistent production from the "concept" cannot resurrect the content in its traditional shape. It can articulate in conceptual form only those elements of the content that implicitly belong to the "concept." To claim anything more would rob it of the evidential force of which it is capable as a conceptual articulation. It would be ill advised if it were induced, by well-meaning or critical demands on the part of religion, to go beyond the sphere of conceptual thinking. On the other hand, the inevitability of such divergences between the conceptual form and the traditionally religious form cannot be seen as an argument against production from the concept. At any rate thought has no occasion to acknowledge the legitimacy of such objections. From its point of view (which it knows to be the true and universal one), where there are discrepancies between the form of the concept and the traditional form, it is the latter that must be sacrificed. The discrepancies are to be understood as an expression of the fact that the traditional form still contains an alien admixture alongside the content. Where Christianity is not in conformity with the concept of religion, it is not the concept that has to be corrected but Christianity that has to be elevated to conceptual form.

The relationship of the levels of the concept and of traditional religion arises in slightly altered form for the question that Feuerbach himself acknowledges to be legitimate: "Does what Hegel depicts as Christianity really conform to it?"[38] It is true that Feuerbach intends this question to be answered also in regard to the difference between religion and philosophy of religion. Its legitimacy, however, derives already from the fact that the lectures contain passages whose aim is none other than to appropriate the representational content of the Christian religion. The philosophy of religion has indeed "to distinguish between how the idea is for the *concept* in the various elements and how this comes to *representational* expression" (*LPR* 3:188). Where it is dealing with the latter topic, conformity can be demanded and lack of conformity made occasion for complaint. To this extent the concern of theological interpretation is recognized within the framework of a philosophical interpretation also. Little argumentative value, however, can attach to any objections bearing on the way the representational form is presented. Greater weight would attach to such objections only if the faulty rendering of the representational form also entailed an inconsistency in the conceptual form. But in general the differences that occur at the representational level—in regard for instance to what is said about the trinity and in particular the position of the Spirit in it—are not due to mere lack of familiarity. Rather, in reproducing the representational form Hegel is influenced by the conceptual form, but not vice versa.

In examining Hegel's philosophy of religion it is therefore essential to focus on its conceptual form. This is not simply to decide the contest of the birds in favor of the Owl of Minerva and against the Dove of the Holy Spirit;[39] nor is it to postpone it on the grounds that an encounter between them is excluded because the owl is a night bird and the dove a creature of the day, a "luminous being."[40] It is, however, only in the form of philosophy that one can discuss

38. Ludwig Feuerbach, *Über Philosophie und Christentum in Beziehung auf den der Hegelschen Philosophie gemachten Vorwurf der Unchristlichkeit* (1839), in *Gesammelte Werke,* ed. W. Schuffenhauer, vol. 8, 2d ed. (Berlin, 1982), p. 250.

39. For this image see Eberhard Jüngel, *God as the Mystery of the World,* trans. Darrell L. Guder (Grand Rapids, Mich., 1983), p. 285.

40. [*Tr.*] The author here engages in a wordplay with the term *Lichtwesen,* which is used in the *Phenomenology* to describe the view of God found in one of the religions, most likely Judaism (see chap. 2, n. 54).

the possibility of a philosophical theology and philosophy of religion. Such discussion would otherwise be subject to criteria it could not accept and liable to arouse expectations it could not credibly fulfill.

4.2. The Differences in Architectonics

Hegel conceives the Christian religion as the one in which the concept of religion has become an object to itself. It could be assumed that the shape of Part III of the lectures was thereby prefashioned by the shape of Part I. But in Part I Hegel arrived at a binding form only later on, and although Part III is relatively stable compared with the other two parts, it does show evidence of changes in conception. Here the divergences are not related to one another as differing stages of development. Nor is it possible, as in the first part, to point to one conception as binding. One can, however, attempt to acquire an insight, in the light of these divergences, into the relationship between the dogmatic content and the philosophical systematization.

The divergences between the lecture series can now be seen from the new edition, and thus we need not describe them in detail. Moreover, we have already discussed elsewhere[41] the relationship between the structural conceptions in the *Encyclopedia*, the manuscript, and the later series—that is, the articulation into three spheres or three elements. This description needs to be supplemented by pointing out that the conception of the manuscript, too, may originally have been different. All three conceptions include elements that can be considered an appropriate form of presentation in at least one aspect. The difficulty in arriving at a valid form for Part III probably lay in the impossibility of combining these elements to form a unity.

The arrangement of "A. Abstract Concept" and "B. Concrete Representation" does not present a problem. In all probability the original conception of the manuscript did not envisage the third section, "C. Community, Cultus," as an independent section. The

41. See the author's *Die Religionsphilosophie Hegels* (Darmstadt, 1983), pp. 93–97.

general survey of the manuscript (*LPR* 1:110–112) gives no information in this regard, and in fact there is no comprehensive summary for Part III at all. The first hint is contained in an addition to the heading for Section B. Hegel explains, obviously following on from the words "Concrete Representation": "or rather determination, i.e., development of the idea – weaves itself by itself into cultus" (*LPR* 3:73 n. 39). Justification for this does not come until the next lecture series, with the structure of the manifestation of the Spirit (*LPR* 3:188). This at once explains why in their treatment of "Determinate Religion" the last two lecture series break through the separation of representation and cultus. The manuscript's allusion to the interweaving of cultus and representation recurs somewhat later in the summary setting out the division of the three spheres: the idea in and for itself, differentiation, and "objectivity as of finite spirit."[42] Here Hegel distinguishes two forms of "the appearance of God in finite spirit": "the history of redemption and reconciliation, the eternal divine history itself"; and "the subjective side of this history, as [it takes place] in finite spirit, in the individual, . . . the form of the cultus" (*LPR* 3:77). This finding is confirmed by the "Loose Sheets" relating to the manuscript. They also speak of the sphere "(γ) objectivity as of finite spirit" and characterize this objectivity as the one "in which God returns into himself in self-consciousness – cultus" (*LPR* 3:379).[43] The third sphere, of which Hegel says that it contains the higher realization of the Spirit (*LPR* 3:87), is thus not the later Section "C. Community, Cultus" but the third sphere of the original plan, encompassing christology and ecclesiology. This way of viewing it is also the one that harmonizes most readily with the three moments of the concept of religion as formulated in Part I of the lectures (*LPR* 1:194–195).

42. [*Tr.*] "Objektivität als des endlichen Geists" (*V* 5:16). *LPR* here translates: "Objectivity [appears] as finite spirit." While this rendering has no real effect on the meaning, it does obscure the parallel with the "Loose Sheets" referred to immediately below.

43. These considerations make it appear doubtful whether the editorial insertion of the heading (γ) before "Cultus – formation of the community" a few lines later was correct (*LPR* 3:379 line 41). [*Tr.* The translation should read here: "[(γ)] Cultus – formation of the community" (cf. *V* 5:296 line 170). The closing bracket was inadvertently omitted.]

Christology and ecclesiology did not originally form merely successive elements of the third sphere. One of the "Loose Sheets" shows how closely Hegel wanted to bind them together. At the same time he distinguishes their function, saying that christology suffices, to be sure, for individuality[44] but not for universal individuality (*LPR* 3:382–383). This is spelled out in the manuscript. Christology forms "only one side of the consummation of the third sphere." It grasps individuality as only *one*, exclusive, and not as universal. Exclusive individuality has initially "*many* single individuals confronting it," whom it has to bring back "into the unity of the Spirit, into the *community*" before it can be "actual, universal self-consciousness" (*LPR* 3:133).

Given this conception of the dual consummation of the third sphere, it could, properly speaking, be expected that the second form of consummation should also be treated as the second part of this sphere. But immediately following the phrase just cited Hegel begins a third *section*, "C. Community, Cultus," and a little later justifies this by referring back to the portrayal of the Christian religion as a whole. The "pure concept of God" and the "manifestation" "in the three spheres of thinking, representation, and actuality" are followed by the region of "subjective immanence," "the kingdom of the Spirit" (*LPR* 3:142). Numerous reasons of a formal nature can be adduced for this deliverance from the third sphere, but taken singly none of them is compelling. We can, however, say with certainty that it cannot have been motivated by the desire for a trinitarian philosophy. For even with this separation, the manuscript is not brought into agreement with a dogmatics articulated on trinitarian lines.

Such an agreement is realized by Hegel only in the last three lecture series. Here he again distinguishes the "Abstract Concept" and

44. [*Tr.*] *Einzelheit*. In *LPR* 3 this term is translated as "singularity" or "singular individual" in order to distinguish it from the term *Individuum*, which Hegel also occasionally uses. The most natural English translation, however, is "individuality." *Einzelheit* is the quality that defines human being as finite spirit, by contrast with the *Besonderheit* ("particularity") of nature. Each human individual is singular (*einzeln*), i.e., unique, as well as "not divisible" into further parts. But Hegel also speaks of a "universal" or communal individuality, and indeed human individuality reaches its fulfillment only in the ecclesial (or spiritual) community.

three "elements." These do not fully coincide with the "spheres" of the manuscript in that the first consummation of the third sphere, christology, constitutes the main content of the second element; and the second consummation of the third sphere, in the community (which the manuscript separates off from this sphere itself), now forms the sole content of the third element. By this means the whole structure of this last part of the lectures is changed. One possible motive for this change may be that the lectures, like the *Phenomenology* before them, show that the community is not the actual self-consciousness of reconciliation, that it does not possess this reconciliation and divinity as actual but still merely as represented and should therefore be dealt with in the framework of "Concrete Representation." But there are several reasons for not assigning it there, such as the enumeration of the moments making up the concept of religion in Part I of the manuscript (*LPR* 1:194–195), and also the insight gained precisely in the 1824 lectures that the manifestation of the Spirit is necessarily a being for others, namely for the community. The original conception of the manuscript does better justice to this, in that it expresses most clearly the unity of christology and ecclesiology. Sections 569–570 of the *Encyclopedia* could also be interpreted as such a unity, assuming that the entire doctrine of the Spirit is encompassed here; in fact, however, this is not the case, and also it is rather improbable given the agreement between the conclusion of § 570 and the conclusion of the third sphere in the manuscript (*LPR* 3:133).

Objections can also be raised to the new way of conceiving the second element, combining what was previously the second sphere, the creation and preservation of nature, the moment of difference, with the third sphere, christology. Here the new conception may be said to have forcibly combined two opposing elements— separation and reunion—into one. But even if this change in conception is understood as a legitimate consequence of systematic insights, it does involve relegating christology to a subordinate position to the extent that it does not go beyond exclusive individuality. This is also borne out by the fact that much greater stress is laid on christology in the manuscript than in the later lectures. The depreciation of christology can be seen further in the fact that the 1827 lectures describe the second element in its entirety as the realm in which spirit "is able to bring to consciousness [only] in this external fashion what God is" (*LPR* 3:272). This formula recalls the concluding sentence of § 568 of the *Encyclopedia*, to the effect that in the moment of particularity spirit, as thinking, is of course also directed toward the eternal, "but stands in an external relation to it." It is only after this that the *Encyclopedia*'s christology ensues, in § 569. Yet, if we must assume a reappraisal of christology in the lectures, this does not correspond to the way it is presented in the *Encyclopedia*. Nor does Hegel later fuse the two conceptions into one. The disparity cannot, however, be explained in terms of the difference between a popular form of conception in the lectures and a systematic one in the *Encyclopedia*. It is also likely to be fruitless to seek to develop valid reasons from the *Encyclopedia*'s general conception of "absolute spirit." On the contrary, its posture vis-à-vis the traditional religious understanding is less problematic. Nothing in fact prescribes that philosophical systematics must accord with the creed—especially since the trinitarian conception of dogmatics remains rather the exception.[45]

The philosophical system, however, must at any rate be presented in a consistent manner. This requirement provides a formal reason for the restructuring of "Concrete Representation" from 1824 on. Its triadic form could be subsumed under the headings that determine the conception of Part I of the lectures, initially by intent and from 1827 on in reality too—namely, "Concept of God," "Representation," "Cultus." This formal unity in the way the "Concept of Religion" and the "Consummate Religion" are developed replaces the unity that exists in the manuscript—a unity that exists, to be sure, not between the systematic shape of the "Concept of Religion" and the original (though not actual) conception of the "Consummate Religion," but rather between the moments of the concept of religion that are enumerated in Part I

---

45. See, e.g., Philipp Marheineke, *Die Grundlehren der christlichen Dogmatik* (Berlin, 1819), and *Die Grundlehren der christlichen Dogmatik als Wissenschaft* (Berlin, 1827). In view of its temporal priority, the question arises whether it was not the first of these works that induced Hegel to adopt a trinitarian schema for the "Consummate Religion."

(*LPR* 1:194–195) and the original conception of Part III. This interpretation can indeed neither explain nor justify the fact that the discrepancy is carried over into the structure of the *Encyclopedia,* which is akin to that of the manuscript. And it is no recommendation for the constructive value of the terms "universality," "particularity," and "individuality" that they remain unaffected by the change in contents. Rather it arouses misgivings about the explanatory power of an interpretation based on logical structure. As long as such fundamental problems concerning the assignment of the dogmatic contents to the differing spheres or elements are not decided, and indeed are not even seen and reflected on, it is appropriate to be skeptical about other interpretations that seek to grasp the fine structure of the argumentation in greater or lesser detail by tying it to the logic.

4.3. The Metaphysical Concept

(1) The treatment of the "metaphysical" or "abstract concept" remains unaffected by these differences in conception. To be sure, the 1827 lectures treat all the proofs of God already in the "Concept of Religion" and not in the framework of the "metaphysical concepts" of "Determinate" and "Consummate Religion." But this is a mere variant of presentation, which is moreover abrogated in the 1831 series.

There were references to the "metaphysical concept" in the earlier published editions as well. But what it was the concept of, or what conceptual role it played within the "Consummate Religion," remained unclear. In the *Werke* the title of this section read "The Metaphysical Concept of the Idea of God," and it came before "The Kingdom of the Father." The metaphysical concept was wrongly combined with the introductory sections. Moreover, it is in no way the metaphysical concept of the idea of God that is involved here but the metaphysical concept of the Christian religion. As for Georg Lasson, while his interest in a trinitarian structure led him to adopt the heading "Kingdom of the Father" from the *Werke,* he did not adhere to the thematic delimitation of this "Kingdom" as found in the *Werke.* He included under this heading the introductory characterization of the Christian religion and the discussion of the metaphysical concept as well. Neither of these belongs to the "Kingdom of the Father." There is indeed a connection between the latter and the metaphysical concept, but it has to be made explicit in its own terms and not implied tacitly by mixing differing spheres.

(2) Under the heading "abstract" or "metaphysical concept" Hegel treats of that proof which is assigned to the Christian religion, namely the ontological. While the assignment of the cosmological and physicotheological proofs within the history of religion varies, Hegel consistently links the ontological proof to Christianity. Yet it is not immediately clear what qualifies it to constitute the formal explication of the concept of the "Consummate Religion"—what is specifically Christian about the idea of the *id quo maius cogitari nequit* or the supremely real or most perfect being. Hegel does not in any event speak here of the *ens necessarium*; and the concept of *causa sui* also occurs only once, in the special materials from the 1831 lectures (*LPR 3:355*). Undoubtedly this proof only came on the scene with Christianity; and this is no matter of chance, for, as Hegel stresses on several occasions, the ancients had not yet attained the profundity of this proof. But even this insight into the relationship of modern to ancient philosophy does not bind the ontological argument so closely to the Christian religion as to make its designation as the metaphysical concept of Christianity beyond all doubt. A further possible objection would be that this proof came on the scene only relatively late in the Christian era, after more than a thousand years of its history. And it can hardly have escaped Hegel's notice that the proof never acquired so unassailed a position as one might have been led to expect from its being named the metaphysical concept of Christianity. Even if Hegel probably never concerned himself in detail with the history of the ontological argument and the differing strategies of proof employed, his treatment of it points in itself to the somewhat sporadic importance he assigned to it. Above all it is not immediately clear where the dogmatic unity of this argument with Christian doctrine is to be found, and especially what its unity might be with the doctrine that Hegel regards as central, that of the trinity. Nor did he ever expressly demonstrate such a link.

(3) Yet the assignment of the ontological proof to Christianity is not merely an expression of an embarrassed search for principles on which to structure the philosophy of religion. The link becomes visible, however, only if one does not establish a direct relation between the ontological proof and Christian doctrine but mediates proof and doctrine alike through what is in fact the metaphysical concept of Christianity. The ontological proof is indeed for Hegel only the reflective shape of the metaphysical concept, which itself is properly speaking nothing other than the identity of concept and reality. Such an identity Hegel does not find adequately explicated in the traditional forms of the ontological proof, whether the Anselmian form or one of the Cartesian forms. He frequently concurs in the critique directed at the forms of the proof. Thus he readily grants the empiricist objection that being is no determination of content (*LPR* 3:354). And he objects to the Anselmian form of the argument on the ground that it merely presupposes the unity of concept and reality in the idea of what is most perfect. It is, to be sure, a perfectly reasonable presupposition, as Hegel maintains contrary to modern critics: if it is permissible to make presuppositions, then it is permissible to make this one. But in philosophy this is not permitted. Hegel therefore regards the presuppositional structure as the defect of the Anselmian proof; but no less does he regard the modern notion of the "concrete, empirical human being" (in contrast with which the concept supposedly appears as something one-sided and defective) as the defect of the more recent debate. Philosophical exposition has to eliminate this defect and spell out the presupposition, namely, that unity of concept and being which Hegel calls "what is most perfect" and "the absolute truth" (*LPR* 3:72).

The proper place for this, however, is not the philosophy of religion but the *Science of Logic* and in particular the concept of the absolute idea. Here for the first time the idea of the unity of subjectivity and objectivity, of concept and reality, is consummated. The traditional ontological proof does no more, in Hegel's eyes, than explicate the absolute idea in terms of the understanding. And it is not the ontological proof in its traditional form but the absolute idea that is the metaphysical concept of the Christian religion. The absolute idea is what contains within itself, and vouches for, the truth of the concepts of God of precritical metaphysics; it is the successor concept to *ens realissimum* as well as *ens necessarium* or *causa sui,* and therefore it is the highest object of philosophical theology. This philosophical-theological dimension is, however, only indirectly derivable from the chapter on the absolute idea at the end of the *Logic.* It is only the philosophy of religion that makes it fully clear that the absolute idea is the proper object of philosophical theology. For it is only here that the content of the idea of the identity of concept and reality has become sufficiently concrete for the idea of God not to remain abstract. It is only here that the highest idea of metaphysics is expressly acknowledged to be identical with the idea of God found in religion. Strictly speaking, this does not occur for the first time at the beginning of the "Consummate Religion," but already in the chapter on the concept of God in Part I of the lectures (see pp. 253 ff. above). To be sure, it is not until 1827 that Hegel makes this reference explicit in Part I. But whereas there he introduces the concept of God only in connection with the systematic development of the *Encyclopedia,* here the point at which the religious idea of God is seen to be identical with the highest idea of logic is attained within the history of religion itself, in the consummate religion.

Thus it does not conflict with the way the system is conceived that the 1827 lectures refrain from treating the ontological proof at this point. To do so is legitimate, not because in these lectures the ontological proof is already taken up in Part I, but because the metaphysical concept, properly speaking, of Christianity is not the ontological proof but the absolute idea, which has only to be referred to parenthetically in the philosophy of religion. One might consider therefore whether the conception of the 1827 lectures does not take precedence over those of the other series. For within the framework of its introduction, after glancing back at the shapes of the history of religion, it leads to this very concept of the absolute idea, which it defines more concretely as absolute subjectivity. In point of intelligibility at least, this conception is preferable to starting with the metaphysical concept.

Furthermore we encounter here formulations that throw significant light on the link between the ontological proof, the absolute idea, and Christianity. The historical stages traversed down to the consummate religion "are encompassed within the infinite, absolute form, in absolute subjectivity, and only the spirit so defined as absolute subjectivity *is* spirit" (*LPR* 3:268). This definition admittedly presupposes the problematic idea of the "resumption" of the history of religion.[46] But it does cite an argument for believing that the idea of the identity of subjectivity and objectivity belongs to Christianity. And it marks very precisely the proper place and also the meaning of references to "absolute subjectivity." Such references presuppose the traversing of finite determinations, not only from the standpoint of the *Encyclopedia* but also historically. "The last stage, however, is that this concept, this subjectivity for which spirit is, is not to remain something external to spirit, but rather is itself to be absolute and infinite subjectivity, infinite form" (*LPR* 3:269). It is characteristic of both concepts that they cannot belong to one side of the religious relationship alone. It is therefore stated, in what follows immediately upon the quoted passage, that infinite form is the circuit of this determining process. This process is the bringing forth of spirit by itself and to this extent also the comprehension of spirit. Without the latter one could not speak of the former. And it is only as this identity of objective development and its self-knowing that spirit is "infinite subjectivity. . . . This, then, is the absolute idea."

These passages in the 1827 lectures afford a sharper insight in two respects than the treatment of the metaphysical concept in the other series. In the first place they interpret the concept of the absolute idea by that of absolute subjectivity.[47] The two terms are in no way tautological. The absolute idea is not spoken of in the same way here as at the end of the *Logic*. For it has here as its sides the

---

46. [*Tr.*] That is, the resumption of the whole of the history of religion into one. On Hegel's idea of "resumption" (*Resumtion*), see above, pp. 136, 141. See also H. S. Harris, *Hegel's Development: Night Thoughts (Jena 1801–1806)* (Oxford, 1983), chap. 4.

47. On the character of this concept as pertaining specifically to the philosophy of religion, see the author's "Absolute Idee—absolute Subjektivität," *Zeitschrift für philosophische Forschung* 35 (1981): 385–416.

process of the genesis of spirit as it traverses its world, and its self-knowing in so doing. This makes this standpoint much richer than that of the conclusion of the *Logic*. Since this argumentation in the 1827 lectures is systematically equivalent to the discussion of the ontological proof in the other series, a sentence from Strauss's excerpts may be cited in support of this interpretation: "what we have in this relationship between the two sides of the ontological proof is God as spirit itself" (*LPR* 3:361). The succeeding statements are also transmitted indirectly by the *Werke* (*LPR* 3:356–357). Thematically, they again accord closely with the 1827 lectures: the identity of concept and being designated in the ontological proof is itself the very identity that is actualized in the process of spirit's self-genesis, diremption, and return into itself. But the process whereby this concept of God acquires concrete shape is linked to the course of the *Encyclopedia* and the philosophy of religion. They make explicit the concept of spirit; at any rate no other concept of it is developed in the framework of Hegel's philosophy. To be sure, this idea of God can be rejected as insufficient—and with all the more reason the more convincing is the conception with which one intends to replace it. But there is little point in imputing to the Hegelian conception, whether with positive or critical intent, another idea of God than that which it develops in philosophical terms.

The second insight could also be gleaned from the other lecture series. But it can be linked in particular to a formulation found in 1827: "what is adequate to the concept is only the concept itself insofar as it has itself as its counterpart or object" (*LPR* 3:269). This suffices to show that in speaking of the ontological proof Hegel is not concerned with being in the sense of that of a hundred thalers, which explains the vehemence of his attacks on a critique of the ontological proof along these lines. What is involved is not the transition to such a mode of being, but the idea of the reality that matches the concept because it is itself nothing other than the concept. It could be said that although the traditional ontological proof seeks to transcend the difference between concept and being, it at the same time reinforces it by emphasizing their heterogeneity. Hegel by contrast seeks to exhibit this transition by grasping concept and reality as one and the same. If there is good reason to understand objectivity in terms of the objectifying of the concept—and this is what the entire development of the system seeks to show—then indeed the idea of their identity in the self-consciousness of absolute spirit no longer forms any special difficulty. And that this idea is not for the first time expounded in a special branch of philosophy but is the basic idea of thought as such—for this Hegel sees evidence in the form in which this idea is present in religion, namely in the representation of the trinity.

4.4. The Idea in the Element of Thought: Speculative Theology

(1) The remarks at the close of the preceding section point to the link betwen the ontological proof and the idea in the element of thought—or "the Kingdom of the Father," as it is called in the last lecture series. The metaphysical concept of Christianity, the idea as the unity of concept and reality, is treated in the ontological proof in the form of the understanding, which holds fast the opposites and so necessarily fails to demonstrate their unity. In the element of thought, by contrast, this idea is the object, not, to be sure, of thinking proper, but of religious representation. The latter has no difficulty in vouching for the unity of concept and reality, but conceptualizing it is another matter. Because of this linkage it is no more possible, in Hegel's view, to renounce the ontological proof in philosophy than the trinitarian idea of God in theology. The ontological proof of precritical metaphysics was condemned to failure because metaphysics sought to conduct it without recourse to the trinitarian idea of God.[48] The ways in which it is formulated in representation and for the understanding, however, remain of themselves inadequate formulations of the truth that philosophy thinks in the speculative concept of God.

---

48. See V 9:141 [forthcoming in English as *Lectures on the History of Philosophy (1825–1826)*, trans. R. F. Brown and J. M. Stewart, vol. 3 (Berkeley, Los Angeles, Oxford, 1990)]. Hegel does not make explicit reference to the ontological proof here, but in general to the "ontotheological problem" of "modern metaphysics," which does, to be sure, develop the antithesis to the point of absolute contradiction, but cannot resolve it since it does not conceive God as triune.

(2) By explicating this concept one at the same time exhibits the inner unity of philosophical theology and the philosophy of religion. The former must pass beyond the abstract idea of God to the concept of the absolute idea as absolute subjectivity, and it is in the philosophy of religion that this occurs. On the other side the philosophy of religion would lack any sort of foundation if it could not be conceived as one moment in the explication of philosophical theology. The idea of God is indeed a product of subjective spirit, but of a spirit that produces its content according to necessity. Unless the philosophy of religion is grounded in philosophical theology this necessity vanishes. While the idea of God would then continue to be a product of subjective spirit, it would no longer be its truth but its projection.

(3) These remarks on the idea in the element of thought seem to be only loosely related to the text of this section. They are, however, based on the function it plays. This can be defined relatively easily because it remains constant in all variants of the lectures, and even in the *Encyclopedia* its content is identical. In the *Encyclopedia* it comes under the heading "Moment of Universality" (§ 567); the manuscript speaks in general of the first sphere, and the later lecture series of the first element; but the *Encyclopedia* too can speak of "spheres or elements" (§ 566). It is only between the further spheres and elements that a difference in scope comes into play. The formal distinction between moments and spheres or elements is defined in §§ 565–566: for representation the moments divide off to form "particular spheres or elements, in each of which the absolute content presents itself." It is only representation that gives the moments of the content "independence and makes them presuppositions toward each other, and phenomena that succeed each other, as well as a nexus of events subject to finite reflective categories" (§ 565).

This makes clear what truth value the philosophy of religion accords to the three spheres or elements. But its responsibility is neither to disregard nor simply to repeat the representational form of the absolute content, but rather to show how the "concept" is at work in it. The first part of the philosophy of religion has developed the concept of religion; the third part shows how this concept becomes objective to itself in religion itself and so in the form of representation.

The sole content of this first sphere is accordingly the way in which religious representation has for its object the absolute idea, although properly speaking this can only be grasped adequately by conceptual thinking. This follows mandatorily from the conception of the lectures, and Hegel endorses it explicitly in all expositions of the first element that are here distinguished. The philosophy of religion cannot present another concept of God than that of the "Concept of Religion" and at the same time the metaphysical concept of the "Consummate Religion." The latter in turn results from the preceding development of the system (see above, pp. 247 ff.): "Absolute spirit . . . is, in terms of content, the essential and actual spirit of nature and [finite] spirit" (*Enc* § 565).[49] Instead of "absolute idea" Hegel does indeed, above all in the 1824 and 1827 lectures, use the term "eternal idea." This is most likely an expression of the fact that here (as already in the metaphysical concept) he is not discussing the absolute idea in the form attained at the end of the logic of the concept (*SL* 824 ff., *GW* 12:236 ff.).

Occasionally, to be sure, Hegel does give the impression that the logical form of the absolute idea is all that is involved. Thus the 1827 lectures maintain that in the first element God is considered "in his eternal idea, as he is in and for himself, prior to or apart from the creation of the world, so to speak" (*LPR* 3:275). The reference is obviously to the well-known formula in the introduction to the *Science of Logic* (*SL* 50, *GW* 11:21). And the manuscript refers to the closing chapter (*SL* 824, *GW* 12:236): "speculative science" has "recognized and demonstrated that this idea [is] the truth, the whole truth, the sole truth" (*LPR* 3:79). But here (as is already the case with the metaphysical concept) the absolute idea probably does not refer solely to "the abstract logical identity of concept and being as immediates" (*LPR* 3:361) but to the substantial identity of spirit, where spirit constitutes both sides of the relationship, as concept and as reality. Strauss's excerpts do not pro-

---

49. [*Tr.*] "Der absolute Geist . . . ist dem Inhalte nach der an und für sich seiende Geist der Natur und des Geistes." We have here partly followed the English translation, which, however, substitutes "God" for "absolute spirit."

vide the only support for this view. It is borne out by the statement in the manuscript that the consummate religion is the one in which the concept of religion "has returned to itself, the one in which the absolute idea—God as spirit in the form of truth and revealedness for consciousness—is the object" (*LPR* 1:111).[50] This accords with the "Concept of Religion," which presupposes not only the logic but also the development of the system in the *Encyclopedia* down to objective spirit. At the same time—and this is the reason for Hegel's repeated references back to the absolute idea—the explication of this substantial identity is here discussed primarily in terms of its general logical content as identity of concept and reality, since the other of concept, namely reality, is here the concept itself.

According to this interpretation of the first element, its content follows seamlessly from the development of the system, without specifically religious or theological presuppositions. Thus it is the case that it is not representational but conceptual thinking that comprehends God as perfect already in the initial sphere of his eternal self-containment and self-communion. But this occurs nowhere else than in the *Logic,* in the thinking that thinks itself, which is "the absolute truth and all truth" (*Enc* § 236). Thus it is only the philosophy of religion that makes transparent the speculative-theological character of the *Logic.* Apart from the *Logic* there is no other special sphere where the divine being would eternally bring itself forth prior to and apart from the world.

One cannot fail to notice here the references to the Aristotelian idea of the *noēsis noēseōs.*[51] Their occurrence is in no way accidental. For Hegel's aim is in fact to show that in the idea of the trinity nothing else is comprehended than the unity of *nous* and *noēton*: in the idea of the identity of concept and reality as the mode of thinking that thinks itself, the trinity is comprehended, and vice

50. [*Tr.*] Translation modified slightly; see *V* 3:28.

51. The interpretation of the relationship of the absolute idea to the *noēsis noēseōs* does not form part of the philosophy of religion in the narrower sense but of the logic. In this connection see Klaus Düsing, *Das Problem der Subjektivität in Hegels Logik* (Bonn, 1976), pp. 305 ff.; and *Hegel und die Geschichte der Philosophie* (Darmstadt, 1983), pp. 124 ff.

versa. This first discloses the meaning of what otherwise appears a mystery.

By this means we have described the conceptual content of what, for religious consciousness, is found in the representational comprehension of the sphere of pure thinking. This reconstruction uses Hegelian formulations in part, and in part considerations relating to the overall conception of the lectures, regarding the unity of the metaphysical concept of the Christian religion with the "Concept of Religion." A multitude of philosophical objections can doubtless be raised to Hegel's idea, and above all to his assertion that this idea is the necessary and certain result of the prior development of the system. Theological objections by contrast are out of place until Hegel goes on to assert that this idea is at the same time the conceptual expression of the immanent trinity. Indeed Hegel readily concedes that the designation of this element as the "Kingdom of the Father" is not wholly apt, for the very reason that here the actual subject matter is the immanent trinity (*LPR* 3:362).

It is indeed incumbent on his philosophy to prove that the doctrine of the trinity is nothing other than the representational form of this idea of the identity of concept and reality—that this identity is apprehended by religion only in "the happily naive forms of representation that are available" (*LPR* 3:79) as the begetting of the Son by the Father and as the unity of the Father and the Son in the Spirit. Such proof could reside solely in mutual recognition on the part of the representational and the conceptual forms. But this recognition, by definition, must come from the side of the conceptual form. For according to Hegel it pertains to philosophy to understand itself and its other, whereas religious representation takes cognizance only of their nonidentity. Insight into the speculative concept of spirit is achieved only by a mode of thinking that itself thinks the identity of concept and reality and to that extent is no longer religious consciousness as such.

This identity is no reason for disregarding the difference between the conceptual form and the traditional religious form. A philosophical account has to distinguish "between how the idea is for the *concept* in the various elements and how this comes to *repre-*

sentational expression" (*LPR* 3:188). Speculative reconstruction of the religious content aims on the one hand at its rational grounding and on the other (as far as necessary) at purifying the church doctrines as a precondition for their being produced in conceptual thought. It is stated explicitly in *Enc* § 567 that God, "as substantial power in the reflective category of causality, is the creator of heaven and earth, but in this eternal sphere rather begets only himself as his Son"; and that the Creed, instead of the immanent trinity, falsely takes into its first article the idea of creation of the world. In the same way it is no error in history of dogma but a deliberate correction of the church's doctrinal representation that under the heading "trinity"[52] Hegel describes a structure that has with good reason been termed a "biunity." For him it is an incorrect way of viewing the matter to say that the Spirit proceeds from the Father and the Son as a *tertium quid*; the Spirit rather is nothing but their real unity (*BSchr* 14). What could be the third to concept and reality, to thought and its other, if not the unity of the two? Neither here nor elsewhere does Hegel draw from this the conclusion that he conceives only a biunity. Inasmuch as the other two have their real being in the Spirit, the Spirit is actually a third element. In Hegel's view, this way of grasping the relationship of Father, Son, and Spirit ensures that what is conceived is a tri-*unity* and not just a triad that stands in a difficult-to-explain relation to the essential unity. A third element that was something other than the real being of the first two and that only proceeded from them would not be the return out of other-being and would not therefore be spirit; rather it would be comparable to the Hindu Shiva, even if Hegel does not explicitly draw this consequence.

There is one further modification to trinitarian theology that Hegel deems necessary. He sees it as an advantage that his solution grasps the trinity as "universal idea" (*LPR* 3:289)—"universal" not only by comparison with the "traces" of the idea that can be discerned in the history of religion. To the objection that, as

52. On Hegel's philosophy of the trinity, in addition to the literature cited by the author in *Die Religionsphilosophie Hegels*, see now especially Dale M. Schlitt, *Hegel's Trinitarian Claim* (Leiden, 1984); see also Herbert Huber, *Idealismus und Trinität* (Weinheim, 1984); and Emilio Brito, *La christologie de Hegel* (Paris, 1983).

such a universal idea, God is not thought of appropriately, Hegel is ready with the answer that it was just the mistake of the Gnostics to think of the universal as a particular, and that it is only when the trinity is conceived as universal idea that its truth is apprehended; and then it provides the supreme illustration of what it means to conceive the idea of Christianity. To the extent that theology holds fast to divine persons, it cannot conceive the trinity as universal idea. From the perspective of pure thinking, it then stands with the Gnostics, despite all its differences from them. In regard to the Gnostics Hegel could say the same thing he did of the prior forms of trinitarian thought: "the ancients [did] not know what they really possessed in these forms, namely, that they contained the absolute consciousness of truth" (*LPR* 3:81).

The question whether and how one has to speak of God's personality—whether of a triad of persons in an essential unity or of a single personality in three moments or modes of being—does not therefore pose itself for Hegel in the same way as for the dogmatic tradition. What he says on the subject is, as is well known, open to one or the other interpretation. This vacillation does not arise from an uncertainty of thought but from the fact that in his eyes this distinction pertains in any event only to the sphere of representation. The idea of God as the unity of concept and reality, as the thinking that thinks itself in the other of itself, stands over against both these dogmatic forms. It is, however, closer to the one that maintains the unity of personality in three moments. This is already plain in the criticism that the *Phenomenology* directs at representation, which "takes the moments of the movement that spirit is as isolated immovable substances or subjects instead of transient moments" (*Phen* 466, *GW* 9:411).

The absolute being known as spirit is conceived by the lectures as absolute subjectivity. The stages traversed in the history of religions "are encompassed within the infinite, absolute form, in absolute subjectivity, and only the spirit so defined as absolute subjectivity *is* spirit" (*LPR* 3:268). In the concept of absolute subjectivity as the infinite form of self-determining and sublating-of-determinacy, Hegel claims to grasp the conceptual truth of what is intended in the Christian tradition in the idea of the personality of God. And because of this concept Hegel denotes subjectivity as the principle of Christianity. This principle found its most commonly quoted but not its most philosophically demanding expression in the affirmation that the subject is the object of God's love. In order to understand the principle of Christianity one must first understand what the idea of absolute subjectivity signifies in the philosophy of religion.

The religious consciousness will deem it an implausible assurance that the personality of God has to be grasped as absolute subjectivity or the trinity as the identity of the concept and itself as the other of itself. Admittedly it does not have to be furnished with an absolute demonstration of speculative truth. It has to be made aware, however, that the foundations on which it believes itself to rest securely have become insecure. To do this is, to be sure, not the genuine task of speculative philosophy. But it does have to exhibit the untruth of the apprehension of God in terms of the understanding; it has, for instance, to criticize the attempt to attribute predicates to God as to a hard-and-fast subject that is of itself indeterminate and to formulate the conditions of their freedom from contradiction (*LPR* 3:270–271). And it is also its task to point to the unsatisfactory nature of other foundational attempts—invoking for example authority, tradition, or history—which grasp the speculative inner content in forms of sense or of the understanding. Hegel did not need to refute such modes of grounding in detail since he regarded them as having already been refuted from another quarter. His problem was that the absolute content itself risked being lost along with the unsatisfactory grounding.

The instruments Hegel employed to reground the absolute content have always been deemed inferior in value to those he regarded as unsuited for the purpose. In itself this is an argument neither in favor of the latter nor against the former. What we have to do here is not discuss the theological relevance of his position but spell out the philosophical features of his attempt to recover the idea of God for theoretical philosophy and in so doing reground the philosophy of religion. The persuasiveness of his endeavor remains bound up with the systematic development of his philosophy in general. There is little sense in introducing something else into his philosophy, whether it be in order to criticize it more readily or to obtain from it a more effective strengthening of one's own position.

The question whether Hegel's philosophical interpretation of the doctrine of the trinity does justice to the religious consciousness or to the requirements of trinitarian theology is wholly independent of its systematic development. Nor does it decide whether Hegel's interpretation is correct. Objections to his solution would have to show that their proposed alternatives not only yielded dogmatically acceptable results but were better grounded. And they would also have to exhibit that, and to what extent, they assigned to the trinity a comparably focal position in thought. In Hegel's view the idea of the trinity, in the concrete form conferred on it here, is not confined to the philosophy of religion. It is seen as a historically extant solution to the basic problem of speculative theology, namely that of conceiving the relation to oneself as a relation to one's other—in other words, of conceiving how freedom is possible. For Hegel's concept of freedom is just this, being-present-to-self in being-other [*Beisichsein im Anderssein*]. For this reason too it is only when the trinity is interpreted as absolute idea that one can make clear the point where the doctrine of the trinity fuses with the philosophy of freedom. The idea of the trinity is not just superimposed on what is properly a logical or even panlogistical system to give it a theological overlay. Nor does it form a merely a posteriori conceptual interpretation of a faith that is presupposed and not rethought by philosophy. The church's doctrine of the trinity is rather an undertaking akin to speculative theology, resulting from analogous ways of posing the problem. The concepts of substance, subject, and the universal form only seemingly accidental means by which to interpret the inner-divine relations. And no one who surveys the formulation of the dogma of the trinity historically will be able to say that there is no evidence for assuming such a kinship.

4.5. The Idea in the Element
of Representation: Speculative Christology

(1) In the lectures considerably more space is devoted to christology than to speculative theology in the narrower sense. More weight also is attached to it in the lectures' subsequent reception. Espe-

cially in christology, the linkage between philosophy and the historical dimension of religion finds unmistakable expression. Yet, unlike speculative theology, christology is subject to conditions that complicate its treatment. To the extent that these conditions are reflected in architectonic differences, they have already been discussed above. These differences too are by no means merely formal in nature. They can be justified only if they reflect a differing evaluation of the material. Otherwise not only would the persuasiveness of the logical paradigms be at stake but also the meaning of the systematic structure as a whole.

(2) The differences in architectonics also affect the question how far the bounds of christology ought to stretch. As Hegel uses it, the expression "Son of God" has a threefold meaning: the traditional one of the divinity of Jesus; that of a theological designation of the world; and finally the meaning associated with the Logos christology, where it is used to designate the second moment of the immanent trinity, the "Son," who remains in original identity with the "Father" (*Enc* § 567). In the interests of the unity of the doctrine of the "Son of God," these different meanings would have to belong to a single systematic structure. In this regard the unity between the "eternal" and the "temporal" Son seems to give rise to lesser difficulties than the relation of the "eternal Son" to the world, though it is the latter relationship that has systematic priority. It is also less problematic than the first.

Hegel in no way asserts the flat identity of the natural world and the "eternal Son." The lectures stress that it is a misunderstanding to suppose that "the eternal Son of the Father . . . is *the same as* the physical and spiritual world—and only this is to be understood under the name 'Son'" (*LPR* 3:87). But this disclaimer would hardly be necessary if this view were not suggested by an analogy in the systematic position of "Son" and world. Here the error seems to be due, not to representation, but indeed to the concept, for what is involved in the first and second spheres is "the same idea implicitly," and "the absolute act of the first division [is] *implicitly* the same as the second," which is understood as creation of a world. Only "representation holds the two apart as quite different grounds and acts" (*LPR* 3:86–87). It divides the single manifestation into successive spheres (*Enc* §§ 565–566) and speaks of the "disintegration of the eternal moment of mediation, of the one Son, into the independent antithesis" of nature and finite spirit (*Enc* § 568). But if it pertains only to representation to distinguish "two eternal activities of God," whereas "God's activity is after all utterly one and the same" and not a manifold, then the view cannot be simply rejected that, for the concept, the world is the same as the "eternal Son." This supposition, which goes back to the Hegel School, is therefore not entirely incorrect. "Son" is after all only the highest expression of difference in general (*LPR* 2:265 n. 90). Indeed, on several occasions Hegel identifies the world and the "eternal Son," and not merely in the lectures on the history of philosophy (*LHP* 2:76, *W* 14:253), where one could presume an inappropriate form of words, but—in virtually the same terms—in the philosophy of religion as well: "As spirit or as love, God is this self-particularizing. God brings forth the world, his Son, posits another to himself and in this other has himself, is identical with himself" (*LPR* 1:437).[53] He puts the point even more bluntly, saying that "all temporal determinacy is to be eliminated, whether in terms of duration or of the now" and only "the simple thought . . . of the other is to be held fast" (*LPR* 3:88). The world is the same as the "eternal Son" inasmuch as both are the *other*. It must accordingly be assumed that it is merely representation that distinguishes them. This is confirmed by the 1824 lectures (*LPR* 3:199). But it is only the isolation of two processes that has to be attributed to representation, the fact of holding them apart in time—holding apart, indeed, a phase of unity, a phase of falling away, and a third phase, in which the divine idea comes forth in this other-being, to use the terms employed in a fragment relating to the 1824 lectures (*LPR* 3:388).

53. [*Tr.*] Translation altered slightly; cf. *V* 3:325–326. The German text reads "Gott . . . die Welt, seinen Sohn erschafft." In *LPR* we translated this as "God creates the world and produces his Son" to avoid the suggestion that the Son is "created" and the world "produced." The verb *erschaffen* has both connotations. But in this way we obscured the identity the author wants here to emphasize. For an English equivalent that will apply to both "world" and "Son" we now use "to bring forth." In the lectures on the history of philosophy, the verb used with reference to both "Son" and "world" is *erzeugen*, "to beget."

On this view the error of representation would not consist in holding the "eternal Son" and the world apart but solely in failing to recognize that what are involved here are not temporal processes and a falling-away but distinguishable forms of other-being that are constantly held in identity. The 1827 lectures in particular stress that the determinacy of other-being too belongs to "the primal division of the idea" and that the determinate entity is released to go forth as an independent object (*LPR* 3:292–293). At the same time Hegel emphasizes here also that this other has no "genuine actuality": "For the world, to be means to have being only for an instant, so to speak, but also to sublate this its separation or estrangement from God. It means to return to its origin" (*LPR* 3:293). He does indeed speak here of a "fall" but at the same time stresses that the idea of the independence of the other is always taken back into the unity of the concept. Since reality is the other of the concept, but precisely *its* other wherein it recognizes itself, and since the existence of the world is also a moment of this reality, there cannot be an actual "fall" here as in other conceptions. To use a term applied to Spinoza, which Hegel takes from contemporary discussion, this could be called his "acosmism" (*LPR* 1:377). And this acosmism suffices in his view to acquit Spinoza of the charge of cosmotheism.[54] The same claim may be made on behalf of Hegel's own conception. If the world is the other of spirit, but precisely what is released as other by spirit, and has no genuine actuality, then the charge of pantheism is, properly speaking, an idle one.

(3) Concerning the third way in which the designation of Son is understood, as a christological title of exaltation, few problems might be expected. The figure of Jesus acquires in Hegel's work an importance matched by few other philosophies. Many features that distinguished Hegel's christology in its time are today so much a matter of course that attention has first to be drawn to their peculiarity compared with then contemporary approaches. Jesus no longer appears as a teacher or as virtuous human being, as in En-

---

54. [*Tr.*] See the editorial annotations in *V* 3:406–407 and *LPR* 3:377 n. 27. "Cosmotheism" is another name for "pantheism" or "atheism" rather than for "acosmism," as the English notation inadvertently implies.

lightenment philosophy or rationalist theology; nor does he appear as an embodiment of a universal idea, an ideal figure of a humanity well-pleasing to God, as in Kant. For this reason the Hegel of Berlin days dismisses the comparison of Jesus and Socrates as an idle consideration over which one need not linger. Philosophy can, to be sure, make Jesus the theme of an external consideration, for instance by the history of philosophy or the philosophy of world history. But in the philosophy of religion Jesus is the object because his destiny is accessible to *religious* consideration, and the latter alone is of consequence. This is reflected in Hegel's treatment of christology. The arrangement of the later lectures is superior to the manuscript in that the manuscript places religious and also speculative considerations first, and only then external considerations, whereas the later lectures proceed in reverse order. To be sure, external consideration as well, in Hegel's eyes, is not merely external. It too is dealt with only insofar as it "is already the start of our being led over to what is higher" (*LPR* 3:367). The differing ways of considering the matter do not, consequently, stand in disconnected juxtaposition. If this were not so, there would be no reason why religious consideration should be concerned with this human being and not another.

(4) The reason why talk of the "eternal Son" and of the world constitutes a unity is that they form, as it were, differing results of one and the same primal division. This conceptual definition of the "Son" as the "other" poses difficulties in the understanding of Jesus as the "Son." The third and more narrowly christological meaning of the "Son" cannot in fact (in a fashion similar to the first two spheres of the manuscript, or to the first element and the first form of the second element) be attributed to a further specification of the absolute division by representation. This is matched by a striking dimunition in the use made of the term "Son" as opposed to the title "God-man" [*Gottmensch*]. The texts that designate Jesus as "Son of God" are almost exclusively quotations or at least paraphrases of quotations from the Bible. But the decisive point is not whether Hegel uses this expression but how the connection between the "eternal" and the "temporal" Son is to be understood. The divine-human unity that is manifest in Jesus runs counter to

the movement of externalization, be it that involved in the immanent trinity or the creation of a world. It cannot be interpreted as a further representational aspect of this movement, but (as the manuscript and the *Encyclopedia* also maintain) falls within another sphere. The function it performs in the system is at odds with the two preceding forms of the "Son." While these are defined as differing forms of otherness, the "temporal Son" is conceived as infinite return and reconciliation of the externalized world with the eternal being. One cannot therefore speak of a structural unity of the three meanings of "Son of God." For Hegel "Son" means in the first place otherness: either the otherness, held in immediate identity, of the "eternal Son," or the otherness that has stepped out to momentary independence, that of the world. In the special christological sense, however, "Son" does not mean otherness but return from otherness. Hegel does indeed attempt to embrace both the "eternal" and the "temporal" Son by maintaining it is "the Son of the eternal sphere transposed into temporality" (*Enc* § 569). No objection can be raised to the extent that the sole intention here is to reiterate an image of religious representation; but a philosophical grounding it is not. Contrary to the common criticism that Hegel does not take the immanent trinity seriously, the "economic trinity" is therefore much more problematical with him than the "immanent." For however much the latter diverges from church doctrine, it has nevertheless a significance certified by the system.

The reason why this relation between the "eternal" and the "temporal" Son remains so vague is not solely their differing function in the system. It also resides in the fact that Hegel's christology in the narrower sense cannot provide philosophical justification for what at least one form of traditional christology conceives as the link between them, namely the preexistence of Christ as the Logos. By contrast, when it comes to the uniqueness of the God-man, his philosophy develops arguments for the rationality of church doctrine.[55] The latter is, to be sure, illustrated but in no way grounded by the once-and-for-all character of the fact. But not all the reasons Hegel adduces for it are convincing. For example, the uniqueness of the God-man does not follow from that of the "eternal Son"

55. See the author's *Die Religionsphilosophie Hegels*, pp. 98–99.

(*LPR* 3:114–115)—even if one were willing to supply the systematic link that Hegel fails to provide. For it could belong to the shape in which the "eternal Son" appears under the conditions of the temporal sphere that uniqueness here degenerates into a multiplicity of God-men. From the requirement that it should be possible to *perceive* the divine-human unity, it is even possible to infer that this unity must constantly appear in at least one new individual, for example in a continuous succession of Dalai Lamas. For perception is only perception of something present.

(5) We have not yet touched on the question what status accrues to a christology in the framework of a speculative philosophy—the question whether and how the inner theological content of christology is at all amenable to a philosophical explication. In few questions is the interpretation of Hegel's philosophy of religion as controversial as in this one; and this is no recent development. The dispute concerning it led, as is well known, to the breakup of the Hegel School in the 1830s. Owing to its great importance for the history of the effect of Hegel's philosophy of religion, it seems appropriate at this point to draw on some aspects that could serve to answer the question concerning the meaning a christology might have for speculative philosophy.

In this respect it is necessary to grasp more precisely than is commonly the case what is at issue in the earlier dispute. It in no way involves merely a predominantly positive or a more negative attitude to religion. The two wings and the center of the Hegel School differ—in the original form of the break—in their attitude to the relationship between idea and history. They differ not only on whether Hegel *had* deduced the fact of the God-man from the idea but also on whether the actuality of the God-man *could* be deduced from the idea of divine-human reconciliation.[56] The possible ambivalence of the relationship between idea and history is reflected in two series of statements by Hegel as cited by Strauss. The one holds fast to the actuality of divine-human unity in the sense

---

56. David Friedrich Strauss, *The Life of Jesus Critically Examined,* trans. G. Eliot, ed. P. C. Hodgson (Philadelphia and London, 1972, 1973), pp. 779–784; *In Defense of My "Life of Jesus" against the Hegelians,* trans. M. C. Massey (Hamden, Conn., 1983). See also below, pp. 373–376.

that Hegel himself once formulated it when speaking of the distinction between Christian and pre-Christian forms of the idea of incarnation: in Christianity this unity is "not imagination, but is *actually the case.*" According to the other, the divine-human unity is actualized in the faith of the community.[57] How the two accounts are to be combined is a question to which no answer has yet been given. Unless one is content simply to confess the inconsistency of Hegel's christology, one is obliged to find a solution.

The first point to be noted is that the two statements do not form a logical contradiction. They become contradictory only when the second is also made exclusive: when it is alleged that the unity is actual only in faith and not also independently of it. This is justified only if there are no valid grounds for demonstrating the factual nature of this unity (even though the fact cannot be dogmatically contested either), or if dogmatic considerations impel one to reject in principle the factual nature of this unity and go back exclusively to faith. Once the problem is formulated in this way, it becomes clear that it cannot be resolved by counting whether there are more instances of the first statement or of the second in Hegel's work. Nor is it a question of a mere predilection for a christology based on fact or on kerygma. The question is rather one of philosophical demonstrability.

No one will condemn a philosophy for not taking a position on christological questions. To the extent that it feels itself called to do so, however, one must ask whether it is simply recapitulating dogmatically reflected, or even naively religious, tenets in philosophical guise, or whether it is offering a contribution of its own.

---

57. [*Tr.*] These two viewpoints, with their differing emphasis, are found in the same passage of the *Phenomenology:* "That absolute spirit has given itself the shape of self-consciousness implicitly, and thus has also given it for its consciousness—this now appears as the *faith of the world* that spirit is present as a self-consciousness, i.e. as an actual human being, that it exists for immediate certainty, that the believing consciousness sees and feels and hears this divinity. Thus this self-consciousness is not imagination, but is *actually the case*" (*Phen* 458, *GW* 9:404–405). The last sentence reads in German: "So ist es nicht Einbildung, sondern es ist *wirklich an dem.*" The Miller translation contains at this point a serious error, reading: "Thus this self-consciousness is not imagination, but is *actual* in the believer." "Es ist an dem," in Hegel's antiquated German, simply means "it is in fact the case."

Only the latter would be philosophical, and moreover only it could be of interest theologically. Hegel's contribution to christology, but also to other doctrinal loci, is indeed relatively brief and also modest compared with doctrinal tradition. The problems referred to are traditionally treated in a decidedly more detailed and thorough fashion. Where one seeks to clarify the rigor and effectiveness of dogmatic conceptions, one will have to turn to systematic theology. It is another question whether philosophy is capable of making its own contribution to the problematical theme of christology. But just this is what Hegel's philosophy of religion promises to do.

This contribution may lie only in the fact that his philosophy reveals how the subject of "christology" can occur in the theoretical form of modern consciousness—and indeed that it *can* occur there. If, however, we are speaking of a specific philosophical contribution, independent of theological justifications and presuppositions, we must avoid always asking too much of it theologically and so undermining it. Hegel's contribution has to be viewed as requiring justification on the basis of philosophical thought itself, and not only on the basis of a presupposed revelation or tradition. Only in this way is it possible to prevent statements of faith from turning up again in the guise of philosophical demonstrations. To clarify the issue, it may serve to reflect on the question what in fact are the possibilities of demonstration in Hegel's philosophy. This is not the place to present an exhaustive analysis of these possibilities, and we can indicate only a few results of such an analysis.

Philosophy cannot, using its own means, demonstrate the *fact* of the divine-human unity. The reasons for this are, to be sure, not the same as those for its inability to deduce single objects such as Krug's pen.[58] In contrast with this, philosophy is quite capable of explicating the *necessity* of the unity of God and humanity. It is not possible, however, for it to identify the fact of this unity historically.

But philosophy is also unable to justify itself by a given fact. The view that has recently been advanced on various sides to the effect

58. [*Tr.*] Wilhelm Traugott Krug was a German popular philosopher and critic of Hegel. See *GW* 4:178 and *Enc* § 250 footnote.

that Hegel bases himself on the "Christian fact"[59] cannot be correct. Moreover, this is contrary to the main thrust of speculative philosophy and ruinous for its philosophical claim and theological relevance alike. This does not, however, in any way expose Hegel's philosophy to the charge of being unhistorical. It has less reason to fear this charge than positions that rely on facticity. Philosophy cannot embark on this road, if only because the fact of the divine-human unity is not, and cannot be, attested historically. The so-called approach based on historical fact always reaches back in the last resort behind the historical to the assumption of a Son of God conceived in terms of substance and nature, an assumption that cannot be introduced into the concept of history. This can already be seen from the early text-criticism of the Enlightenment period, for instance by Hermann Samuel Reimarus, and from the discussion of these problems in Lessing's polemical writings. From his early years on, Hegel paid attention to this discussion—and it would hardly lead to respect for his position had he failed to take its results seriously. His founding of the truth of Christianity on the idea responds to a situation in the history of theology and philosophy that is molded by Lessing's insight into the impossibility of providing a historical foundation for eternal truths. Had Hegel disregarded this insight, his approach would perhaps have been the expression of a pious consciousness that seeks its fulfillment in a flatly acquiescent affirmative. It would be a relapse from the insight his contemporaries had gained into the relationship between truths of reason and of history, as well as between historical science and dogma, and it would have to be rejected as outmoded from the start. But this is not a question of the concept of philosophy, but of reflection on the foundational power possessed by a fact as such. This is why Hegel seeks a new line of approach in order to show that the uniqueness of the God-man is rational: it is not the case that a fact functions as norm for the idea, but rather that the fact is validated when it is recognized as strictly adequate to the idea (*LPR* 3:145).

---

59. As representative of this interpretation, see James Yerkes, *The Christology of Hegel,* 2d ed. (Albany, 1983), esp. p. 207.

At the same time the interpretation outlined here does not see Hegel's position as governed by a complete disjunction between the truths of reason and of history. Nor does it see it as characterized by a forgetfulness of the significance of such a disjunction, properly defined. That he, unlike many of his interpreters, was fully conscious of this problem is clear from his very lapidary hermeneutical principle: "The history of Christ is also narrated by those upon whom the Spirit has already been poured out" (*LPR* 3:323 n. 199). This insight into the impossibility of a recourse to the external history of Jesus undermines the opposition of the Spirit and the letter, and it does so by totally renouncing knowledge of a historical actuality independent of the Spirit.

It is the task of speculative philosophy to explicate the truth of the absolute idea. It is also part of this truth that it should manifest itself, it should appear in finitude. This and nothing else is what the philosophical trajectory as portrayed in the *Encyclopedia* describes. To this extent, demonstration of the advance to individuality also pertains to the necessity of the idea. Philosophy has "*to grasp conceptually what [already] is*. What is must be *actual* on its own account, before philosophy comes—[it must] not just [be] what is true implicitly, but [must be] in general empirical consciousness" (*LPR* 3:144). The necessity involved here is not merely what is subjectively required. That would not be a sufficient argument for passing over to individuality. Above all, no such requirement would exist unless it had been called forth by the movement of the absolute idea, the movement of positing and sublating finitude.

If it is impossible for speculative philosophy to deduce a fact, and if it is likewise illegitimate for it to take a fact as its scientific and not merely historical starting point, then it is necessary to demarcate the limit of its demonstrative power. Hegel designated this limit very precisely on several occasions. Speculative philosophy can spell out the need for and the necessity of reconciliation. Indeed, it can go a step further and argue that a plurality of God-men is inappropriate to the idea. But it cannot prove which particular individual has to be recognized as the God-man. The circle can, however, be drawn more tightly thanks to another mode of grounding, that based on the philosophy of history. A sentence that in

Lasson's edition is so distorted as to be meaningless says very clearly: "To make this one into its holy one also has a local and exclusive occasion" (*LPR* 3:115). From this it seems that in addition to the local grounds there are also other grounds for designating a particular human being. Another passage expresses itself even more precisely. The sole basis on which the actuality of the divine-human unity can be demonstrated is the philosophy of history: "'When the time had come, God sent forth his Son'; and *that* the time had come can only be discerned from history" (*LPR* 3:215).

But there is one thing verification based on the philosophy of history cannot do, namely demonstrate in which individual the divine-human unity becomes actual. If philosophy wants to make use of such knowledge, it must have recourse to something whose attestation lies outside itself. But this in no way means that such a presumption is arbitrary. The required certainty cannot be the certainty of an external fact for the reason that has been given, namely that such a fact cannot be demonstrated. It then remains questionable, however, what legitimates the divinity of the God-man. Hegel had good reason not to follow the contemporary assumptions as to Jesus' freedom from sin or peculiarity of self-consciousness. For a historical proof of sinlessness would be a curiosity indeed, while a historical proof for a divine-human self-consciousness, assuming it could be conducted, would remain irrelevant to the question of truth.

There are, however, few problems about acknowledging that the community has experienced the actuality of the divine-human unity, and has attained the perception of being reconciled, in one particular individual. This is likewise a historical fact, but of a different kind than the acknowledgment of the facticity of a God-man. But philosophy cannot simply accept this fact of the community's consciousness either. There may be several such reports, referring to competing individuals. What it means for philosophy to acknowledge this fact is that it finds the fate of this individual appropriate to the idea—and it finds it to be so because of its conformity to the systematic exposition of the nature of the concept. It is only for this reason that philosophy can accept this presupposition. And even this does not result in the rehabilitation of the fact in the sense of external history. For the story of Christ is quite inconceivable as external history, for obvious methodological reasons. The history that is acknowledged to be appropriate to the idea is also not a fact accessible to profane history. It is attested only by those upon whom the Spirit has already been poured out; only in the form in which it is experienced and handed down by the community is it in conformity with the idea. It is not this or that feature that is a product of this spiritual comprehension, indeed not even only that wherein the religious history as a whole differs from external comprehension, but the external history itself, insofar as it too is recounted only by those upon whom the Spirit has been poured out. This is not a rationalistic singling out and reinterpreting of individual features. It follows logically from a method which, using the modern term, one can describe as based on "kerygmatic history." Strictly speaking, this entails consequences for the systematic structure of the "Consummate Religion," namely that "representation," the content of the second element, always means the representation of a community. The way the matter is presented in the *Encyclopedia* could be interpreted as alone doing justice to this connection, since it includes christology in the "moment of individuality" as a "presupposition."

This result of the nondemonstrability of the external fact would be misunderstood if it were viewed as the expression of a docetic flight from history, or a residual uncertainty vis-à-vis what is historical, or however these objections may be worded. Nor can it be argued that some phrases sound as though more than kerygma is involved, after all. Such criticism betrays only a misunderstanding of what is required for grounding a philosophy of religion, and what it is methodically possible for it to know with certainty. This result makes it necessary, therefore, to take up a position on the question posed by Strauss, in favor of the view that the divine-human unity can be comprehended solely in the faith of the community. What has been said so far does not, to be sure, prove that it is not "actually the case." But there is no way one can see by which to prove an external fact of "divine-human unity." Such a fact only becomes comprehensible once it is mediated through the actuality of the Spirit in the community. Even if there are statements to the contrary in Hegel's work, and even if these prove to be more numerous than the restriction to the faith of the community, the fact remains that on the basis of Hegel's philosophy as philosophy, only the recourse to the faith of the community is legitimate. This unavoidably seems to imply that on the basis of the theoretical means at his disposal Hegel is not entitled to go on to affirm that the unity "actually is the case." Bruno Bauer thus seems to be right in saying that in Hegel critical arguments and orthodox ways of speaking are found side by side, and that this ambivalence is unavoidable from the standpoint of Hegel's own philosophy[60]—notwithstanding the fact that it is only the left-Hegelian interpretations that actually treat Hegel's statements on the theoretical basis his philosophy affords. It is indeed customary today to dismiss left-Hegelian interpretations as inappropriate. But the right-Hegelian view can be criticized for going beyond what speculative philosophy can prove or even totally disregarding the question what its demonstrative possibilities are. In the strict sense of Strauss's distinction, today virtually all interpreters probably belong to the left, including those who claim to favor a right-Hegelian interpretation of the philosophy of religion. For no one in all probability will any longer profess to be able to deduce a fact qua fact from the idea.

(6) It would remain unsatisfactory, however, to resolve what is an undeniable tension by regarding the first series of statements as utterly inappropriate to Hegel's systematic presuppositions. Hegel is, after all, obviously of the view that the unity in question is "actually the case"—a fact and not a mere fiction. In accord with the methodological guideline that a distinction should be made between the way something is for the concept and how it comes to representational expression (*LPR* 3:188), it could easily be shown how the problem is solved for conceptual thought. The point at issue, however, is just the right of religious consciousness to hold fast to the "is" also at the level of representation. Only in this way

---

60. See Bruno and Edgar Bauer, *Briefwechsel während der Jahre 1839–1842 aus Bonn und Berlin* (Charlottenburg, 1844), letter to Edgar Bauer, 15 March 1840.

can the supposed discrepancy between Hegel's approach and individual utterances be overcome. And only in this way is he exonerated from the suspicion that he is incapable of deciding between his philosophical insight and relics of orthodoxy or even requirements of a political nature. A solution should be proposed, therefore, that makes it possible to hold fast to the "is," to the actual presence of God in the finite. The nature of this solution could be indicated and at the same time concealed by the title "Lutheran christology." It recognizes the fact that Hegel was a Lutheran and also professed to be one—at a time when this was not at all so opportune from the standpoint of religious politics. Despite his public profession it is difficult to say whether confessional elements influenced his philosophy and, if so, how.[61] An easier question to answer is the function that Protestantism played in his philosophy, although this too is not as obvious as his emphasis on the "Protestant principle" might suggest.

It is only in the doctrine of the eucharist that an explicit reference to Luther is to be found. As is well known, Hegel declares that the Lutheran version of it—strictly speaking, not of eucharistic doctrine itself but of the antinomy of freedom and grace—is, even if not speculative, nevertheless "the most ingenious" (*LPR* 3:157). The Reformed view, which he knows only in the form of Zwingli's teaching, lacks in his view the element of the "is." The Catholic view does hold fast to the "is," but Hegel criticizes it for making the holy something external, with all the consequences that stem from this, by accepting a change in the substance of the host and the wine. Eberhard Jüngel has drawn attention to a figure of thought that is implicit in Lutheran doctrine, and of which Hegel himself was possibly unaware. Hegel's references to the death of God are, Jüngel maintains, in line with the Lutheran version of the doctrine of *communicatio idiomatum,* the interchange of divine and human properties.[62] These two aspects (eucharist and *com-*

61. There is no getting away from this despite Ulrich Asendorf's attempt to define the systematic relationship between Luther's and Hegel's conceptions; see his *Luther und Hegel* (Wiesbaden, 1982). On Hegel's "Lutheran christology" see also *LPH* 415, W 9:500.

62. Jüngel, *God as the Mystery of the World,* pp. 96–97.

municatio) do not, in Hegel, seem to be directly linked. Yet it is possible to discover in his interpretation evidence of the link that does in any event exist between them, and to put this link to good use for interpreting his christology.

Before trying to explain this connection it seems appropriate to make plain what, if anything, can be meant by "Lutheran christology." Certainly it does not mean Luther's christology, in the way that one speaks of the christology of Karl Barth or others. "Lutheran" is meant in the confessional sense. Yet christology does not seem to be primarily the field in which the confessions diverge. Hegel too shares the view that they only differ in their cultus (*LPR* 3:154). The christological differences between them are little if any greater than those between theologians belonging to the same confession.

What we are in search of is a model that—notwithstanding the impossibility of a historical proof of the fact of the divine-human unity and a philosophical demonstration of its particular individuality—reaches back behind the sphere of the faith of the community and expresses the actuality of this unity at the representational level also. To find such a model one can look for helpful analogies, and such an analogy can be found in the Lutheran doctrine of the eucharist[63]—though, strictly speaking, only in one specific understanding of this doctrine, an understanding that does indeed adhere to it in the main but leaves out of account a series of genuinely Lutheran elements. In this regard it can be left open whether this understanding is originally Hegelian or whether he is here following an interpretation that was widespread at the time.

In Hegel's view the distinguishing feature of the Lutheran doctrine is that it regards the host as actual "only in faith and in the partaking. This [is] its consecration in the faith and the spirit of each individual" (*LPR* 3:155). The 1824 lectures expand on this, saying that "the sensible is first spiritualized in the subject. . . . The

63. In addition to the well-known earlier treatments of this subject, see now Gunther Wenz, "Für uns gegeben," in *Mahl des Herrn,* eds. M. Garijo-Guembe, J. Rohls, and G. Wenz (Frankfurt, 1988), pp. 223–338. A work still reflecting the subsequent effect of Hegel's lectures is Franz Hildebrandt, *Est: Das Lutherische Prinzip* (Göttingen, 1931).

crucial point in this interpretation is that transubstantiation takes place only in the partaking of communion, in faith, and only in a spiritual fashion" (*LPR* 3:236). The 1827 lectures emphasize that "the movement does indeed begin with something external, which is an ordinary, common thing, but the communion, the self-feeling of the presence of God, comes about only insofar as the external thing is consumed—not merely physically but in spirit and in faith. God is present only in spirit and in faith." And special material from the 1831 lectures stresses that "apart from communion and faith, the host is a common, sensible thing: the process is genuine only within the subject's spirit" (*LPR* 3:338 incl. n. 244).

The uniform tenor of these passages brings out clearly where Hegel's conception accords with the Lutheran, and where it diverges from it. He leaves out of account the latter's realistic features, which lead to problems concerning the *manducatio impiorum,* and emphasizes instead the spiritualization of the sensible in the subject. For this reason he is not faced with the problem to which Luther's doctrine could provide a consistent solution only with difficulty, if at all, namely the extent to which the divine is present even leaving aside the sacramental *actio*. Hegel also does not refer to the constitutive significance of the introductory words of the eucharist. Their function he assigns rather to faith, to which, we are told, belong "consecration" and "transubstantiation." What he has in common with Lutheran doctrine is the link to the accomplishment of the sacramental action and the stress laid on the real presence of the divine.

From a christological point of view, Hegel's "Lutheran" conception of the eucharist can be amplified as follows: what is given immediately and can be demonstrated is the community's faith that Christ is present in the host. Although this stipulation refers in immediate fashion only to faith, it equally implies the "is"—despite the apparent fact that the host is just any piece of bread. What is given and demonstrable is faith alone, and yet from it and from it alone is inferred the actuality of the "is." The reason why this is legitimate is that the statement concerning faith is not coupled with another that would be susceptible of and need a grounding of its own. Instead the "is" is understood as analytically implied by the statement concerning faith: there is an immediate transition from certainty to being.

This makes the "Lutheran" version of eucharistic doctrine an apt paradigm for christology. There can be few doubts as to the justification for such a transference. The introductory words of the eucharist are expressly christological statements, no less than the "I am" passages in the Gospel of John. It must therefore be possible to transform eucharistic christology into general christological statements. And Hegel's conception of the religious representation of Jesus can be viewed as one such retranslation of the christology of the "Lutheran doctrine of the eucharist" into general christological statements—even if he never expresses this in so many words. What is involved in his doctrine of the eucharist as in his christology is a specific conception of the unity of the divine and the human. We are, it may be supposed, entitled to demand that this unity should have the same character in both cases. The unity of the divine and what is externally present in the sacrament can then be thought of as a paradigm for the divine-human unity that actually exists in Christ.

This conception has the effect of excluding a prior transubstantiation, which makes the divine something that also exists in natural form. According to the Lutheran doctrine of the eucharist, there is no reason to suppose that the substance of the host has been changed by the consecration of the priest and that the unity therefore also exists independently of the sacramental action—or, as Hegel puts it, independently of partaking and faith. Nor is there any reason to regard such a transubstantiation as an indispensable precondition for the actuality of the divine-human unity. And there is also no cause to assign as it were a natural status to the interchange of properties, irrespective of the Spirit in the community. Whoever accepts the Lutheran form of the *communicatio idiomatum* in the doctrine of the eucharist has no valid reason to contest its applicability to christology. Just as it is not a sufficient argument against the presence of the divine in the sacrament to dispute a prior transubstantiation or even the actuality of the *communicatio idiomatum* before the sacramental action, so also it is not an argument against the actuality of the divine-human unity in Christ to regard the interchange of properties in him as not occurring, as it were, in a natural form.

And not only is there no cogent reason for assuming such a "christological transubstantiation" or for acknowledging a doctrine of two natures, but also Hegel would reject the presumption of a difference in substance and the accompanying two-natures doctrine as a misunderstanding of the way in which the divine can alone become present. Instead of laying the foundation for a correct understanding of the divine-human unity, it tends to cast doubt upon it. A difference in substance of this kind ultimately entails the traditional doctrine of the incarnation, which places the divine-human unity at the beginning of the life of Jesus, as well as its subsequent dogmatic elaboration; and such a difference is a mystery not only for the understanding but also for reason. Not only is it philosophically indemonstrable, but also, according to Hegel, even within the framework of religious representation it is the expression of a misunderstanding of the very idea it is meant to safeguard. This is why he says in unusually sharp fashion: "'Divine and human nature' is a puzzling and difficult expression, and the kind of representation we associate with it should be forgotten" (*LPR* 3:211–212).

The opposite extreme, however, is no less to be rejected. It cannot be said that the community came to perceive the divine-human unity in this one man despite the fact that he himself was a mere human being. It is not merely claimed of this human being that he symbolized the unity; the unity is also asserted to be actual. Judged in terms of the demonstrative possibilities of philosophy, Hegel might have been content with the mere *significat,* with affirming that for the faith of the community Christ has acquired the "significance" of the divine-human unity—the implication being that this was indeed no more than a question of faith. But as with the doctrine of the eucharist, such a solution would, for Hegel, not only not be a speculative solution, it would not even be "ingenious."

So although Jesus is the son of a carpenter, and the divine-human unity is tangible only in the Spirit-guided faith of the community, it is nonetheless necessary to hold fast with undiminished intensity to the "is." The "is," the immediate transition to reality, resides in faith itself, in precisely the same way as in the believer's partaking of the sacrament, or (in Lutheran terms) in the reciting of the introductory eucharistic words in the context of sacramental action. So what may appear as a contradiction between the naturalness of the human Jesus and the actuality of reconciliation can be mediated according to the model based on "Lutheran eucharistic doctrine." In holding fast to the humanity of Jesus and consequently rejecting the traditional doctrine of the incarnation, while at the same time stressing the actuality of the divine-human unity, Hegel is as little falling into contradiction as the Lutheran doctrine of the eucharist. More correctly, he is *no more* falling into contradiction—that is, from the point of view of the understanding, which either rejects this unity or demands that its actualization be preceded by an alteration of substances, an alteration that must admittedly remain no less inexplicable. Just as the real presence of the divine in the eucharist does not presuppose an alteration in substance or a presacramental *communicatio idiomatum,* the actual divinity of Jesus does not entail it either. Any other solution conceives the unity between the divine and the finite in such a way as though, in order to be really present, the unity had initially to become actual outside the Spirit and the community, as it were in a separate act.

Obviously Hegel's "Lutheran christology" is the christology neither of Luther nor of the Lutherans as such. In this respect Hegel may even be more consistent than Luther, who in the doctrine of the incarnation accords to the *communicatio idiomatum* the status of existing in natural form, whereas in the doctrine of the eucharist he ties it to the community's accomplishment of the sacramental act—to the "Spirit"—and denies that it is naturally existent other than in *usus,* however inconsistent this may ultimately be.

(7) This conception poses problems, both for theology and for Hegel's philosophy. One has to inquire of systematic theology whether it has taken sufficiently into account this connection between eucharistic doctrine and christology. There is no doubt that the link is not unknown, and considerable weight was attached to

it in the doctrinal debates of the time of the Reformation.[64] But it was not determined there in the radical form that Hegel's conception calls for: the doctrine of the incarnation was not reformulated on the basis of the sacramental form of the *communicatio idiomatum*. The accentuated differences in eucharistic theology must, however, also entail equally accentuated differences in christology. In terms of content, priority should indeed be given to christology. Then it would be consistent to modify sacramental doctrine in light of the common doctrine of christology. It seems as though, on this point too, Hegel had a sharper eye for dogmatic connections than is the case in certain areas of dogmatic theology—in much the same way as Eberhard Jüngel has shown to be the case for the link between trinitarian doctrine and *theologia crucis*.[65]

For Hegel, this unity of eucharistic doctrine and christology is not, to be sure, an explicit theological proposition, but neither is it an accidental discovery, so to speak. His philosophy of religion provides a general and a specific methodological grounding for the postulate of the unity between the two. For one thing, the proper sphere in which the truth of the Christian religion, and the other religions as well, becomes manifest is not, for Hegel, representation and religious doctrine, that is, the "kingdom of the Son," but the third element, the cultus. In the cultus truth has its existence in the actual self-consciousness of the community. It is therefore only in this third element too that it becomes evident what it means to conceive God as infinite subjectivity (*LPR* 3:140). The specific foundation is to be found in the dictum that all differences between the confessions derive their meaning from the differences in eucharistic theology (*LPR* 3:338 n. 240). This remark for which the sources previously afforded no confirmation is now borne out by Strauss's excerpts (*LPR* 3:372). It relates directly to the confessions' attitude to questions of the political sphere and to the conception of a universal ethical life in which everything positive, all external authority, would be dissolved, and freedom and the actual divinity of ethical life would for the first time be realized. But inasmuch as the

---

64. See Theodor Mahlmann, *Das neue Dogma der lutherischen Christologie* (Gütersloh, 1969); and Walter Sparn, *Wiederkehr der Metaphysik* (Stuttgart, 1976).
65. Jüngel, *God as the Mystery of the World*, pp. 92 ff.

dictum formulates a universal principle, it may prompt one to suppose that even where no differences between the confessions seem to be discernible, they have nonetheless to be postulated—even if they do not become as obvious as on the political level.

Only the interpretation presented here frees Hegel's philosophy from the fundamental ambiguity that led to the schism in his school; it alone saves it from the reproach that it is incapable of deciding between holding fast to facticity and going back to the faith of the community. These two positions can be combined in the manner described: the "is" becomes actual in the Spirit of the community and not in an external actuality. This solution is not only analogous to the "Lutheran doctrine of the eucharist" but also accords with Hegel's interpretation of Protestantism. It is important to bear in mind his dictum that in modern times—which he always thought of as the period of Protestantism—subjectivity is recognized as an absolute moment (*LPR* 3:166). The idea of seeking reconciliation outside subjectivity betrays, then, a misunderstanding of the problem.

Hegel's "Lutheran christology" also serves to demonstrate what it means that philosophy presupposes religion. It can and must accept from religion the idea of the divine-human unity—but only insofar as it can rethink the content in its own terms in the course of obtaining methodically secure knowledge. As the invariable result of this rethinking, philosophy is capable of comprehending religion—better indeed than religion understands itself. It can therefore correct christology in light of the cultus, and it can do this not only when the transition is made to conceptual thought but already at the level of representation. At the same time it is evident how one should understand Hegel's claim that now philosophy is essentially orthodox: it is so because, in contrast with some of the theological christologies of Hegel's contemporaries, it holds fast to the actuality of the divine-human unity, and it does so on the basis of an argument that at least in the Protestant context cannot be regarded as heterodox.

(8) A further question concerns the consequences of this solution for Hegel's philosophy. The preceding remarks are indeed not intended as dogmatic considerations, but as a contribution toward

solving the problem of grounding Hegel's christology, a problem that was first formulated in all its sharpness by Strauss. It might appear as though the ambiguity impugned by Strauss could indeed be overcome by referring to Luther's doctrine of the eucharist, but only at the cost of introducing into Hegel's philosophy the not inconsiderable problems posed by this doctrine—a sort of theological Trojan horse. But this solution is indispensable if one is to have any chance of maintaining the importance of christology for Hegel's philosophy. It alone makes it possible to formulate the religious representation of the divine-human unity in a way that is not opposed to Hegel's solution of the ontological problematic in either method or content. Only it can preserve the unity of religiophilosophical and ontological argumentation. The alternative to this would be not only that the actuality of the divine-human unity would remain indemonstrable for philosophy but also that the representation of the unity of the divine and the human would have to be rejected in principle, insofar as traditional "non-Lutheran christology" is conceived in the sense of the Chalcedonian two-natures doctrine. And against this Hegel constantly raises the objection, for which he obviously has in the first place his early study of Spinoza to thank, that one must not base oneself on a dualism of substances, and as a consequence human nature is not utterly opposed to the divine nature (see above, pp. 121–122).

Hegel uses ever new turns of phrase to express the unity of divine and human nature, and he does so already in the Jena system draft where his philosophy of religion for the first time assumes systematic form: "The divine nature is no other than human nature" (*GW* 8:280). The Berlin lectures put it the same way: "What it [this unity] posits is that divine and human nature are not intrinsically different" (*LPR* 3:214). Hegel sees the inmost idea of Christianity in the fact that "these extremes, divine and human nature, are not in themselves extremes, but the truth is their identity instead" (*LPR* 3:211). His conception thus forms the opposite pole to the assertion "that God became human in Jesus Christ in order to distinguish definitively between God and humanity forever" (see above, p. 132). From Hegel's point of view this robs the incarnation and Christianity as such of all religious meaning. It makes the incarnation into a didactic lection regarding something that in Judaism was in any case little disputed. And it also robs the incarnation of its philosophical meaning. For what consciousness learns from the incarnation is that the opposition of natures is sublated, and not just on the basis of a historical datum but intrinsically: the other becomes known as one moment of a God who is not merely self-enclosed in abstract fashion. If the significance of the incarnation lay in an accentuated dualism of substances and natures, Hegel would perhaps not be alone in believing that this sufficed to make it nonsense.

Hegel's "Lutheran christology" contests on the one hand the attribution to Jesus of a special kind of substance and, on the other, the idea that to contest this is to surrender the real presence of the divine. Yet, Hegel does little to explain in concrete terms how this "is" is to be more precisely thought of at the level of representation. His attention is directed to the actuality of reconciliation and its confirmation. But the few indications that he gives toward an interpretation of the "is" can be combined into a rounded picture. Though this picture does involve similar problems to those confronting modern theological christologies, it also leads in principle beyond them; but the direction in which it leads is one that theology may well be able to follow only at the price of self-surrender.

The *communicatio idiomatum* is actual in "the Spirit" and nowhere else. Thus it too can be conceived solely on the basis of the formation of the community. Hegel binds, as few others before or since, the knowledge of the divine-human unity to the sublation of the sensible individual and the actuality of the Spirit in the community. He mentions only once Jesus' consciousness of his identity with the Father (*LPR* 3:121), and this reference, strictly speaking, cannot form an exception to this rule. And even the references to the death of God must be subsumed under this approach. His christology is thus the most consistent "christology from below" that can be conceived—even if at first appearances it seems otherwise. For a connection with the "eternal Son" of the first element is only established verbally (*Enc* § 569) and is neither required nor demonstrable for Hegel's conception. By contrast, theological positions that are not based on a prior incarnation in the sense of the two-natures doctrine but on the resurrection[66] also find themselves obliged to assume a divinity that is already existent, in a manner that each has to define for itself more precisely. How such a divinity might be conceived does indeed present considerable difficulties. Seen in the light of the analogy to eucharistic doctrine, however, the problems confronting such christologies appear somewhat comparable to the question whether before the sacramental action the host is not after all something more than just a piece of bread.

(9) These considerations enable us to affirm the consistency of the Hegelian christology, that is, of the very element of his teaching whose supposed inconsistency furnished the occasion for the schism of his school. They make Hegel's statements compatible with one another as well as with his method and, finally, with his ontology. In no other way could his christology be integrated into his system, nor, would it seem, readily into any other. Yet it can be understood as expressing the reconciliation of the divine and the human in such a way that this can also be conceived by philosophy—with other means, to be sure, yet in an analogous fashion.

The philosophy of religion has the task not solely of explicating religious representation but also of demonstrating how it can be combined with conceptual thinking. The way in which conceptual thinking sees the truth of christology, however, has only been touched on. We must therefore still indicate the changes that occur if christology is conceived not only according to the paradigm of what Hegel calls the "ingenious" Lutheran doctrine of the eucharist but, going beyond this, speculatively.

It is Hegel's ontological principle that whatever is not one implicitly cannot be posited as one (*LPR* 1:193). Faith too can give expression to the divine-human unity only because it is implicitly actual. Nor does the two-natures doctrine seem to affirm anything else. It makes the actuality of the unity a presupposition for its being known in the community. But representation takes implicit being for an external state. Hegel achieves this insight through the debate concerning an original state at the beginning of history (see

66. See, e.g., Wolfhart Pannenberg, *Jesus—God and Man* (Philadelphia, 1968).

above, p. 168). Already in the *Phenomenology* he deploys it as an argument against having recourse to "the historical Jesus" and the primitive Christian community: representation "confuses 'origin,' as the immediate existence of the first appearance, with the simplicity of the concept" (*Phen* 463, *GW* 9:409). In the same way it mistakenly takes what is implicitly existent to be a singular fact. Implicit being, however, expresses the universal. This is the Hegelian sense of the twice-mentioned "once is always" (*LPR* 3:115, 133). Certainty only expresses, with regard to this individual human being, what is the case in general: "The implicitly subsisting unity of divine and human nature must be revealed to humanity in an objective way; this is what happened through the incarnation of God" (*LPR* 3:314 n. 173). Certainly this truth is not the truth of ordinary consciousness. For this reason religious representation sets it over against itself as an other (*LPR* 3:313), and indeed as something exclusive; for, "as spirit, God contains the moment of subjectivity and uniqueness in himself; his appearance, therefore, can only be a single one, it can take place only once" (*LPR* 3:315 n. 173). In several single individuals, divinity would become an abstraction (*LPR* 3:114). And adherence to the one individuality forms at the same time the precondition for passing over to universality.

The basis of Hegel's christology is the idea of the implicit unity of the divine and the human. One could therefore ask whether, on this basis, it makes sense to speak of a *communicatio idiomatum*. It does seem justified, however, because the unity in question, as is always the case with Hegel, is no mere immediate coincidence, no uniformity without differentiation; the *idiomata* are distinct. Yet the communication between them must not be conceived as a single point in history. Its conceptual form is founded in the *Logic,* especially in the concept of true infinity and ultimately in the concept of the absolute idea; and it is explicated religiophilosophically in the part of the "Concept of Religion" that sets out the concept of God as well as in the "metaphysical concepts" of the "Consummate Religion." But this means that the communication is for Hegel not something that happens just at one particular time, whether it be in the life of Jesus or in the sacrament. This communication is "the nature of spirit," which also contains within itself finitude, the "moment of immediate existence" (*LPR* 3:315 n. 173); it is the implicitly subsisting foundation of all actuality in general, in other words an ontological principle.

4.6. The Idea in the Element of Self-Consciousness: Speculative Pneumatology

(1) These christological problems already impinge on the last section of the various lecture series, not only because Hegel treats the paradigm of christology, the doctrine of the eucharist, first under the heading "The Subsistence of the Community," but also because the community forms the material prerequisite of christology. For this reason it was Hegel's original intention to discuss community and christology jointly in the third sphere, as the manifestation of the absolute idea as finite spirit (see above, pp. 292–294). By severing the "community" from christology and making discussion of it an independent unit forming a third part of the "Consummate Religion" or a third element, he made it more difficult to perceive this material connection.

Hegel conceives the transition from christology to the community as one from exclusive to universal individuality (*LPR* 3:133). The manuscript interprets the transition from the one human being to the universality of the community likewise as a transition from representation to actuality, to the self-consciousness of reconciliation. The last three lecture series, by contrast, no longer oppose the "community" as the actuality of reconciliation to the three spheres of representation, but discuss it as the last such sphere.

(2) This change is probably not made solely in the interests of formal harmonization or to impart a trinitarian pattern consistently. It expresses the insight that even the prior "actuality" of reconciliation still bears a strong imprint of representation. The community does not in fact renounce "consciousness and its representations in the form of doctrine, etc." This relativizes the actuality of reconciliation: "The 'now' of communion dissolves in its representation, partly into a beyond, an otherworldly heaven, partly into the past, and partly into the future. But spirit is *simply present to itself*; it demands a fulfilled present, it requires more than

merely confused images. It requires that the content should itself be present" (*LPR* 3:237). Thus it is the two moments that appear indispensable for religion in general and eucharistic theology in particular that lead Hegel to criticize the community so sharply, namely the hardened distinction it draws between its present life and the historical event of reconciliation, and the fact that it links the real presence in the sacrament to particular points in time. And Hegel here couples these two moments with an even sharper attack on eschatology than the attacks he directed against it in the *Early Theological Writings* and in the *Phenomenology* (*Phen* 478, *GW* 9:420–421). In his view, eschatology merely expresses the inability to recognize the actuality of reconciliation. Such a recognition, according to him, can indeed happen only in the form of the concept and not in the medium of representation. The confused view afforded by representation is therefore neither accidental nor avoidable: it resides in the essence of representation itself.

(3) This depreciation of the community makes it difficult to understand that Hegel nevertheless assigns such an exalted status to it, both in his manuscript and in the later lectures, asserting that in it divine self-consciousness breaks forth (*LPR* 3:233). In the 1827 lectures Hegel expresses this in even more striking fashion: "the community itself is the existing Spirit, the Spirit in its existence [*Existenz*], God existing as community" (*LPR* 3:331). And the provocation offered to religious consciousness is further heightened by the fact that this divine self-consciousness should break forth for the first time here and not in the two preceding spheres. Yet this follows logically from the approach adopted by the speculative philosophy of religion. Part I of the lectures defines religion as the self-consciousness of God, and religion is nowhere actual save in the community. The beginning of Part III takes up this idea. Religion is, according to it, the consciousness of God as "the absolute object; but [it is] God's consciousness and subjectivity; the genuine object is the whole. That God whom we designate as a mere object *over against* consciousness is an abstraction" (*LPR* 3:62).[67] To this

---

67. [*Tr.*] At the author's suggestion we have modified our translation slightly. The German text reads: "*des absoluten Gegenstandes –*, aber sein *Bewusstsein, Sub-*

corresponds the concept of the division of the substantial unity into itself and a knowing for which it exists as such. The substance is spiritual substance (*Enc* § 554), in the sense of the concept of spirit as developed in the *Encyclopedia*: the subjective spirit that has traversed the spheres of the logic and of the philosophies of nature and of spirit knows spirit as its own essence and as all actuality (see above, pp. 249 ff.); it knows spirit as absolute subjectivity. Religious representation assigns this element of spirituality to a divine subject as self-consciousness. Speculative philosophy, however, knows nothing of such an exclusive divine subject—or, at most, it recognizes it surreptitiously. It does not, however, need simply to confess its ignorance, but can conceive the idea of the substantial identity of spirit in the context of the development of the system. And in the light of this idea it must reject as an abstraction the representation of a self-conscious God who is nonetheless only an object of consciousness; this is an abstraction that necessarily occurs at the standpoint of representation and of consciousness because the idea of absolute subjectivity is missing from it. The sphere of pure thought "prior to or apart from the creation of the world" is, by definition, not accessible to representation in its appropriate form. The representational idea of God does not therefore suffice either for the concept of substantial identity (from the standpoint of the *Encyclopedia*) or for the demand that consciousness and self-consciousness should be identical (from the standpoint of the *Phenomenology*). The element of knowing in this totality is religion's mode of knowing the truth. To assert another form of self-consciousness would be unsound in method and empty of content.

(4) The right to conceive this knowledge of God on the part of the community as the existence of God as community follows from Hegel's understanding of particularity and individuality as manifestations of the divine idea. The individuality that is represented as the exclusive unity of divine and human nature is in actuality first brought to completion in bringing back the many into the unity of the Spirit, and in so doing it exists as actual, universal self-

---

jektivität – der *wahrhafte Gegenstand* ist *dies Ganze;* jener Gott, den wir bloss Gegenstand *gegen* Bewusstsein nennen, ist *Abstraktion"* (V 5:1).

consciousness (*LPR* 3:133). This self-knowing of the Spirit is "the infinite return into itself, infinite subjectivity, not represented but actual divinity, the *presence* of God" (*LPR* 3:140)—that is, the self-consciousness of God. It is this alone that for Hegel makes the Christian religion the religion of spirit.

The constituting of this actual, present divinity does not, to be sure, need just a mere plurality of particular individuals, but rather individuals as universal—a community. For their knowledge of the Spirit as their essence cannot be the knowledge of any particular essence. It is therefore only constituted by the community. The community begins with faith in the divinity of the one human being and at the same time first constitutes this faith. The 1824 lectures express this in a seemingly paradoxical way: "It is the community as it begins from faith; but on the other hand, it is the faith that is brought forth as spirit, so faith is at the same time the result" (*LPR* 3:226). Even the historical, external form of faith is the result of the community, and still more so genuine faith; and by "community" is meant not only the primitive community but the community and the church in general in their historical development.

The manuscript in particular devotes a great deal of space to the "origin of the community." The most important statements on the community, however, are not to be found under this heading (*LPR* 3:142 ff.). All that is discussed there is the question of verification, which Hegel later deals with in the second element. More important is what he has to say at the beginning of the section on the community (*LPR* 3:133 ff.).[68] Here he considers the constitution of the community not merely from the angle of the development of knowledge. Consciousness of the divine idea as the absolute unity of the universal and the individual is here primarily grasped as "infinite love that exists only as infinite anguish" (*LPR* 3:137). This love binds the individuals together as universals. It destroys particularity and accords value to the individual only as universal. It is therefore "precisely the concept of spirit itself." And it is not the

68. [*Tr.*] In the English version we have taken as a heading for the introductory paragraphs to "C. Community, Cultus" a phrase from the margin of the manuscript, "Standpoint of the Community in General" (cf. *V* 5:69 n. 917). It is this material that is now under discussion.

knowledge of the community (which is limited to the form of representation and thus of separation) but this *love* that is said to be for individuals "spirit—the *Holy Spirit*" (*LPR* 3:140).

The manuscript makes this concept of infinite love from infinite anguish the focal point of the community. This implies that Hegel distinguishes this sphere as that of actual reconciliation from the one where reconciliation is merely represented. But the later lecture series no longer speak of this love. Their conception of the origin of the community is based solely on the formation of faith, on religious representation. Yet Hegel does also hold fast here to the concept of the Holy Spirit. The secondary materials contain the statement that "in this shape of actuality, the Spirit is, as it were, the 'third person'" (*LPR* 3:231 n. 183). How one is to think of the relationship of this Spirit to individual subjects is reflected in illuminating fashion in Strauss's excerpts: the working off of naturalness is "on the one hand . . . the doing of the subject, and on the other of the Holy Spirit; but the Holy Spirit is nothing external to the subject—it is its own spirit, whereon it believes" (*LPR* 3:372). This is no subsequent, left-Hegelian distortion. Rather this formulation applies exactly to the relationship between individual and universal spirit, and it is also expressed in the concept of the witness of spirit to the Spirit: "My spirit knows itself, it knows its essence" (*LPR* 1:389). And finite spirit's knowledge of its essence is precisely the divine self-consciousness (*LPR* 3:233). But in religion it is not for the individual subject to know that it is its own spirit whereon it believes. And the only reason why philosophy of religion is feasible as philosophical theology is that what is involved in religion is not an external relationship to a being alien to self-consciousness, but the concept of spirit, which is the essence of individual spirit.

(5) Religion has indeed, in Hegel's view, a history, inasmuch as it is a form of spirit's self-knowing, and spirit does not immediately know itself as it is. But it must not in any way be inferred from this that historical methods are therefore appropriate in religion and in theology. Initially Hegel does still seem to invoke history as the starting point for the elevation into spirit. He says for instance that the infinite idea could attach itself only to Christ and not to the countless other divine figures of Greek mythology or the syn-

cretism of late antiquity (*LPR* 3:145). His references to an initially historical faith also point in this direction. By contrast the 1831 lectures reveal a profounder insight into the relationship of spirit and history by affirming that history, too, is narrated by those upon whom the Spirit has already been poured out (*LPR* 3:323 n. 199).

Hegel's repudiation of historical theology is, for the most part, condescendingly classed as a sign of his lack of insight, his failure to understand the discipline of historical-critical theology, which was still at that time in its infancy, or even as an expression of animosity toward competing approaches. Such assessments, however, do not measure up to his position. If they are presumed to be self-evident, this is only because it is not recognized that the historical approach has already surrendered those contents which it claims the better to preserve. Two of Hegel's insights have even today lost none of their relevance. The first concerns the impossibility of proving historically the divinity of Jesus. Historical verification relates only to external circumstances; but faith is not concerned with external things (*LPR* 3:226–227), and a historical proof that Jesus was the Son of God would be nonsensical. Hegel was by no means the first to have this insight. On the contrary it was well known at the time, at least since Lessing's polemical writings. But a historical proof is also precluded because here there are no "historical facts." Hegel does not become entangled in fruitless attempts to hold fast to the unity of dogma and history. Such attempts still color Schleiermacher's approach—and not to its advantage, as is also clear from Strauss's transcript of Schleiermacher's lectures on the life of Jesus. For Hegel, by contrast, the content cannot be justified by history but by philosophy alone: "What spirit does is no history" (*LPR* 3:232).

Hegel might well have been less categorical about rejecting the historical character of the content and the use of historical methods for comprehending it if he had not known himself to be in possession of a better understanding, namely that the content proved itself to be true by corresponding to the nature of spirit. The immediate form of this verification is spirit's witness to the Spirit; the mediated form is the demonstration by speculative philosophy that the content corresponds to the systematically developed concept of spirit.

Otherwise the content would be a matter of indifference. But that the historical content coincides with thought is not the result of a preestablished harmony, or of the circumstance that thought accommodates itself to history, or conversely of the supposition that historical events follow upon one another in a way determined by thought. It is due rather to the fact that the historical content is brought forth by thought itself: "Only in thought does history first achieve the form by which it has absolute interest for spirit" (*LPR* 3:230). Reason recognizes the content to be true in and for itself when it recognizes its own "counterpart" in it (*LPR* 3:228). Hegel consequently repudiates the historical method: "Make of Christ what you will, exegetically, critically, historically. . . . The only question is, what is the idea or the truth in and for itself" (*LPH* 325–326, *W* 9:395–396).

Yet it would be incorrect to see no more in the historical approach than a method that necessarily fails to achieve success for the reasons indicated. This would not require the demonstration that the religious content is speculative in character. Historical treatment, however, tends to disguise the content's distinctive character. It sets the finite subject in an incorrect relationship to this content by implying that the content does not concern the essence of spirit—that it is not a spiritual content in the sense described. In any event, historical treatment is not so much the cause as the expression of such a misconception of the absolute content: "When [religious truth is] treated as historical, that spells an end [to it]; then it no longer [lives] in immediate consciousness, i.e., in actuality" (*LPR* 3:160).

(6) In Hegel's view, the historical mode of treatment and the moral form of interpretation are the complement to the basic conviction of his day, that God is unknowable. This assessment impels him to end his manuscript "on a discordant note" (*LPR* 3:158). But although his judgment concerning the justification for historical and moral interpretation—and also, in all probability, his judgment concerning the fate of the religious community as such—does not change, he replaces the last section of the manuscript in the ensuing years by passages relating to the realization of faith or of the spirituality of the community. These shift the focus of his discus-

sion of the community from the first part, the origin of the community, to the last part. In the 1824 lectures, the realization of faith is broken down into three forms of objectivity—in the heart, in reflection, and in the concept. These passages combine historical insights and conceptual arguments. Clarity is helped by the distinction drawn in the 1827 lectures between the real stages and the ideal side of realization (*LPR* 3:342). In considering the former, Hegel places the realization of faith in the context of world history. The manuscript already says of world history that it is the exhibition of the truth, namely of the unity of divine and human nature (*LPR* 3:144). The series of unsuccessful attempts to reconcile religious piety and worldliness is seen by Hegel as coming to an end in his day in the idea of ethical life. The principle of freedom has now penetrated into the worldly realm too, so that this realm, "because it has been thus conformed to the concept, reason, and eternal truth, is freedom that has become concrete and will that is rational" (*LPR* 3:341–342). Thinking, the freedom of reason, has indeed been acquired in religion, which has preserved the absolute content down to the present day. But thinking now turns against the residue of "merely spiritless externality and servitude, for the latter is utterly opposed to the concepts of reconciliation and liberation" (*LPR* 3:343). As the complement to this abstract universality of the understanding typical of the Enlightenment, Hegel denotes the pious life of feeling of Pietism—probably not without a side glance at the growth of Neopietism in the 1820s. He criticizes both alike for "volatilizing" the content.

The connection between denying the objectivity of God and that of all other determinations of thought that are valid in and for themselves is described in the 1824 lectures in especially pregnant terms, terms that read like a paraphrase of Jacobi's warnings: "Our moral convictions all vanish if we lose the sense of an original moral being as a moral, that is, a personal, being who wills and performs the good" (*JW* 4:xlvii). Hegel does not, however, allow himself to be constrained by this appeal to reestablish the idea of the objectivity of such an original being beyond the subject, the reason being that he regards the consequence of which Jacobi warns as the necessary result of an erroneous idea of God: if thinking renounces the concrete knowledge of God, the loss of all objectivity is indeed unavoidable. Elsewhere Hegel stresses that there "is no ground for supposing that faith in the content or in the doctrine of positive religion can still persist when reason has convinced itself of the contrary" (*LPR* 1:134). The loss of objectivity, the standpoint of abstract subjectivity, is not something that comes on the scene in merely arbitrary fashion, the consequences of which it would be possible to avoid. He sees it as an "infinite demand that the content of religion should be confirmed by thought, and this requirement cannot be turned aside" (*LPR* 3:342 n. 253).[69] But it is not Hegel's intention to describe in this way the tragic aspect of thinking: rather "the process of thinking consists in carrying through this opposition until it arrives at reconciliation" (*LPR* 3:346–347).

Thus the debate between thought and religion does not necessarily end in a concept of subjectivity in which all content "fades away" (*LPR* 3:344). This fear would be justified if abstract subjectivity and abstract thought did not have over against them another concept of thought and of subjectivity: this is the concept "that subjectivity develops the content from itself, to be sure, but in accord with necessity. It knows and acknowledges that a content is necessary, and that this necessary content is objective, having being in and for itself" (*LPR* 3:345). Hegel's entire philosophy is directed to the elaboration of such a concept of subjectivity. He can therefore hold out the prospect of the content of religion finding refuge from the threat it faces from *abstract* thinking by recourse to *concrete* thinking, to the concept. The concept produces the truth, but at the same time recognizes it as something not produced, as subsisting in and for itself (*LPR* 3:345). What this means would seem to be made clearer by the philosophy of religion than by any other part of the system. For while it first comes into contact with the absolute content as something merely given, it transcends this form of givenness and reconstitutes the same absolute content in the form of the concept and by means of the latter's own rules of evidence. Only in this way does the absolute content, the con-

69. [*Tr.*] Translation slightly modified; see *V* 5:265 n. 395.

cept, obtain also an absolute form, the form of the concept. The actualization of this identity is already defined in the manuscript as the task of the philosophy of religion (see above, pp. 221–222). Whether it is successful in this task, whether speculative theology has been successfully regrounded along with the philosophy of religion—this is to be judged not by the criterion of a seamless concurrence with the traditional form of the religious content, but rather by that of the inner systematic consistency of Hegel's philosophy.

(7) The manuscript itself ends with the idea of such a reconciliation of reason with religion. It stresses, however, that this reconciliation is only "partial" (*LPR* 3:162). As to whether the conflict between thought and religion is to be resolved also in actuality, the manuscript's judgment is one rather of resignation. It dates from the same period as the *Philosophy of Right,* which likewise does not yet contain the idea of the mediation of religion and ethical life in the mature shape that it assumes in the last two editions of the *Encyclopedia.* It is only the later lecture series that hold out the prospect of eliminating the "discordant note" in actuality too— in the conception of an ethical life that, like religion and philosophy, rests on the principle of subjectivity. This idea completely changes the conclusion to which the philosophy of religion leads. Instead of a resigned withdrawal into reconciliation within philosophy we have the idea of the reconciliation of religion with worldliness. And this idea is not an external accretion to the idea of a reconciliation within philosophy. Both rest on the idea of infinite subjectivity, of freedom, which has the urge to realize itself, to develop the content out of itself, including the content of philosophy as well as that of actuality.

Hegel places this last section of the later lecture series under the heading "The Realization of Faith" (1824) or, more aptly, "The Realization of the Spirituality of the Community" (1827). A realization of the contents of the Christian religion will be discernible here only to the extent that it can be shown how the concept of infinite subjectivity coheres with Christianity. Hegel did explicitly link the two together on several occasions, including one passage on Greek religion (*LPR* 2:183). The infinite character of subjectivity presupposes the mediation of universality and individuality. This mediation has not yet been effected in other religions, a point Hegel illustrates by reference to Greek religion: the particular always remains for the finite subject something otherworldly. The Christian religion by contrast is characterized by the idea of providence, the conviction that the particular too is encompassed within the divine activity. This conviction is validated by the idea of the incarnation and the trinity, which has as its basis the unity of universality and individuality.

This argument is convincing only if the religious content is itself interpreted in a speculative manner. The same is true with a second way of relating the concept of infinite subjectivity to Christianity, namely the assertion that as an object of divine grace the subject "already has infinite value in virtue of its vocation," and that it is known "as spirit's certainty of itself" (*LPR* 3:340). The first statement can be formulated within the traditional framework of religion, the second only in a speculative interpretation. In other examples too Hegel has difficulty in making the reference to a traditionally representational religious content plausible. Even if it could be made clearer, it would remain undeniable that what is involved is in no sense a linking of the subjectivity principle to exclusively religious contents. For religion too is concerned with spirit's knowledge of itself. And it is only to the extent that it comprehends this that subjectivity becomes infinite.

The stimulus for such comprehension does indeed, in Hegel's view, come from religion itself. He regards the contemporary cleavage between thought and religion, which leads to this insight, as produced by religion itself. As evidence for this we need only recall the introduction to the manuscript. There it is stated that, notwithstanding the evident antithesis between the two, the Christian religion "contains cognition within itself essentially and has stimulated cognition to develop in all its consistency as form, a world of form" (*LPR* 3:106–107). The credibility of this assertion also depends on the extent to which religion is conceived in speculative fashion. The references to realization—of faith, of the spirituality of the community, or finally of the self-consciousness of freedom as the principle of Christianity—presuppose in each case the speculative interpretation of the Christian religion. Otherwise the link remains unconvincing. Whoever, for instance, denies that the conceptual content of the doctrine of the trinity and of the idea of incarnation lies "in the thoroughgoing unity of universality and individuality" has, according to Hegel, little inducement to understand in the light of this tradition the reconciliation of thought and religion or even the actual rationality of the state, the unity of the universal substantial will and subjective freedom (PR § 258 W 8:313). And whoever does not accept that in faith self-consciousness has the consciousness of its essence, has little justification in Hegel's view for regarding the "self-consciousness of freedom" as the principle of Christianity (LPR 3:164). By contrast, the extent to which speculative philosophy succeeds in making credible such insights into the internal constitution of religion and the connection between religion and other forms of spirit, determines the extent to which the philosophy of religion lives up to its program, "to show forth the presence of reason in religion" (LPR 3:247).[70]

---

70. [Tr.] "die Vernunft der Religion zu zeigen" (V 5:175). It is from this statement, in part, that the author derives the leitmotiv of his work, "die Vernunft in der Religion." Hence we have modified LPR, which reads, "to show forth the rational content of religion."

CHAPTER IV

THE CONTROVERSY OVER THE
SPECULATIVE PHILOSOPHY OF RELIGION

1. The Themes and Limits of the Controversy

(1) Hegel's attempt to win back the idea of God for theoretical philosophy, to reestablish a philosophical theology in unity with the philosophy of religion, serves a dual purpose. On the one hand the philosophy of religion concludes the system of philosophy—at least in the broad sense that "religion" designates the highest sphere of the system as a whole, the sphere in which spirit does not direct itself to something else but turns itself back to the knowledge of itself as absolute spirit. This purpose accordingly falls solidly within the framework of the Hegelian system as a whole. Its coherence with it would be much less plausible, and would indeed be quite unintelligible, if the philosophy of religion did not conceive the idea of spirit as the truth of those matters that form the subject of the individual disciplines making up the system. Without the philosophy of religion the advance of speculative philosophy by returning into its ground would lead nowhere. Only the sphere of absolute spirit inwardly completes the system; for Hegel there is nothing pejorative about this idea. To this extent it is not just the idea of God in general that is constitutive of the systematic form of philosophy (as is the case for other systems) but only the idea of God fully explicated. And this explication does not occur until the sphere of absolute spirit is reached. Only here are the consummation of knowledge and the constitution of infinite subjectivity attained. And although the philosophy of religion in the narrower sense only stands here alongside the philosophy of art and philosophy itself, Hegel nonetheless describes this subjectivity-

consummating and system-concluding function much more precisely in the context of this discipline than in that of the other two.

In addition to this purpose of showing the self-contained character of the system, the philosophy of religion also serves a practical purpose (at least in the three later lecture series), that of exhibiting the occurrence of reconciliation in actuality. It argues that the condition of rupture or cleavage in actuality is to be understood as an opposition within a single principle, the principle of subjectivity and the self-consciousness of freedom. From this standpoint even what is supposedly opposed to religion appears as nonetheless conditioned by it. To be sure, this is the case only because Hegel formulates this principle of Christianity already in a way that is not confined to the religious sphere in the narrower sense but as a philosophical and at the same time a world-historical principle. The prospect of healing the discord of the time is not independent of the way in which the conception that propagates such healing is formulated. It is bound up with the degree of insight possessed by the philosophy of religion and the heed paid to its call to take refuge in the concept. Such refuge could preserve the absolute content of religion in an altered form, and not in a merely esoteric form, hidden as it were from the world. Taking refuge in the concept is rather the indispensable prerequisite for being able to comprehend the shape of reality, with all its cleavages, as the realization of the principle of subjectivity and freedom. But this is the case only if one breaks free from the still limited conception of the 1821 manuscript. It is not a question of mere preference as to whether one inclines to the more "pessimistic" outcome of the manuscript or the more "optimistic" outlook of the later lecture series. Rather, in the manuscript this whole realm of the realization of the spiritual principle in actuality has not been fully considered. Yet there can be no disputing the fact that within the framework of Hegel's conception such consideration is called for.

(2) Hegel's call to take refuge in the concept has, however, never met with much response. The reasons for this are indeed quite varied. The main reason probably is that no need for such a refuge has been seen. The call must in fact be judged to make little sense to anyone who does not subscribe to Hegel's diagnosis in both its

aspects, the one pertaining to religion internally and the other offering an analysis of the present day. Only those who believe themselves threatened see the need to seek refuge. We can presume, therefore, that neither the threat presented by the understanding and its way of thinking, which empties heart and heaven alike, nor the discord of the age in fact attained the proportions that Hegel thought he could not merely predict but also, in his own time, diagnose.

A second argument against seeking refuge in the concept might well be that the proffered refuge appears even more uncertain than the religion under threat, whether that threat is supposed or actual. At any rate the history of the influence of Hegel's philosophy bears out such misgivings. Even at the time when it, and in particular the philosophy of religion, were most influential, there were few who had confidence in its ability to provide religion with a refuge from the threat it faced. And today it is only in theological discussion that the speculative philosophy of religion, threatened by indifference and oblivion, seems to find an asylum ensuring its survival, even if only in the mode of being ceaselessly contradicted. The relationships of forces that decide who is providing a refuge for whom, and when, are of course not purely argumentative in nature. But Hegel's dictum is concerned with philosophical arguments and nothing else.

Finally the decision to seek refuge assumes that he who takes it is not certain in so doing to lose what he aims to keep. But taking refuge in the concept necessarily seemed bound up with a surrender of the traditional form of religion. In that case it was always preferable to defy the assaults of the understanding and of history— even if only by maintaining that they had long since been rebuffed—rather than to lose one's own identity in the form of the concept. From the 1820s on, many were of the view that the greatest threat to religion and theology came not from the reflective thinking of the understanding or from historical science but from the very quarter that proclaimed itself to be a refuge. To be sure, there were also voices that emphatically supported Hegel's call: "The Hegelian philosophy is the last place of refuge, the last rational support of theology. In the same way that Catholic theologians once became de facto Aristotelians, so Protestant theologians must now become de jure Hegelians, in order to be able to combat 'atheism.'" But this endorsement of Hegel's dictum served little to arouse confidence in it; rather it discredited it still further: it comes after all from Feuerbach's *Vorläufige Thesen zur Reformation der Philosophie* (*FGW* 9:258).

(3) For these various reasons, the history of the influence exerted by Hegel's philosophy of religion was limited to the two decades following its first publication. The actually productive phase is limited further to the decade between 1833 and 1843; the expositions of subsequent years were more in the nature of historical analyses and secondary reflections. Borrowing Franz Overbeck's literary-historical concept, this early phase could therefore be called the *Urgeschichte* of the controversy over Hegel's philosophy of religion. It is doubtless also possible to find traces of the philosophy of religion in the century following this brief period and to draw individual lines of connection to it even in areas, both philosophical and theological, where it received no extensive consideration. On the whole, however, these remain isolated instances and confirm the absence rather than the presence of anything that can be called a "history of influence" [*Wirkungsgeschichte*]. The reason for this break in the continuity of the speculative philosophy of religion and its living influence can be seen in the course of the unusually intensive reception and critique devoted to it in the 1830s and 1840s. For the result of these one or two decades can be summed up as acknowledgment of the complete failure of the Hegelian conception. The reasons given for this are, to be sure, widely opposed, ranging from the anthropological reduction of religion on the left to the supernaturalistic restoration of orthodoxy on the right.

This whole area of discussion has not yet been the subject of any monograph, whether issue-oriented or historical. Only one sector has so far been researched in detail, namely the controversy within the Hegel School. It is indeed inside the School that the controversy concerning Hegel's philosophy of religion crystallizes.[1] But it is not

---

1. The most important survey for the investigation of this period is provided by Karl Löwith, *From Hegel to Nietzsche* (New York, 1964). A comprehensive portrayal of the debates within the School is found in Hans Martin Sass, *Unter-*

limited to the School, and its course cannot ultimately be made intelligible without looking beyond the School. For the opposing positions within the School did not develop by a process of immanent interpretation. They arose in the course of the controversy that opposed the School to contemporary outside commentators. We are not thinking here so much of the views advanced by Jakob Friedrich Fries, Karl Christian Friedrich Krause, Bernard Bolzano, Johann Friedrich Herbart, and Moritz Wilhelm Drobisch, who indeed played no part in the debates in which the School engaged. But Franz Xaver von Baader, Friedrich Wilhelm Joseph Schelling, Christian Hermann Weisse, and Immanuel Hermann Fichte did intervene in the discussion from the side of philosophy, as did the circle of speculative theists that formed around Weisse and Fichte—in particular Carl Philipp Fischer and Jakob Sengler.

Decidedly more fragmented and difficult to take in at a glance is the circle of antagonists from the side of theology. On the Protestant side it extends from the neoorthodoxy of Ernst Wilhelm Hengstenberg and the *Evangelische Kirchenzeitung* circle to the latter-day theological rationalism of Heinrich Eberhard Gottlieb Paulus, Julius Friedrich Röhr, Karl Gottlieb Bretschneider, and the *Allgemeine Kirchenzeitung* circle; in between are found the Neopietism of Friedrich August Gottreu Tholuck and Julius Müller, and the early mediating theology of Carl Immanuel Nitzsch and others. On the Catholic side it was above all the Catholic Tübingen School, especially Franz Anton Staudenmaier and Johann Evangelist Kuhn, but also Anton Günther and Johann Heinrich Pabst, who intervened in this dispute.

And a further factor exerted no less an influence on the debate over Hegel's philosophy of religion than the weightiest of the arguments deployed in it, namely the political developments marking these years. As the situation became gradually more acute in the late 1830s, culminating in a complete reversal at the beginning

---

suchungen zur Religionsphilosophie in der Hegelschule 1830–1850 (Münster, 1963). See also Peter Cornehl, Die Zukunft der Versöhnung (Göttingen, 1971). No detailed references are provided here to the literature on the Hegel School because the works of his students and their opponents are themselves relevant to Hegel only as "secondary literature."

of the 1840s, the lines of demarcation were drawn for the corresponding accentuation and ultimate breakdown of the contemporary philosophical-theological debates.

(4) The controversy over the speculative philosophy of religion concerned primarily its results.[2] It was not conducted, however, as an unprejudiced critique of the way in which Hegel had conceived the idea of God and religion in general, or as a comparison with the philosophical theology and interpretation of religion of the Enlightenment. It concerned almost exclusively the question whether the speculative philosophy was Christian in character—whether it accorded in particular with the idea of God but also with other contents of the Christian religion, such as christology or the doctrine of sin. In this regard the opponents of the philosophy of religion were helped by the fact that it seemed itself to recognize such a Christian character as a criterion. Indeed, it taught the identity of content of philosophy and religion, and even affirmed that philosophy did nothing other than to conceive the idea of Christianity.

It has been indicated above (pp. 288 ff.) how this program is to be understood—not in the sense of a flat sameness in the utterances of Christian religion and speculative philosophy but as a concurrence that includes a difference of form. What this means more precisely has been illustrated in regard to the trinitarian idea of God, christology, and ecclesiology. Despite major differences Hegel holds fast to the concurrence with Christianity because he takes the view that when the content is raised into the form of the concept, when it is developed in the context of a speculative philosophy, while differences inevitably emerge yet identity can be recognized in the differing forms. In the broadest sense the identity of content of philosophy and religion consists in the fact that they both have as their subject spirit that knows itself—spirit that no longer has something other as its object, but its own self, its own essence, and is thus conscious of itself.

2. Unlike the preceding chapters (especially the second and third), reference is made here on several occasions to sources that in part are not well known, since the information given on the status of research on Hegel's philosophy of religion in the author's *Die Religionsphilosophie Hegels* does not cover this area of the debate between students and opponents. But the citation of literature in the following pages does not in any way claim to be comprehensive.

(5) It was only after Hegel's death that the actual history of the influence of the systematically developed philosophy of religion of the Berlin years began—not because his death allowed divergences that in fact already existed between his students to unfold but because the textual basis for a detailed discussion was previously lacking. Marheineke's edition of the philosophy-of-religion lectures for the first time made available comprehensive materials that were also sufficiently concrete to provide a basis for discussing the questions that were causing general concern. It therefore marks the end of the prehistory and the start of the history of the influence of the philosophy of religion, at least in its systematic form. But this history of influence is, unlike most other comparable cases, a history of the controversy over that which forms its substrate.

A philosophical controversy—such as that which arose between Friedrich Heinrich Jacobi and Schelling after 1811 concerning "divine things"—might in general be said to be characterized by the fact that one side contests the correctness of the premises or the force of the arguments and conclusions of the other side. In the controversy concerning Hegel's philosophy of religion a further dimension came into play, namely whether its results were compatible with Christianity. The discussion was constantly marked by the complex situation that what had to be decided was not simply Hegel's acceptance or rejection of traditional theological propositions but the delicate question whether the way in which he interpreted them should be regarded as satisfactory or rejected as a gross misrepresentation. The decision on this was complicated from the outset by the fact that not enough had been done to clarify what was involved in arriving at a plausible identification of biblical and ecclesiastical doctrines with their speculative interpretation. A further difficulty that arose after Hegel's death was the necessity of first checking the conformity of each and every supposedly speculative interpretation with the philosophy of religion itself—a task that soon called for the same attentiveness as was needed to judge whether the speculative interpretation could be reconciled with positive doctrine.

Furthermore, the statements under dispute were for the most part contained not in texts that their author had published himself or at least prepared for publication, but in a posthumous edition of lecture transcripts. The methods used in composing the transcripts and in their editorial compilation gave rise to fears concerning the reliability of the texts. The suspicion was also soon voiced that the opposing interpretations might be due to ineptitude in handling the sources—if indeed not to deliberate manipulation. These considerations led to the decision to issue a new edition, though this too proved incapable of solving the problem of interpretation and only became entangled more deeply in the suspicion of deliberate one-sidedness (cf. *LPR* 1:24–30). Only now is it possible to adjudge that the textual basis is of no significance for the antithetical character of interpretation. The reason for the controversy lies deeper, in the problem whether the representational content of the philosophy of religion can be identified with its conceptual form.

Even today the view is still heard that Hegel's philosophy of religion is marked by an ambiguity of conception that actually invites conflicting interpretations. In support of this view an unexceptionable historical witness is cited, namely the rupture of the School into a "right" and a "left," each of which can invoke in its behalf an array of proof texts. In this case it would indeed be a sign of faulty interpretation if one sought to persuade the texts to agree (something that in other cases is not the least of virtues). At all events it seems that a tally is called for to determine which side can adduce the greater number of proof texts.

The School itself in no way denied the existence of such tensions between individual statements and between groups of statements. David Friedrich Strauss for his part devotes a great deal of attention to the arguments that speak in favor of one or the other side. He does not, however, draw the conclusion that one can now simply persist in one or the other of the differing positions or decide the matter by counting. Philosophically speaking, the question ultimately is not whatever Hegel may have said but what he *could* say—in other words, what statements a philosophy is entitled to make on the basis of a specific method. For according to Hegel too, it is not so much the concern of philosophy to formulate concepts as to prove them—even if in a fashion that is different from what is generally customary.

If the question is posed in this fashion, the oft-conjured ambiguity disappears. It then becomes clear that there is only one way in which to interpret Hegel's statements consistently in the context of his system. To be sure, this does not mean that after it has been put in unambiguous form, Hegel's philosophy is no longer a two-edged sword: it remains at one and the same time apologia and critique of Christianity. To the extent that one takes the preconceived view that it can only be one or the other, one will misinterpret this as ambiguity.

The School did not initially perceive its progressive fragmentation as refutation of Hegel's philosophy. It formulated various interpretations that justified continued adherence to it. Even if it was going too far to explain the divergences in terms of examples drawn from the history of Christianity and the confessions, they could be explained by analogy to the *Logic* as particularization of the universal, that is, as particularization of the principle of the philosophy of religion that Hegel had developed.[3] This interpretation did indeed entail a sublation of the particular in the universal—not in the sense that the particular interpretations would be destroyed, but that they would show themselves to be particularizations of one principle. The School broke up when the differing standpoints could no longer be understood as particulars of a single universal (after 1839). In its first phase (1832–1835) differing standpoints could express themselves side by side, without each seeking to supplant the others. Splintering only set in when the differing standpoints were drawn beyond the framework of the inner-philosophical discussion to enter into the debate concerning the relationship between theology and history (1835–1839).

2. The Prehistory of the Controversy

(1) The controversy concerning the Christian character of Hegel's philosophy is not confined to the philosophy of religion or to the

---

3. Cf. Carl Ludwig Michelet, *Geschichte der letzten Systeme der Philosophie in Deutschland von Kant bis Hegel* (Berlin, 1838), 2:637–638; Karl Rosenkranz, *Kritische Erläuterungen des Hegel'schen Systems* (Königsberg, 1840), p. xxxv; Philipp Marheineke, *Einleitung in die öffentlichen Vorlesungen über die Bedeutung der Hegelschen Philosophie in der christlichen Theologie* (Berlin, 1842), pp. 20, 29.

Hegel School. It even predates the debates concerning the philosophy of religion as a component discipline of the system. For Hegel's broad assertion of the identity of content of religion and philosophy, as well as his specific claim to be in agreement with Christianity, were almost unanimously rejected outside his School even in the 1820s—that is, before publication of the *Lectures*—on philosophical as well as theological grounds. For the School, in addition to Hermann Friedrich Wilhelm Hinrichs, mention should here be made in particular of Isaak Rust—to say nothing of Carl Friedrich Göschel and the speculative theologians Carl Daub and Philipp Marheineke.[4] C. H. Weisse, who stood close to the School up to the time of Hegel's death, also lamented the confusion of form and content, of concept and thing itself, as well as the inappropriateness of the logical categories for the purpose of conceiving "living faith," and he disputed the identity of content of religion and philosophy.[5] Anyone who misunderstood the logic as the theory not of objective but of abstract thinking was bound to reject its theological pretension as a "strange deification of the abstract, logical, or metaphysical world of the concept,"[6] and to repudiate its claim to grasp the truth of Christianity in the form of thought as impossible to redeem if not dishonest.[7] Other critics were less reticent in condemning it, protesting that Hegel placed a "stiff, dead form of knowing" above "living faith"—the "gibberish of concepts" above "pious movements of the heart."[8]

4. Hermann Friedrich Wilhelm Hinrichs, *Die Religion im inneren Verhältnisse zur Wissenschaft* (Heidelberg, 1822), p. xvi; Isaak Rust, *Philosophie und Christenthum oder Wissen und Glauben* (Mannheim, 1825); Kasimir Conradi, *Selbstbewusstseyn und Offenbarung* (Mainz, 1831); Carl Friedrich Göschel, *Aphorismen über Nichtwissen und absolutes Wissen* (Berlin, 1829); Carl Daub, *Die dogmatische Theologie jetziger Zeit* (Heidelberg, 1833); Philipp Marheineke, *Die Grundlehren der christlichen Dogmatik als Wissenschaft* (Berlin, 1827).

5. Christian Hermann Weisse, *Ueber den gegenwärtigen Standpunct der philosophischen Wissenschaft* (Leipzig, 1829), pp. 209, 213.

6. C. H. Weisse, *Ueber das Verhältniss des Publicums zur Philosophie in dem Zeitpuncte von Hegels Abscheiden* (Leipzig, 1832), p. 27.

7. This latter criticism of Hegel's philosophy of religion is rejected by Weisse; see his *Gegenwärtiger Standpunkt*, p. 210.

8. Carl August Eschenmayer, *Die Hegelsche Religions-Philosophie verglichen mit dem christlichen Princip* (Tübingen, 1834), p. 30; Hülsemann, *Ueber die Hegelsche Lehre* (Leipzig, 1829), p. 230; K. E. Schubarth and K. A. Carganico,

It was obviously easier for theology, and in particular a theologizing philosophy, to come to terms with the result of the Enlightenment critique of religion, namely that the existence of God is unprovable. This at least left the door open to postulating the existence of God for the sake of the possibility of moral action. Moreover it had already become clear in the 1790s that once God had been postulated, it was not difficult to furnish him subsequently with whatever predicates were regarded as necessary for the sake of theology or religion. It was more difficult to come to terms with a philosophy that purported to be able to give very definite information regarding the concept of God and the content of religion in general, but obviously conceived of God in a way that was not widely communicable, and moreover presented considerable differences from the traditional Christian view and threatened to alter the character of religion as such. Hegel failed to make clear that his philosophy of religion did not aim to replace piety by the study of logic but to elaborate the inner content of the Christian religion, a content that resided in reason itself, and thus to place the truth of Christianity, whose validity was currently threatened, on a more secure foundation.

The affirmation of the identity of content of philosophy and religion in general, and of agreement with Christianity in particular, is indeed credible if it is understood in the light of Hegel's precise explanations. But these were seldom taken into account in the contemporary discussion. Rather the debates of the late 1820s already displayed a characteristic that can be traced down to the present day: the standard adopted in the controversy over the Christian character of the philosophy of religion was only seldom that of a theologically considered concept of the Christian religion. It was much more frequently a prescientific, naive understanding of what was Christian that was brought into play against Hegel's attempt to conceive it. Since such explicit recognition of the legitimacy of testing its Christian character formed part of the claim advanced by the philosophy of religion, it was thought unnecessary to pay

---

Ueber Philosophie überhaupt, und Hegels Encyclopädie der philosophischen Wissenschaften insbesondere (Berlin, 1829), p. 148.

heed to the rules that necessarily follow from Hegel's theorem concerning the difference of form between religion and philosophy. The polemic conducted against the philosophy of religion from the standpoint of naive religious feeling implicitly affected at the same time broad sectors of theological science—and not only where it invoked the "religious sense of the German people" and its "depth of soul," or where it objected to Hegel's proof of the truth of Christianity; revealed religion is true, it was said, not because of its concurrence with reason but because it is *divine* revelation and "as divine revelation . . . [it is] in every respect divine revelation."[9] These first reactions to Hegel's philosophy of religion—later intensified in the controversy over Strauss and Bruno Bauer—already accomplished an important step along the road that severed naive religious consciousness from scientifically conducted theology.

(2) The first phase of the controversy over the Christian character of Hegel's philosophy (1828–1831) was marked by such a methodologically naive critique. It was also conducted on a narrow textual basis. The *Lectures* had not yet appeared, and Hegel himself was taking steps to ensure that transcripts prepared from students' notes did not fall into the wrong hands and that he was not made responsible for the content of such compilations (*V* 3:xv). By contrast the chapter of the *Phenomenology* devoted to religion played only a subsidiary role in this phase of the controversy—despite the fact that the *Phenomenology* had greatly influenced the way in which the philosophy of religion was received within the School. It was in fact the older students, such as Georg Andreas Gabler and H. F. W. Hinrichs, who were often reproached in the later School controversy for not having advanced beyond the phenomenological standpoint. This was true of the earliest study of the philosophy of religion to emerge from the School, Hinrichs's *Die Religion im inneren Verhältnisse zur Wissenschaft* (1822); it was less true of C. F. Göschel's *Aphorismen über Nichtwissen und absolutes Wissen* (1829), but again so in large measure of Kasimir Conradi's *Selbstbewusstseyn und Offenbarung* (1831). The same applied to

9. Hülsemann, *Ueber die Wissenschaft der Idee* (Breslau, 1831), pp. 210, 14; cf. Hülsemann, *Hegels Lehre*, p. 230.

what later became the Hegelian left. Even the choice of proof texts in Strauss's *In Defense of My "Life of Jesus"* (1837) reveals the importance of the *Phenomenology* for his understanding of the philosophy of religion. And the extent to which Feuerbach was influenced by the *Phenomenology*, even though he had also attended the 1824 philosophy-of-religion lectures, is patently clear from his *Essence of Christianity* (1841). It can be left an open question whether the main reason why the "Religion" chapter of the *Phenomenology* was ignored in the early stages of the controversy was that it posed major difficulties of understanding or that the critics were anxious to address current issues.

Initially at any rate, the controversy focused on the speculative theological character of the logic—in particular the logic of the *Encyclopedia* (and the *Encyclopedia* as a whole). Above all, the latter became important for the discussion, and rightly so, since Hegel in the second edition (1827) had inserted into the "Preliminary Conception" [*Vorbegriff*] of the *Encyclopedia* logic a discussion of the three "attitudes of thought to objectivity." The third of these attitudes concerns the foundations of the philosophy of religion insofar as Hegel here, in the context of the theory of objective thinking, sublates the traditional antithesis of faith and reason, of mediated and immediate knowing. Because this text was more detailed than the "Religion" chapter of the *Encyclopedia*, it afforded a better basis for discussing the scope and limitations of faith, immediate knowledge, intuition, and thought. For this reason Hülsemann's second indictment of Hegel, which also appeared anonymously, and accused him this time not of pantheism but of atheism, focused exclusively on this "Preliminary Conception." Here the logical and epistemological foundations of the philosophy of religion were portrayed more clearly than in any other text prior to the appearance of the lectures.

(3) The charge of pantheism, atheism, and paganism leveled against Hegel's philosophy drew the polemical consequences from the dual claim of the *Logic* to constitute both the true speculative theology and the foundation underlying the system. This charge sought to shift the debate regarding the God-concept of speculative philosophy into the emotional and political realm and there to reap

more easily the fruits of the polemic that otherwise remained out of reach. The weight that attached in those days to such accusations is evident from the violent dispute over Spinoza's pantheism and (not three decades previously) the "atheism controversy," which resulted in Fichte's losing his professorial chair in Jena. If the almost-concurrent "Halle dispute" (1830) regarding Julius August Ludwig Wegscheider and Wilhelm Gesenius[10] had no dramatic outcome, this is not due to those whose denunciations sparked it off but to the cool-headed reaction of the minister who was responsible, von Altenstein, who sympathized with Hegel's philosophy.

Hegel's philosophy was termed pantheism at least as early as 1823, in an anonymous work by Tholuck (*LPR* 2:574 n. 172). In the second edition of his *Encyclopedia* Hegel sought on several occasions to counter the "definite prejudice" that his philosophy taught pantheism. After already broaching this theme in the preface, he embarked on a detailed refutation of the charge of pantheism in § 573, far transcending the framework of a corollary in the process. Yet it remained without effect, for the pantheism from which Hegel distanced himself was conceived much too narrowly, namely as the literal deification of everything. The failure of the refutation gave a fresh impulse to the accusers. They were so sure of being in the right that they expressly distinguished Hegel's pantheism (correctly from a historical point of view) from earlier forms, Spinozism in particular, but only in order to reject it the more decisively.[11]

10. On the Halle dispute, see Wilhelm Schrader, *Geschichte der Friedrichs-Universität zu Halle* (Berlin, 1894), 2:165 ff.

11. Hülsemann, *Hegels Lehre*, pp. 196 ff.; Hülsemann, *Wissenschaft der Idee*, pp. 196, 204. Gottlob Benjamin Jäsche, *Der Pantheismus nach seinen verschiedenen Hauptformen* (Berlin, 1826–1828), 1:73, defines pantheism as the assumption that God is not God without the world—exactly what, according to Hotho, Hegel himself maintains (see *LPR* 1:308 n. 97). At the beginning of vol. 2, Jäsche makes several references to Hegel's second edition of the *Encyclopedia* (pp. xxii, xxvii, xliv). See also Carl Friedrich Bachmann, *Ueber Hegel's System und die Nothwendigkeit einer nochmaligen Umgestaltung der Philosophie* (Leipzig, 1833), p. 288; Friedrich Julius Stahl, *Die Philosophie des Rechts nach geschichtlicher Ansicht* (Heidelberg, 1830), 1:308–309. For Schelling, too, Hegel's pantheism is "not the pure, silent pantheism of Spinoza" but an artificial pantheism "in which the divine freedom is all the more ignominiously lost for one's having pretended to seek to save it and sustain it" (*SW* 10:159–160).

The charge of pantheism was not based on the chapter of the *Encyclopedia* devoted to religion but on the theological claim advanced by Hegel's speculative logic. Attempts to refute it by specifically religiophilosophical arguments were therefore countered with an obstinacy that would otherwise be unintelligible. The God of whom metaphysical definitions were formed from pure categories of thought was not credited with personality even when he later came to be addressed in the philosophy of religion as "absolute subjectivity"—especially since the conception of the philosophy of religion was regarded, rightly, as dependent on the logic and was therefore rejected as a case of inappropriate experimentation with the logical method.[12] To be sure, it was only seldom that the indictments of pantheism and atheism led beyond a trivial polemic.[13] But in particular, their denunciation of Hegel for placing his teaching above Christianity and himself above the apostles, indeed above Christ himself,[14] invested these accusations with such political weight that Hegel could not avoid confronting them.[15]

Already in the late 1820s it is a feature of the discussion that it bore only on the question whether Hegel's philosophy was pantheistic; the meaning and legitimate limits of a philosophical treatment of the concept of God were not considered at all in a principled way. Hegel's philosophy is in fact immunized against a

12. Hülsemann, *Hegels Lehre*, p. 206.

13. The most acute analysis of the problem is by Weisse; see his *Verhältnis des Publikums*, pp. 23–35; and *Die Idee der Gottheit* (Dresden, 1833), pp. 151 ff., 222 ff. He even sees himself tempted "not just to place Hegel's error on a par with other forms of pantheism but to declare it forthright to be *atheism*, or indeed *nihilism*, since it is said at the same time that the idea (which is precisely pure form) is all in all" (p. 225). In his first anonymous attack Hülsemann does, to be sure, include the word "pantheism" sloganlike in his title, as he does two years later with "atheism"; but he is so little aware of the problem that he misconstrues Hegel's rejection of the charge of pantheism as the defense of a term used by Hegelian philosophy to designate itself (cf. *Hegels Lehre*, p. 197). The extent to which the polemics directed against Hegel are ill considered from a philosophical-theological perspective is evident, for example, in the naive understanding of revelation that Schubarth and Carganico invoke in opposition to Hegel in their *Über Philosophie*, p. 155.

14. Hülsemann, *Hegels Lehre*, pp. 187, 210.

15. See Hegel's review of Hülsemann's *Hegels Lehre* and of Schubarth's and Carganico's *Über Philosophie* in *BSchr* 330–402.

straightforward charge of pantheism because it sees its distinctive characteristic in the very fact that it conceives substance as absolute subjectivity. The sole question that could have been put to Hegel's philosophy on internal grounds concerned the results it arrived at in executing its program. In this regard attention would have had to be paid in particular to the transition that Hegel makes from the concept of subjective and objective spirit to the concept of God as the truth of the preceding development of the system (see above, pp. 248 ff.). This philosophical consideration of the relationship of God to the world would hardly have sufficed to dispose of the doubts as to Hegel's orthodoxy. But the problems involved in re-grounding a philosophical theology, and also the necessity of so doing, could have emerged clearly from it.

What was generally addressed under the label of pantheism, by contrast, was the gulf between such a philosophical concept of God, encompassing God as subjectivity, and the traditional representational contents of religious consciousness. It was the fate of Hegel's philosophy of religion that it was unable to erase the impression that the concepts it developed were intended also to satisfy the aspirations of a pious heart. This made it seem unnecessary for the religious consciousness to undertake critical reflection on the limits of a mode of discourse about God that was philosophically as well as theologically scientific; it found itself in the role of judging the orthodoxy of philosophy and deemed it none of its own concern to have to justify the argumentative use of the truths of faith within the territory of a philosophy of religion. If Hegel's philosophy could be shown not to have succeeded in expounding the personality of God in a manner acceptable to "living faith," then it seemed to be refuted not only by a demand addressed to it from outside but also from within. Moreover, this could easily be demonstrated: Hegel's philosophy of religion, as philosophy, could not keep pace with the way in which the "pious heart" communed with the divine personality, uninhibited by any critical reflection; moreover, it belied all such ambitions, dissolving the antitheses between transcendence and immanence, personality and substance, finitude and infinitude, as philosophically unfounded. Once the criterion of "Christian character" was tailored in this way to the exalted, divinely inspired heart—and this epitomizes large areas of the debate in its early stage—it was hardly surprising that Hegel's philosophy was found wanting. It was only with the fruitful discussion that took place in the 1830s that it became clear that speculative philosophy is in principle incapable of honestly overcoming the gulf between the results of philosophy of religion and the representations of "living faith"—not least in regard to the concept of God as absolute subjectivity.

3. The Personality of God and the Immortality of the Soul

During the initial phase of the discussion of the philosophy of religion I. H. Fichte wrote a work on the personality of God and the immortality of the soul, while at its close Carl Ludwig Michelet justified his lectures on these same topics by contending "that the history of philosophy in the last ten years is, properly speaking, only the history of the controversies that have arisen in the lap of philosophy concerning these matters." The two problems, he asserted, are not merely related but are even "absolutely identical"—the one only a "reflection" of the other.[16] They now stood in a closer connection than in the traditional *metaphysica specialis*.

To speak of "personality and immortality" at the beginning of the 1830s was in no way to embark on a new theme. The suspicion that Hegel's philosophy abandoned the personality of God already constituted the premise on which it was arraigned for pantheism and atheism. It had long been surmised that the form of immortality that was conceivable on the basis of the system had nothing in common with that taught by Christianity. K. E. Schubarth and K. A. Carganico had held it against Hegel that his system failed to mention the immortality of the soul, in all probability not accidentally. Instead of a convincing *démenti*, Hegel's review responded

16. C. L. Michelet, *Vorlesungen über die Persönlichkeit Gottes und die Unsterblichkeit der Seele* (Berlin, 1841), pp. 7 ff.; Immanuel Hermann Fichte, *Die Idee der Persönlichkeit und der individuellen Fortdauer* (Elberfeld, 1834). A similar view is expressed by Ludwig Feuerbach in *The Essence of Christianity*, trans. George Eliot (New York, 1957), p. 172.

with a counterattack on their understanding of immortality. But his argument was in no way suited to dispose of the doubts that existed as to whether the speculative concept of immortality was Christian in character.[17] At the same time the problem of immortality did not initially stand at the center of the discussion since the only sources that were available did not permit any reasoned critique. This was also why Feuerbach's *Thoughts on Death and Immortality* did not receive any greater attention. Despite the fact that they appeared anonymously, they debarred their author for the rest of his life from a professorial chair; but they did not evoke in scholarly discussion the wide echo they would surely have elicited a little later. It was Friedrich Richter's writings on eschatology and immortality that, more or less coinciding with the publication of the lectures, marked the beginning of the debate.[18]

On behalf of the Hegel School Göschel undertook the task of demonstrating against Richter that individual immortality was a consequence of the Hegelian system. His supposed apologia for Hegel unwittingly made clear, however, at what points in the speculative philosophy of religion conclusive objections were to be found to accepting a belief in immortality. With respect to the concept of time, the idea of infinite duration had to be rejected as substituting for eternity the progression into a false infinite represented by an endless time. Furthermore the theorem of an eternal individualizing of universal spirit in no way involved the continuation into a false infinite of this or that single individual. Göschel's review did not therefore close the issue in the manner hoped, but gave the impetus for an intensive dispute in which the legitimacy of philosophical and theological discourse on immortality was explored in depth.[19]

17. Cf. Schubart and Carganico, *Über Philosophie,* pp. 146–147, and Hegel's review (*BSchr* 389–390).

18. Friedrich Richter, *Die Lehre von den letzten Dingen,* vol. 1 (Breslau, 1833); and *Die neue Unsterblichkeitslehre* (Breslau, 1833).

19. See above all C. F. Göschel, "Rezension zu Fr. Richter," *Jahrbücher für wissenschaftliche Kritik* (1834), and *Von den Beweisen für die Unsterblichkeit* (Berlin, 1835). A view similar to Hegel's was expressed by K. Conradi, *Unsterblichkeit und ewiges Leben* (Mainz, 1837); C. L. Michelet, *Persönlichkeit und Unsterblichkeit,* and *Die Epiphanie der ewigen Persönlichkeit des Geistes,* vol. 1 (Nuremburg, 1844); Ferdinand Christian Baur, *Die christliche Gnosis* (Tübingen,

In the philosophy of religion the problem of immortality had been mentioned only marginally. For those students who, like Michelet, maintained Hegel's position, little more remained than to elucidate these passages. Moreover, their tenor is clear: in the idea of immortality the religious consciousness figuratively represents the infinitude of spirit that it is incapable of grasping as eternal presence. By contrast with this somewhat remote topic (as Hegel saw it), the debate over the concept of God touched on the very foundations of the philosophy of religion. Whereas the fusion of logical and specifically religiophilosophical considerations in Hegel's concept of God—that is, the relationship of absolute idea and absolute spirit—had heretofore been only dimly discernible, after publication of the lectures it was plain beyond any possibility of doubt. Admittedly Hegel's God was no longer simply to be equated with the absolute idea of the logic. Yet as absolute spirit God seemed also to be linked with the logic: God conceived as dialectical process, but not as living personality to whom one can pray, and also as an incomplete God who must first come to himself and who needs not merely the world, as affirmed in Hegel's (in fact, Hotho's) even then oft-quoted dictum (*LPR* 1:308 n. 97), but also

1835), pp. 707 ff.; Julius Schaller, *Der historische Christus und die Philosophie* (Leipzig, 1838), pp. 72 ff.; Johann Snellmann, *Versuch einer speculativen Entwicklung der Idee der Persönlichkeit* (Tübingen, 1841). On the critique offered by the speculative theists see Fichte, *Idee der Persönlichkeit*; C. H. Weisse, *Die philosophische Geheimlehre von der Unsterblichkeit des menschlichen Individuums* (Dresden, 1834); Hubert Beckers, *Ueber C. F. Göschel's Versuch eines Erweises der persönlichen Unsterblichkeit vom Standpunkt der Hegelschen Lehre aus* (Hamburg, 1836); Jakob Sengler, *Ueber das Wesen und die Bedeutung der speculativen Philosophie und Theologie*, 2 vols. (Mainz, 1834; Heidelberg, 1837), and *Die Idee Gottes*, 2 vols. (Heidelberg, 1845–1847); Johann Gustav Friedrich Billroth, *Vorlesungen über Religionsphilosophie*, 2d ed. (Leipzig, 1844). The position of naive theism underlies the attacks of Eschenmayer, *Hegels Religionsphilosophie*, pp. 120 ff.; and Bachmann, *Hegels System*, p. 309, and *Anti-Hegel* (Jena, 1835), pp. 167 ff. On Bachmann see K. Rosenkranz, *Hegel: Sendschreiben an den Hofrat und Professor der Philosophie Herrn Dr. C. Fr. Bachmann in Jena* (Königsberg, 1834), pp. 134 ff.; and Feuerbach, *FGW* 8:62–127. On Rosenkranz's position see further his *Kritische Erläuterungen*, pp. 348 ff. It should be noted in passing that the advocates of individual immortality, contrary to what they claimed, argued for the *immortalitas animae* of the *psychologia rationalis* rather than for the biblical belief in resurrection.

humanity, without whom God remains at best a spiritless and self-less totality of moments that does not even attain to consciousness.[20] A blind polemic ultimately saw the God of the philosophy of religion as "a papier-mâché idol," "a glass marionette from the Hegel factory on the Kupfergraben in Berlin," or "an idol of reason that the philosopher generates for himself from his own bowels."[21] In sharp contrast with this, the Old Hegelians—represented by Göschel, who thanks to Hegel's friendly review of his *Aphorismen* had become spokesman of the School—believed in the possibility of combining Hegel's concept of God with Christianity.[22] It was only in the later phases of the discussion that more and more voices came to be heard contrasting Hegel's speculative concept of God with church teaching yet finding that no reason for rejecting it.[23]

The debate over the concept of the personality of God, like the

20. See esp. I. H. Fichte, *Idee der Persönlichkeit*, pp. 10 ff., 33 ff., and *Beiträge zur Charakteristik der neuern Philosophie*, 2d ed. (Sulzbach, 1841). Also Carl Philipp Fischer, *Die Idee der Gottheit* (Stuttgart, 1839), pp. iv ff.; idem, *Der Uebergang von dem idealistischen Pantheismus der Hegelschen Philosophie zum Theismus* (Tübingen, 1843); idem, *Speculative Charakteristik und Kritik des Hegel'schen Systems* (Erlangen, 1845). Also Weisse, *Idee der Gottheit*, pp. 222 ff.; Sengler, *Ueber das Wesen* 2:315 ff.; Billroth, *Religionsphilosophie*, p. 53. Even before the controversy began, Fichte called the knowledge of the personality of God the highest goal of speculation: *Sätze zur Vorschule der Theologie* (Stuttgart and Tübingen, 1826), p. xxxviii. On the criticism of Hegel and the alternatives presented by Weisse, Fichte, and Schelling, see below, sec. 7.

21. Bachmann, *Hegels System*, p. 282, and *Anti-Hegel*, p. 161; Eschenmayer, *Hegels Religionsphilosophie*, p. 57.

22. Cf. C. F. Göschel, *Der Monismus des Gedankens* (Naumburg, 1832); idem, *Beiträge zur spekulativen Philosophie von Gott und dem Menschen und von dem Gott-Menschen* (Berlin, 1838), pp. 11 ff.; and esp. idem, *Beweise für die Unsterblichkeit*, pp. 263–272. Also J. Schaller, *Die Philosophie unserer Zeit* (Leipzig, 1837), p. vi; Georg Andreas Gabler, *De verae philosophiae erga religionem christianam pietate* (Berlin, 1836); K. Rosenkranz, *Enzyklopädie der theologischen Wissenschaften* (Halle, 1831), and *Sendschreiben an Bachmann*, pp. 133 ff.; Johann Eduard Erdmann, *Vorlesungen über Glauben und Wissen als Einleitung in die Dogmatik und Religionsphilosophie* (Berlin, 1837), and "Die Religionsphilosophie als Phänomenologie des religiösen Bewusstseins," *Vermischte Aufsätze* (Leipzig, 1845), pp. 62–117; Conradi, *Selbstbewusstseyn und Offenbarung*.

23. Cf. Baur, *Christliche Gnosis*, pp. 707 ff.; Michelet, *Geschichte*, pp. 643 ff.; idem, *Persönlichkeit und Unsterblichkeit*, pp. 172 ff.; idem, *Entwicklungsgeschichte der neuesten deutschen Philosophie* (Berlin, 1843), p. 388; K. Conradi, *Christus in der Gegenwart, Vergangenheit und Zukunft* (Mainz, 1839), pp. xiii-xiv.

previous discussion of the concept of immortality, only appeared to yield no results. While it did not produce any universally accepted decision as to whether Hegel's concept of God was Christian in character, it did clarify the conditions under which philosophical discourse about God can be meaningful. It was shown to be all too facile to reject Hegel's categories as unsuited to the knowledge of God on the ground that they belonged "to the sphere of our categories and reflective determinations" and to demand instead other attributes for God than those "which derive from our categories"— namely, "uncreated," "eternal," "infinite," "primordial."[24] Such naïveté rightly met with derision from the School. To oppose God to the world in the manner advocated in the riposte to Hegel's alleged pantheism could also clearly be shown to be questionable by means of the religiophilosophical dialectic. The call to conceive God as self-conscious spirit existing prior to and outside the world invited the objection that "spirit" was then only an empty word of which nothing definite could be thought. The self-consciousness of a God that existed prior to and outside the world could be rejected not merely as an indefensible anthropomorphism but also as a theoretical sleight of hand. And whoever criticized Hegel's concept of a necessity of creation as inappropriate to God could find himself having to show that the notion of a creation that occurred "at some point in eternity" through a divine act of will was better suited to the concept of God—to say nothing of the philosophical problems entailed in such a notion.

Finally, Hegel's students were long convinced that just his philosophy of religion was the fortunate possessor of the constitutive condition for meaningful talk of the personality of God, namely the trinitarian concept of God. The latter had become largely alien to the theology of the time, whether that of Schleiermacher or of Tholuck—as opposed to the speculative theology of Daub and Marheineke, which had a great deal in common with Hegel. The School's insistence on Hegel's trinitarian idea invited, to be sure, the retort that Hegel's doctrine of the trinity no longer had any-

24. Eschenmayer, *Hegels Religionsphilosophie*, pp. 3–4.

thing in common with the Christian doctrine beyond the mere name.[25] But this did not affect the systematic connection between the doctrines of the trinity and of the personality of God. And this was nowhere more convincingly established than in Hegel's philosophy of religion. For even if one still held fast to an objectivity of God conceived in terms of the immanent trinity, this did not necessarily have to be thought of as personal or indeed tripersonal. Fichte for instance was obliged to distinguish his conception from church doctrine no less than from Hegel's. He was opposed to taking over the designations Father, Son, and Holy Spirit from the economic trinity into the immanent in order to designate the moments of the "primordial personality," that is, of God's one self-consciousness. Instead he called for a new conception of the immanent trinity, a "speculative-theistic" conception that accepted the unipersonality of God in three moments.[26]

What made the speculative philosophy of religion systematically relevant was not the fact that by means of it the royal road of philosophical knowledge ultimately brought one to the traditional notions based on scriptural and church authority, which were thus simply better grounded than previously. Its relevance lay rather in the fact that it made clear the unbridgeable gulf between positive doctrine and traditional dogmatics on the one hand and speculative truth on the other—for the very reason that what it claimed was to *conceptualize* the idea of Christianity. The assertion that this gulf was at the same time merely one of form separated the School as a whole from its opponents. One group of opponents, arguing on theological (for the most part trivially pietistic) grounds, set the unattainable sanctity of revelation over against all philosophy.[27] The debate with this group was philosophically unrewarding. Basically it took the form of polemical exchanges.[28] Of philosophical sig-

---

25. Bachmann, *Hegels System,* p. 309, and *Anti-Hegel,* pp. 109–110; Eschenmayer, *Hegels Religionsphilosophie,* p. 61; Fichte, *Charakteristik,* pp. 985 ff.

26. On Weisse's concept of personality, which is trinitarian but is differently grounded than Hegel's, see his *Idee der Gottheit,* pp. 14, 252 ff.; see also below, pp. 400 ff. On Fichte, see *Idee der Persönlichkeit,* pp. 70 ff.; *Charakteristik,* p. 986; and below, pp. 411 ff.

27. Especially Eschenmayer, *Hegels Religionsphilosophie,* pp. 25, 44 ff.

28. Cf. David Friedrich Strauss, *In Defense of My "Life of Jesus" against the*

nificance, by comparison, is the School's debate with Weisse and Fichte and those close to them, such as Fischer and Sengler—in general the circle that formed around Fichte's *Zeitschrift für Philosophie und spekulative Theologie*. These "speculative theists" held fast to a "philosophy that offers a true reconciliation with religion and empirical science."[29] In Hegel's system, because of its faulty concept, such reconciliation had necessarily failed, they said. In it God was grasped "solely as dialectical process, as absolute reason, as primordial thought." Since speculative thought was an "adequate reflection of this divine, primordial thought," the a priori knowledge of God was, to be sure, consummated in it—but not the knowledge of God in general. Speculation could not, however, use the a priori thread to ascend "to the idea of a *personality* of primordial reason."[30] It would be quite impossible to introduce the ideas of personality and immortality into the self-contained speculative system without their losing their specific sense. It was not therefore the absence of these ideas that was seen as a defect; instead their absence, wholly consistent given the way in which Hegel's system was interconnected, provided the motive for going beyond it in principle—a project that necessitated a new ontological grounding.[31]

Fichte's attempt to clarify the scope of speculative philosophy in general raised the level of discussion between the Hegel School and speculative theism above that at which it was a matter of arguing whether this or that assertion of the philosophy of religion should be understood in the theistic sense. Göschel's apologetic accumulation of quotations did not therefore rise to the level of the debate. He should have started by emending Fichte's interpretation of Hegel's philosophy as an inwardly consistent nexus of dialecti-

Hegelians, trans. M. C. Massey (Hamden, Conn., 1983); Rosenkranz, *Kritische Erläuterungen*, pp. 267 ff., 309 ff.

29. Weisse, *Verhältnis des Publikums*, p. 41.

30. Fichte, *Idee der Persönlichkeit*, pp. 10–11.

31. Such a new ontology was sketched by C. P. Fischer, *Die Wissenschaft der Metaphysik im Grundrisse* (Stuttgart, 1834); Weisse, *Grundzüge der Metaphysik;* and I. H. Fichte, *Grundzüge zum System der Philosophie*, part 2, *Die Ontologie* (Heidelberg, 1836).

cal, rational knowledge, and have shown the possibility of theistic utterances in the context of the philosophy of religion. The form of exposition represented by Göschel, however, remained stuck in the twilight zone between dialectical rational science and affirmations of Christian faith. It thereby unwittingly became the principal ally of theistically minded critique. In the eyes of contemporary critics, the right-Hegelian attempt to conceive God as absolute personality or absolute subjectivity in the sense of the logical idea, and at the same time to conceive him as the highest individual, simply plunged the false but well-ordered Hegelian system into inconsistencies, evasions, and contradictions.[32] Above all, the right-Hegelian plea for the necessity of a philosophical grounding of the traditional notions of personality and immortality could be used as an argument against the truth-claim of the philosophy of religion. The critics reckoned it to the credit of the right-Hegelians to have gone beyond Hegel on this fundamental question, even if without being clearly aware of having done so.[33]

Contemporaries had an entirely different picture of the various tendencies of the School from that afforded by our current perception, which is that it was the Old Hegelians who preserved the pure doctrine. Because the right-Hegelian interpretation advanced to the ideas of personality and immortality, it was regarded as "progressive," whereas what later became the center and the moderate left seemed to adhere obstinately to the standpoint of the system. In their interpretation of the philosophy of religion, Hegel's opponents came to essentially the same conclusions as the center- and left-Hegelians, whereas they agreed with the right-Hegelians that philosophy too must issue in the traditional Christian doctrines. The great, often unrecognized, and today no longer repeatable interpretative achievement of the center and left lay in two directions.

32. Cf. Fichte, *Idee der Persönlichkeit,* pp. 24–25. Schelling's polemic is also directed against Göschel, *SW* 13:91–92 (see below, p. 416).

33. Cf. Fichte, *Idee der Persönlichkeit,* p. 8; and Fischer, *Idee der Gottheit,* pp. 38–39. A similar view is expressed later, in regard to Gabler, by Franz Anton Staudenmaier, *Darstellung und Kritik des Hegelschen Systems* (Mainz, 1844), pp. 867–868.

First, they maintained the formal nonidentity of representation and concept. Second, trusting to the power of rational thought invoked by Hegel, they showed the truth of the speculative philosophy of religion, positively, by the conceptual elaboration of specific broad topics pertaining to the philosophy of religion, and negatively, by a critique of the representational foundation together with the philosophical propositions based on it. By contrast, the lengths to which the right-Hegelians went in leveling out the differences of form between religious representation and conceptual thought, and in so doing going beyond Hegel (or rather falling behind him), were to be seen above all in the question that was to prove decisive for the fate of the School.

4. The Primacy of the Idea or of History

The divergences that arose within the School on the doctrine of the personality of God and the immortality of the soul can be readily seen in numerous writings and reviews by its members. What occasioned the splintering of the School was not this dispute, nor was it logic and metaphysics, nor the political sensation caused by the philosophy of right, but a topic that forms no part of the traditional stock of philosophical problems, namely the life of Jesus. It was from this angle that the interconnected problems of the philosophy of religion that were initially glossed over in the discussion could be rendered most transparent. In D. F. Strauss, Hegel's philosophy of religion found the interpreter of genius who was capable of doing this. Though Strauss in no way concerned himself with the entire stock of problems in the philosophy of religion, he did seize on the topic that linked it most closely to the current discussion, that is, the relationship between idea and history. Strauss made this point the criterion for the splintering of the School: "To the question of whether and to what extent the gospel history is proven as history by the idea of the unity of the divine and human natures, there are three possible answers: either the entirety of the history is proven by this concept, or merely a part of it, or finally, neither as a whole nor in part is it to be confirmed as historical by the idea."[34]

How this question is to be solved has already been indicated above (see pp. 000 ff.). All that needs to be discussed here is its significance for the course of the controversy over the philosophy of religion. For today Strauss's motivation and arguments are no longer immediately intelligible; their context in the history of theology has long since been swept away. Hegel had criticized his age for its loss of objective truth. To the extent that this loss was imputable to theology, it was the logical consequence (once the hypothesis of inspiration had been demolished) of the insight into the impossibility of grounding Christianity historically. Lessing had formulated this insight in compelling terms, and its correctness was continually (even if only implicitly) borne out by the way in which historical-critical research had expanded since its beginnings. The mythical interpretation, initially confined to the early chapters of Genesis, was extended beyond the themes of "creation" and "the primordial history of humanity" to embrace, first, the remainder of the Old Testament and, later, parts of the New Testament. This process, which took in one area of historical knowledge after another, in strictly consistent fashion, left only two possibilities open: either to salvage what remained of pseudohistorical legitimation (such as by Schleiermacher's playing off the Fourth Gospel against the Synoptics, with the dire consequences that was to have later) or to find a way out by seeking a nonhistorical foundation for Christian truth. Hegel had already learned to despise supernaturalism during his student days; he had demonstrated in his lectures the weaknesses of the so-called "rational theology" (*LPR* 1:154 ff.); and he had rejected as involving the loss of all objective truth the approaches of the theology of feeling and of Schleiermacher. His solution of this fundamental problem lay in the theorem of the identity of content of religion and philosophy, together with the consequences that stemmed from it, namely that if truth was to be firmly based, it had to be produced from the concept,

34. Strauss, *In Defense of My "Life of Jesus,"* p. 38. On the problem as a whole see D. F. Strauss, *The Life of Jesus Critically Examined,* trans. G. Eliot (Philadelphia and London, 1972–1973), pp. 778 ff.

but also that religious representation had to be raised into the concept.

Strauss's manner of proceeding seemed to run directly counter to this solution. Whereas Hegel had always expressed himself unfavorably with respect to a theology that was limited to criticism and history, Strauss was the author of the work that, more than any other, marks the beginning of the historical-critical study of the New Testament, namely *The Life of Jesus*. Typical of this work is the reinterpretation of the concept of myth and its application to the totality of biblical writings. If the myths thus revealed were merely historical, the mythical interpretation, while eliminating much that was repugnant, would be incapable of certifying the truth of the content. Strauss, however, interprets the myths as philosophical; the failure of a historical grounding necessitates having recourse to the concept. To this extent Strauss's procedure is strictly in line with Hegel's insight: just as the truth cannot be demonstrated by historical research, so it cannot be refuted by it either. The result he arrives at is in no way revolutionary. It was accepted by Hegel too, but merely as something presumed on the basis of his diagnosis of the time, not as something demonstrated: only the concept can authenticate the truth of Christianity.[35] But Strauss is astonishingly acute in the way he recognizes that Hegel's dismissal of the fledgling historical theology fails to equip the system with safeguards against attacks from that quarter. Thus he defines the value that alone can attach to historical criticism under the conditions of the speculative philosophy of religion. The mythical interpretation becomes the moment of self-mediation of the speculative concept through the exclusion of everything historical. It provides a posteriori legitimation for Hegel's rejection of a historical grounding of Christianity. What Hegel only anticipates, Strauss brings to pass. Historical criticism demolishes what in Hegel's day still seemed the intact bulwark of Christianity and compels it to take refuge in the concept.

35. This function was also clearly brought out by Strauss's sharpest critics on the right wing of the School; cf. Bruno Bauer, "Rezension zu Strauss' *Leben Jesu*," *Jahrbücher für wissenschaftliche Kritik*, 1835: 885–886; or Göschel, *Beiträge*, pp. 51–52.

Strauss did not, to be sure, acquire his strategy solely from an interpretation of the philosophy of religion. It presupposes a far-reaching insight into current tendencies in the history of theology. The weight that attaches in this connection to his very copious extracts from Schleiermacher's lectures on the life of Jesus has not yet been taken properly into account. These extracts testify to the impossibility of mediating dogma and history,[36] which Strauss interprets as necessitating the taking of refuge, not in history, but in the concept. Nowhere is this necessity more patently expressed than in these extracts and in Strauss's *Life of Jesus*. In order to assess his strategy of grounding the speculative standpoint on the critique of history, it is immaterial whether this strategy can already be found prefigured in a review by his friend Wilhelm Vatke.[37] For the latter too leads back to Hegel's philosophy of religion. And the philosophy of religion does not provide only a posteriori support for Strauss's strategy. His methodological reflections show that it was not only conducive to his conception but made it possible: by founding the truth of Christianity on the speculative concept, one is set free from the rigid and at the same time futile adherence to history that Strauss regards as typical of the theology of his day. By so doing, one makes the historical a matter of indifference, and moreover unintentionally unburdens historical research from the manifold dogmatic considerations which at that time it would otherwise have been incapable of casting off. It counts as one of the decisive turns of events in the history of the influence of Hegel's philosophy of religion that, once historical research is set free, it no longer needed this link and contributed to discrediting the grounding of truth on the basis of self-thinking reason.

The vehement controversies over Strauss's conclusions opened up a new stage in the debate over the Christian character of Hegel's philosophy of religion. For these conclusions were viewed, not un-

36. On Strauss's insight into the impossibility of a mediation, see the author's "Paralipomena Hegeliana zur Wirkungsgeschichte Schleiermachers," in *Internationaler Schleiermacher-Kongress, Berlin, 1984*, ed. K.-V. Selge (Berlin and New York, 1985), pp. 1157–1169.

37. Cf. Wilhelm Vatke, "Rezension zu de Wette: *Lehrbuch der historisch-kritischen Einleitung in die kanonischen Bücher des Neuen Testaments*," *Jahrbücher für wissenschaftliche Kritik*, 1832: 868–869.

justly, as resulting from Hegel's approach—at least to the extent that they concerned the relationship between idea, philosophical myth, and history, even if not the other question as to whether there were one or more God-men. That a philosophy should have difficulties expressing in dogmatically correct fashion the personality of God and immortality was at least not unintelligible and scarcely other than what was expected. But that it should contribute to dissolving the life of Jesus into a myth inevitably brought down censure on its head. Nor was this the only objection to this fruit of speculation that contemporary critics felt constrained to raise: Strauss's interpretation also lent itself to revolutionary political conclusions. Much of the extensive literature devoted to the Hegelian left and right has failed to notice and has consistently disregarded the fact that it was this which transformed a debate on the philosophy of religion into a political debate.[38] In this way the favorable moment seemed to have come to dispose politically of this obnoxious speculative philosophy of religion; moreover, this saved the trouble of discussing it theoretically.

Only now did the divergences within the School become accentuated to the point of an open split. Strauss sealed it by distinguishing a "right" and a "left" wing and a "center" party.[39] The right-Hegelians—Johann Eduard Erdmann, B. Bauer, Julius Schaller, G. A. Gabler, H. F. W. Hinrichs, and above all C. F. Göschel—vehemently disputed whether Strauss could properly be associated with Hegel and proposed to formulate their own position in continuity with the philosophy of religion. Yet they too did not form a uniform front. It is noteworthy that Schaller largely accepted Strauss's mythical interpretation, although he did not understand it properly. Even Göschel could not refrain from coming to the aid of Strauss on numerous points and protecting him against unjus-

38. See the author's "Urmenschheit und Monarchie," *Hegel-Studien* 14 (1979): 73–107, and Marilyn Chapin Massey's *Christ Unmasked: The Meaning of "The Life of Jesus" in German Politics* (Chapel Hill and London, 1983), esp. pp. 81–94.

39. Strauss, *In Defense of My "Life of Jesus,"* pp. 38 ff. On Michelet's classification of the School, see his *Geschichte*, pp. 637 ff., and his *Entwicklungsgeschichte*, pp. 313 ff.

tified attacks. But this defense was at the same time a self-defense. What lay behind the critique of Strauss can be discerned more closely from Göschel's text than from those of the other right-Hegelians. It was essential to draw a sharp dividing line between oneself and Strauss in order to prevent whoever was opposed to Hegel from rejecting the speculative philosophy of religion for having produced such consequences. In the face of calls on the part of theology to grasp the evil at its root, namely Hegel, Göschel recommended the master's philosophy of religion as a proven remedy against Strauss's aberrations.[40] But this was possible only for an interpretation that regarded not only itself but also Hegel's philosophy of religion as closer to Hengstenberg's *Evangelische Kirchenzeitung* than to Strauss. Philosophical differences apart, Göschel's supposed apologia for Hegel was prompted by tactical considerations, and not solely in the face of the attacks from rationalist and neoorthodox circles. The immediate occasion for his work was an undisguised challenge by the Prussian Minister for Religious Affairs, von Altenstein. And his argumentation culminated in a political theology that recalls Franz von Baader but would also have been worthy of the age of Constantine.[41]

The writings in which the Hegelian right sought to defend the speculative philosophy of religion unwittingly revealed their distance from it even more starkly than previously, with respect to the problems of divine personality and individual immortality. Erdmann had recourse to a theory of developmental differentiation in the attempt to make some of Strauss's testimony less objectionable: admittedly it was offensive to religious feeling, but it pertained to Hegel's Jena notebook on the history of philosophy and was therefore of less significance than his mature philosophy of religion.[42] This argument is surprising in that it was precisely the

40. Cf. Göschel, *Beiträge*, p. 278; also Schaller, *Historischer Christus*, p. v.

41. See the author's "Urmenschheit und Monarchie." A noteworthy counterpart, relating not to the controversy over the life of Jesus but to theism in general, is found in Schelling: the demand for the personality of God is matched, in the state, by the desire for a king, whom the individual can love and before whom all are equal, as they are before God (*SW* 11:569–570).

42. J. E. Erdmann, *Versuch einer wissenschaftlichen Darstellung der Geschichte der neueren Philosophie*, vol. 3, part 2 (Leipzig, 1853), p. 846. On Erdmann's interpretation of the philosophy of religion, see his *Glauben und Wissen*.

edition of Hegel's works prepared by Hegel's students that obscured the developmental differences; moreover it was a delicate
matter to give preference to subsequent student transcripts over a
text in Hegel's own hand that had indeed come into being at the
same time as the *Phenomenology*. Even Göschel did not hesitate to
accord a place on numerous occasions to unclear or immature passages in the philosophy of religion, while doing all he could to
downplay their importance.[43] Yet even the topics on which he believed himself to be in complete agreement with Hegel betrayed a
considerable discord, which did not escape contemporary critics
either. This is true above all of his attempt to link the speculative
philosophy of religion to historical evidence and even declare it
consonant with a residual belief in miracles.[44] The fact that such
intentions underlay its argumentation lowered the extreme right's
interpretation to a level inferior to Hegel's philosophy of religion,
and inferior also to Schleiermacher—namely to the level of an orthodoxy rigged out with speculative adornments. As such it was
rejected on the center and the left as well as by Hegel's philosophical opponents. By contrast the center and the middle left acknowledged Strauss's standpoint to be a legitimate exposition of
the philosophy of religion, even if on essential problems they took
up positions against Strauss—primarily on the question whether a
single God-man was established by the idea or by spatiotemporal
circumstances, and also on the question of the basis of Christ's
divinity. Within the School these and other questions gave rise to
a relatively high level of discussion.[45] But this group was much
smaller than the number of those who, while equally convinced of

43. Göschel, *Beiträge*, pp. 16 ff., 45.

44. Ibid., pp. 35–40. The desperate efforts to safeguard miracle made by
Bauer, with the same end in view, in his "Rezension zu Strauss' *Leben Jesu*," pp.
689–690, also make a painful impression. See also Schaller, *Historischer Christus*,
pp. 19 ff.; and the ambiguous position of Rosenkranz in *Kritische Erläuterungen*,
pp. xxiv ff.

45. See, e.g., K. Rosenkranz, *Kritik der Schleiermacherschen Glaubenslehre*
(Königsberg, 1836), pp. xvi ff.; and *Kritische Erläuterungen*, pp. xx ff. Michelet
sought to adhere to the middle position between Strauss and Rosenkranz; cf. his
Persönlichkeit und Unsterblichkeit, pp. 186 ff., 194, and *Entwicklungsgeschichte*,
p. 391. Cf. further W. Vatke, "Beitrag zur Kritik der neueren philosophischen
Theologie," *Hallische Jahrbücher* 3 (1840); Baur, *Christliche Gnosis*, pp. 700 ff.;
and Snellmann, *Idee der Persönlichkeit*, pp. 7 ff.

the appropriateness of Strauss's interpretation, saw in it only renewed evidence of the dangerous nature of Hegel's philosophy of religion.[46]

A decisive contribution to the outcome of the controversy was made by the unexpected support the latter group of critics received from a man who had himself earlier belonged to the circle around Hegel, namely Heinrich Leo. Leo's attack on "the Hegelians" was, to be sure, formally directed only against the Young Hegelians. But since he saw the main contrast between them and Hegel in the fact that Hegel "had not in fact expressed himself clearly as to the pernicious consequences of his doctrine as far as the religious consciousness of the people is concerned,"[47] his attack applied no less to the philosophy of religion of the master. Leo's short text, which was greatly expanded one year later, consists essentially of lengthy quotations from works by Michelet and Karl Theodor Bayrhoffer, on which it comments in polemical footnotes. The probable reason why Leo dispensed with an argued analysis was that he believed the quoted "blasphemy" spoke for itself, and that the "hell-born progeny" of Young Hegelians would in any event strangle each other.[48] Nor are the accusations assembled in the preface in any way new. The Young Hegelians, according to Leo, teach "atheism"; they claim "that the Gospel is a form of mythology," "a religion confined to this world alone." Leo's fourth item of accusation, namely that the Hegelians nonetheless introduce by sleight of hand a "toleration of Christian promises and of external participation in Christian sacraments," indicates that the controversy over the philosophy of religion was now entering a new phase of exacer-

46. On the critique advanced by speculative theism, see, e.g., Fichte, *Charakteristik*, pp. 1000 ff.; Sengler, *Wesen und Bedeutung* 2:xiv; Hermann Ulrici, *Ueber Princip und Methode der Hegel'schen Philosophie* (Halle, 1841), p. 290; Fischer, *Idee der Gottheit*, pp. xxvi, 38–39. Critiques were also advanced from the side of Protestant theology, e.g. by K. G. Bretschneider and E. W. Hengstenberg in the *Allgemeine Kirchenzeitung* and the *Evangelische Kirchenzeitung* in 1836 and 1837, and from the side of Catholic theology, especially by J. E. Kuhn; but these were no more conducive to the philosophical resolution of the question than the trivial attacks in the style, e.g., of Ernst Joseph Gustav de Valenti, *Hegel-Strauss, und der Christusglaube* (Basel, 1843).

47. Heinrich Leo, *Die Hegelingen* (Halle, 1838), p. 7 n.

48. Ibid., p. 26 n.

bation in which it was no longer a matter of testing its truth but of denouncing its sociopolitical consequences and calling for state intervention. In this way the debate was brought down to a level where a discussion concerning the philosophy of religion conducted in a scholarly and academic tone was in danger of not being heard.

5. Hegel's Philosophy Anti-Christian or Christian?

(1) The former right-Hegelian Bruno Bauer drew the consequences from the threatening situation that had developed. Assuming the mask of piety of one extravagantly armed with biblical quotations, he consigned Hegel to everlasting damnation with his "trumpet of the last judgment"—*Die Posaune des Jüngsten Gerichts über Hegel den Atheisten und Antichristen.* Leo's indictment was directed solely against the left and center-left wings, and he formally condemned these groups as sects. Bauer by contrast insisted on the agreement between the left-Hegelian interpretation and Hegel's philosophy of religion: the left-Hegelians were the master's true disciples, whereas the right misread the philosophy of religion through its theistic spectacles, and so, whether deliberately or not, disguised its revolutionary potential. Formally speaking, this reading coincides with the polemic aimed at Hegel by speculative theism, even if Bauer's trumpet is blowing a different tune. His strategy, to help the left-Hegelian interpretation impose itself by branding it as heretical, is unprecedented in the history of philosophy. At the same time his text is comparatively short on arguments that lend themselves to discussion. Its conception exempts the author from the necessity of interpreting in a consistent manner the quotations he has shown such acumen in selecting. The sole defense he allows against Hegel the Antichrist is to renounce unconditionally all philosophical argumentation and revert to a pietistic standpoint. Any philosophical critique of Hegel is denounced as dalliance with the whore of reason, the only effect of which is to plunge more deeply into ruin—as the self-destruction of speculative theism shows. It is not merely Hegel's doctrine of the identity of reason and revelation but also all non-Hegelian attempts to mediate religion and philosophy that Bauer unmasks as works of the devil in

terms so emphatic as to make it appear ultimately inevitable to take the devil's side. Nowhere is the failure of Hegel's proclaimed reconciliation between religion and philosophy more crassly expressed than here.

The subtly feigned concern over Hegel's subversive attitude toward church, state, and ethical life is stylized in the manner of Leo. The actual theme of Bauer's work is the theoretical consequence of the philosophy of religion, namely atheism, which he believes to be concealed beneath a double veil. The first veil, its Christian character, could only deceive fools. But beneath it there is a second veil, that of the philosophy of absolute substance or pantheism, which can be removed only by the critical knife of faith. The "dreadful, horrifying kernel of the system, destructive of all piety and religious sentiment," then at last stands exposed to view, namely that "the religious relationship is nothing but an inner relationship of self-consciousness to itself."[49]

In thus restricting the kernel of the philosophy of religion to the "sole sovereignty of self-consciousness,"[50] Bauer falls short of the mark. Had he developed Hegel's standpoint as that of reason, or even of spirit, he would scarcely have been able to sustain his thesis as to the incompatibility of religion and philosophy. Yet this thesis distills the quintessence of a decade of discussion concerning the philosophy of religion. Up to the end of the 1830s, the main nerve of the philosophy of religion, the thesis of the identity of content, had been contested almost exclusively in the name of religion. As a result of this bitter resistance toward the identity of reason and religion, not only was any effort to cling to this identity rendered illusory; in addition, the parallel enterprise of mediation on the part of speculative theism showed that if reason was overly impatient in calling for mediation, it soon found itself once more subject to a revelation that was no longer in harmony with reason. Shortly before the appearance of Bauer's book, irreversible consequences had been drawn from this insight into the actual failure of media-

---

49. Bruno Bauer, *Die Posaune des jüngsten Gerichts über Hegel den Atheisten und Antichristen* (Leipzig, 1842), p. 48. See also his *Hegel's Lehre von der Religion und Kunst von dem Standpuncte des Glaubens aus beurtheilt* (Leipzig, 1842).
50. Bauer, *Posaune*, p. 127.

tion on the part of the philosophy of religion. One of the surprising turns of events in the modern history of philosophy—though in retrospect it can be seen to be consistent—is that a defense of Hegel called forth by this situation gave rise to a point of view that shortly came to regard itself as having overcome idealist philosophy together with its traditional critique.

(2) The complex argumentative strategy Ludwig Feuerbach adopted in regard to Hegel's philosophy of religion differs radically from that of all other Hegel students. His *Zur Kritik der "positiven" Philosophie* and *Über Philosophie und Christentum*—planned as reviews of works by Sengler and Leo—are not primarily designed to absolve Hegel's philosophy of religion from the odium of un-Christian character. Whether it is in conformity with the Christian religion is "not only a distasteful but also an absolutely idiotic and senseless question that mistakes the essence of philosophy" (*FGW* 8:250). By contrast, the question whether what Hegel affirms to be Christian is in conformity with Christianity is justified, but must be considered with regard to the "infinite difference between the object in the philosophy of religion and the same object in religion itself." This difference, in Feuerbach's view, does not lie in an identifiable error in the philosophy of religion, but follows necessarily from its character as philosophy.[51] All of Hegel's students had previously interpreted the divergence between the philosophy of religion and Christianity by means of the theorem of the identity of content and difference of form between religion and philosophy. The attacks directed against the speculative philosophy of religion, however, had increasingly made it clear that while this theorem opened the door to the critique of religious representation by means of the concept, it also conversely exposed speculation to critique from the side of representation. In order to remove philosophy from the province of such inspection, Feuerbach's double-edged apologia surrendered the basic theorem of the speculative philosophy of religion, substituting for it the affirmation that there is an "unbridgeable gulf" between religion and philosophy: the content

51. Feuerbach's viewpoint is supported by Julius Frauenstaedt, *Studien und Kritiken zur Theologie und Philosophie* (Berlin, 1840), pp. ix-x, 108.

of the latter is thought, of the former "imagination and feeling" (*FGW* 8:220).

From the emphasis he laid on the gulf between Christianity and philosophy in general, and the philosophy of religion in particular, the conclusion could just as well have been drawn that it was better wholly to renounce such an essentially un-Christian philosophy. Orthodoxy too had stressed the irreconcilability of reason and revelation and inferred from this the emptiness of philosophy. To support his emancipation of philosophy from the tutelage of religion, Feuerbach therefore turned the charge of being un-Christian against the theology of his time—against the modern "ivory tower belief [*Doktorglauben*]," which was "only something cultivated in a hothouse, a refined product of reflective disbelief" (*FGW* 8:235–236). As the measure of true Christian piety he took pre-Constantinian Christianity, and thus he denied the Christian character of both present-day philosophy of religion and contemporary philosophy in general; under the conditions of the modern world, any return to this early form remained out of the question.

Feuerbach's critique of Hegel's opponents constitutes the last attempt at a productive interpretation within the universe of discourse to which the conception of the speculative philosophy of religion originally belongs. Yet his apparent apologia calls the latter in question more thoroughly than even the most vehement attacks of its opponents. His strategy is clear, but the execution rests on a chain of decisions that are not discussed. Hegel's claim that his philosophy of religion is in accord with Christianity cannot be shaken by Feuerbach's methodologically questionable and unhistorical playing-off of a pure origin against a contemporary degeneracy. Nor can Hegel's doctrine of the identity of faith and reason be invalidated by the mere assertion of an extremely restricted conception of religion, confined to the stirrings of a pious disposition. At this phase of his thought, Feuerbach does not justify the dissolution of the identity of content of religion and philosophy. But the fact that he does not subscribe to this fundamental theorem of the speculative philosophy of religion is already evident ten years previously, from the letter with which he sent his dissertation to Hegel (*L* 547 ff., *Br* 3:244 ff.). His subsequent polemic shows that under the impact of the philosophy-of-religion controversy this early view was reinforced, making a total divorce between religion and philosophy appear inevitable in the interests of reason too.

The demonstration of the essentially un-Christian character of Hegel's philosophy of religion does not inhibit Feuerbach from revealing theology to be the hidden element in speculative philosophy in his *Vorläufige Thesen zur Reformation der Philosophie* and *Principles of the Philosophy of the Future*. In Hegel's philosophy the departed spirit of theology wanders about like a ghost (*FGW* 9: 243, 247). Feuerbach's newly won standpoint levels out the differences between the disciplines of the system. It is not the philosophy of religion but the theological character of the system as a whole that is held against it. The problems relating specifically to the philosophy of religion on which the discussion centered in the 1830s consequently recede into the background. If all theological propositions are rooted in human desire, what is required can no longer be to clarify questions about the personality of God, individual immortality, and the actuality of the God-man, but in principle to transcend the level at which such questions can meaningfully be discussed. And this is the level at which the speculative philosophy of religion also is located.

In an occasional piece dating from this period, Feuerbach once again gives a detailed statement of his attitude toward Hegel's philosophy of religion. He took the occasion to stress the contrast between himself and Hegel, who, unlike Schleiermacher, misunderstood the essence of religion. But the conclusion he draws from this assessment is Hegelian: if subjectively the crux of religion is feeling, then the only possible conclusion is that "objectively God himself is nothing but the essence of feeling" (*FGW* 9:230). Whereas Hegel places the content of religion in thinking, Feuerbach sees himself constrained by the course of the discussion to fall back on an analysis similar to Schleiermacher's. Only in the practical consequences he derives from this does he still agree with Hegel. He regards it as "a moral necessity, a sacred duty of humanity, to bring the dark and furtive essence of religion wholly under the scrutiny of reason" (*FGW* 9:234). And he sees proof of Hegel's failure to overcome "world-historical hypocrisy" in the fact that both orthodoxy and heterodoxy invoke speculative philosophy in their behalf.

Feuerbach is constantly in search of new ways of formulating the immanent contradiction in the philosophy of religion. While it is the negation of theology, it still rests on the soil of theology[52] and is not its complete negation, free of contradiction. This contradictory character conditions Feuerbach's ambivalent attitude to speculation. He supports it insofar as it accomplishes "the rational or theoretical elaboration and dissolution of God, who is, for religion, other-worldly and nonobjective."[53] But he rejects it to the extent that in so doing it falls into the error of all theology: while recognizing reason as the truth of the divine being, it again separates it off and opposes it to human being as an alien, independent mode of being—the phantom of absolute spirit. Feuerbach no longer bothers to investigate how far speculative philosophy actually accomplishes the theoretical crystallization he imputes to it. In the light of his new, postidealist recourse to "sensuality" and "actuality" and also his radical critique of religion, the antithesis between Hegel's speculative interpretation and religion in the traditional sense is increasingly seen by Feuerbach to be of no importance. The plausibility of his critique accordingly disappears to the extent that one recognizes the left-Hegelian interpretation as the appropriate way to read the philosophy of religion. And it also disappears to the extent that one does not accept Feuerbach's concept of religion, namely that its crux is feeling. This was indeed an understanding shared by a series of critics on the right as well as on the left. Its accuracy can scarcely be regarded as proven. But it did prejudice the outcome of the controversy over the speculative philosophy of religion. For if feeling is not the most important thing in religion, as Feuerbach and the critics on the right maintained, then God cannot be spoken of either as the essence of feeling. And in any event there are good reasons for affirming that God is not the highest feeling but the highest thought.

(3) The apparently confusing multiplicity of standpoints and ar-

52. Ludwig Feuerbach, *Principles of the Philosophy of the Future*, trans. Manfred Vogel (Indianapolis, 1966), p. 22.

53. Ibid., pp. 5–6. The translation omits "and nonobjective" (cf. *FGW* 9:266).

guments in the discussion of the philosophy of religion thus turns out to be an astonishingly coherent process. The critique of *theologia naturalis* had placed in question the possibility of a knowledge of God acquired through reason and thus cast doubt upon the recently proclaimed unity of reason and revelation, while historical criticism had undermined the seemingly historical foundations of Christianity. As an alternative to the response to this situation that consisted in grounding religion on subjectivity in the narrow sense, Hegel sought to show that the foundation of the truth of Christianity was the speculative concept. The philosophy of religion was designed as a counter to the approach based on abstract subjectivity and to historical criticism. It could be neither corroborated nor refuted by the latter. Strauss's mythical interpretation did not therefore go beyond Hegel's own approach. It simply supplied the supplementary evidence needed to support Hegel's solution, which was far in advance of its time. Feuerbach was therefore justified in presenting his critique of religion as superior in principle to Strauss's mythical interpretation and at the same time assailing Hegel's philosophy of religion as the last refuge of orthodoxy. For he discovered the path that still remained open for criticism—irrespective of whether such criticism was ultimately justified. Speculative philosophy might well offer objective truth a refuge against historical criticism. But it was no more capable than the subjectivist approach it criticized of protecting Christianity against the interpretation offered by psychology of religion—against the theory of projection elaborated by Feuerbach in his productive encounter with speculative philosophy. For by this means Hegel's philosophy itself was placed in question—whether rightly or not could be determined only by a separate discussion. To be sure, it was essentially objections to the logic that led to Feuerbach's break with speculative philosophy. But it was only in the context of the critique of religion in *The Essence of Christianity* that his critique of the mode of thought that is concerned only with itself and loses contact with "actuality" became historically operative. The foundational problems that arose in this connection elevated the critique of religion into the model for the critique of speculative philosophy, in fact of all philosophy. In line with what Feuerbach had already called for in his attack on Leo, not only was theology revealed to be the clue to philosophy, but also anthropology was revealed to be the clue to theology; thus in principle the curtain could be lowered on the controversy over the identity of content of religion and philosophy, the personality of God and individual immortality, and the facticity of the God-man.

6. The End of the Original Controversy Over Hegel's Philosophy of Religion[54]

(1) "For Germany the *criticism of religion* has been essentially completed."[55] Karl Marx's much-quoted pronouncement drew the closing line to the debate that had been conducted with utmost vigor for a decade and more. This is not to be understood as implying that Feuerbach's premises, to which Marx is here alluding, are beyond all further question. Feuerbach's critique of Christianity did, however, bring to an end the period of direct appropriation and criticism of the speculative philosophy of religion, a period of which Michelet had good reason to say that the basic philosophical decisions had been made in the debate over Hegel's philosophy of religion.[56] The studies that subsequently appeared on the problem of the speculative philosophy of religion no longer derived from a living encounter with contemporary philosophical problems, but (where they dealt with Hegel) addressed themselves to something that was already historically distant. It was only in the controversy over Schelling's late philosophy, as well as for the breakup of speculative theism and the formulation of Kierkegaard's position, that Hegel's philosophy of religion proved to be still a systematic force.[57]

54. [Tr.] In the German text this heading reads "Das Ende der 'Urgeschichte'"; the *Urgeschichte* of the controversy, as defined by the author, refers to the decade between 1833 and 1843 (see above, p. 352).

55. Karl Marx, "Toward the Critique of Hegel's Philosophy of Law: Introduction," *Writings of the Young Marx on Philosophy and Society*, eds. L. D. Easton and K. H. Guddat (Garden City, N.Y., 1967), p. 249.

56. Michelet, *Entwicklungsgeschichte*, pp. 315–316; and *Persönlichkeit und Unsterblichkeit*, p. 7.

57. Indicative of this change is the appearance of what is even today the standard biography, Karl Rosenkranz's *Hegels Leben* (Berlin, 1844). An exception to this historicizing tendency is the attempt by Moritz Carriere to ensure a future-

This greater independence from current polemics might have encouraged a more nuanced examination of the speculative philosophy of religion. But the newly-emerging studies of the history of philosophy were only rarely capable of abandoning the well-worn lines of apologia and critique. To be sure, the tenor of critique changed from occasionally life-threatening polemic to objectivizing description, but the themes and consequently the slogans remained the same. Historical distance had no beneficial effect as long as the criterion for assessing the philosophy of religion remained unchanged. A discussion of the philosophical foundations of Hegel's theory of religion was still largely replaced by an examination as to whether it was compatible with a pious heart or with dogma. Any question about the appropriateness of this criterion was quickly resolved by reference to Hegel's claim that the content of religion and philosophy is identical. But since the standpoint of Christianity was identified with the representational position that Hegel endeavored to sublate into the concept, there could never be any question about the fact that Hegel's form of Christianity was not the "true" one.[58] His idea of the trinity was rejected,[59] as was

---

oriented relevance for the philosophy of religion by taking up again the Jena schema of a historical succession of Catholicism, Protestantism, and New Gospel; see his *Die Religion in ihrem Begriff, ihrer weltgeschichtlichen Entwicklung und Vollendung* (Weilburg, 1841), pp. 178 ff., 156 n. It is significant that Carriere traces his reception of the philosophy of religion back to Eduard Gans, for it was Gans, the teacher of Marx, who in the debate over the philosophy of right stressed the fact that the actualization of the rational had not yet been achieved. On the debate between the Hegel School and Schelling, see, e.g., P. Marheineke, *Zur Kritik der Schellingschen Offenbarungsphilosophie* (Berlin, 1843); F. Bauerheim, *Die Grundlehren der Neu-Schelling'schen und der Hegel'schen Philosophie in ihrer gegenseitigen Beziehung* (Reutlingen, 1847); Anonymous, *Schellings Offenbarungsphilosophie und die von ihr bekämpfte Religionsphilosophie Hegels und der Junghegelianer* (Berlin, 1843).

58. It was above all Staudenmaier's work, characterized by a great breadth of treatment, which sought to legitimate itself by this methodological reflection; see his *Darstellung und Kritik*, p. 5. See also Eschenmayer, *Hegels Religionsphilosophie*, p. v.

59. Staudenmaier, *Darstellung und Kritik*, pp. 817–818; Ulrici, *Prinzip und Methode*, p. 263; Fichte, *Charakteristik*, pp. 986 ff. Fichte strikes a new note inasmuch as he is generally unwilling to retroject the terms Father, Son, and Spirit from the economic into the immanent trinity; and he criticizes Hegel for also conceiving

his concept of revelation.[60] As previously, however, criticism was directed primarily at his supposed pantheism. This reproach had now been systematically extended to the point of encompassing all other objections that had previously been raised separately, though from the point of view of content no new arguments had been introduced. F. A. Staudenmaier's prolix discussion of "logical pantheism" was based on Gottlob Benjamin Jäsche, while the identification of Hegel with Gnosticism went back to Ferdinand Christian Baur.[61]

(2) The broadening of the textual basis did result in a few new initiatives. The difference between the religion chapter of the *Phenomenology* and the philosophy-of-religion lectures had thus far been referred to essentially only for the controversy as to whether the philosophy of religion was Christian in character, not for a philosophical interpretation. Even where there were indications to this effect, they rapidly ended in charges that one's opponents remained shackled to the phenomenological standpoint.[62] The methodological differences between the religion chapter of the *Encyclopedia* and the lectures were considered by Hermann Ulrici, along with others, but he did not pursue this possible avenue of interpretation in a consistent manner.[63] In addition to these differences that

---

the economic trinity as self-actualization and thus obscuring the distinction between the two forms of the trinity. A different view is taken by G. A. Gabler, *Die Hegel'sche Philosophie* (Berlin, 1843).

60. Cf. Staudenmaier, *Darstellung und Kritik*, pp. 24 ff.; Ulrici, *Prinzip und Methode*, pp. 246 ff.; Ludwig Noack, *Der Religionsbegriff Hegel's* (Darmstadt, 1845), pp. 24–25, 28. Noack was editor of the *Jahrbücher für spekulative Philosophie und die philosophische Bearbeitung der empirischen Wissenschaft* (Darmstadt, 1846–1848), a journal that contains several articles of importance for the debate over Hegel's philosophy of religion.

61. Staudenmaier, *Darstellung und Kritik*, pp. 32 ff., 63 ff. Cf. Jäsche, *Der Pantheismus nach seinen verschiedenen Hauptformen*, esp. 2:xxviii; and Peter Volkmuth, *Der dreieinige Pantheismus von Thales bis Hegel* (Cologne, 1837). On the link to Gnosticism, see Baur, *Christliche Gnosis*.

62. The dominant influence of the *Phenomenology of Spirit* is especially evident in Hinrichs, *Die Religion;* Gabler, *Die Hegelsche Philosophie;* and Conradi, *Selbstbewusstseyn und Offenbarung.* On the relationship between philosophy of religion and phenomenology, see Erdmann, "Religionsphilosophie als Phänomenologie."

63. Ulrici, *Prinzip und Methode*, pp. 245–277, esp. 253.

were already known, others now came to light. Karl Rosenkranz's biography for the first time made known Hegel's youthful critique of religion and his historical construction of Christianity in line with Schelling, dating from the Jena years.[64] A decade earlier the partial publication of Hegel's early writings would have been bound to cause a sensation. Now the discussion had already advanced too far for these texts to receive greater attention than they did.[65]

A stimulus to interpretation of the philosophy of religion was, however, provided by the new edition of the lectures (1840), which diverged from the first edition in important passages. These differences could only be of limited value for the discussion, since the conception of the new edition, like that of the old, did not permit any sure judgment as to Hegel's process of thought. Statements by the editors spread additional confusion. Marheineke's note to the effect that the later edition had greater recourse to Hegel's manuscript and notes led to the presumption that the newly incorporated material consisted of passages from the manuscript—which, however, was mostly not the case.[66] For his part Bruno Bauer declared categorically that the new edition revealed more clearly Hegel's atheism.[67] The contrary, to be sure, comes closer to the truth, but even today there are some who give credence to the provocative blast of Bauer's trumpet.

I. H. Fichte was the only one to gain insights from the difference between editions which modified his earlier judgment. Whereas on the basis of the first edition he had regarded Strauss's reading alone

64. Rosenkranz, *Hegels Leben*, pp. esp. 45 ff., 132 ff., 462–537; somewhat later, Rudolf Haym, *Hegel und seine Zeit* (Berlin, 1857), pp. 16–61.

65. Eduard Zeller sought to introduce into the debate the information made available by Rosenkranz in his "Ueber Hegel's theologische Entwicklung," *Theologische Jahrbücher* 4 (1845): 192–206. The same year Noack in his *Religionsbegriff* turned his attention to the early writings, but at the same time looked essentially for guidance to the later system.

66. Marheineke in W_2 11:vii. On the basis of Marheineke's indications, Ulrici took a passage from Griesheim's transcript of the 1824 lectures to be an integral part of Hegel's lecture manuscript; the same confusion was evident in Fichte's *Charakteristik*, pp. 992 ff. On this matter see also *LPR* 1:29–30.

67. Bauer, *Posaune*, p. 149; but cf. Bruno Bauer and Edgar Bauer, *Briefwechsel während der Jahre 1839–1842 aus Bonn und Berlin* (Charlottenburg, 1844), p. 50.

as appropriate, he now found traits that for the first time made intelligible for him what motivated the right-Hegelian interpretation. But this new tension between right- and left-Hegelian *dicta probantia* did not lead Fichte to try again to resolve the matter. He simply distinguished between the principle of the system and Hegel's private views, imbued (as he perceived them) with deep belief. While such a distinction usually serves to legitimate a position that is accepted in general terms but viewed as less successful in elaboration, its function here was the contrary: the principle was rejected, and whatever could still be regarded as acceptable in the philosophy of religion appeared to be something alien to the principle. Fichte absolved Hegel as a private individual from the sins of his philosophical system precisely because he had remained "inconsistent, neither one thing nor the other," and his "intellectual and spiritual powers far surpassed the immediate results of his principle."[68] Fichte can hardly have been unaware of the necessarily ruinous consequences of such an apparent apologia for the truth-claim of the philosophy he exonerated.

From the philosophical point of view the speculative concept of religion still formed the principal objection to the philosophy of religion. The discussion here involved a peculiar intertwining of a left-Hegelian interpretation with a right-Hegelian position and vice versa, as was the case also with the controversies over the philosophy of right. In left-Hegelian fashion, Staudenmaier saw absolute spirit immanentized by Hegel to become the hypostasis of finite spirit. From his theistic viewpoint he therefore criticized absolute spirit as an anti-Christian self-deification of human being. Ludwig Noack by contrast interpreted absolute spirit in right-Hegelian fashion as objective, divine being, and since religion was supposed to form such a being's self-consciousness, he several times posed the urgent question whether any place remained in the philosophy of religion for human being—a question that since Feuerbach had acquired a new, sharper resonance.[69] It betrayed the fact,

68. Fichte, *Charakteristik,* p. 996.
69. Staudenmaier, *Darstellung und Kritik,* pp. 872 ff., 836; Noack, *Religionsbegriff,* pp. 12, 21, 31 et passim. The two views are directly opposed to one another by Reinhold Schmidt, *Der philosophische Absolutismus des Hegelschen Systems* (Berlin, 1845), p. 17: according to the one, God is "the monstrous egoist,

however, that Hegel's intention was no longer understood. For the speculative concept of religion utterly precludes any such opposition of God and human being. One can, to be sure, object that the mediation it envisages fails to come about, but not that it leaves "human being" out of account.

(3) Rudolf Haym gathered together in a definitive way the arguments deployed against the philosophy of religion, producing a polemic whose biting sarcasm could scarcely be surpassed. According to it, Hegel's concept of religion was a merely superficial consequence of the *Logic,* which for its part obtained its nourishment by preying on living matter.[70] The eradication of piety and religious disposition ignored the characteristic essence of religion, and the sublation of representation into the concept was an "out-and-out terrorist proceeding," which under the semblance of conserving religion brought about its evaporation into a schema and the disintegration and destruction of its most basic elements.[71] At the same time, as far as the relationship of the logical sphere to the philosophy of religion is concerned, Haym's polemic remains in principle captive to the position that Feuerbach had already repudiated in 1838–39, using Hegel's argument that it was not the task of the philosophy of religion to generate or conserve piety but solely to pose the question of the conceptual truth of religion. And insofar as Haym's objections concern the relationship between idea and facticity, they do not attain Strauss's level of reflection. He deplores the depreciation of the historical aspect of religion as the obverse of its reduction to logic.[72] The *Phenomenology,* in his view, formed the turning point in Hegel's attitude to the historical, in that it merged the historical with the speculative; and the philosophy of religion completely betrayed the historical sense of the young Hegel in favor of the "sorriest confusion" of speculation and history.[73]

---

who knows nothing and wills nothing but himself and consumes the whole world for his purposes"; according to the other, Hegel allots "all actuality and truth to the human spirit," which is "the focus and in fact the vehicle of the entire movement."

70. Haym, *Hegel und seine Zeit,* pp. 408, 417.

71. Ibid., pp. 408, 413.

72. Ibid., pp. 414 ff.

73. Ibid., p. 417. The charge that Hegel confuses the logical and the historical

Haym too sees as the deciding point between speculation and history the problem that Strauss projected into the center of the controversy over the philosophy of religion, namely that of Jesus as God-man. His critique is very similar to Fichte's *Beiträge zur Charakteristik der neueren Philosophie,* which is sharply critical of the disparity between the stress Hegel lays on the actuality of the divine-human individual and his simultaneous "straying into the metaphysical realm," arguing that it is absurd to transform facticity into metaphysical concepts and so seek to endow them with eternal significance.[74] Haym rejects as "philosophical frivolity" or even as "sleight of hand" Hegel's attempt to justify the appearance of the God-man on the basis of the idea and then to sublate it once again into the idea—his attempt to conceive the history of Christ and the self-destruction of this history simultaneously.[75] His and Fichte's criticism has the merit of having once again made clear the folly of harboring such expectations from the speculative construction of historical facts—even if only in the face of demands that were and are made of Hegel in this sense. Neither Haym's nor Fichte's criticism affects the speculative philosophy of religion, which, as has been shown by Strauss, conceives not the brute fact but the fact of faith on the basis of the idea (or more precisely the need) of reconciliation. In order to be guilty of the *metabasis eis allo genos* imputed to him, Hegel could not have been the "intimate of Lessing" (*L* 32, *Br* 1:21). A form of criticism that removes the spiritual element from Hegel's "spiritual interpretation" in order to make it into the proof of a "factual theophany," or the logical deduction of the "unity of natures" in Christ, or the speculative version of Chalcedon—such a criticism has an easy time of it. But it is its own doing to incorporate "all the crudities of ecclesiastical litany . . . into the speculative schema"; it alone endows the philos-

---

was one that in substance had already been voiced by Schelling and the speculative theists as well as by Noack, *Religionsbegriff,* p. 66. Cf. also Karl Schwarz, *Zur Geschichte der neuesten Theologie* (Leipzig, 1856), p. 25.

74. Fichte, *Charakteristik,* pp. 1002–1003.

75. Haym, *Hegel und seine Zeit,* pp. 422 ff.

ophy of religion with the "apologetic-restorationist tendency" for which it condemns it.[76]

(4) For all its intensity, the controversy produced no ultimately convincing critique of Hegel's subtle response to the basic questions posed by philosophy of religion. His carefully worked-out solutions were for the most part trumped by cheap claims that believed they were under no necessity of testing their systematic premises and conclusions. Another factor unfavorable to the philosophy of religion was that its diagnosis of the contemporary forms of and threats to Christianity was not widely shared. The treatment it offered met, therefore, with incomprehension. In erecting the philosophy of religion on the basis of the logic, Hegel was indeed drawing the consequences of the failure of a historical grounding of the truth of Christianity and, along with it, of an approach that limited the content of religion to the sphere of inwardness. Anyone who failed to appreciate this motivation was inevitably bound to accuse Hegel of treason—whether against history, or against revelation, or against both. Haym's attempt to go beyond Hegel relapses, like that of other critics, into the antitheses that it was the aim of the speculative philosophy of religion to overcome. Against the grounding of God-manhood on the idea, he deploys Hegel's early approach to Jesus in terms of subjective "certainty of oneness with God,"[77] which is not susceptible of historical proof any more than it is relevant to the argument. In opposition to Hegel he salvages piety or "living faith"—but such faith once again is wholly devoid of any objective content because it is at the same time contrasted with the "shadow-image" of orthodoxy. This is clear from Haym's understanding of dogma as stemming from a need for theoretical insight dissociated from religion and his brief allusions to the history of dogma. For the revolution that had been wrought in the history of theology by Strauss's mythical interpretation, Haym is totally devoid of understanding.

No direct answer to the question whether the philosophy of reli-

76. Ibid., p. 421.
77. Ibid., p. 421.

gion is possible can be arrived at by means of arguments drawn from the philosophy of religion itself. The conditions of its falsifiability were never comprehensively formulated in the discussion of that time. Ultimately they reside in the fundamental problem of the Hegelian system as such, namely the truth of objective thinking. If this theorem remains unassailed, the philosophy of religion too is open only to partial objections. If it is disputed, however, as it was in particular by Feuerbach and also by Schelling and the speculative theists, then the philosophy of religion necessarily is affected too. For this reason the young Feuerbach's criticism of Hegel's doctrine of the identity of content of religion and philosophy remained initially an assertion devoid of force. It was only after he had contested in principle the truth of the *Logic* that he was able to undertake his pioneering critique of religion. It was only rarely, however, that the discussion of the philosophy of religion extended beyond the debate over the Christian character of individual theorems to attain this level of principle. Thus the opportunity for an appropriate investigation of the foundations of the philosophy of religion was thrown away in favor of precipitous agreement on the one side and over-hasty criticism on the other. Nor did the subsequent pronouncements by the Hegelian School pose the problem in its fundamentals any longer; rather they exhausted themselves in repetitions.[78] And the ensuing half-century was to show that there was even less prospect of such investigation after the foreclosure of the discussion initiated by "German idealism." For this foreclosure not only meant giving up any systematic discussion of the philosophy of idealism; it also undermined any historical knowledge of the level of problems with which idealism was concerned.

7. The Controversy over the Concept of Philosophy

(1) Despite the range of themes covered and the confusing multiplicity of charges, rebuttals, and rejoinders, the debates over the speculative philosophy of religion essentially followed a consistent

---

78. This is the view of K. Rosenkranz, *Hegel als deutscher Nationalphilosoph* (Leipzig, 1870), pp. 199 ff.

course. A decade after publication of the lectures, virtually all possibilities of interpretation and critique had been exhausted. From this multiplicity of possible viewpoints two opposing options basically took shape. The first lies in affirming the traditional idea of God and of religion—whether in the form of the right-Hegelian belief that Hegel himself took this option, or in bitter polemic directed against him. In either case the orientation toward a traditional, at times even a radically orthodox, understanding of God and religion spells the intentional or unintentional surrender of Hegel's approach. The motives for this step are not philosophical but religious in nature. In both cases truth is regarded as given by religion in advance, and one's attitude to philosophy depends on whether one understands it to be compatible with this truth.

The second option, radical surrender of the traditional understanding of God and of religion, also abandons Hegel's approach, although it is not true of it in the same way that its motives are nonphilosophical in nature. To be sure, they may in part—as for example with Feuerbach—have taken shape at an early stage in the individual development of those who were later to become critics. But they only became manifest in the debate over the philosophical character of the philosophy of religion. In this dispute the critics increasingly find themselves constrained to recognize the nonidentity of religion and philosophy and so give up the central theorem of the speculative philosophy of religion. This is evident from the way in which Bruno Bauer's writings, as well as Strauss's or Feuerbach's, developed. But the result of this option, like the first, is to point away from philosophy—although only from a philosophy as traditionally understood, in favor of a "new philosophy" oriented to the paradigm of sensuous nature [*Sinnlichkeit*]. To be sure, considerations critical of metaphysics are what first led to the break with philosophy as traditionally understood; but they are bound up with considerations critical of religion as such.

To speak of the discussion as following a consistent course refers to this trend toward the progressive clarification of what is implied by the speculative philosophy of religion, whether it be judged affirmatively or negatively. It does not mean, however, that no options apart from these two are conceivable—such as the option of a strict adherence to the Hegelian standpoint, disregarding all assaults from the side of religion or the right or from the critical philosophy of the left. As representative of this tendency, more so than Rosenkranz, Michelet could be mentioned. But even the spectrum of critique of the philosophy of religion is not exhausted by the two options referred to. An influential group of critics cannot be assigned to either category, namely the critique emanating from Schelling and the so-called late idealists. And Kierkegaard's criticism is different again, though it has several points of contact with this group.

(2) Søren Kierkegaard's analysis of Hegel's philosophy of religion does not actually stand in the context of the internal or external controversies of the Hegel School, although in point of time it belongs to this period and his knowledge of Hegel is partly derived from the writings of his students. There are also some surprising analogies, for instance to Feuerbach's critique of present-day Christianity and of Hegel's claim to reconcile Christianity and reason. The thrust of his critique is partly analogous to Schelling's, to the extent that it defines the limits of a philosophy that seeks to base itself on mere reason instead of submitting to the suprarationality and even irrationality of revelation. At the same time it goes beyond it, insofar as in principle it abandons the objective mode of philosophical search for truth that is common to Hegel and Schelling alike.

Kierkegaard's critique, as it can be ascertained in particular from *Either/Or* and *Fear and Trembling,* or from the *Philosophical Fragments* and the *Concluding Unscientific Postscript,* is not carried out systematically, as is the case with his thought generally. Essentially he accuses the speculative philosophy of religion of three misunderstandings. These do not relate to marginal questions but to the very core of Hegel's approach, namely the role played by logic in the system: (1) the confusion of logic and actuality; (2) the leveling of the boundaries between logic and ethics; and (3) the obliteration of the distinction between the logical and the religious—what it means to exist as a Christian. In Kierkegaard's view this threefold misunderstanding results in Hegel's evaporation of Christian existence into dogmatics, and of dogmatics into logic. This is evident to him especially in the way Hegel defines the central idea of Christianity, the divine-human unity. Christianity, which is essentially "subjectivity," cannot be attained by the objective dispassionateness of speculation. The form of thought to which Hegel subjects Christianity lowers it in Kierkegaard's eyes to the level of mystification on the one hand and to paganism on the other. What matters is the experience of the absolute paradox of faith and not an understanding accessible to reason of an objective truth of Christianity, or indeed recourse to the philosophy of history to trace how the Christian principle is actualized. Objective cognition of the truth of Christianity is replaced by existential praxis—the problem of living as a Christian. For Hegel this is a problem that has to be disposed of before embarking on philosophy; in other words, it is not a philosophical problem. It is for this reason that Kierkegaard's objections aim more strongly even than Feuerbach's critique at a revision of the concept of philosophy.

It has always been difficult to determine, however, to what extent Kierkegaard was affected in working out his position by a productive encounter with Hegel's philosophy. Leaving this problem of Kierkegaard research aside, it must be borne in mind, when we pay closer attention to his reception and criticism of the speculative philosophy of religion, that his approach does not merely shy away from any explicit (even if critical) assessment of the systematic fundamental problems of the philosophy of religion, but is so confrontational in its tendency that any productive discussion of the fundamental questions that have been left open by this approach becomes difficult, if not impossible, even subsequently.

(3) Unlike Kierkegaard's critique, that of Schelling and the late idealists does not go beyond the framework of the traditional understanding of philosophy, even if each modifies it in his own fashion. This group of critics has already been referred to in passing, especially in connection with the topics of the personality of God and the immortality of the soul. The importance of these critics, however, is not confined to the objections they raised in that regard. It lies in the fact that, in dialogue with Hegel (even if partly unavowed), they worked out and introduced into the current debate alternatives to the speculative conception of the philosophy of reli-

gion that came to exert a major influence on the debate's progress and conclusion. The epoch-making importance of the controversy over Hegel's philosophy of religion is also clear from the fact that these supposedly better alternatives, which at that time did not venture beyond the territory of traditional philosophy, could be rejected as even less firmly secured than the system they aspired to improve or to overcome.

We do not intend in any way to present this group as if it were inwardly uniform. Walter Schulz has rightly protested against the idea that Schelling was, as it were, the head of the late idealists. On the contrary, he tends to trace the late idealists back to Hegel in all too unbroken fashion. But the chief motives for the late-idealist critique of Hegel do not derive from an encounter with his philosophy; they predate it, and have some aspects in common with Schelling's thought. Above all, the late idealists do not in any way propose a uniform critique or an identical alternative to the speculative philosophy of religion. At the beginning of the discussion, in the early 1830s, it might indeed appear that this was the case. But as the debate proceeded it became clear that the divergences between Fichte and Weisse, for example, were no less serious than those between Schelling and Weisse. No detailed account has yet appeared of the way in which these divergences developed until they led to the complete fragmentation and open rupture of the circle centering on the *Zeitschrift für Philosophie und spekulative Theologie* in the 1840s. Such an account would also have to consider the different stages of development in the numerous works published by the individual members of this circle in the nearly forty years between 1826 and 1862.[79]

Notwithstanding all the differences between them, the late idealists are at one in proclaiming the need to pass beyond Hegel's idea of God to a "living," "free," "actual," "personal" God. But the path to this goal is described in very differing fashion. In part it leads beyond idealism. Rather than speak of "late idealism" it might thus be more correct to refer to this group as "speculative

---

79. In addition to C. H. Weisse and I. H. Fichte, see especially J. Sengler, C. P. Fischer, H. Ulrici, U. Wirth, and H. M. Chalybäus.

theists"—provided that theism is not defined as excluding the idea
of an immanent trinity. The speculative theists also agree with one
another and with Schelling in perceiving that there is a necessary
connection between Hegel's a priori approach and his results. This
distinguishes them from the right-Hegelians, who as it were expect
the tree of the Hegelian system to bear fruits that are quite incapable of growing on it. For this reason the speculative theists,
with Schelling, call at least for a revision of the method, if not for
the replacement of the Hegelian concept of philosophy by a new
one that does not methodically preclude attainment of the goal in
view, namely knowledge of the personality of God.

(4) Let us here refer briefly to three of these counterproposals to
the speculative philosophy of religion—those of Weisse, Fichte, and
Schelling. They make plain the difficulty of arriving at an alternative conception that at the same time keeps to the soil of traditional
philosophy. Of these three, C. H. Weisse's conception comes closest
to Hegel. He alone was accounted a sympathizer of the School in
his early years. He nevertheless expressed the difference between
himself and Hegel at an early date. His writings prior to the mid-
1830s formulate it even more sharply than his portrayal of Hegelian philosophy in his *Sendschreiben* to Fichte of 1842, which forms
the high point of the controversy between the speculative theists
and the speculative philosophy of religion.

The early writings are full of sharp invective against Hegel's idea
of logic, against the transformation of the world in all its bloom
"into the shadow-image of a metaphysical ghost."[80] The accusations contained in these writings betray all too clearly a misunderstanding of the idea of the logic. Hegel too can call logic abstract
or term it the science of form—but not without adding that it is
the science of pure, absolute form, which manifests itself as actuality. For Weisse, by contrast, it remains pure, abstracted form, and
content only begins once such form is left behind. He therefore
criticizes the logic for confusing form and content, ground and essence, concept and idea,[81] asserting that it hypostatizes absolute

80. Weisse, *Verhältnis des Publikums*, p. 26.
81. Weisse, *Gegenwärtiger Standpunkt*, p. 209.

knowledge or the idea of truth "into an objective reality that is regarded as immediately one and the same as this idea."[82] This understanding of the logic forms the presupposition for Weisse's critique of Hegel's speculative theology and philosophy of religion. In his eyes Hegel is not simply guilty of misunderstanding what logic actually is and can do. He believes that Hegel compounds this misunderstanding by reducing speculative theology and the philosophy of religion to logic. This brings about the "deification of the abstract, logical, or metaphysical world of the concept"; it confuses the logical idea "with the most wonderful and superabundant of all ideas, the idea of divinity."[83] Putting it even more incisively, Hegel's pantheism substitutes "the nothingness of the concept for the superabundant depth and fullness of the Christian Godhead."[84] And Weisse accordingly accuses Hegel's philosophy not only of pantheism and atheism but even of nihilism.[85]

Weisse's view of the logic can be described as a sheer misunderstanding but also as an intentional critique of it. For the divergence between him and Hegel is based on the fact that he rejects the ontological proof as Hegel understands it.[86] Yet it is a simple error on his part that he regards Hegel's speculative theology and also the philosophy of religion as limited to the logic; thus he maintains the error of Hegel's system to reside in the fact that "the intuitions and representations, feelings and doctrines of religion have no other content than this form of the pure concept as a basis."[87] This erroneous assessment of speculative theology in the narrower sense as well as of the philosophy of religion does, to be sure, date from the years preceding publication of the lectures on the philosophy of religion. It is based on Hegel's statement in the Heidelberg *En-*

---

82. Weisse, *Idee der Gottheit,* p. 226.
83. Weisse, *Verhältnis des Publikums,* pp. 27, 32.
84. Ibid., p. 35.
85. Weisse, *Idee der Gottheit,* p. 225.
86. See Dieter Henrich, *Der ontologische Gottesbeweis* (Tübingen, 1967); cf. also Harald Knudsen, *Gottesbeweise im deutschen Idealismus* (Berlin and New York, 1972), pp. 204 ff.
87. Weisse, *Gegenwärtiger Standpunkt,* p. 212.

cyclopedia that at the close of the system the logic acquires the signification of speculative theology.[88]

Unlike Weisse's *Ästhetik* of 1830, the significance of these early writings as far as the philosophy of religion is concerned resides in Weisse's critique of Hegel's conception (or what he deems to be Hegel's conception). An alternative to Hegel's standpoint is indicated more in negative terms than positive. What Weisse *wants* to prove is clearer than how he proposes to go about it. For him the goal is to bring about a "new period of philosophy, a philosophy that offers a true reconciliation with religion and empirical science and no longer contrives to bring about the appearance of such a reconciliation by means of metaphysical formulae."[89] Despite the fact that Weisse formulates this goal in explicit opposition to Hegel, it does not differ, in the abstract way it is formulated, from the concern of the speculative philosophy of religion. Nor, taken abstractly, does the other stipulation voiced in the same context diverge from Hegel's program, namely that the exalted belief in God that first emerged in Christianity be expressed in a form that also satisfies the requirements of a methodologically rigorous philosophy. It is only in the execution of this program that the contrast between Hegel and Weisse becomes evident.

Weisse's first exposition of his counter-concept is in his treatise *Die Idee der Gottheit* (1833). He notes in the preface that he had been able "while in press still to make use of and take into account"[90] Hegel's lectures on the philosophy of religion, which had appeared a short time previously. This came too late, however, to have any effect on the conception of his text. Weisse continues to deplore the fact that Hegel had "foisted off" the idea of speculative

---

88. *Enc* 1st ed. § 19. The reason why Hegel did not repeat this observation in the later editions of the *Encyclopedia* is probably that it tends to obscure the way in which the concept of God, as it unfolds, leads beyond the logic. Weisse does indeed note that Hegel did not repeat this statement in the second edition (cf. *Gegenwärtiger Standpunkt*, pp. 117–118); but he regards this as meaning that "the interest of logical thought is treated throughout as one and the same with interest in knowledge of the divine."

89. Weisse, *Verhältnis des Publikums*, p. 41.

90. Weisse, *Idee der Gottheit*, p. vii.

truth as such as the idea of divinity.[91] His protest against identifying logic with speculative theology accounts for the fact that the latter is dealt with only at the close of Weisse's system, following his treatment of aesthetics. His work in fact covers only the first part of speculative theology, the idea of divinity. The other two parts, "philosophy of religion" and "religious ethics," were not expounded in corresponding fashion. We do not therefore know how Weisse intended actually to link speculative theology in the narrower sense, the "idea of divinity," and the philosophy of religion. But the part we do have already treats the problems that show whether his criticism of Hegel is justified.

The striking claim made by his treatise is that it leads to secure philosophical knowledge of God. It promises not only the knowledge of God as such, but knowledge of the actual God, not simply the abstract, dead God of Hegel's logic. Weisse seeks to attain to the actual idea of divinity (part 3) or to the teleological concept by passing through the ontological concept of God (part 1), which is identified with pantheism, and the cosmological concept, which is identified with deism (part 2). Part 1 comprises the dialectical deduction of the concept of divinity from the ideas of truth and beauty; part 2, God's extramundane character and his personality; and part 3, the concept of the divine trinity. As far as can be seen from these declarations of intent, Weisse's program is still very similar to Hegel's. The similarity is further underlined by his verbal adherence to the "dialectical method." But the way in which Weisse carries out his project contrasts sharply with this proclamation as well as in general with his boastful claim to have arrived at a fundamental and vital insight. It is clear from the execution that, for all his assertions that he is improving Hegel's system, the philosophical horizon of the speculative philosophy of religion has been obscured for Weisse by the desire to demonstrate the personality and extramundane character of the trinitarian God. The question of the constitution of pure thinking as well as of absolute subjectivity has all but vanished even from historical reminiscence.

91. Ibid., p. 162.

This characteristic of the post-idealist approach is evident above all in the three dialectical deductions we have referred to. Certainly Weisse conceals the arbitrariness of each of his "dialectical transitions" behind lengthy expositions. But even this cannot make any of them convincing. The decisive step beyond Hegel would have to lie in the deduction of the extramundane character and the personality of God. The shaky ground on which this step is taken is clear from Weisse's own formulation. The dialectical transition he indicates from the ontological concept of divinity to the cosmological is supposed to be proof of the extra- and supramundane existence of God.[92] Yet it consists in nothing other than the plea for a "higher unity" of the ideas of truth and beauty—a "unity of being, . . . which as such forms the common substance of truth and beauty, but is related to every individual thing that is true and beautiful as the spiritually absolute ground, which, without surrendering its unity and selfhood, moves into the world of phenomenal existence as into the externally infinite, fragmented counterpart of its inner and yet utterly present infinitude." This brings us no closer to demonstrating the supramundane personality of God. As a mediating element Weisse therefore introduces the further assumption that the "content of the idea of truth and beauty grasped in the shape of particularity and singularity . . . is conceived under the name of *world* as what is grounded, over against divinity as the ground." And, for Weisse, it is in fact the moment of beauty that for the first time comes to consciousness in the concept of world, driving this concept beyond itself, and shaping itself "into the certainty of an otherworldly ground of the world . . . because it is beauty that is guardian of that concept of unity that has been lost in the concept of world but . . . can never be eradicated."[93]

It would probably be difficult to find a less convincing demonstration of the idea of God as such or of the extramundane character of God in particular. Yet the manifest lack of logical rigor is even more evident in the case of the proof of the personality of this God, concerning which Weisse also undertakes to render an "exact

92. Ibid., p. 157.
93. Ibid., pp. 158–159.

account." He elevates the concept of genius to the level of an "anticipation of the divine personality in the aesthetic field," and calls for this progress in the definition of absolutely spiritual consciousness to be reflected also in the higher fields of scholarship: "The highest concrete unity of spiritually absolute consciousness, the hypostatized idea of truth, to which the totality of the aesthetic sphere has to trace its origin, must receive from it the attribute of self-consciousness."[94] Nor do Weisse's other attempts really take him any closer to the desired goal—such as the assertion that it is "above all the necessity of finding a ground and a concrete unity for the already known content of absolute spirit that leads to the concept of divine personality."[95]

The cognitive value of such deductions is discussed by Weisse in a subsequent passage. The view he expresses there is that in fact pantheism and deism—in other words, the transition to the concepts of divinity as well as personality and extramundane character—lead only to nihilism because they ground only "an extratemporal, metaphysical category of divinity, but not the knowledge of a God who is eternally and at all times actual." For Weisse this ultimate step is reached only with the deduction of the doctrine of the trinity. This deduction is, however, open to objections similar to those brought against the two preceding ones. As long as the method remains the same, it is not possible to see what could raise the third step above the level of category to actuality. Weisse refers here to the teleological proof, indeed to both the physico- and the ethicotheological proofs: faith in a personal creator of the world, he tells us, finds itself conditioned in this regard "by the demand for an omnipotent actualizer of the idea of the supreme good."[96]

In this third part also his highly self-conscious exposition nowhere attains insight into the level of problems encountered in the speculative philosophy of religion. It cannot be said that his approach demands a change in the concept of philosophy. Externally Weisse's concept of philosophy preserves continuity with ideal-

94. Ibid., pp. 165–166.
95. Ibid., p. 167.
96. Ibid., p. 242.

ist philosophy—hence his repeated assurance that he is following Hegel's dialectical method. But in fact other elements have become determining. They occasionally surface in methodological reflections, for example in the statement that what is involved in the concept of divine personality is "whether the dialectic of the universal concept that has been attained must remain an empty formalism, or whether it can be filled in by a . . . representational content."[97] As far as the nature of his advance is concerned, the decisive factor is that the general thread of his treatment is determined by elements of nonphilosophical provenance, namely the self-imposed task to demonstrate, in opposition to Hegel, the personality of God and the immortality of the soul. The unsatisfactory element in his approach might therefore be held to reside in the fact that as speculative—just as Hegel's approach had been—it was unsuited for realization of its self-appointed end. But this impression cannot be maintained in regard to Weisse's speculative theology because his conception—if only because of its depreciation of logic and disregard for the problems posed by the constitution of pure subjectivity—is totally unaffected by the constellation of problems that characterizes idealism as a whole.

After his *Idee der Gottheit*, Weisse assessed his relationship to Hegel's philosophy of religion, in part implicitly, in part explicitly, on several other occasions. His *Metaphysik* (1835) enters of course into only one sector of the problems, and his *Philosophische Dogmatik* (1855–1862) dates from a period when the controversy over Hegel's philosophy of religion is already a thing of the past. But he does take up this issue in his *Sendschreiben* to Fichte, in a much more nuanced manner than before. And he carefully distances himself from his position in the *Idee der Gottheit*.[98] His new attitude to Hegel's philosophy is, to be sure, not entirely consistent. There are several vacillations of judgment; these are probably due either to the polemical purpose of the *Sendschreiben* or to the necessity of bringing his position into the closest possible harmony with Schelling's late philosophy. His new assessment of Hegel's philos-

97. Ibid., p. 159.
98. C. H. Weisse, *Das philosophische Problem der Gegenwart: Sendschreiben an I. H. Fichte* (Leipzig, 1842), pp. 211–212.

ophy rests on two insights. The first of these did not actually stem from a deepened study of Hegel's philosophy but from his taking over Schelling's distinction between negative and positive philosophy.[99] With Schelling he now deals more justly with the *Logic* than in his previous critique: in the *Logic*, he tells us, Hegel recognized the *prius*—the absolute idea—"for what it in truth is, namely something subsistent and absolute [*ein Seiendes und Absolutes*]." Yet at the same time he joins Schelling in censuring Hegel for having "treated the *prius* as though it were already on its own account the totality of the genuinely subsistent, the absolute."[100] The new appreciation of the *Logic* also extends to the judgment regarding its theological dimension: as pure science of reason, as science of the absolute *prius*, metaphysics can "also lay claim directly on its own account to the meaning of speculative theology." Its categories are ipso facto determinations of divinity—although not of the personal, free God. Yet it is only in the logic that the truth of the concept of God is to be sought. For Weisse, unlike Fichte or even Rosenkranz, the logic therefore needs no prior "original subject" [*Ursubjekt*] to which the logical determinations can be ascribed as attributes. In affirming this theological dimension of the logic, Weisse acts as though he has to defend it against Hegel, whom he reproaches with having been led by a striving for popularity to delete from the Heidelberg *Encyclopedia* the statement that at the end of the system the logic acquires the meaning of a speculative theology.[101]

Weisse's emphasis on the justified theological claim of the logic stands in contrast, however, with the second insight modifying his

99. Ibid., p. 91.
100. Ibid., p. 103. For his critique of this confusion, see pp. 115, 118 ff., and 131.
101. Ibid., p. 209. On the question of the personality of God, see pp. 139, 159–160. Weisse distorts Hegel's definition of the theological dimension of the logic when he says that Hegel attributed "to this science, transposed to the end of the system, the meaning of speculative theology" (p. 137). What Hegel is concerned with is not a "transposition" of this sort or a repetition of the logic at the end of the system, but the fact that it is only from the end that the authentic meaning of the logic can be clearly seen. For only from the end can it be seen that the real sublates itself and returns into the pure idea, and that logical universality is not something particular alongside the wealth of the real world, but contains the latter within itself and thus is true and concrete universality. See above, pp. 401–402.

assessment of Hegel's philosophy of religion, and also with his critique of the conception underlying Hegel's system as a whole. The philosophy-of-religion lectures show Weisse that Hegel does not confine speculative theology to logic. Now he even acknowledges that the philosophy of religion recognizes a living, personal God.[102] This modifies his judgment as to the extent to which Hegel's system as a whole qualifies as philosophy of religion. But Weisse is no longer capable of discerning the connection between the idea of God in the logic and in the philosophy of religion. It follows from his view that the logic (or the system in general) and the philosophy of religion fall apart in total unrelatedness.[103] To make the gulf between them crystal clear, Weisse again debases the idea of God in the logic, asserting that it is nothing but a "dead abstraction, disposed of once and for all, derived from a common, not a Christian, theism."[104]

By contrast with Hegel's supposed lack of mediation between the ontological and religiophilosophical ideas of God, Weisse regards his own system as characterized by a necessary connection between these two factors in the concept of God. He fails to recognize the inner unity of speculative theology and philosophy of religion in Hegel's system, although the elaboration of this unity had been the unifying principle of the system since Hegel's Jena period. In several respects Weisse's conception even displays extensive similarity with Hegel's, for instance in his acceptance of a "dialectical progression to be achieved gradually from the concept of the world, via the whole of the philosophy of the real, to the concept of God."[105] Indeed, this process coincides with the demonstration of the necessity of the religious standpoint. Hegel never surrendered the idea of such a demonstration, but only removed it in successive stages from the philosophy of religion itself. Even the attempt to match the individual stages of the constitution of the idea of God with the ontological and cosmological (and with it the teleological) proofs is carried through by Weisse in a fashion similar to Hegel. He even

102. Ibid., p. 257.
103. Ibid., esp. pp. 257, 258, 309.
104. Ibid., p. 257.
105. Ibid., p. 211.

tries to establish an explicit unity between Hegel's ontological and religiophilosophical ideas of God by identifying the former with the abstract moment of the "Father," in other words, with the first moment of the trinitarian idea of God in the philosophy of religion.[106]

At the same time Weisse adheres to his conception of a gulf between Hegel's system and the philosophy of religion, and on the basis of his premises he is right to do so. For he believes it possible to discern in the philosophy of religion the idea of a personal and extramundane God—an idea that surely cannot be introduced into a system that Weisse classifies by and large as a "negative philosophy" even if its tendency is to break through the limits this implies. Thus it is just because he misunderstands the philosophy of religion that Weisse can see in it "an instinct of genuine Christian orthodoxy"[107] and attain an affirmative attitude to it, yet reject the system.

This dilemma confirms once again the choice that exists between a consistent interpretation of the Hegelian system, including the philosophy of religion, and the specific form that the idea of a personal God has come to have in the Christian religion. This choice not only causes the gulf that Weisse criticizes in Hegel's system but also affects his own approach. For his claim is that he does not derive the idea of a personal and extramundane God from prior revelation. To be sure, he recognizes the doctrine of the trinity in its ecclesiastical form as a kind of spiritual norm from which one cannot deviate without prejudicing the knowledge of truth.[108] In this regard Weisse initially proposes the procedure of supplementing and filling out the "empty ontological possibility" by means of "intramundane facts of revelation," that is "by a content that for the first time gives me the concept of an *actual* God, a God who *is* and *exists*." A little later, however, he lays great weight on the fact that he develops not merely the ontological idea of God but also that of a personal, living God, not from revelation but "from other premises."[109] He does indeed endeavor to do so—but fails in the

106. Ibid., pp. 275–276.
107. Ibid., p. 264.
108. Ibid., p. 265.
109. Ibid., pp. 215, 217.

attempt, not because of an avoidable error or a personal incapacity, but on objective grounds. A "dialectical deduction" of the living, personal God "from other premises" would in fact undermine Schelling's distinction between negative and positive philosophy, to which Weisse now rallies for the sake of his critique of Hegel. Thus he tries to bring about on his own a concept of philosophy that conjoins the rigorous method of dialectical knowledge and the idea of God of the Christian religion in its traditional form. The failure of this attempt is a further argument in favor of renouncing one or the other in the interests of consistency. Either Hegel's idea of God is recognized as the outcome of philosophical inquiry into the nature of God, an inquiry that is conducted in terms of pure thought and leads to a result that is consistent in method and appropriate in content; or, at least in the theoretical situation that obtained at the time, one is driven to accept the view of Fichte and Schelling that the absolute is not accessible to such inquiry.

(5) I. H. Fichte also underwent a clear change in his understanding and critique of the speculative philosophy of religion, and his own approach changed accordingly. Two elements, however, persist virtually unchanged throughout his numerous writings: that it is the highest goal of speculation "to recognize the personal God in the unconditioned," and that speculation is solely a propaedeutic to the doctrine and the spirit of Christianity, to which it is therefore subordinate.[110] Initially Fichte claims to have deduced, in "a purely speculative and consistent fashion," even the character of the true redeemer as he appeared in the human race.[111] He also indicates initially that the personality of God is imperceptible, to be sure, but not unthinkable.[112] Here already the theme of "experience" is announced.[113] Following Hegel's death and the publication of the philosophy-of-religion lectures, Fichte became an increasingly sharp critic of speculative philosophy. He calls for a "new philosophy" negating Hegel's, "a philosophical theology of personality, of

110. Fichte, *Vorschule*, pp. xxxviii, 236.

111. Ibid., p. 225.

112. I. H. Fichte, *Ueber Gegensatz, Wendepunkt und Ziel heutiger Philosophie* (Heidelberg, 1832), p. xxiii.

113. Ibid., pp. xxiv ff.

the freely self-revealing deed, whereby one might finally hope to reconcile apriorism and intuition, history and speculation."[114] To Hegel's assertion of the necessity of the concept Fichte opposes freedom—the philosophy of freedom in contrast to the philosophy of the concept.[115] And over against Hegel's "complete emptying of all content from Christianity," Fichte stresses "the deeply personal qualities of the highest personality."[116] He regards this idea of the personality of God as so important that he criticizes Hegel and also Weisse's *Idee der Gottheit* because both of them put this idea only at the end of philosophy, whereas its place is at the beginning—in ontology or even epistemology.[117]

Fichte is well aware that such a change of place within the system cannot be effected at will. Placed at the beginning of the system, the idea of God cannot be the result of the cognitive knowledge furnished by the logic and the whole of the philosophy of the real. In any event Fichte does not envisage a cognitive appraisal of this kind, regarding it as nothing short of an expression of philosophical hubris. Speculation must turn back from exclusive apriorism "to humility and studiousness," leaving behind the "insolence of an a priori mode of knowing."[118] Elevation to the idea of personality necessarily involves severance of the a priori thread. A priori knowledge, the entire dialectical development of the concept, is in Fichte's eyes no more than a subordinate form of knowledge.[119] This corresponds to his constantly reiterated understanding of the propaedeutic function of a speculative logic.

In his writings of the early 1830s Fichte takes the view that there is a consistent linkage in Hegel's system between his method and his idea of God, since both are erroneous.[120] But he rejects in the sharpest way possible the efforts of the right-Hegelians to seek as-

114. I. H. Fichte, *Religion und Philosophie in ihrem gegenwärtigen Verhältnisse* (Heidelberg, 1834), p. v.

115. Ibid., pp. 4–5.

116. Ibid., pp. 17–18.

117. Ibid., p. 30.

118. I. H. Fichte, *Ueber die Bedingungen eines speculativen Theismus* (Elberfeld, 1835), p. 43.

119. Fichte, *Idee der Persönlichkeit*, p. 11.

120. Ibid., p. 10.

surance of the personality of God and individual immortality by recourse to dialectical knowledge based on reason. One can accept unreservedly the justice of this criticism. If one does so, it would seem plausible to have renounced all knowledge of God. But this cannot be said for Fichte's attempt to substitute for Hegel's conceptual thinking a new mode of cognition suited to the goal that had eluded Hegel—whether it appears under the pretentious title of a "speculative-intuitive knowing"[121] or in the somewhat more modest and in fact inconsequential assertion that we are capable of conceiving absolute self-consciousness, the "original I" or original personality of God, because we are ourselves persons.[122] It remains uncertain how one is to conceive of such a "positive mode of knowing the divine spirit, penetrating into the secret of its personality, its thoughts and decisions."[123] Fichte does indeed regard the complete knowledge of God, "according to his a priori concept of form," as not only possible but already achieved in his *Ontologie,* and he regards this as also covering the idea of spirit and of personality. But the latter is achieved only in the transition from the *Ontologie* to the *Spekulative Theologie.*[124] Methodologically speaking, the relationship between these parts of the system corresponds to the transition from negative, contradiction-resolving dialectic to positive dialectic. But even the latter is not yet positive knowledge properly speaking. For in Fichte's view the inaccessible secret of God's personality can be unlocked only "by the free act of revelation." It lies beyond all apriority, whether negatively or positively dialectical.[125]

Here again it is doubtful whether use of a negative-dialectical method to expound the concept of the personality of God in §§ 293 ff. of the *Ontologie* achieves Fichte's aim of exhausting

121. I. H. Fichte, *Grundzüge zum System der Philosophie,* part 1, *Das Erkennen als Selbsterkennen* (Heidelberg, 1833), pp. 311 ff.

122. Fichte, *Idee der Persönlichkeit,* p. 70.

123. Fichte, *Ontologie,* p. 38.

124. [Tr.] *Die speculative Theologie oder allgemeine Religionslehre* (Heidelberg, 1846) is the third part of Fichte's *Grundzüge zum System der Philosophie,* of which *Die Ontologie* (1836) is the second part and *Das Erkennen als Selbsterkennen* (1833) is the first part.

125. Fichte, *Ontologie,* pp. 34 ff.

the form of actuality of the absolute; it is doubtful whether he succeeds in showing the ascent "from the concept of the unifying all-consciousness to the necessity of the eternally one self-consciousness" in the elevation of the concept of absolute thought to the personality of God.[126] Section 297 cites the arguments for the transition: "the unity of purpose in the infinite," "the infusion of every individual thing with infinitude," and "the ideal preexistence of the original image of the world."[127] None of these premises can be conceived without contradiction, according to Fichte, unless the personality of God is presupposed. But this can for good reasons be contested: above all it is doubtful whether the premises are justified. But if one concluded that Fichte's argumentation is valid, one would also have to acknowledge that he had succeeded—again without going beyond a priori knowledge and the negative-dialectical method—in expounding the concept even if not yet the actuality of a personal God—assuming one is willing to accept this distinction.

Yet Fichte himself a little later no longer seems convinced on this score. His reply to Weisse's *Sendschreiben* explicitly rejects the separation of the concept and the reality of God as well as Schelling's distinction between negative and positive philosophy.[128] In numerous other respects too he succeeds in correcting Weisse's understanding of Hegel's philosophy and rejecting Weisse's doctrine of the personality of God as lacking foundation.[129] From this he infers the need to turn one's back wholly on pure formal thinking and the coercion of logical thought, to forsake the deceptive soil of dialectic with its spinning out of mere conceptual abstractions, and to move into the realm of experience. He now sees the world of pure concepts as a soft, easily malleable element.[130] Instead of digging in the sterile desert of the a priori for fountains of living water, he would have us bathe in the one eternally flowing spring of life

126. Ibid., p. 513.
127. Ibid., p. 515.
128. I. H. Fichte, "Der Begriff des negativ Absoluten und der negativen Philosophie," in *Vermischte Schriften zur Philosophie, Theologie und Ethik* (Leipzig, 1869), pp. 165–166.
129. Ibid., p. 204.
130. Ibid., pp. 207, 216.

constituted by the real. And he interposes another argument for switching from speculation to an empirical approach, an argument that is not to be reckoned among the strongest—namely that by adopting an approach based on actuality and truth even those who are speculatively less talented could with a modicum of diligence achieve some results.[131]

Using this alternative approach, Fichte now seeks to realize the old goal of a nonspeculative knowledge of God's personality. It is open to question, however, whether the change in the concept of philosophy really brings him closer to this goal. At all events he now believes he has shown that the immanence of divine spirit in the world rests on the absolute transcendence of a divine personality that is free from the world, self-conscious and all-conscious. He even invokes his scientific proofs "that the universe subsists only through the presence of divine spirit in it"; and he sees in such reasoning "true philosophy" and the "true religion of the future."[132] And he forswears not only a priori speculation but also the historical element in Christianity, which is in any case no longer believed—in favor of a new faith whose world-saving power may soon manifest itself more profoundly "than in any previous epoch since Christianity came on the scene."[133] The terms in which he proclaims this new faith and the age of divinely illumined science, both here and in the preface to the slightly later *Spekulative Theologie,* are such as to throw doubt on Strauss's right to the title of "cultural philistine."[134] But beyond this, Fichte's account affords no evidence of any more far-reaching contribution to solving the problem of idealist philosophy, a problem to which Hegel's conception of the unity of speculative theology and philosophy of religion consistently claimed to provide an answer.

(6) Fichte's critique of the speculative philosophy of religion, and to an even greater extent Weisse's, were fanned by varied reports that were circulating concerning Schelling's late philosophy. It was

131. Ibid., p. 210.
132. Ibid., pp. 210–212.
133. Ibid., pp. 212–213. Cf. *Spekulative Theologie,* esp. p. xx.
134. [Tr.] It was Friedrich Nietzsche who bestowed this title upon Strauss in his *Untimely Meditations,* trans. R. J. Hollingdale (Cambridge, 1983), pp. 7 ff.

reported that Schelling had distinguished between two methodologically distinct sides of a single philosophy, the positive and the negative side, which, already in Schelling's own terms, were in danger
of being understood as two different forms of philosophy. In particular the distinction Schelling drew between the absolute *prius* as
the negatively universal, without which no knowledge is possible,
and the positive, through which knowledge comes about (*SW* 10:
213–214), contributed to a better understanding of the methodological scope and the speculative-theological competence of logic,
even if this distinction finally was not adopted by Weisse and was
expressly rejected by Fichte. And apart from these two, Schelling's
intimations formed, during the 1830s and early 1840s, a point of
reference and criterion for discussion that were all the more fruitful
because it was none too clear just what his own view was.[135]

Schelling's philosophical approach during these later years can
be directly understood as providing a measure to assess the theological and religiophilosophical dimension of speculative philosophy. As such it acquired considerable importance in the debates
between Hegel's students and his critics from the theist camp. But
neither Schelling's later approach nor his own explicit criticism of
Hegel belongs in the context of these debates. He refers only occasionally to Hegel's students or to the speculative theists. When he
does condescend to do so, his utterances could not be more sharp
and disdainful. The efforts of the speculative theists he regards as
"moutarde après diner"; and concerning the "sentimental and
pietistic phrases" of the right-Hegelians (he obviously has Göschel
in mind) we are told that they could "only excite disgust in any
thinker worth his salt" and that Hegel has to be defended against
the affront inflicted on him by his partisans (*SW* 13:92).

Schelling's critique of Hegel's philosophy of religion is not as
explicit as might have been expected given its importance and also
its value for an understanding of his own philosophical develop-

---

135. [*Tr.*] Schelling's Berlin lecture manuscripts on *Philosophie der Mythologie*
and *Philosophie der Offenbarung* were not published until after his death in 1854
as the second division of *SW*—now generally numbered continuously with the first
division as vols. 11–14. The concluding volume of the first division, *SW* 10, contained mostly unpublished shorter writings from 1833 to 1850.

ment. For he is at pains to reduce Hegel's philosophy in general to the level of an "episode," and a sorry one at that.[136] Furthermore, his late philosophy is conceived before the publication of Hegel's philosophy-of-religion lectures. Finally, his distinction between positive and negative philosophy represents such a fundamental critique of Hegel's philosophy of religion that it may have seemed neither necessary nor sensible to enter extensively into detail. In the light of this distinction, Hegel's approach necessarily appeared as a supreme example of a failed negative philosophy, which, heedless of its limits, seeks to reach out beyond the bounds of a philosophy based on mere logical reason and to pass itself off as positive philosophy (*SW* 13:80).

Schelling's critique is therefore primarily a critique of the logic and its foundational function for Hegel's system—a critique of the claim to transcend the realm of merely logical knowledge and to be capable of grasping actuality, a claim that makes it the most repulsive and petty logical dogmatism (*SW* 13:82). From Schelling's opposition of positive and purely rational philosophy stem a number of further objections: to Hegel's understanding of revelation as manifestation of the concept; to the thesis, already implied in this, that God is wholly revelatory; to the merely logical, abstract formulation of trinitarian doctrine, which prevents God from being genuinely conceived as person; to the supposedly free externalization of the idea to become nature (regarding which Schelling refers to the change in viewpoint from the *Logic* to the *Encyclopedia*); and finally to Hegel's assertion that God is not God without the world and only in subjective spirit attains his self-consciousness. Despite the seemingly fragmentary nature of the direct and indirect critical references with which the *Philosophie der Offenbarung* (*SW* 13–14) is strewn, these—together with the chapter devoted to Hegel in the *Vorlesungen zur Geschichte der neueren Philosophie* (*SW* 10:126 ff.)—form the most complete internal critique of the content of Hegel's philosophy of religion. For their starting point is not the interpretation of individual passages but reflection on

136. See *SW* 10:125; also *Aus Schellings Leben*, ed. G. L. Plitt (Leipzig, 1869–1870), 3:63.

what is in fact conceivable for a philosophy that rests on a merely logical basis.

The distinction between negative and positive philosophy forms the most egregious criterion for evaluating Hegel's philosophy. If one accepts it, then Schelling's judgment regarding the Hegelian system is unavoidable. But it is doubtful whether his principle of a dual structure of philosophy in general is appropriate to the assessment of Hegel's system. Undoubtedly Hegel's philosophies of nature and spirit move into regions that, according to Schelling's classification, are reserved for positive philosophy. For their object is not mere possibility but the real, that is, actual processes and events (SW 13:89). At the same time Hegel's philosophy does not, by reason of methodological considerations, go as far as Schelling's positive philosophy aspires. It does, to be sure, aim at actuality, but at knowing reason in actuality, without thereby making actuality merely rational. If, for example, it is seeking reason in religion, it does not in any way understand religion as something purely rational, as something that moves exclusively within the limits of reason alone. The distinction drawn between negative and positive philosophy is not therefore a sufficient objection to Hegel's concept of philosophy. To refute this concept it would be necessary to show that it is impossible and senseless to look for the rational in actuality—and for reason in religion.

The fact that for Hegel this is the goal means that the limits to what his philosophy of religion can affirm are much narrower than what Schelling is willing to accept for his positive philosophy. Because Hegel's philosophy of religion does not regard itself as positive philosophy in Schelling's sense, it does not proceed to the results Schelling allows his empiricism, namely "that the true God is not mere universal being, but is himself at the same time a particular or empirical being" (SW 10:216). Had it been Hegel's view that his philosophy could assert this—and this was the opinion of the right-Hegelians—he would indeed have offended against his concept of philosophy. Schelling's barbed words against Hegel's dogmatism would then be justified. But as has been shown in chapters 2 and 3 above, especially in regard to the bitterly disputed themes of the personality of God and christology, such an assumption is erroneous.

Schelling's fundamental distinction is at odds with Hegel's concept of philosophy. It also severs the link that for Hegel holds the system together, namely the unity of speculative theology and philosophy of religion. Indeed, it is only on the basis of the final discipline of the system, the philosophy of religion, that the logic can be viewed as speculative theology. And it is only at the end of the system that the idea of God, the first metaphysical definitions of which form the first categories of the logic, is explicated in appropriate form. If it is to be in any way truth, the idea of God cannot, in Hegel's view, be divided into a negative and a positive part of philosophy. The methodological unity of philosophy is in his eyes a sine qua non for the divine to be known both in the logic and as it is manifest in the philosophy of the real, including the philosophy of religion.

Hegel thus conceives the unity of the system in terms different from those in which Schelling sees the interface between negative and positive philosophy (*SW* 13:92–93). But he also conceives purely rational philosophy in terms different from those in which Schelling understands negative philosophy. For in Hegel's view the ontological proof in its new speculative formulation means that in the logic the division between essence [*Wesen*] and existence [*Existenz*]—*that* something is and *what* it is—is sublated. And there are grounds for assuming that the reason why Schelling cannot effectively contest the argumentative justification of this proof in Hegel's work is that his own concept of "unpreconceivable being" [*unvordenkliches Sein*] also necessitates the same transition from concept to being.[137] Fichte, therefore, is not wrong when, in countering Weisse's invocation of the fundamental distinction in Schelling's late philosophy, he refers to Schelling's earlier insight that with the concept of God complete actuality is given too—and that all other assumptions are only indications of the fact "that within the world of ideas, too, it is not God that has been posited."[138]

137. See Henrich, *Der ontologische Gottesbeweis*, pp. 223–224, 237.
138. Fichte, "Begriff des negativ Absoluten," p. 165.

From the point of view of Hegel's approach as well as this insight (if we are willing to call it that), and also in order that Schelling's late philosophy may be regarded as a consistent development, the thinking that led him to pose the question in the way he there did can be seen, not as a step toward the consummation of German idealism, but as a withdrawal behind previous insights. And it is not only the idea of negative philosophy that is open to criticism. We are equally justified in asking: With what right does Schelling speak of what is above being as the Lord of being (SW 13:93)? How is the move made from the negative metaphysical differentiation between pure activity and thinking, and the designation of such activity as the absolute, to positive philosophy? And finally, what philosophical status can positive philosophy have when Schelling emphatically stresses that it neither needs nor is susceptible of any grounding (SW 13:93)? In other words, in what is the philosophical character of positive philosophy grounded if not the a priori, which is, properly speaking, the theme in it too?

Schelling viewed his late philosophy as destined and in a position to replace and surpass Hegel's system—and especially Hegel's principle of the unity of speculative theology and philosophy of religion. Yet Schelling himself was largely responsible for the fact that, instead of a reconstruction of genuinely philosophical arguments and motifs for the shape of the late philosophy, other interests thrust themselves into the foreground. According to his own testimony the "signal for the reversal and hence for positive philosophy" is given by the will of the ego, which cries out for a personal God and for redemption: "*Him, him,* will it have, the God who acts, who comes equipped with providence . . . and who, in a word, is the *Lord* of being" (SW 11:566). Schelling expressed this demand in phrases reminiscent of his opponent Jacobi. And in this demand he must have known himself to be united with virtually all other critics of the speculative philosophy of religion—except for the extreme left, which saw precisely in such demands the proof that such a conception of philosophy had to be left completely behind. To determine whether Schelling's late philosophy did justice to this demand *as philosophy* would require an interpretation that discussed his approach not in its own terms but in light of the contemporary debates. The latter indeed afford a wealth of arguments that make success appear unlikely.

What brought to an end the history of the reception of the speculative philosophy of religion was undoubtedly not the reproach that Hegel's philosophy of religion had accomplished too much, a reproach that at that time emanated from the left and in another form is still heard today. It was rather the opposite view that Hegel had failed to meet this demand addressed to philosophy. His philosophy in fact did not promise the positive knowledge of a personal God "outside the idea" (*SW* 11:570). Yet he did not rest content with the negative knowledge of a nonactual God enclosed within the idea, but went on to conceive God *as* the idea and religion as the self-knowing of this idea in human being. And he believed he could demonstrate that this concept of God and this conception of the philosophy of religion were not only philosophically possible but also necessary—necessary for the consummation of philosophy, for the constitution of the concept of absolute subjectivity. Further demands on philosophy he would have rejected with the words of the elder Fichte: "We need no other God, nor can we conceive any other."[139]

139. See above, pp. 104, 251.

BIBLIOGRAPHY

1. Original Sources

Works by Hegel are found in the list of abbreviations at the beginning of the volume and are not repeated here. In the case of Feuerbach, J. G. Fichte, Kant, Schelling, Friedrich Schlegel, and Schleiermacher, only complete German editions are listed, not individual works, although English translations of individual works by these authors to which reference is made in the footnotes are included. Names of authors that are bracketed indicate works originally published anonymously.

[Anonymous.] *Schellings Offenbarungsphilosophie und die von ihr bekämpfte Religionsphilosophie Hegels und der Junghegelianer: Drei Briefe.* Berlin, 1843.

Bachmann, Carl Friedrich. *Anti-Hegel.* Jena, 1835.

————. *Ueber Hegel's System und die Nothwendigkeit einer nochmaligen Umgestaltung der Philosophie.* Leipzig, 1833.

[Bauer, Bruno.] *Hegel's Lehre von der Religion und Kunst von dem Standpuncte des Glaubens aus beurtheilt.* Leipzig, 1842. Reprint, Aalen, 1969.

————. *Die Posaune des jüngsten Gerichts über Hegel den Atheisten und Antichristen: Ein Ultimatum.* Leipzig, 1842. Reprint, Aalen, 1969.

Bauer, Bruno. "Rezension zu Strauss' *Leben Jesu.*" *Jahrbücher für wissenschaftliche Kritik,* 1835, nos. 109–113: 879–894, 896–912; 1836, nos. 86–88: 681–704.

Bauer, Bruno, and Edgar Bauer. *Briefwechsel während der Jahre 1839–1842 aus Bonn und Berlin.* Charlottenburg, 1844. Reprint, Aalen, 1969.

[Bauerheim, F.] *Die Grundlehren der Neu-Schelling'schen und der Hegel'schen Philosophie in ihrer gegenseitigen Beziehung: Ein Beitrag zur objektiven Würdigung beider Philosophieen.* Reutlingen, 1847.

Baur, Ferdinand Christian. *Die christliche Gnosis oder die christliche Religions-Philosophie in ihrer geschichtlichen Entwiklung.* Tübingen, 1835.

Bayrhoffer, Karl Theodor. *Die Idee und Geschichte der Philosophie.* Marburg, 1838.

Beckers, Hubert. *Ueber C. F. Göschel's Versuch eines Erweises der persönlichen Unsterblichkeit vom Standpunkt der Hegelschen Lehre aus: Nebst einem Anhang über die Anwendbarkeit der Hegelschen Methode auf die Wissenschaft der Metaphysik.* Hamburg, 1836.

Billroth, Johann Gustav Friedrich. *Vorlesungen über Religionsphilosophie.* Edited by J. E. Erdmann. 2d ed. Leipzig, 1844.

Carriere, Moritz. *Die Religion in ihrem Begriff, ihrer weltgeschichtlichen Entwicklung und Vollendung: Ein Beitrag zur Verkündigung des absoluten Evangeliums und zum Verständnis der Hegel'schen Philosophie.* Weilburg, 1841.

Conradi, Kasimir. *Christus in der Gegenwart, Vergangenheit und Zukunft: Drei Abhandlungen, als Beiträge zur richtigen Fassung des Begriffs der Persönlichkeit.* Mainz, 1839.

———. *Selbstbewusstseyn und Offenbarung, oder Entwickelung des religiösen Bewusstseyns.* Mainz, 1831.

———. *Unsterblichkeit und ewiges Leben: Versuch einer Entwicklung des Unsterblichkeitsbegriffs der menschlichen Seele.* Mainz, 1837.

Dahlenburg, Johann Friedrich. *Philosophie und Religion der Natur, für gebildete Menschen.* 3 vols. Berlin, 1797.

Daub, Carl. *Die dogmatische Theologie jetziger Zeit oder die Selbstsucht in der Wissenschaft des Glaubens und seiner Artikel.* Heidelberg, 1833.

Erdmann, Johann Eduard. "Die Religionsphilosophie als Phänomenologie des religiösen Bewusstseins." In *Vermischte Aufsätze*. Leipzig, 1845.

——. *Versuch einer wissenschaftlichen Darstellung der Geschichte der neueren Philosophie*. Vol. 3, part 2. Leipzig, 1853.

——. *Vorlesungen über Glauben und Wissen als Einleitung in die Dogmatik und Religionsphilosophie*. Berlin, 1837.

Eschenmayer, Carl August. *Die Hegelsche Religions-Philosophie verglichen mit dem christlichen Princip*. Tübingen, 1834.

——. *Die Philosophie in ihrem Uebergang zur Nichtphilosophie*. Erlangen, 1803.

Feuerbach, Ludwig. *The Essence of Christianity*. Translated by George Eliot. New York, 1957.

——. *Gesammelte Werke*. Edited by Werner Schuffenhauer. Vol. 8, *Kleinere Schriften I*. Vol. 9, *Kleinere Schriften II*. 2d ed. Berlin, 1982.

——. *Principles of the Philosophy of the Future*. Translated by Manfred Vogel. Indianapolis, 1966.

Fichte, Immanuel Hermann. "Der Begriff des negativ Absoluten und der negativen Philosophie: Antwortschreiben an Herrn Dr. theol. Ch. H. Weisse auf dessen Sendschreiben an Fichte: 'Das philosophische Problem der Gegenwart' 1843." In *Vermischte Schriften zur Philosophie, Theologie und Ethik*. 2 vols. in 1. Leipzig, 1869. Reprint, Aalen, 1969.

——. *Beiträge zur Charakteristik der neueren Philosophie, oder kritische Geschichte derselben von Des Cartes und Locke bis auf Hegel*. 2d ed. Sulzbach, 1841.

——. *Grundzüge zum System der Philosophie*. Part 1, *Das Erkennen als Selbsterkennen*. Heidelberg, 1833. Reprint, Aalen, 1969. Part 2, *Die Ontologie*. Heidelberg, 1836. Reprint, Aalen, 1969. Part 3, *Die spekulative Theologie oder allgemeine Religionslehre*. Heidelberg, 1846. Reprint, Aalen, 1969.

——. *Die Idee der Persönlichkeit und der individuellen Fortdauer*. Elberfeld, 1834.

——. *Religion und Philosophie in ihrem gegenwärtigen Verhältnisse*. Heidelberg, 1834. Reprinted from the *Heidelberger Jahrbücher der Literatur*.

————. *Sätze zur Vorschule der Theologie.* Stuttgart and Tübingen, 1826.

————. *Ueber die Bedingungen eines speculativen Theismus; in einer Beurtheilung der Vorrede Schellings zu dem Werk von Cousin: Ueber französische und deutsche Philosophie.* Elberfeld, 1835.

————. *Ueber Gegensatz, Wendepunkt und Ziel heutiger Philosophie. Erster kritischer Theil.* Heidelberg, 1832.

Fichte, Johann Gottlieb. *Attempt at a Critique of All Revelation.* Translated by Garrett Green. Cambridge, 1978.

————. *Gesamtausgabe der Bayerischen Akademie der Wissenschaften.* Edited by Reinhard Lauth, Hans Jacob, and Hans Gliwitzky. Div. 1. Stuttgart–Bad Cannstatt, 1964 ff.

————. "On the Foundation of Our Belief in a Divine Government of the Universe." In *Nineteenth-Century Philosophy,* edited by Patrick L. Gardiner, pp. 19–26. New York, 1969.

Fischer, Carl Philipp. *Die Idee der Gottheit: Ein Versuch, den Theismus speculativ zu begründen und zu entwickeln.* Stuttgart, 1839.

————. *Speculative Charakteristik und Kritik des Hegel'schen Systems und Begründung der Umgestaltung der Philosophie zur objectiven Vernunftwissenschaft, mit besondrer Rücksicht auf die Geschichte der Philosophie.* Erlangen, 1845.

————. *Der Uebergang von dem idealistischen Pantheismus der Hegelschen Philosophie zum Theismus, mit besonderer Rücksicht auf die Schrift: "Die Hegel'sche Philosophie: Beiträge zu ihrer richtigen Beurtheilung und Würdigung," von Georg Andreas Gabler.* Tübingen, 1843.

————. *Die Wissenschaft der Metaphysik im Grundrisse.* Stuttgart, 1834.

Forberg, Friedrich Karl. "Entwicklung des Begriffs der Religion." *Philosophisches Journal* (Jena and Leipzig), 8, n. 1 (1798).

Frauenstaedt, Julius. *Studien und Kritiken zur Theologie und Philosophie.* Berlin, 1840.

Fries, Jakob Friedrich. *Neue oder anthropologische Kritik der Vernunft.* 2d ed. Heidelberg, 1831. Newly edited by G. König and L. Geldsetzer. Aalen, 1967.

———. *Wissen, Glaube und Ahndung.* Jena 1805. Newly edited by G. König and L. Geldsetzer. Aalen, 1968.

Gabler, Georg Andreas. *Die Hegel'sche Philosophie: Beiträge zu ihrer richtigen Beurtheilung und Würdigung.* Berlin, 1843.

———. *De verae philosophiae erga religionem christianam pietate.* Berlin, 1836.

Göschel, Carl Friedrich. *Aphorismen über Nichtwissen und absolutes Wissen im Verhältnisse zur christlichen Glaubenserkenntniss: Ein Beitrag zum Verständnisse der Philosophie unserer Zeit.* Berlin, 1829.

———. *Beiträge zur spekulativen Philosophie von Gott und dem Menschen und von dem Gott-Menschen: Mit Rücksicht auf Dr. D. F. Strauss' Christologie.* Berlin, 1838.

———. *Der Monismus des Gedankens: Zur Apologie der gegenwärtigen Philosophie am Grabe ihres Stifters.* Naumburg, 1832.

———. "Rezension zu Fr. Richter." *Jahrbücher für wissenschaftliche Kritik,* 1834, nos. 1–3, 17–19.

———. *Von den Beweisen für die Unsterblichkeit der menschlichen Seele im Lichte der spekulativen Philosophie: Eine Ostergabe.* Berlin, 1835.

Goethe, Johann Wolfgang von. *Faust.* Translated by Walter Kaufmann. New York, 1961.

———. *Goethe's and Schiller's Xenions.* Translated by Paul Carus. Chicago, 1896.

[Grohmann, Johann Christian August.] *Ueber Offenbarung und Mythologie: Als Nachtrag zur Religion innerhalb der Grenzen der reinen Vernunft.* Berlin, 1799.

Haym, Rudolf. *Hegel und seine Zeit: Vorlesungen über Entstehung und Entwickelung, Wesen und Werth der Hegel'schen Philosophie.* Berlin, 1857. Reprint, Hildesheim, 1962.

Herder, Johann Gottfried. *Aelteste Urkunde des Menschengeschlechts.* 2 vols. Riga, 1774–1776. Vol. 6 of *Sämtliche Werke.* Edited by B. Suphan. Berlin, 1883.

Heydenreich, Karl Heinrich. *Betrachtungen über die Philosophie der natürlichen Religion.* 2 vols. Leipzig, 1790–1791.

———. *Brief über den Atheismus.* Leipzig, 1796.

———. *Encyclopädische Einleitung in das Studium der Philosophie nach den Bedürfnissen unsers Zeitalters: Nebst Anleitungen zur philosophischen Literatur*. Leipzig, 1793.

Hinrichs, Hermann Friderich Wilhelm. *Die Religion im inneren Verhältnisse zur Wissenschaft*. Heidelberg, 1822. Reprint, Brussels, 1970.

Hölderlin, Friedrich. *Über Religion*. In *Sämtliche Werke* 4:275–281. Stuttgart, 1961.

[Hülsemann.] *Ueber die Hegelsche Lehre oder: Absolutes Wissen und moderner Pantheismus*. Leipzig, 1829.

———. *Ueber die Wissenschaft der Idee*. Div. 1, *Die neueste Identitätsphilosophie und Atheismus oder über immanente Polemik*. Breslau, 1831.

Jacobi, Friedrich Heinrich. *Open Letter to Fichte*. In *Philosophy of German Idealism*, edited by Ernst Behler. New York, 1987.

———. *Werke*. 6 vols. Leipzig, 1812–1825. Reprint, Darmstadt, 1976.

Jäsche, Gottlob Benjamin. *Der Pantheismus nach seinen verschiedenen Hauptformen*. 2 vols. Berlin, 1826–1828.

Jakob, Ludwig Heinrich. *Die allgemeine Religion: Ein Buch für gebildete Leser*. Halle, 1797.

———. "Philosophische Abhandlung: Ueber die Religion." *Annalen der Philosophie und des philosophischen Geistes von einer Gesellschaft gelehrter Männer* (Leipzig), 2 (1796).

Kant, Immanuel. *The Conflict of the Faculties*. Translated by Mary J. Gregor. New York, 1979.

———. *The Critique of Judgement*. 2 vols. Translated by James Creed Meredith. Oxford, 1928.

———. *Critique of Practical Reason*. Translated by Lewis White Beck. New York, 1956.

———. *Critique of Pure Reason*. Translated by Norman Kemp Smith. London, 1930.

———. *The Fundamental Principles of the Metaphysic of Ethics*. Translated by Otto Manthey-Zorn. New York, 1938.

———. *Gesammelte Schriften*. Edited by the Royal Prussian Academy of Sciences, the German Academy of Sciences in Berlin, and the Academy of Sciences in Göttingen. Berlin, 1900 ff.

———. *Lectures on Philosophical Theology*. Translated by Allen

W. Wood and Gertrude M. Clark. Ithaca, N.Y., 1978.

———. *Religion within the Limits of Reason Alone*. Translated by Theodore M. Greene and Hoyt H. Hudson. La Salle, Ill., 1934.

Köppen, Friedrich. *Ueber Offenbarung, in Beziehung auf Kantische und Fichtische Philosophie*. 2d ed. Lübeck and Leipzig, 1802.

Leo, Heinrich. *Die Hegelingen: Actenstücke und Belege zu der s.g. Denunciation der ewigen Wahrheit*. Halle, 1838.

Lessing, Gotthold Ephraim. *The Education of the Human Race*. Translated by F. W. Robertson. London, 1881.

———. *Eine Parabel* (1778). In *Sämtliche Schriften*, edited by K. Lachmann, 3d ed. prepared by F. Munker, vol. 13. Leipzig, 1897.

[Maass, Johann Gebhard Ehrenreich.] *Kritische Theorie der Offenbarung: Nebst Berichtigung der Schrift: "Christus und die Vernunft."* Halle, 1792.

Marheineke, Philipp. *Einleitung in die öffentlichen Vorlesungen über die Bedeutung der Hegelschen Philosophie in der christlichen Theologie: Nebst einem Separatvotum über B. Bauers Kritik der evangelischen Geschichte*. Berlin, 1842.

———. *Die Grundlehren der christlichen Dogmatik*. Berlin, 1819.

———. *Die Grundlehren der christlichen Dogmatik als Wissenschaft*. Berlin, 1827.

———. *Zur Kritik der Schellingschen Offenbarungsphilosophie: Schluss der öffentlichen Vorlesungen über die Bedeutung der Hegelschen Philosophie in der christlichen Theologie*. Berlin, 1843.

Marx, Karl. "Toward the Critique of Hegel's Philosophy of Law: Introduction" (1844). In *Writings of the Young Marx on Philosophy and Society*, edited by Loyd D. Easton and Kurt H. Guddat, pp. 249–264. Garden City, N.Y., 1967.

Michelet, Carl Ludwig. *Entwicklungsgeschichte der neuesten deutschen Philosophie mit besonderer Rücksicht auf den gegenwärtigen Kampf Schellings mit der Hegelschen Schule*. Berlin, 1843.

———. *Die Epiphanie der ewigen Persönlichkeit des Geistes. Eine philosophische Trilogie*. Vol. 1. Nuremberg, 1844. Vol. 2. Darmstadt, 1847. Vol. 3. Berlin, 1852.

————. *Geschichte der letzten Systeme der Philosophie in Deutschland von Kant bis Hegel.* Part 2. Berlin, 1838.

————. *Vorlesungen über die Persönlichkeit Gottes und Unsterblichkeit der Seele oder die ewige Persönlichkeit des Geistes.* Berlin, 1841.

Nietzsche, Friedrich. *Untimely Meditations.* Translated by R. J. Hollingdale, with an introduction by J. P. Stern. Cambridge, 1983.

Noack, Ludwig. *Der Religionsbegriff Hegel's: Ein Beitrag zur Kritik der Hegel'schen Religionsphilosophie.* Darmstadt, 1845.

Novalis (Friedrich von Hardenberg). *Schriften.* Vol. 1. Edited by P. Kluckhohn and R. Samuel in collaboration with H.-J. Mähl and G. Schulz. 3d ed. Darmstadt, 1983.

Philosophisches Journal einer Gesellschaft Teutscher Gelehrten. Edited by F. I. Niethammer and J. G. Fichte. 10 vols. Neu-Strelitz, 1795–1796. Jena and Leipzig, 1797–1800.

Platner, Ernst. *Philosophische Aphorismen: Nebst einigen Erläuterungen zur philosophischen Geschichte.* 3d ed. Leipzig, 1793.

Pölitz, Karl Heinrich Ludwig. *Beitrag zur Kritik der Religionsphilosophie und Exegese unsers Zeitalters: Ein Versuch auf Veranlassung der neusten zur Begründung einer reinen Religionswissenschaft angestellten Untersuchungen.* Leipzig, 1795.

Reinhold, Karl Leonhard. *Beyträge zur Berichtigung bisheriger Missverständnisse der Philosophie.* Jena, 1790.

Richter, Friedrich. *Die Lehre von den letzten Dingen: Eine wissenschaftliche Kritik, aus dem Standpuncte der Religion unternommen.* Vol. 1. Breslau, 1833. Vol. 2. Berlin, 1844.

————. *Die neue Unsterblichkeitslehre: Gespräch einer Abendgesellschaft, als Supplement zu Wielands Euthanasia.* Breslau, 1833.

Rosenkranz, Karl. *Enzyklopädie der theologischen Wissenschaften.* Halle, 1831.

————. *G. W. F. Hegel's Leben.* Berlin, 1844. Reprint, Darmstadt, 1963.

————. *Hegel als deutscher Nationalphilosoph.* Leipzig, 1870.

————. *Hegel: Sendschreiben an den Hofrat und Professor der Philosophie Herrn Dr. C. Fr. Bachmann in Jena.* Königsberg, 1834.

———. "Hegel's ursprüngliches System, 1798–1806: Aus Hegel's Nachlass." In *Literarhistorisches Taschenbuch,* edited by E. R. Prutz, vol. 2. Leipzig, 1844.

———. *Kritik der Schleiermacherschen Glaubenslehre.* Königsberg, 1836.

———. *Kritische Erläuterungen des Hegel'schen Systems.* Königsberg, 1840. Reprint, Hildesheim, 1963.

———. "Rezension zu Schleiermacher: *Der christliche Glaube.*" *Jahrbücher für wissenschaftliche Kritik* 2 (1830): 872–874.

Rust, Isaak. *Philosophie und Christenthum oder Wissen und Glauben.* Mannheim, 1825. 2d ed. 1833.

Salat, Jakob. "Geht die Moral aus der Religion, oder diese aus jener hervor? Einige Winke zur neuern Geschichte und Kritik der Religion." *Philosophisches Journal* (Jena and Leipzig), 5, no. 3 (1797).

———. *Grundlinien der Religionsphilosophie: Eine Vorarbeit in Hinsicht auf die zweyte, ganz von Neuem ausgearbeitete Auflage seiner Darstellung derselben.* Sulzbach, 1819.

———. "Noch ein Beitrag über die moralische Begründung der Religion." *Philosophisches Journal* (Jena and Leipzig), 8, no. 4 (1798).

———. *Die Religionsphilosophie.* Landshut, 1811.

Schaller, Julius. *Der historische Christus und die Philosophie: Kritik der Grundidee des Werks "Das Leben Jesu" von Dr. D. F. Strauss.* Leipzig, 1838.

———. *Die Philosophie unserer Zeit: Zur Apologie und Erläuterung des Hegelschen Systems.* Leipzig, 1837.

Schelling, Friedrich Wilhelm Joseph. *Aus Schellings Leben: In Briefen.* Edited by G. L. Plitt. 3 vols. Leipzig, 1869–1870.

———. *Historisch-kritische Ausgabe.* Published by the Schelling Commission of the Bavarian Academy of Sciences. Edited by H. M. Baumgartner, W. G. Jacobs, H. Krings, and H. Zeltner. Stuttgart, 1976 ff.

———. *Of Human Freedom.* Translated by James Gutmann. Chicago, 1936.

———. *On University Studies.* Translated by E. S. Morgan. Athens, Ohio, 1966.

————. *Sämmtliche Werke.* Edited by K. F. A. Schelling. 14 vols. Stuttgart and Augsburg, 1856–1861.

————. *System of Transcendental Idealism.* Translated by Peter Heath. Charlottesville, Va., 1978.

Schiller, Friedrich. *Werke: Nationalausgabe.* Vol. 20. Weimar, 1962.

Schlegel, Friedrich. *Kritische Friedrich-Schlegel-Ausgabe.* Div. 1, vol. 2, *Charakteristiken und Kritiken (1796–1801).* Edited by Hans Eichner. Munich, Paderborn, Vienna, Zürich, 1967.

————. *Friedrich Schlegel und Novalis: Biographie einer Romantikerfreundschaft in ihren Briefen.* Edited by Max Preitz. Darmstadt, 1957.

Schleiermacher, Friedrich Daniel Ernst. *Aus Schleiermachers Leben: In Briefen.* Edited by L. Jonas and W. Dilthey. 3 vols. Berlin, 1860–1863.

————. *Kritische Gesamtausgabe.* Div. 1. Berlin and New York, 1980 ff.

————. *On Religion: Speeches to Its Cultured Despisers.* Translation of the 1st edition of 1799 by Richard Crouter. Cambridge, 1988.

Schmidt, Reinhold. *Der philosophische Absolutismus des Hegelschen Systems: Eine Abhandlung.* Berlin, 1845.

Schubarth, K. E. and K. A. Carganico. *Ueber Philosophie überhaupt, und Hegels "Encyclopädie der philosophischen Wissenschaften" insbesondere: Ein Beitrag zur Beurtheilung der letztern.* Berlin, 1829.

Schwarz, Karl. *Zur Geschichte der neuesten Theologie.* Leipzig, 1856.

Sengler, Jakob. *Die Idee Gottes.* 2 vols. Heidelberg, 1845–1847.

————. *Ueber das Wesen und die Bedeutung der speculativen Philosophie und Theologie.* General Introduction. Mainz, 1834. Special Introduction. Heidelberg, 1837.

Snellmann, Johann. *Versuch einer speculativen Entwicklung der Idee der Persönlichkeit.* Tübingen, 1841.

Stahl, Friedrich Julius. *Die Philosophie des Rechts nach geschichtlicher Ansicht.* Vol. 1. Heidelberg, 1830.

Staudenmaier, Franz Anton. *Darstellung und Kritik des Hegelschen*

Systems: Aus dem Standpunkte der christlichen Philosophie. Mainz, 1844.

Storr, Gottlob Christian. *Bemerkungen über Kant's philosophische Religionslehre: Aus dem Lateinischen: Nebst einigen Bemerkungen des Uebersezers über den aus Principien der praktischen Vernunft hergeleiteten Ueberzeugungsgrund von der Möglichkeit und Wirklichkeit einer Offenbarung in Beziehung auf Fichte's "Versuch einer Critik aller Offenbarung."* Tübingen, 1794. Reprint, Brussels, 1968.

Strauss, David Friedrich. *In Defense of My "Life of Jesus" against the Hegelians.* Translated and edited by Marilyn C. Massey. Hamden, Conn., 1983.

———. *The Life of Jesus Critically Examined.* Translated by George Eliot. Edited by Peter C. Hodgson. Philadelphia and London, 1972–1973.

Ulrici, Hermann. *Ueber Princip und Methode der Hegel'schen Philosophie: Ein Beitrag zur Kritik derselben.* Halle, 1841.

Valenti, Ernst Joseph Gustav de. *Hegel-Strauss, und der Christusglaube.* Basel, 1843.

Vatke, Wilhelm. "Beitrag zur Kritik der neueren philosophischen Theologie." *Hallische Jahrbücher* 3, nos. 1–8 (1840).

———. "Rezension zu de Wette: *Lehrbuch der historisch-kritischen Einleitung in die kanonischen Bücher des Neuen Testaments.*" *Jahrbücher für wissenschaftliche Kritik,* 1832: 868–869.

Volkmuth, Peter. *Der dreieinige Pantheismus von Thales bis Hegel.* Cologne, 1837.

Weisse, Christian Hermann. *Grundzüge der Metaphysik.* Hamburg, 1835.

———. *Die Idee der Gottheit: Eine philosophische Abhandlung: Als wissenschaftliche Grundlegung zur Philosophie der Religion.* Dresden, 1833.

———. *Philosophische Dogmatik oder Philosophie des Christenthums.* 3 vols. Leipzig, 1855–1862.

———. *Die philosophische Geheimlehre von der Unsterblichkeit des menschlichen Individuums.* Dresden, 1834.

————. *Das philosophische Problem der Gegenwart: Sendschreiben an I. H. Fichte.* Leipzig, 1842.

————. "Über die eigentliche Grenze des Pantheismus und des philosophischen Theismus: Mit besonderer Beziehung auf Hegels *Vorlesungen über die Philosophie der Religion*" (1833). In *Die Flucht in den Begriff* (see Secondary Sources), pp. 64–96.

————. *Ueber den gegenwärtigen Standpunct der philosophischen Wissenschaft: In besonderer Beziehung auf das System Hegels.* Leipzig, 1829.

————. *Ueber das Verhältniss des Publicums zur Philosophie in dem Zeitpuncte von Hegels Abscheiden: Nebst einer kurzen Darlegung meiner Ansicht des Systems der Philosophie.* Leipzig, 1832.

Wolff, Christian. *Theologia naturalis methodo scientifica pertractata. Pars prior, integrum systema complectens, qua existentia et attributa Dei a posteriori demonstrantur.* New ed. Frankfurt am Main and Leipzig, 1739. *Pars posterior, qua existentia et attributa Dei ex notione entis perfectissimi et natura animae demonstrantur.* 2d ed. Frankfurt am Main and Leipzig, 1741.

Zeller, Eduard. "Hegel's *Vorlesungen über die Philosophie der Religion* (2. Aufl. 1840)" (1841). In *Die Flucht in den Begriff,* pp. 114–139.

————. "Ueber Hegel's theologische Entwicklung: Mit Beziehung auf Rosenkranz' *Leben Hegel's.*" *Theologische Jahrbücher* 4 (1845): 192–206.

2. Secondary Sources

Only those titles are listed to which reference is made in the text or footnotes. For a more complete survey of the literature, see Jaeschke, *Die Religionsphilosophie Hegels,* as well as "Die Flucht vor dem Begriff: Ein Jahrzehnt Literatur zur Religionsphilosophie (1971–1981)," *Hegel-Studien* 18 (1983): 295–354.

Asendorf, Ulrich. *Luther und Hegel: Untersuchungen zur Grundlegung einer neuen Systematischen Theologie.* Wiesbaden, 1982.

Beck, Lewis White. *Commentary on Kant's Critique of Practical Reason.* Chicago, 1960.

Becker, Werner. "Über Schellings Konstruktion des Christentums." In *Subjektivität und Metaphysik: Festschrift für Wolfgang Cramer*, edited by D. Henrich and H. Wagner, pp. 1–20. Frankfurt am Main, 1966.

Brito, Emilio. *La christologie de Hegel: Verbum Crucis*. Translated by B. Pottier, S.J. Paris, 1983.

Cassirer, Ernst. *The Philosophy of the Enlightenment*. Translated by Fritz Koelln and James Pettegrove. Princeton, 1951.

Cornehl, Peter. *Die Zukunft der Versöhnung: Eschatologie und Emanzipation in der Aufklärung, bei Hegel und in der Hegelschen Schule*. Göttingen, 1971.

Delekat, Friedrich. *Immanuel Kant: Historisch-kritische Interpretation der Hauptschriften*. 3d ed. Heidelberg, 1969.

Düsing, Klaus. *Hegel und die Geschichte der Philosophie: Ontologie und Dialektik in Antike und Neuzeit*. Erträge der Forschung, vol. 206. Darmstadt, 1983.

————. *Das Problem der Subjektivität in Hegels Logik: Systematische und entwicklungsgeschichtliche Untersuchungen zum Prinzip des Idealismus und zur Dialektik*. Hegel-Studien, Beiheft 15. Bonn, 1976.

————. "Das Problem des höchsten Gutes in Kants praktischer Philosophie." *Kant-Studien* 62 (1971): 5–42.

Fackenheim, Emil L. *The Religious Dimension in Hegel's Thought*. Bloomington, Ind., and London, 1967.

Feiereis, Konrad. *Die Umprägung der natürlichen Theologie in Religionsphilosophie: Ein Beitrag zur deutschen Geistesgeschichte des 18. Jahrhunderts*. Leipzig, 1965.

Die Flucht in den Begriff: Materialien zu Hegels Religionsphilosophie. Edited by F. W. Graf und F. Wagner. Stuttgart, 1982 (with an extensive bibliography).

Gawoll, Hans-Jürgen. "Karl Heinrich Heydenreich: Zwischen Spinozismus und Kantianismus." Manuscript of Special Research Group 119 of the Deutsche Forschungsgemeinschaft, Ruhr University, Bochum.

Gethmann-Siefert, Annemarie. *Die Funktion der Kunst in der Geschichte: Untersuchungen zu Hegels Ästhetik*. Hegel-Studien, Beiheft 25. Bonn, 1984.

Harris, H. S. *Hegel's Development: Toward the Sunlight, 1770–1801.* Oxford, 1972.

———. *Hegel's Development: Night Thoughts (Jena 1801–1806).* Oxford, 1983.

Hartlich, Christian, and Walter Sachs. *Der Ursprung des Mythosbegriffs in der modernen Bibelwissenschaft.* Tübingen, 1952.

Heede, Reinhard. "Die göttliche Idee und ihre Erscheinung in der Religion: Untersuchungen zum Verhältnis von Logik und Religionsphilosophie bei Hegel." Diss. Dr. phil., Münster, 1972.

———. "Hegel-Bilanz: Hegels Religionsphilosophie als Aufgabe und Problem der Forschung." In *Hegel-Bilanz: Zur Aktualität und Inaktualität der Philosophie Hegels,* edited by R. Heede and J. Ritter. Frankfurt am Main, 1973.

Heimsoeth, Heinz. *Transzendentale Dialektik: Ein Kommentar zu Kants Kritik der reinen Vernunft.* Berlin, 1969.

Henrich, Dieter. *Der ontologische Gottesbeweis: Sein Problem und seine Geschichte in der Neuzeit.* 2d ed. Tübingen, 1967.

Herms, Eilert. *Herkunft, Entfaltung und erste Gestalt des Systems der Wissenschaften bei Schleiermacher.* Gütersloh, 1974.

Hildebrandt, Franz. *Est: Das Lutherische Prinzip.* Studien zur systematischen Theologie, no. 7. Göttingen, 1931.

Horstmann, Rolf Peter. "Jenaer Systemkonzeptionen." In *Hegel: Einführung in seine Philosophie,* edited by O. Pöggeler. Freiburg and Munich, 1977.

Huber, Herbert. *Idealismus und Trinität, Pantheon und Götterdämmerung: Grundlagen und Grundzüge der Lehre von Gott nach dem Manuskript Hegels zur Religionsphilosophie.* Weinheim, 1984.

Jaeschke, Walter. "Absolute Idee—absolute Subjektivität: Zum Problem der Persönlichkeit Gottes in der Logik und in der Religionsphilosophie." *Zeitschrift für philosophische Forschung* 35 (1981): 385–416.

———. "Äusserliche Reflexion und immanente Reflexion: Eine Skizze der systematischen Geschichte des Reflexionsbegriffs in Hegels Logik-Entwürfen." *Hegel-Studien* 13 (1978): 85–117.

———. "Christianity and Secularity in Hegel's Concept of the State." *Journal of Religion* 61 (1981): 127–145. A revised version of "Staat aus christlichem Prinzip und christlicher Staat" (see below).

———. "Early German Idealist Reinterpretation of the Quarrel of the Ancients and Moderns." *Clio: Interdisciplinary Journal of Literature, History, Philosophy of History* 12 (1983): 23–36.

———. "Hegel's Last Year in Berlin." In *Hegel's Philosophy of Action: Proceedings of the Joint Conference of the Hegel Society of Great Britain and the Hegel Society of America in the Fall of 1981*, edited by L. S. Stepelevich and D. Lamb, pp. 31–48. Atlantic Highlands, N.J., 1983.

———. "Kunst und Religion." In *Die Flucht in den Begriff*, pp. 163–195.

———. "Paralipomena Hegeliana zur Wirkungsgeschichte Schleiermachers." In *Internationaler Schleiermacher-Kongress, Berlin, 1984*, edited by K.-V. Selge, pp. 1157–1169. Schleiermacher-Archiv, edited by H. Fischer, vol. 1. Berlin and New York, 1985.

———. *Die Religionsphilosophie Hegels*. Erträge der Forschung, vol. 201. Darmstadt, 1983.

———. "Staat aus christlichem Prinzip und christlicher Staat: Zur Ambivalenz der Berufung auf das Christentum in der Rechtsphilosophie Hegels und der Restauration." *Der Staat* 18 (1979): 349–374.

———. "Urmenschheit und Monarchie: Eine politische Christologie der Hegelschen Rechten." *Hegel-Studien* 14 (1979): 73–107.

———. "Zur Logik der Bestimmten Religion." In *Hegels Logik der Philosophie: Religion und Philosophie in der Theorie des absoluten Geistes*, edited by D. Henrich and R. P. Horstmann, pp. 172–188. Internationale Hegel-Vereinigung, vol. 13. Stuttgart, 1984.

Jauss, Hans Robert. *Literaturgeschichte als Provokation*. Frankfurt am Main, 1970.

Jüngel, Eberhard. *God as the Mystery of the World: On the Foundation of the Theology of the Crucified One in the Dispute between Theism and Atheism*. Translated by Darrell L. Guder. Grand Rapids, Mich., 1983.

Kimmerle, Heinz. "Die von Rosenkranz überlieferten Texte Hegels

aus der Jenaer Zeit: Eine Untersuchung ihres Quellenwerts."
Hegel-Studien 5 (1968): 83–94.

———. "Zur Chronologie von Hegels Jenaer Schriften." *Hegel-
Studien* 4 (1967): 125–176.

Knudsen, Harald. *Gottesbeweise im deutschen Idealismus: Die
modaltheoretische Begründung des Absoluten dargestellt an
Kant, Hegel und Weisse.* Berlin and New York, 1972.

Löwith, Karl. *From Hegel to Nietzsche: The Revolution in Nineteenth-Century Thought.* Translated by D. E. Green. New York,
1964.

———. "Hegels Aufhebung der christlichen Religion." In *Hegel-
Tage, 1962: Vorträge und Dokumente,* edited by H.-G.
Gadamer. *Hegel-Studien,* Beiheft 1. Bonn, 1964.

Mahlmann, Theodor. *Das neue Dogma der lutherischen Christologie: Problem und Geschichte seiner Begründung.* Gütersloh,
1969.

Massey, Marilyn Chapin. *Christ Unmasked: The Meaning of "The
Life of Jesus" in German Politics.* Chapel Hill and London,
1983.

Pannenberg, Wolfhart. *Jesus—God and Man.* Translated by Lewis
L. Wilkins and Duane A. Priebe. Philadelphia, 1968.

Sandberger, Jörg F. *D. F. Strauss als theologischer Hegelianer: Mit
unveröffentlichten Briefen.* Göttingen, 1972.

Sass, Hans Martin. "Untersuchungen zur Religionsphilosophie in
der Hegelschule 1830–1850." Diss. Dr. phil., Münster, 1963.

Schlitt, Dale M. *Hegel's Trinitarian Claim: A Critical Reflection.*
Leiden, 1984.

Schneider, Helmut. "Zur Dreieckssymbolik bei Hegel." *Hegel-
Studien* 8 (1973): 55–77.

Scholtz, Gunter. *Die Philosophie Schleiermachers.* Erträge der Forschung, vol. 217. Darmstadt, 1984.

Schulin, Ernst. *Die weltgeschichtliche Erfassung des Orients bei
Hegel und Ranke.* Göttingen, 1958.

Schulz, Walter. *Die Vollendung des Deutschen Idealismus in der
Spätphilosophie Schellings.* 2d ed. Pfullingen, 1975.

Sparn, Walter. *Wiederkehr der Metaphysik: Die ontologische Frage in der lutherischen Theologie des frühen 17. Jahrhunderts.* Stuttgart, 1976.

Szondi, Peter. *Poetik und Geschichtsphilosophie I: Antike und Moderne in der Ästhetik der Goethezeit.* Edited by S. Metz und H.-H. Hildebrandt. Frankfurt am Main, 1974.

Theunissen, Michael. *Hegels Lehre vom absoluten Geist als theologisch-politischer Traktat.* Berlin, 1970.

Timm, Hermann. *Gott und die Freiheit: Studien zur Religionsphilosophie der Goethezeit.* Vol. 1, *Die Spinozarenaissance.* Frankfurt am Main, 1974.

————. *Die heilige Revolution: Das religiöse Totalitätskonzept der Frühromantik: Schleiermacher–Novalis–Friedrich Schlegel.* Frankfurt am Main, 1978.

Trede, Johann Heinrich. "Mythologie und Idee: Die systematische Stellung der 'Volksreligion' in Hegels Jenaer Philosophie der Sittlichkeit (1801–1803)." In *Das Älteste Systemprogramm: Studien zur Frühgeschichte des deutschen Idealismus,* edited by R. Bubner. *Hegel-Studien,* Beiheft 9. Bonn, 1973.

Wagner, Falk. *Was ist Religion? Studien zu ihrem Begriff und Thema in Geschichte und Gegenwart.* Gütersloh, 1986.

Weischedel, Wilhelm. *Der Gott der Philosophen: Grundlegung einer Philosophischen Theologie im Zeitalter des Nihilismus.* Vol. 1, *Wesen, Aufstieg und Verfall der philosophischen Theologie.* Darmstadt, 1975.

Wenz, Gunther. "Für uns gegeben: Grundzüge lutherischer Abendmahlslehre im Zusammenhang des gegenwärtigen ökumenischen Dialogs." In *Mahl des Herrn: Ökumenische Studien,* edited by Miguel Garijo-Guembe, Jan Rohls, and Gunther Wenz, pp. 223–338. Frankfurt am Main, 1988.

Wohlfart, Günter. *Der spekulative Satz: Bemerkungen zum Begriff der Spekulation bei Hegel.* Berlin and New York, 1981.

Yates, Thomas Vance. "Hegel and the Natural Religion of Modern Philosophy." Diss., Freiburg, 1975.

Yerkes, James. *The Christology of Hegel.* 2d ed. Albany, 1983.

INDEX OF CITATIONS

This index provides an overview of citations from and references to Hegel's works which are found in the text and footnotes. The works are listed in chronological sequence—printed works according to the date of original publication and manuscripts according to the probable date of composition. In addition to titles, the German editions from which citations are made in this study are indicated by abbreviations (see pp. xiii–xv), as are the available English translations. The abbreviation "Fr" designates the numbering of the fragments of Hegel's early writings established by G. Schüler, "Zur Chronologie von Hegels Jugendschriften," *Hegel-Studien* 2 (1963): 127–133. As is now customary, these and other untitled fragments are identified by their opening words. The numbers in the left-hand columns are the page numbers of the cited texts; those in the right-hand columns are the page numbers of this volume. With the exception of the *Lectures on the Philosophy of Religion*, for which only the page numbers of the English edition are given, it is the German editions that are indexed here; corresponding pages of English translations, when they exist, can be obtained from the in-text English/German references on the indicated pages.

Briefe von und an Hegel (*Br*) (Eng. tr. *L*)

Theologische Jugendschriften (*J*) (Eng. tr. *ETW* and *TE*)

Notizen zum absoluten Geist (1817–18), edited by H. Schneider, *Hegel-Studien* 9 (1974)

Vorlesungen über die Philosophie der Weltgeschichte (1822–31) (W 9) (Eng. tr. *LPH*)

INDEX OF NAMES AND SUBJECTS

Designer: U.C. Press Staff
Compositor: Prestige Typography
Text: 10/13 Sabon
Display: Sabon
Printer: Bookcrafters
Binder: Bookcrafters